Achieving Service-Oriented Architecture

Achieving Service-Oriented Architecture

Applying an Enterprise Architecture Approach

RICK SWEENEY

WILEY

John Wiley & Sons, Inc.

Published by John Wiley & Sons, Inc., Hoboken, New Jersey.
Published simultaneously in Canada.

The figure "The Maturity Levels," from the slide show "CMMI Overview," © 2005 Carnegie Mellon University Mellon University, is used with special permission from its Software Engineering Institute.

Any material of Carnegie Mellon University and/or its Software Engineering Institute contained herein is furnished on an "as-is" basis. Carnegie Mellon University makes no warranties of any kind, either expressed or implied, as to any matter including, but not limited to, warranty of fitness for purpose of merchantability, exclusivity, or results obtained from use of the material. Carnegie Mellon University does not make any warranty of any kind with respect to freedom from patent, trademark, or copyright infringement.

This publication has not been reviewed nor is it endorsed by Carnegie Mellon University or its Software Engineering Institute.

For general information on our other products and services or for technical support, please contact our Customer Care Department within the United States at (800) 762-2974, outside the United States at (317) 572-3993 or fax (317) 572-4002.

Wiley also publishes its books in a variety of electronic formats. Some content that appears in print may not be available in electronic books. For more information about Wiley products, visit our web site at www.wiley.com.

Library of Congress Cataloging-in-Publication Data:

Sweeney, Rick, 1954–
    Achieving service-oriented architecture : applying an enterprise architecture approach / Rick Sweeney.
        p. cm.
    Includes bibliographical references and index.
    ISBN 978-0-470-60451-9 (cloth)
    1. Information technology–Management.   2. Management information systems.
3. Service-oriented architecture (Computer science) I. Title.
    HD30.2.S93 2010
    658.4′038011–dc22

                                                                                2009050977

Printed in the United States of America

10   9   8   7   6   5   4   3   2   1

Contents

PART IV   DEVELOPING YOUR PLAN FOR ACHIEVING
                 SERVICE-ORIENTED ARCHITECTURE

Acknowledgments

I would like to thank Shelley Therrien for grammatically reviewing this book and helping me put it together. I would also like to thank my wife, Linda, for putting up with me for months while I focused on writing.

Introduction

This book is *not* about the technical capabilities and technologies required to build a service-oriented architecture (SOA) application. There have been many books written on this subject. Some are very good. I highly recommend Michael Rosen, Boris Lublinsky, Kevin T. Smith, and Marc J. Balcer's *Applied SOA: Service Oriented Architecture and Design Strategies* (Hoboken, NJ: John Wiley & Sons, 2008) for anyone wanting to build technically sound and highly flexible SOA applications.

This book is about an architectural approach to the *cultural, organizational,* and *operational* changes that must be made across the corporate landscape to successfully achieve SOA. Thus this is an enterprise architecture business organization and management practice book. Both the technical knowledge provided in books like *Applied SOA* and the business organization and management practices defined in this book are critical to realizing the full value of SOA. Adopting one without the other will limit your SOA success.

I wrote this book because SOA has changed the entire landscape for planning, designing, implementing, and supporting business "applications." The success of SOA requires a major paradigm shift in the fundamental core of how information technology (IT) organizations and the business in general operate. Adopting SOA as an architectural strategy will force you to challenge every aspect of your corporate culture and current practices, which will effect a transformation that impacts every aspect of your company.

This book will show you how to set up your IT and business organizations and practices to successfully implement and run your SOA "application" development life cycle under an architecturally driven SOA paradigm. Its content is based on years of experience of promoting architecture under a "service-based" philosophy well before the concept of SOA became popular. SOA has simply validated this philosophy and brought focus to its virtues to the entire audience of vendors, consultants, IT departments, and business in general.

I hope that you will find value in the contents of this book. At a minimum, it will provoke many discussions that will challenge the traditional approaches that many of you have been using. For those of you who agree with all or most of what is stated in this book, it will be a useful tool for you to accelerate SOA's adoption in your company. The more people within your IT organization, business units, and vendors/partners who read the book, the more consistent and accelerated that adoption will be.

Who Should Read This Book?

Clearly this book targets the chief information officers, chief technology officers, and chief architects of corporations. These individuals and the positions they hold have the best possibility of effecting a transformation and paradigm shift in their company. Rarely does a corporate transformation occur without a top-down commitment of the executive leadership.

This book also targets the architecture practice within IT. The architects will have to invest the biggest commitment and do most of the work to implement what is presented in this book.

Everyone else in IT should read this book as well. They need to understand how this paradigm shift will affect them and their departments and be committed to the transformation as well. Having everyone in IT on the same page will certainly accelerate SOA's adoption.

This does not mean that business leaders should not read it as well. The business leaders from the executive level down may not understand (or care to understand) some of the technical examples described in this book. Nevertheless, the multitude of value propositions presented will certainly ring true and be readily recognized by these leaders.

There is also value to guiding business leaders to specific sections of the book. For those businesspeople participating in governance activities, the governance chapter (Chapter 8) presents an excellent tool for teaching and educating them as to the critical role they must play and the new responsibilities they must embrace. For those involved in specifying or documenting business requirements for IT projects, Chapter 9, "SOA System Development Life Cycle," and Chapter 11, "People Involved in the SOA Process," are critical. There is value in this book for every leader in the company. The more these leaders read and understand, the higher the probability of their acceptance and support.

Finally, any IT partners and vendors you have (such as outsource developers) or business partners with which your IT people interact (such as an outsource call center partner that integrates or uses your systems to service your customers) should read the book as well. An effective and comprehensive internal SOA practice has tremendous value. Having a synergistic extension of that practice embedded in your external partner and vendor environments provides even more value.

SOA Adoption Has Been Slow

The concept of SOA has been around for several years now. Technologies that provide SOA capabilities are also maturing. Yet SOA has not reached the level of penetration that was expected. The reason its adoption has been slow is not because of technology restrictions but because of architectural restrictions. These architectural restrictions in the context of people, policies, and practices have not adapted and transformed to support the SOA architectural paradigm.

Achieving a successful SOA vision will depend more on how effective you are with people skills and at establishing these new SOA policies and practices than on the successful implementation of the technologies themselves. The establishment of these new SOA policies and procedures will, in effect, create a major paradigm shift in the culture of the corporation. Don't get me wrong: A strong technical architecture is key to successfully realizing the value of SOA, but attempting to do so solely from a technical perspective, without focusing on the policies, procedures, and practices, will almost certainly fail to achieve all that SOA has to offer.

The absence of this transformation of the practices used in the corporation is why SOA's adoption has been slow. It is because successfully implementing SOA is not simply the implementation of a vendor product or technology. Nor is it the use of Web services. Successful implementation requires a major paradigm shift in how the company thinks about, manages, and uses its IT assets.

This adoption failure has been further exasperated by the relatively short-term focus of corporations. The mentality of corporate culture has evolved to such a point that anything that cannot be completed, or at least have a major milestone, within six months is almost impossible to even start. All SOA vendors will "sell" you on one relatively simple short-term project to begin your SOA process. They sell this approach not because they necessarily believe it is the best way to be successful at SOA but because it is the best way to sell their product.

Perhaps a more accurate description of what is described in this book is service-oriented enterprise architecture. This book applies enterprise architecture practices and principles to SOA. The goal of enterprise architecture is to maximize utilization and efficiency of the IT assets and to identify synergistic opportunities and values for the business. Interestingly, the goal of SOA is to maximize utilization and efficiency of IT investments through services and to create synergistic opportunities and values for the business using those services.

The barriers to maximizing the goals of *enterprise architecture* have traditionally been the size and age of the legacy application portfolio and the lack of a more effective model to architect and build business applications. The barriers to maximizing *SOA's* goals have been the lack of people, processes, and practices defined from an enterprise architecture perspective to support the SOA model. This book brings enterprise architecture practices and principles to the SOA model. It defines all the things architects usually define (governance, system development life cycle [SDLC], frameworks, models, etc.) but defines them to specifically support and maximize SOA.

Throughout my years of developing and evolving a service-based architecture approach to business systems, I had to rely on a lot of experience-based intuition and trial and error to set up the practice. There was nothing out there that documented how to do it. Even today there is still very little, which is why I wrote this book. I am providing you with my insight and knowledge as it relates to over 25 years of IT leadership experience and over 15 years of driving a service-based philosophy for business application design. This book was written to help others learn from my experience and avoid having to figure it out on their own. Even if you do not embrace the contents of this book 100 percent, I am confident that you will get significant value out of the experiences and examples I provide.

The Business Is Already Involved in Architecture; It Just Does Not Know It

The two largest reasons for adopting and "institutionalizing" an architecture practice are the rapid expansions of technologies in terms of viable technical alternatives and the business's perceived rights for involvement in technical decisions. These are realities that the architects must manage and control. New technologies and capabilities will continue to be introduced, and nontechnical businesspeople will continue to be exposed to them through avenues like the Web and vendor contacts. This presentation will be heavily weighted toward the positive, or "sizzle," business values of the technology and very little toward the support, integration, and architectural synergy with the rest of the enterprise.

All these events have contributed to create a world where architecture can no longer be perceived as an IT function. Architecture needs to be perceived as a business function at the tactical and strategic levels. This requires that the business take ownership of the architecture. There is a difference between selling the value of an architecture practice to the business and having that business drive the architectural value through co-ownership.

To this end, the architecture practice must facilitate this transformation from IT ownership to business ownership. Doing so will require an entirely new perspective of the IT process throughout the organization, a major paradigm shift in corporate culture, processes, and accountabilities. It also requires a whole new set of policies, procedures, and standards within the architecture practice arsenal to help the organization achieve this paradigm shift.

The architecture practice must learn to proactively live and exist in this new world to be successful. The architects must spend a significant amount of their effort on communicating and educating both the business community and the business application vendors that reach out to that business community. The old days of waiting for the business to bring a project to IT before assessing the architecture implications are long gone. Recognizing that the business will become aware of technical solutions to meet some of its business needs and institutionalizing a process and culture where the business understands enough about the value and need of the architecture practice to involve it up front will help tremendously in achieving a long-term SOA vision.

Pragmatism Is Also Important

Architects must be pragmatic. New technologies and business application solutions are hitting the market and businesses are being exposed to them at light speed. Any bureaucratic process that slows or derails this process in the eyes of the business will fail. In this new world, the architects are incapable of stopping purchased business applications and often the noncompliant technologies and platforms they use from being introduced into the environment. By getting up front in the acquisition process (especially before a purchase commitment has been made to the vendor), the architects have the opportunity to influence these decisions and to minimize the impact by proactively establishing vendor compliance commitments in future releases. If the business is prepositioned to view and validate these solutions in the context of an architecture that it has taken ownership of, the probability of a more positive (architecture-compliant) outcome rises significantly.

Since more and more companies buy business applications rather than build them or alternatively partner with someone else to use or "lease" their business applications (e.g., application service providers), the traditional architectural approach around development does not apply. The advent of vendors providing software as a service (SaaS) further extends this model. The new approach cannot just focus on data and integration concerns but must also focus on maximizing the architectural compliance and SOA interoperability of these purchased or leased solutions. Conducting architectural discussions with these vendors and reaching an architectural vision and compliance agreement with them prior to signing a contract to purchase their business applications helps to move all business applications used by the company toward the SOA vision, not just the ones custom built in-house.

SOA *Is* the Way

No other architectural approach to business applications provides the capability to achieve the maximization of efficiency and flexibility that SOA can offer. If you think of SOA as a way to transform all the physical aspects of business applications into standardized, logical, and consumable "views" of the underlying application code, you have taken the first step down the right path. If you now understand that these logical views or services can be structured to support their delivery to a consumer over any number of delivery channels without replicating their underlying functionality, you have taken the next step in the right direction. Finally, if you recognize that an architecture practice is required to ensure that the business applications delivered are designed to provide the flexibility, adaptability, and reusability promised, you have take the final step toward a belief in and commitment to SOA. If you can get vendors who promote business solutions to your business to understand these beliefs as well, and get them to agree to support the architecture in future releases of their products, you will remove a large barrier in your quest to achieve the end state SOA vision.

Not an Introduction to Enterprise Architecture or Service-Oriented Architecture

This book is not an introduction to enterprise architecture or SOA. It assumes anyone implementing the model and the practices it defines has a strong base of experience and knowledge in architecture principles, processes, and practices. Its intent is to show how to transform your enterprise architecture practice so that SOA is the predominant strategic approach for applications utilized in the company and how the enterprise architecture organization can facilitate this rise of SOA to prominence.

SOA Is Here to Stay

SOA is here to stay. Its prominence will become more and more evident to more people as time goes on. I think back to when relational database technology came to the market. The biggest knock was that it was too inefficient to support transaction processing. Most of its early adopters used it to replicate data for reporting purposes. Advances in database efficiencies coupled with increased computing power and disk input/output performance have led us to today where very few online transaction processing (OLTP) systems applications do not have a relational database engine. It can be argued that some technical people saw the virtue of relational databases for OLTP and together with the hardware and software vendors evolved multiple technologies (CPU, memory, storage, database performance tools, etc.) to make the technology not only pragmatic but also desirable. It took many instances of proven adaptations of the relational database technology and the publication of these successes as repeatable processes before the tipping point for relational databases was reached.

The (relatively) slow adoption of SOA has been the result of similar factors. Proven, repeatable experiences with SOA that can be readily understood and adopted by others are lacking. They are lacking because the repeatable experiences that are out there are technical implementation experiences, not architectural experiences. This has hindered the ability of architects to show and promote SOA's value as a core, prominent strategy for the company to adopt. What is lacking is a repeatable SOA SDLC, a repeatable SOA governance process, and a repeatable SOA enterprise architecture framework.

This is what this book hopes to provide. It lets the reader "see" the entire architectural approach to SOA and how all the pieces of the approach fit together and complement each other. It provides all the definitions and documentation needed to implement the approach. It provides comprehensive, repeatable architectural processes that can be adopted and implemented in your company.

The enterprise SOA architects still need to investigate and learn more about your environment and *transform* your company to the SOA model defined in this book based on your unique corporation. The final chapter in this book (Chapter 14) shows you how to do this.

Architects Need to Be Proactive

It is important that architects recognize that they need to be proactive, not reactive. If architecture waits for a new technology or a new approach like SOA to be introduced at a project level, it is already too late to architect the solution from an enterprise perspective. It becomes a tactical implementation exercise, not a strategic one. The architects need to be proactively ahead of the business from a technology perspective in addition to the practice perspective. What role will business process management systems play? Wireless access protocol? Security assertion markup language (SAML)? Web Services 2.0? Describing their role in the context of the as-is and to-be architecture instead of as a single business application project has a profound impact on many decisions that will be made, not the least of which is vendor contracting, pricing, and infrastructure capacity.

What You Will Learn in This Book

Reading this book will provide you with a complete and comprehensive methodology and framework for adopting and managing an SOA environment including:

- Direct linkage and management of all SOA activities to the corporate strategy and business plans.

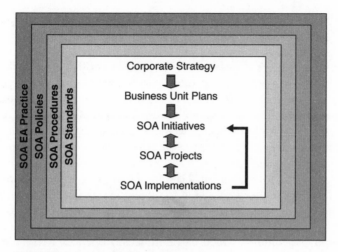

EXHIBIT I.1   SOA~EAF Methodology

- Direct mapping of the business (conceptual) view of the SOA assets to the design (logical) view of those SOA assets and their implemented (physical) representations.

The book also shows you how to set up and run your SOA enterprise architecture practice using this methodology and framework and how to leverage existing architecture artifacts into this new framework. An overview of the methodology is presented in Exhibit I.1.

This SOA Enterprise Architecture Framework (SOA~EAF™) Methodology diagram and the associated architecture framework that supports it are defined in detail in Chapter 5.

This book provides everything you need to set up and manage the methodology and framework. It will show you how to set up and run the SOA SDLC to develop architecture-driven SOA applications. It will define the governance processes to effectively and efficiently manage this SOA SDLC. The book also defines all the resources needed to implement all the processes in terms of their roles, responsibilities, and capabilities. It tells you how to leverage the SOA model to evolve and migrate your legacy application environment to modernize and maximize these investments going forward. It shows you how to address different business and IT organization models and how to deal with them. Finally, the book shows you how to assess your current business and IT SOA enterprise architecture maturity. You will be able to identify gaps between your current people, processes, platforms, and practice capabilities and the ones defined in this book. You will be able to build your own SOA business strategy and roadmap for bridging this gap.

How This Book Is Organized

This book is organized into four parts.

> **Part I** discusses the value of SOA and architecture in general. It discusses how a new architectural approach is required to achieve all the value that SOA has to offer.

Part II defines the SOA~EAF and the methodology that uses this framework. This part also discusses how to integrate and leverage your existing enterprise architecture assets into this new framework.

Part III defines the SOA processes and practices within the methodology that need to be implemented to effect the paradigm shift throughout the corporation and realize SOA's advantages. It defines the different types of resources and skills needed within the company to transform the organization and effectively manage the transformation. It also redefines the roles and responsibilities of the business participants in the SOA application development process.

Part IV provides information on how to assess your company's SOA maturity and how to use that assessment to develop your SOA business strategy and roadmap to implement the SOA model and practice defined in this book.

Three appendixes are provided as references. Appendix A contains templates of documents and forms described in the book that you can modify and use in your own practice. Appendix B defines the different types of SOA services discussed throughout the book and describes their applicability. Appendix C provides an example of the architectural principles and considerations that must be addressed when defining an enterprise architecture approach for SOA. It uses the enterprise SOA security development framework as an example. These appendices are provided so they can be pulled out and referenced by business architects, solution architects, and project architects. In addition, there is a glossary of acronyms used in this book.

Closing Remarks

This book provides a repeatable process and shows a pragmatic way to achieve all that SOA has to offer. It also provides insight into how an architecture practice can play an even larger strategic role within the organization. Throughout this book I have provided many examples based on my experiences. While the exact situations you encounter may be different, the architectural process and management techniques I used to resolve them are the points I want to make with those examples. I hope they will help you when you encounter similar processes and management issues in your unique environment.

I am interested in your feedback and comments. You can leave them on my blog, www.soaistheway.wordpress.com. I will gladly respond and use your input to improve the next edition of this book.

Good luck, and let the journey begin!

About the Web Site

My blog (www.soaistheway.wordpress.com) is dedicated to the promotion and advancement of the service-oriented architecture approach to business systems design. The purpose of the site is to provide a forum where people like myself, who believe that SOA is the next baseline of the business application evolution, can share and express ideas and help advance the institutionalization of SOA throughout the business domain. You will also find electronic versions of the template documents and forms provided in Appendix A to help facilitate their use and adaptation. Feel free to use them within your company as is or modify them to suit your own business needs. If you are using the templates or variations of the templates for commercial reasons or include them in documents distributed to entities outside your company, I ask that you honor the copyright laws and include the following copyright disclosure at the bottom of each template page:

Achieving Service-Oriented Architecture

PART I

Value of Enterprise Architecture and SOA

CHAPTER 1

What Is an Architecture Practice, and Why Do You Need One?

I have been studying and practicing architecture from an information technology and business strategy perspective for more than 20 years. While the concept of architecture was not well defined, well understood, or well communicated in those early years, the advancements in computing technologies were forcing the concept to the surface due to unmanaged complexities in information technology (IT) that were impacting efficiencies and costs. IT organizations were being further impacted by a rapidly accelerating trend of computer literacy by the nontechnical business community. Systems were no longer being perceived as magical "black boxes," and the business involvement was not limited to business requirements. In some cases today the business jumps right over the pragmatic assessment of requirements into the selection of a prebuilt vendor solution for IT to "install."

Since the beginning of multiplatform computing, much has been written about the value of an enterprise architecture practice. Most revolves around the "selling" of architecture to the business leaders. This material is essential for obtaining buy-in and commitment. As architects, however, we recognize there is a more fundamental underlying reason why architecture is important. That reason is simply that computing technology and systems have become increasingly more complex. The number of technologies, the ways those technologies are being adapted and utilized, and the multitude of alternatives available as solutions to any given business need seem to grow exponentially each year. The result is that there are literally thousands of ways that technology can solve any one business need. While this is good in terms of competitiveness and pricing, it is bad in terms of complexity and overhead. In other words, the good news is we have many alternatives and options for solving a problem technically. The bad news is we have many alternatives and options for solving a problem technically, and without an architecture you end up implementing many different ways to solve different instances of the same problem.

Business Organizations and Departments Do Not Operate as Isolated Islands

The obstacles begin to emerge when it is realized that individual business needs are not self-contained or isolated islands. All or a portion of any one business's needs may, and often do, have value to other business units and other business processes. While the ability to enter and validate an order from a customer was originally perceived as an internally bounded business activity, today many customers are provided the capability to directly enter the order through the Web or through a partner web site supporting your business. These add-on systems are directly influenced and impacted by the way the order system works. Adding the capability to identify high-value customers for premier services or to cross-sell customers through any of these add-on mechanisms will depend largely on how the underlying application operates and how the add-on solutions are implemented.

The point is, adapting to any of these evolutionary changes without consideration of an architecture has a high probability of incurring excessive costs for duplicity and support and may not even be attainable for technical or financial reasons.

Thus, in addition to providing guidance and traceable links to the business strategy and business unit plans, an architecture provides fundamental, basic analytical, and management capabilities to ensure that everything aligns properly and works efficiently.

If you think about building a home, the architect shows you, the customer, floor plans and layouts, even perhaps a scale model. He may even show the plans or model in the context of a high-level architecture (i.e., where it sits on the lot or how far it is set back from the street). What he does not show you is how all the plumbing and wiring is laid into the building and interconnected or where the heat ducts are. He may not show where the utilities are brought in from the street. Rest assured, however, that all of these specifications are documented and will be part of the delivery. They are specified not only based on your input in terms of the size of the building and its layout, but also on the zoning and building codes of the community. There is an expectation that the customer does not have to worry about these code and zoning requirements. The architect takes care of them. Do you as the customer take the blame and responsibility if the building inspector finds a violation?

Now let us think back to when the Pilgrims first settled in America. Certainly they applied basic building principles, but there were no building or zoning rules. As our country grew and became more crowded and complex, the need for these regulations became more apparent. Similarly, as the size and complexity of our technology infrastructure grew, we recognized the need for these basic standards and principles as well.

An enterprise architecture practice is an organization within the company that manages the complexities of the IT environment and applies principles and techniques to reduce the complexities, improve efficiencies, and reduce capital and operational expenditures. This alone should be enough to justify an architecture practice. Architecture, however, can provide an even more critical service. Architecture can help the business take advantage of the IT infrastructure to gain competitive advantages over the competition. An architecture-compliant environment and strategic architecture principles can provide opportunities and advantages not possible without these capabilities.

As a way to illustrate how technology complexity has evolved, I would like to present a brief history of computing. I will focus on some key technological milestones that have played a major role in this evolution. Understanding the past helps us deal with the future. We need to use what history has taught us to help us avoid similar mistakes in the future. We also need to realize that taking advantage of new technologies and approaches can be accelerated if we understand how the adoption of previous technologies evolved.

Looking at the Past to Understand the Future

Technology advancements are for the most part an evolution. Each new technology concept is based on improving what already exists. Companies that can recognize these improvements early on and adopt them are usually the ones that gain the greatest competitive advantage from them. Understanding how computing has evolved historically and the roles that technologies played in that evolution can help us assess where technologies of today might lead us in the future.

In the beginning, business use of computers was simple and straightforward (although it may not have seemed so to those adopting it). It consisted of punch cards in, green bar printouts, and assembler language in the middle. There were not many options involved for how to do things.

Three key technology advancements resulted in the next major leap in business computing. First was the development of a new program language called common business-oriented language (COBOL) designed for writing business applications. The second advancement was the introduction of magnetic disks allowing data and programs to be readily accessible in real time. The third advancement was the introduction of the real-time terminal device based on the customer information control system (CICS) from IBM. These technologies brought us out of the world of batch processing into real-time processing, at least at a rudimentary level. As a result of these advancements, the type and volume of business applications exploded. In addition to performing traditional financial batch processes, such as general ledger and payroll, computers were now being used to price and process orders, generate invoices, and manage inventories and purchases.

The next major milestone was the introduction of the mini- and super-minicomputers that exploded the competitiveness of the computer hardware market and started the continuous advancements in the price performance of computer hardware that continues to this day. People walk around today with devices in their pocket that have more processing power and storage capacity than a computer with a footprint the size of a football field in the 1960s!

There was, however, a downside to this era of the computer evolution. The downside was the proliferation of redundant data and duplicity of business logic through the explosion of silo business applications.

Businesses began extracting data from the mainframe to their minis, tweaking duplicated business logic to support a slightly different set of processes, and providing a custom user interface to support them. And thus the era of multiple "stovepipe" applications with significant redundancy of data and logic began.

The next two technology advances did not create a new era of computing, they simply extended the boundaries of the existing proliferation era and slapped a new label on it. These two advances were:

1. Significant advancements in networking and network interoperability
2. The introduction of the macrocomputer known as the personal computer (PC)

For the first time there was availability of computing power at the desktop and connectivity to tap into it. The new label attached to applications developed in this phase was *client-server*. Now business data (especially reference and edit/validation supporting data) and business logic were not being duplicated on a few minicomputer platforms. They were being proliferated to hundreds, if not thousands, of desktop PCs throughout the company.

At this point most businesses had reached the epitome of what I call the resource-consumption model. Every new application:

- Was more costly and time consuming to develop and deploy.
- Added to the total year-over-year fixed cost expenses of operations.

More important, but seldom recognized, this proliferation did not improve, but instead eroded, the flexibility and adaptability to business changes.

In fact, many companies were backed into a corner where their only option was to build or buy another silo stovepipe solution even though they recognized the long-term impact of these decisions. Some companies were lucky enough to recognize the value of middleware and adopted an enterprise application integration (EAI) framework. This helped to minimize the number of point-to-point connections among the systems and reduced the need for some redundant business data and logic. Those that did adopt a middleware EAI strategy were better positioned to move to the next layer of sophistication.

The next major technology advancements were unique in that they came from an entirely different direction. They were not focused on helping businesses improve their internal systems, but they ended up revolutionizing the way we conduct business. I am talking, of course, about the Web browser and World Wide Web technologies.

While many companies were successfully extending their systems externally to their customers and suppliers, they did so without the availability of a globally accepted ubiquitous channel to do so. Customer and vendor penetration was limited in that it often required that they also make a significant investment to participate in this electronic relationship. (Bulletin Boards were the exception.)

The World Wide Web changed all this. What started out as a mechanism to help find information more easily on the Internet and more intuitively through a graphical user interface ended up providing a globally accessible ubiquitous user interface for processing business transactions. Business transactions were now capable of traversing multiple companies and multiple industries through partnerships that heretofore were unheard of. We only have to look at the online travel web sites like Orbitz® or Priceline® to see the synergistic market value of partnerships across multiple industries with a common goal (selling travel services).

The World Wide Web explosion was fueled by the introduction of another technology: fiber optic networks. Fiber optics not only geometrically expanded the bandwidth globally, but its proliferation did to the cost of wide area networks what chip advancements did to the cost of computers. Not only was bandwidth cheap and plentiful, but a standard ubiquitous interface called the Web browser was made available to take advantage of it! Wireless technologies are now taking away the physical restrictions of this new world. It truly is now anytime, anyplace.

Which brings us to today. On the positive side, we have this wonderful capability to reach out to anyone, anywhere, and conduct business. We have the ability to blend our strengths with those of our partners and even competitors to increase exposure and market share. On the negative side, we have this portfolio of redundant and stovepipe internal business applications on a massive heterogeneous set of technologies requiring heavy human involvement to navigate them when performing business activities.

If you think about what has evolved, it is ironic that we have actually come full circle from where we started. When we started there was only *one* system (one that was relatively simple by today's standards), the big mainframe with punch cards in and green bar printout. We have now evolved to where we are again at *one* system. Scott McNeely from Sun Microsystems once said, "The network is the system." As business looks at its need to get at whatever information or processes it needs, whenever it needs it, wherever it needs it, is it not looking at the entirety of systems as one? The distinction between yesterday and today is that systems were originally viewed as physical by the business. Today they are viewed as conceptual.

This is both good and bad for architects. On the good side, it gives us the ability to highlight and communicate the value of the logical and conceptual components of architecture. On the downside, our need to maintain an up-to-date and accurate mapping of the conceptual-to-logical and logical-to-physical components of our environment is absolutely critical.

Thus the evolution of technologies and the capabilities they provided have had as great an impact on how businesses operate as anything else they have encountered. They have also been responsible for the single largest expenditure increase year over year. Even though the cost of many technologies has shrunk considerably over the years, the total amount IT spends has increased significantly over that same period. This is partly due to the fact that companies today use more technologies and have more business applications than they ever had before. What is not necessarily understood by the business is the fact that the acquisition of most of these technologies and business applications was not made based on architectural principles and added a significant amount of costs associated with redundancy, duplicity, and complexity. There is a lot of waste and a lot of unnecessary overhead in most IT operations today. Therefore, it is critical that the architects are aware of the technologies and capabilities coming down the pipe. Many of these may be beneficial to or desirable by the business. Architects need to proactively understand what will be required to minimize the architectural impact of these technologies and maximize their effectiveness if they are brought in-house.

Summary

The answer to why we need an architecture practice is:

- To ensure that all the IT investments will hang together and work the way they are suppose to work and when they are supposed to work.
- To proactively ensure that any new technologies, platforms, or solutions introduced into the environment are the best solutions from a business *and* architecture perspective.

- To be the agents of advancement of the business's understanding of and participation in an architectural approach to IT systems.
- To leverage and exploit the understanding and participation of the business to identify strategic opportunities and maximize the return on investment on IT expenditures.

While any one of us may have taken on a project to build a shed in the backyard or finish off a room in the house without a formal plan, none of us believe we could build a skyscraper without architects. We would not, however, use architects if they were not formally trained in and knowledgeable about the architectural design principles and practices as well as all the regulations and laws applicable for the development environment. We must believe that this is also true for our IT systems as well.

None of us would go out and buy a prebuilt spare bedroom to attach to our house without an architecture design for how that room will be integrated with the existing house. Buying a prebuilt business application without considering the architectural impact can result in similar restrictions and complexities when implemented.

CHAPTER 2

Why Is a Service-Oriented Architecture So Valuable?

In Chapter 1 it was suggested that we have come full circle in terms of our view of systems and that business today functions as if there is just one system. This is not 100 percent true. What is more truthful is that business *needs* business applications to be one system, as evidenced by the way businesses want to use those systems. Unfortunately, neither businesses nor IT follow a model or process that actually allows the separate stovepipe business applications to become a single system. As more project-based point solutions are built or purchased, organizations move farther away from a single-view model.

The pain comes once the immediate need has been met by the point solution. The business will naturally carry the point solution to the next level, that is:

- What other value can this solution provide?
- What other organizations are questioning if there is value in the solution for them?
- Or worse, has the business changed again, and do we need a different view?

The conflict between what the business really needs and what IT delivers will continue to exist until the model and processes are transformed to a new paradigm. That paradigm is service-oriented architecture (SOA). Attempts to continually enhance stovepipe applications to become something that they fundamentally are incapable of becoming will continue to be futile and frustrating to businesses. Providing a single view of the business applications is impossible when each of those systems has its own proprietary application-specific user interfaces. Continuously creating new stovepipe applications that create new views needed by the business for specific initiatives but delivering them through yet another proprietary application-specific user interface provides only temporary relief; when the business changes again, these new solutions will be just as inflexible and costly to enhance as all the other applications.

SOA is the only architectural approach that I am aware of that is specifically designed to solve this problem. Notice that I call it an architectural approach, not a technology. Implementing SOA as a technology will not solve this problem.

The problem with stovepipe solutions is that they are not designed to play in a virtual, logical world. The typical stovepipe solution encapsulates the entire architectural domain of the specific function it performs. By that I mean it usually controls not just the business logic needed for the specific function, but also the physical and logical user interface/presentation layer used to access the business logic. Stovepipe solutions are not necessarily designed to expose their business logic through mechanisms other than their proprietary presentation layers; nor do they access business logic from other business applications through their presentation layer interfaces. Their embedded security systems are also not designed to authorize access to the business logic outside their own presentation interface.

Traditionally, these applications were leveraged by other business areas through data layer integration, either by replicating the stored data to other databases or by writing new logic to process the application data, which could be accessed independently from the initial application's logic and security. The problem with this approach was that it could not leverage any of the business logic in the application (stored procedures are the exception). In many cases some or all of the logic associated with the application had to be rewritten to support the new need. Another new presentation layer was also required to access and display the new logic, and a new security mechanism to control it. The net effect of this approach was the physical implementation of another stovepipe application. This physical approach is a costly one in terms of all the duplication, redundancy, and complexity introduced each time one of these implementations occurred.

Where Does SOA Fit In?

The difference between an enterprise architecture (EA) and an SOA from a technical perspective is that an EA practice will capture and identify this wasteful duplicity and unnecessary complexity and an SOA will provide a pragmatic, evolutionary design approach to ultimately eliminate them.

Therefore, an SOA sits squarely in the middle of the answer to the question: How do we get from where we are now to where we want to be?

The three key tenets to the understanding of the architectural framework and methodology defined in this book are:

1. Understanding the flaws and restrictions of what we have built in the past and how we built them.
2. Recognizing the technology advancements that exist today that eliminate these restrictions.
3. Learning a methodology and framework for evolving existing and new applications to take advantage of these capabilities.

As these tenets highlight, successfully taking advantage of SOA is not a technology implementation or a product purchase. It is called a service-oriented *architecture,* not a service-oriented *technology* or service-oriented *product* for a reason. To architects, it must represent an approach and a philosophy. SOA has qualities and characteristics that make it unique and distinguishable. These architectural qualities and characteristics, not the technical qualities and characteristics, are what makes SOA so valuable and are the basis for choosing it over other architectures.

How Has Technology Been Evolving and Advancing to Solve These Problems?

Our traditional stovepipe applications are problematic because their design creates barriers to creating a single view of the company's systems. SOA is an approach that can actually move us toward achieving a single-system view of the environment by removing or circumventing these barriers. New technologies built to support SOA are providing the capabilities to eliminate or diminish these barriers. An effective SOA approach shifts the entire corporate mind-set from a physical focus to a conceptual and logical focus.

This transition away from a physical focus has, in fact, been the natural order of progression of technology since the inception of computers. When is the last time any of us dealt with IRQ and port conflicts when installing device drivers? These physical complexities are now hidden from users, who only have to deal with some logical decisions presented by an installation wizard when the device is being installed. As the complexity of computing increased, the technologies evolved to solve or resolve the lower-level physical complexities. As more of the physical complexities were resolved, making the physical complexities less of an issue, the focus began to shift into complexities in higher layers (i.e., the logical complexities). The physical complexities of computer hardware were resolved and hidden by representing and resolving them logically through software. In the example just given, all the data and analysis to ensure resource conflicts do not occur when installing new devices still needs to take place, except now it is done through the installation software and the firmware on the devices being installed.

Networks represent perhaps the largest class of technologies that have advanced their ease of use and hence their adoption. Many in my generation remember excruciatingly well the difficulties interconnecting local area networks (LANs) with different data link layer protocols or connecting LANs and wide area networks (WANs) using different network layer protocols. We also remember painful experiences in trying to resolve IRQ and port conflicts in DOS when installing network cards on personal computers. Technology and technology standards have taken care of all of these problems. Today the biggest network challenge we face may be entering the wired equivalent privacy (WEP) key accurately when running the "Connect to Network" wizard. Today people with absolutely no technical network training are installing and configuring multiuser LANs and LAN to WAN routing networks in their own homes! We have evolved to where it does not matter how we connect; we expect that we can get access to the network and get what we need.

Exhibit 2.1 reflects examples of how technical advancements in networking have resolved all the complexities and incompatibilities to where any network component, whether it is embedded in a computer or a stand-alone network device, can be (technically) interconnected to any other network device.

The same evolution and advancements have been occurring for technologies that support software applications. If we think of the (logical) application layers as data and data logic at the lowest layer, business logic at the middle layer, and presentation logic at the top layer, we see that technology advances have resolved many of the interoperability issues of the past. We no longer spend significant time and resources figuring out, for example, how a JAVA application running on a UNIX server can use a structured query language (SQL) database running on a

Layers	Implementation Options
Physical Layer	Twisted Pair, Coax Cable, Wireless. It doesn't matter.
Link Layer	Ethernet, Token Ring, Packet Switch, Time-Division Multiplexing (TDM). It doesn't matter.
Network Layer	Internet Protocol (IP), Systems Network Architecture (SNA), Internetwork Packet Exchange (IPX). It doesn't matter.

EXHIBIT 2.1 Advancements in Network Connectivity

Windows server. Interoperability at the data layer has been significantly improved by technology to the point where today little concern is expended at this layer.

Interoperability at the business logic layer is a much more complex problem. There are many languages, platforms, and approaches used at the business logic layer. Data layer interoperability has been solved through the development of technologies that provided a layer of abstraction above the physical data stores through standardized application program interfaces (APIs) and the adoption of data access standards (e.g., SQL) and data formats (e.g., extensible markup language [XML]). Logical device technologies like open database connectivity (ODBC) and Java database connectivity (JDBC) provided a standardized way to logically access data from many different data platforms and technologies. Today there are *no* physical or logical restrictions that force us to duplicate data for different business applications.

Note

Data duplication is not the same as data replication to support wide geographical performance or replication to support client-side validations. Where data are replicated, it is for the sake of efficiency/performance rather than for processing's sake.

As fewer issues remained at the data layer, vendors shifted their focus to the business logic layer. The question here is the same as the one at the data layer. Instead of asking the data question, "How we can use existing data in its existing storage location instead of duplicating it?" we are now asking, "How do we use existing business logic instead of duplicating it?" The evolution of solutions to this question has evolved from modular programming with exit routines to remote procedure calls (RPCs) to middleware technologies like IBM WebSphere MQ and object request brokers (ORBs) to Web services.

Thus the major focus of technological advancements at the data and business logic layers has been on providing capabilities to eliminate the wasteful duplication of data and business logic. This has been forcefully driven by the customers who have seen a continuous increase in the annual IT spending go to supporting this duplication and its associated complexity. It has also been accelerated by the introduction of browser technology that provides a ubiquitous user interface technology. Applications written to take advantage of a browser client achieve three major objectives:

1. They eliminate a significant amount of the duplication needed to support multiple client platforms.
2. They provide the capability for client access to the application without having the application preinstalled and/or preconfigured on those clients.
3. Any browser client on any internal or external authorized network can access the application.

Today, technology has solved:

- The requirement to access business data on different platforms that use different technologies.
- The requirement for accessing business logic written in different languages on different platforms.
- The ability to orchestrate the extracted data and business logic into new and different business processes.
- The ability to distribute these new processes over different multiple channels.
- The need to have a single client-side platform that anyone can use to present these processes.
- The ability to access these clients from anywhere at any time.

Exhibit 2.2 shows how application-level advancements and standards have done for application interoperability what the network enhancements and standards did for network interoperability depicted in Exhibit 2.1.

Advancement	Benefit
HyperText Markup Language (HTML), Browser	Universal User Display
Portals	Universal Service Choreography
Extensible Markup Language (XML)	Universal Data Recognition
Web Services	Universal Code Recognition
Simple Object Access Protocol (SOAP)	Universal Code Delivery
Internet	Universal Connectivity
Secure Sockets Layer (SSL) Security Assertion Markup Language (SAML)	Universal Security

EXHIBIT 2.2 Advancements in Application Interoperability

Where the network technology and standards advances in Exhibit 2.1 make it possible today to *connect* to anyone anywhere at any time, the technology and standards advances in Exhibit 2.2 allow us to *interact* with anyone anywhere at any time! These advancements, however, will have limited value if we are unable to deliver the business services and business processes that can operate within these standards. Being able to deliver them efficiently and effectively is important as well.

The loosely coupled, granular approach of SOA and the capabilities to "plug and play" these loosely coupled SOA components into multiple configurations of delivered capabilities is the first interoperability benefit of SOA. The ability to extract and abstract the business capabilities from the legacy systems and incorporate their capabilities into the loosely coupled SOA components is the next interoperability benefit of SOA. The ability to architect the SOA components that utilize and leverage the standards in Exhibit 2.2 is the final interoperability benefit of SOA. No other architecture can support and, more importantly, maximize these three benefits.

Where Do We Need to Focus Today?

The technologies that exist today allow us to isolate and hide the physical restrictions that were built into applications in the past and leverage standards to deliver capabilities to anyone anywhere. Just as networking advances solved the network interoperability issues from a physical and logical perspective, application technology advances have solved the interoperability issues at the physical and logical layers.

Now the focus needs to shift to the conceptual layer. People know they can get e-mails on their phone as well as their computers. They know that e-mails read on or replied to on one of these channels can be revisited later on the other channel. Almost none of them understand how this physically or logically happens. They just know conceptually that it does.

This is where we need to take the business in terms of their business applications. People need to be able to conceptually describe what they want and not have to worry about how it is logically or physically accomplished. This is a difficult task to achieve because IT has spent years training people to address and deal with the physical and logical issues of their business applications. They have evolved to the point where their business requirements are laced with technical solutions and platform recommendations. So it is not just IT, but the business as well, that has to transform and adopt a new philosophy and approach.

There will be many businesspeople who will not be willing to make this transformation without hard physical evidence that their needs and requirements expressed at the conceptual level are truly reflected and accurate in the logical and physical implementations. The SOA Enterprise Architecture Framework (SOA~EAF™) and methodology defined in this book provides the tractability and evidence across these layers to comfort their unease and gain their acceptance.

How Do We Express the SOA Value from a Business Perspective?

While the technical value of SOA is important, the most important value of SOA is that it provides us with an approach for transforming all the physical aspects of our business application assets into standardized, logical, and consumable views that can be presented to the business holistically and conceptually in a way users can understand. It also provides an opportunity for IT and the business to communicate and interact with each other at a highly efficient and equally understood level. That common, equally understood language is the language of services. The highly structured and easy-to-understand mechanism for describing and managing those services is through one of two perspectives:

1. Those who supply (provide) the services
2. Those who use (consume) the services

Imagine a world where the entire conversation between the business and its IT organization is based on discussions on service consumer and service provider requirements. It would not matter if those discussions were in terms of specifying requirements, planning future capabilities, or meeting performance expectations. They would all be described and communicated in terms of the person who needs to use it and the people who need to provide it. At a minimum, it creates a common, level playing field across all business units so that funding trade-offs and delivery prioritization's can be evaluated from an apples-to-apples perspective. At a maximum efficiency level, it exposes previously unseen commonalties and efficiencies across those business units and new opportunities for expanding stakeholders and buy-in.

Transforming the Old Physical and Logical Business-IT Language to the Conceptual Language of Services

Early in my career (back when the business seldom got involved with technical or physical systems issues), I received some wise advice from a consultant who came in to help me with my project. I was frustrated in that I was not getting any buy-in from business leaders to implement a major component of an application suite as a front end to the order system. The consultant said, "Let's look at the message you've been communicating." He read from my presentation:

This module will increase the system throughput by 40% and provide more accurate validations of orders resulting in a 25% improvement in the order throughput rate.

He revised my presentation by stating:

Installing this module will allow us to get all the orders received during the crunch at the end of each quarter booked without increasing order staff and running second and weekend shifts. It will also allow us to reduce the number of orders entered incorrectly that cause the sales reps to go back to the customer, wasting their time and the customer's time. The improvements from this system will result in an annual order booking expense savings of $500K at current order levels.

The fact is, I knew inherently that the throughput and accuracy improvements would result in savings and a return on investment (ROI). I assumed that the business leaders would recognize this as well. The problem is that I did not quantify it and relied on them to make this leap. Unfortunately, the business was focused on the conceptual aspects of running the business in terms of the workload of their sales force and the satisfaction of customers. I was presenting a technical recommendation based on a system's performance and efficiency.

The lesson learned is, if you want to make a point when presenting something of value, you need to do so by understanding the recipients' frame of reference for measuring value and present the metrics that they can relate to and act on. That frame of reference must be based on their world, not yours. Architects deal in efficiencies and improvements. Business leaders deal in revenues, expenses, and ROI.

What we are attempting to do is to establish a new communication language and communication vehicle between IT and the business. We are attempting to replace conversations around *IT terms and concepts* (such as users and system user interfaces) with conversations around *business terms and concepts* (such as constituents and service consumers). We are attempting to replace conversation about *physical concepts* (such as databases and servers) with conversations about *conceptual concepts* (business processes and business functions).

We are trying to solve two problems here:

1. We are trying to get the business back to focusing on its business needs rather than a technical solution.
2. We are trying to get IT to talk in terms and concepts that the business understands, not ones that IT understands.

Earlier in this book I talked about the evolution of technologies and how they have changed the way we develop systems. There has also been an evolution in how business and IT perceive technology and how they represent it. When I first started my career, I never had a businessperson tell me what they needed in terms of a technical solution. I would venture to guess that if any of you looked back at business requirement documents produced for previous projects, you will find examples of technical solutions in these business requirements. Some examples include:

- Need an extract of the order database loaded onto the financial analysis server.
- Need to add e-mail address field on the order review screen.

Even worse, the first time you hear about a business requirement may be when the businessperson hands you a vendor's sales brochure and says, "The company wants to buy this product that was shown in a demo by the vendor last week."

The issue is that the two business requirement examples and the vendor product solution may turn out to be the right solution, but only after the due diligence is completed. By this I mean:

- The real business requirements are understood and documented.
- The solution is assessed in the context of the enterprise set of requirements, not just requirements of one business unit.

- The compatibility and compliance of the solution with the established corporate policies, standards, and guidelines as well as any external regulatory or contractual compliance are assessed and vetted.
- The recommended solution or vendor product solution is the best technical solution.

I use the e-mail address field example because it relates to a situation that happened to one of my solutions architects on a project. The order department had submitted a project two years earlier. It was not approved. Since then it had hired its own "business analyst" and produced the detailed business requirements document for the project. This document, however, did not use the company's standard business requirements gathering template or the specified standards within that template (use cases, swim lanes, etc.). The original proposal was not written up as an SOA initiative and did not use the business architecture template or the SOA initiative proposal format. The project was now being resubmitted for funding approval and sent to the business architecture representative along with the full set of completed business requirements for review.

The business analyst hired by the business documented this e-mail field requirement for the order review screen. When asked why this was needed, the business analyst responded, "So the order administrator can e-mail the sales rep when the order is accepted." The business analyst was next asked how the field would be populated. He referred to another requirement in a different section of the requirements document that stated, "Sales reps will be required to enter their e-mail address on each submitted order." The discussion led to a third requirement in yet another section of the requirement document that stated, "The order administrator will send an e-mail notification to the sales rep informing them if the order was approved or denied using the sales rep e-mail address entered on the order." It was further discovered that this would be accomplished by cutting and pasting the e-mail address from the order screen into the TO: field on the e-mail client with a typed message as to the acceptance or rejection of the order (including a reason why for rejected orders). Each administrator would have a sheet with a standard list of reasons for rejections.

The problem here is that the business analyst documented a solution that was not very efficient. It required the reentry of the sales rep's e-mail address on every order, even though that information existed in the mail directory system. It required a manual cut-and-paste of the information to an e-mail client and the manual keying of rejection reasons.

When asked why the business defined the requirements this way, the analyst responded, "They were trying to minimize the cost of developing the system so they could have a better chance of getting it approved."

The requirements were full of similar statements presenting other solutions for the same reason (to save development costs). What they failed to factor in was the efficiency cost of the extra manual steps they were implementing! These are often seen as hidden costs that do not factor into the financial decision. They were trading off higher human resource costs and system inefficiencies for lower system development costs in the hopes of getting a lower-priced project approved.

If the requirements-gathering process focused on services and the requirements of those services from both the service consumer and service provider perspective, leveraging the business architecture framework defined in this book, the resulting business requirement document would have been very different.

First there would not have been a technical solution specified in the requirement. The "OrderStatusNotification" service would have defined a requirement that simply stated: "The order status notification process will provide a service that notifies the sales rep of the status of the order when the order is booked." The second distinction that would have occurred if the service approach was followed is that the *service provider* (in this case order administration) would not have defined the requirements of the *service consumer* (in this case the sales reps). Since this was well before the popularity of the BlackBerry and cell phone e-mail, many of the sales reps did not check their e-mails even daily. Many of them were on the road and often did not have access to their e-mail.

The other flaw in the service provider's perception was the fact that most of the sales reps did not enter their orders themselves. Most of them used faxes or overnight delivery services to send them to the district office where they were keyed in by office staff. Many of the follow-up activities to resolve rejected orders were handled by these individuals, not the sales reps. Therefore, notifying these individuals of rejections was as important, if not more important, than notifying the sales reps.

The solution for the office administrators ended up being an e-mail to the office staff individual for rejected orders with the e-mail address pulled from the e-mail directory server based on the order entry ID stored on the order record. The solution for the sales reps was the sending of a text message to their cell phone for every order booked using their sales ID number from the order to look up their cell phone number in the corporate directory server. The text notification request along with the phone number and contents of the text message was sent as a message to the monitoring platform used by network services, which had the ability to receive external alert messages and send out the text messages for those alerts. The order status rejection codes and descriptions used for the notifications were pulled directly from the order system and the order records.

The final business requirement definition of the "OrderStatusNotification" service was:

> *The Order Status Notification Process will provide a service that notifies the sales rep of the status of the order when the order is booked. It will also notify the sales office staff person that entered the order of all orders that are rejected and the reason for the rejections. The preferred notification mechanism for the sales reps is a text message to their cell phone. The preferred notification mechanism for the district office administrator is an e-mail to their personal mailbox.*

I went through this very lengthy detailed example because the points it brings across are very important to understand as you transition into a service-based model for requirements gathering. The first key point is that the service model approach removes physical and technical solutions from the business requirement definition. Even though the requirement just defined mentions text messaging and e-mail, these terms are being represented from a conceptual perspective, not a physical perspective. The requirement did not say "text messages sent through a HP network monitoring console to cell phones on a Sprint network."

Business analysts and business architects must constantly be on guard to make sure that business requirements stay at the conceptual level and understand the distinction between technology definitions from a conceptual view versus a physical or even logical view. The second key point is business analysts and business architects must clearly understand which requirements represent the needs of the service consumers and which represent the needs of the service providers and ensure that the individual or individuals specifying the requirement represent those communities. This does not mean that they should not document a requirement expressed by one party on behalf of the other party. They should, however, recognize that it is coming from the other side and validate those requirements with the other party.

The first problem with the original approach used for requirements gathering was that it thought of and documented the requirements at a functional level in the context and mind-set of a traditional stovepipe application solution. The second problem was that the requirements were gathered exclusively by the providers of the capabilities, not the consumers of the capabilities.

A major reason why SOA is so valuable is that it drives the business to define requirements at a conceptual service level, focusing in on the business process as it relates to those consuming the service as well as those providing the service. In the earlier example, which of the two approaches resulted in the better business solution? Which approach provided a better view of how the *business* operates rather than how a *system* operates? The value of SOA is that it helps to deliver better solutions to the business to help them do what they need to do, when they need to do it, and how they need to do it.

If you are using use cases to gather business requirements, you are already on the right path. A slightly modified version of the use case modeling technique is the mechanism used in the SOA~EAF methodology defined in this book to gather business requirements from a top-down consumer-centric perspective. In fact, the use case model is the basis for the SOA business architecture model as well. The modification is the insertion of a *channel layer* between the actor and the services. Channels are defined in Chapter 4.

Even if the solution ends up being a purchased vendor product versus an in-house development, we must still conduct the due diligence around the business requirements and the architectural compliance. This is especially true as we move more toward compliance with our SOA model. Any solution including purchased solutions need to be evaluated in terms of their ability to plug in to the SOA architectural framework. This is further explained in Chapter 7.

Getting IT and the business to this utopia may never happen completely, but making significant inroads toward it is very doable. It will not, however, be easy or quick. Many operational and foundational support activities must be transformed for it to become a reality. The first step, which is discussed in the next chapter, is to fully explain and help the business understand this new model of operation. Once this is accomplished, the transformation will be much easier to bring about.

Getting On the Same Page

The point that will be continuously made throughout this book is that SOA as an architectural approach, rather than a technology implementation, presents a wonderful opportunity to create a whole new way for business and IT to interact.

At one extreme is a belief held by many that you build some Web services and you are doing SOA. While there may be inherent value to these services, they have little chance of helping you realize the values of SOA. At the other extreme, which is the basis of this book, there is a highly efficient, easily understood, and (business and IT) shared process that transforms the company into a highly competitive and efficient organization leveraging and maximizing its IT assets and doing so in all the right places (i.e., where it has the highest value and where it is needed most).

Properly designed SOA applications following architectural tenets and principles can be structured to support a consumer over any number of delivery channels without replicating their functionality. Investments in SOA components at every layer of the architecture will add to the flexibility and competitive advantages available to the business heretofore unseen. Both IT and the business need to understand these will not happen if an architectural approach to SOA is not adopted. Everyone needs to be on the same page and working toward the same vision.

Value of SOA from a Financial Perspective

As mentioned in Chapter 1, most companies find themselves spending more on IT each year. Even though the price/performance of hardware has improved exponentially since computer processing was introduced, the spend rate continues to increase. Not only does spending increase, but there is a general business perception that they seem to get less and less each year for that spend.

Most companies would probably be shocked if they truly understood how much of the annual IT spend covers the cost of maintaining and managing the duplication and complexity from prior years' IT spend. Companies that attempt to hold their year-over-year IT spend flat soon find that the percentage of dollars available for new developments and enhanced capabilities dwindles as the percentage of dollars spent on maintenance and support increase. This is why I call the stovepipe approach to application development (or acquisition) the resource consumption model. The process, effect, and result of the old approach are listed next.

Process
- Data is duplicated rather than reused at the source.
- Business logic to manage and process the new data source is redeveloped out of necessity instead of using existing business logic processing existing data.
- New presentation logic has to be created to display the new business logic and data since every stovepipe legacy application has its own user interface.
- In most cases the new application needs to be secured so new security functionality is built for the application.

Effect
- Resources are needed to design and set up the new data store, even if it is the same schema on the same technology platform.
- More disk space is needed to store the duplicate data.
- Business conditions may require changes to the data structures that have to be accommodated in each duplicate store (e.g., expanding a customer number or order number field to accommodate more numbers).

- Processes used to replicate or synchronize the data between the different stores may be required.
- Resources are needed to define or validate the duplicate business logic, and to design, code, test, and deploy the duplicate logic.
- Resources are needed to design, code, test, and deploy changes to existing logic that is duplicate in the applications. (All the applications need business and presentation logic changes to handle the increase in the size of the customer and order number fields in the example just given.)
- More support resources are needed to keep more applications up and running and healthy.
- More resources are needed to test the applications when changes that affect them all, such as the customer and order number examples, are made.
- In many cases resources are needed to certify new client software and deploy the software to tens or hundreds of client devices.
- Business and/or IT resources are needed to manage and maintain another security system.

Result (Under a Flat Spend Model)

- Dollars that were available last year for development and enhancements are now being spent to maintain and support last year's developments and enhancements.
- The amount of dollars left for development and enhancement each year is less.
- The cost of doing developments and enhancements is increasing because the increasingly complex environment takes more time to understand and validate to ensure that changes are made everywhere they need to be made and new instances of duplicate data are fed from the right source.
- Eventually no money will be left for developments and enhancements and, unless the spend rate is increased, maintenance and support will be cut.

I did not have to list as many effects as I did. A few would have been sufficient to make the point. When you see all of them, however, it drives home just how big an impact a poor development approach and the wrong architecture can have on a company.

The problem with the traditional project approach is that the assessment of the impacts of these effects is evaluated at a micro project level. From an overall IT spend perspective, the cost of duplicating one database needed for the project is probably negligible. The same is probably true for the duplicated business logic, presentation logic, and security logic as well. Letting this happen once is okay, but what if it happens year after year, 100 times a year or more? The cost is no longer so insignificant. More important, the cost of just maintaining this increased complexity gets higher and higher. Even more important, the time it takes for IT to deliver new systems or enhance old systems to support new or changing business conditions increases as the overall complexity of the environment increases.

The resource consumption effect of traditional architectures not only prevents us from focusing on strategic and competitive advantages through the use of IT, but also, as time passes, continues to decrease our ability to provide basic IT services. Since effective IT is such a significant part of the ability of our business units to function, the business as a whole suffers from these impacts.

An SOA enterprise architecture approach is designed to develop 180 degrees opposite of the traditional approach and to explicitly eliminate the complexity and duplicity produced by the old approach. SOA's focus is on reuse of data *and* business logic. It focuses on developing loosely coupled granular capabilities that are easy to adapt to changing conditions and provide a high level of reuse and reconfiguration, allowing plug and play of functional activities into new and different business services.

A lot of people who have implemented SOA as a technology rather than as an architecture have complained that SOA adds complexity, not reduces it. They are, in fact, telling the truth. This is because nothing in the technical implementation they developed was based on an architectural strategy. When EA integration tools like middleware were introduced, they added complexity to the environment as well. Eventually, as they started to be used following an enterprise architecture approach instead of a technical implementation approach, the number of complexities they eliminated and the monies they saved became more evident. If they never adopted an EA approach, the environment would have continued to get more complex. The same will be true for SOA. The financial value of all the savings in all the areas (development, enhancement, maintenance, and support) will be increasingly greater and increasingly more evident as time goes on.

Summary

An enterprise architecture approach to SOA offers tremendous advantages and benefits over other architectures. This includes advantages to the business in terms of competitive adaptability and flexibility as well as better-quality solutions that are more in line with how the business wants to operate. It provides benefits to IT by giving the IT department back the control and accountability of the physical and logical aspects of implementations and moves the business away from these concerns. It has financial value in the long-term savings that a highly leveraged and heavily reused architecture that eliminates duplicity and unnecessary complexity provides. Most important, it is the approach that will ultimately allow the business to think of its business application portfolio as one conceptual system.

CHAPTER 3

A New Architecture for a New World

The way companies operate continues to change, forcing the applications that support them to change. Technologies continue to advance and, in some cases, can change the way companies operate. In other words, business drives technology as vendors try to address the changing needs of their user base. At the same time, technologies drive business as different applications of those technologies are discovered.

Businesses want the adaptation of existing systems and implementation of new systems to occur as fast as human changes occur. They want the entire corporate portfolio of business applications, especially the mission-critical applications, to be able to change as fast as their personal applications on their PCs can change. They want to be able to plug and play new technologies and have them fully integrated immediately with all the other capabilities they use. Businesses now include technology and its business usage in their conceptual vision of how they want to operate and function.

Businesses are also thinking more and more from a top-down, consumer-centric perspective rather than a bottom-up, IT systems perspective. They are thinking more holistically from an internal and external perspective. Key stakeholders today think in terms of what they need, where they need it, and when they need it. They think in terms of access both within the traditional boundaries of the company and outside those boundaries. Salespeople want every asset at their disposal when they are at the office to be at their disposal when they are on the road. Customers that receive support and service want to have direct access to those capabilities so they can "do it themselves."

This Is Not Your Grandfather's World

This current business state demands more and more exposure of the company's capabilities to external consumers. This requirement is the largest driver behind the paradigm shift in how we think about, design, and implement all our business applications. It is forcing us to think about any new application or application enhancement in the context of its exposure. This exposure relates not only to a set of employees but to certain external groups as well. It forces us to think not only about the inherent functionality that the new application or enhancement will provide but also where and how it will be used and what impact it will have on users' overall experience. In other words, it forces us to think holistically about how this new capability will fit in with existing interactions and experiences. The only way to assess and implement this properly is through a top-down, consumer-centric approach.

This is very different from the world our grandparents grew up in. Most of our grandparents never interacted directly with the computer systems of the companies they consumed from. Any interaction was probably with a phone telephony application, and this was done by accident, not by choice (all they did was dial a phone number). My mother, who is in her eighties, has never used an ATM, let alone a PC. My children have been using PCs and the Internet since before they started their formal schooling. They use them for everything from ordering pizza delivery, to buying music, to "socializing" with their friends. My mother's expectations of how the companies she consumes from should support and interact with her is so fundamentally and profoundly different from my children's perception that it is almost impossible for her to comprehend their view.

Unfortunately, in many cases, some of the systems companies use today to support and interact with their customers were in existence when my mother represented their largest consumer demographic. While she found the person using these systems very helpful in assisting her, my children found them annoying and a waste of time by forcing them to involve somebody else in solving a problem or processing a transaction. Companies need to show their customers that they are not getting their father's Buick!

What Are Business Applications, and What Is Wrong with Them?

Fundamentally we recognize that a *business application* is the automation of a business process, or at least the automation of business functions. We also fundamentally recognize that the purpose of automating business processes and business functions is to:

- Improve the productivity of the workers and the quality and consistency of their work.
- Capture data in electronic form that can be turned into information. The aim is not just to support the business processes or functions of the hosting application but also to make that data available for producing valuable information and other automated business functions and processes to other business units across the enterprise.

When the use of these business applications was limited to a small, controlled number of people who were the only conduit to the functions and processes performed by the application, there was no need to decompose these applications and modularize their capabilities. There was no need to expose subsets of the application's functionality so they could be accessed and used by a larger audience of users in a new or different way. Unfortunately, when this need did occur, the early model adopted was to replicate the necessary data and duplicate the necessary logic to provide this subset of capabilities in new, separate applications. This was a very costly and time-consuming approach. Because of this cost and time overhead, most of the time the way that we bridged the need for information across multiple business applications to support a business process was through the infusion of a *human* into the process. These approaches are still the norm in many companies today.

In the old days (before our external constituents interacted directly with our systems), our traditional bottom-up, stovepipe approach, which required users to have access to several applications and knowledge of multiple user interfaces to effect a business activity, was plausible. It was plausible because the company controlled the user (employee) and had the commitment and time to invest in giving them the training and knowledge needed to navigate and use all the needed business applications. We could invest in the training and skills they needed to know all the systems used to do their job because of an ongoing daily relationship with the employee. These employees had a motivation to understand these system complexities and understand them well. Their motivation was called employment. In many cases, even the most proficient employees may have perceived their interaction with these systems as cumbersome and ineffective. They also recognized that they needed their job and lived with it.

These complexities were hidden to the external consumer on the phone. The ability to service that external consumer was based on a combination of the various systems used by the company and the experience and skills of the employee navigating those systems, but none of this was visible to the consumer on the phone. Sometimes, however, the interaction with the external consumer required access to information or processing a transaction that was not performed (authorized) by the employee who took the call. Perhaps the consumer wanted to increase their credit limit, and only authorized credit department personnel could perform this function. In this case, the dreaded "transfer to another department" would occur. Hopefully the company had put mechanisms in place to make this transfer effective and efficient, but in many cases the external consumer would be forced to recommunicate all or a significant portion of their need. While this need to be transferred and restate your problem to someone else was acceptable to our parents, it is totally unacceptable to today's generation. Exhibit 3.1 shows this traditional interaction.

The world today, however, has changed, and changed dramatically. Businesses no longer think in terms of human-to-human boundaries of the traditional stovepipe applications. They no longer accept the human intervention requirement of bridging these systems to support their needs.

The world has also changed in that the corporate walls are no longer a boundary of corporate applications. Corporations are demanding that their customers, vendors, and partners have access to their business processes and services as well. In some cases it is the customers, vendors, or partners themselves that are driving this demand. These are being pushed by the business not only to remain competitive with others in their market, but also because of the internal resource cost savings and improved satisfaction of the consuming external constituents.

Unfortunately, the world of how we define, fund, and implement our business applications has not evolved to keep pace with these changes. Even though the company may think and strategize this new way, our traditional methodology and processes used to develop business applications do not help us to develop solutions this way. When we expose our capabilities directly to the external consumer, we need to fix the associated black holes that are created by the lack of the presence of that skilled employee. (See Exhibit 3.2.)

Customer's single point of contact was a *person.*

A customer calls into customer services to conduct business.

Service associates have a host of stovepipe applications at their disposal to help them process the customer's request. Navigating multiple systems is time consuming and complex. Associates have had extensive training on the systems to make them more efficient.

Often the service associates do not have the answer and need to contact someone else in the organization (or forward the call from the customer) who has a different set of systems at his or her disposal to process the customer's request.

This chain can go down many levels depending on the complexity of the request.

EXHIBIT 3.1   Traditional Customer Interaction Model

As we extend access of our systems to external consumers outside our borders, we cannot expect that these individuals have the skills and knowledge to navigate multiple user interfaces to get what they need. We also need to recognize that they may not have the knowledge of which interface to start with. Thus, most companies today provide external consumers an access point designed to facilitate finding what

The Web Impact
When the customer's single point of contact is the *Web*, not a person...

There's no person available who knows all the systems and how to navigate and use them

Service associates have a host of stovepipe applications at their disposal to help them process the customer's request. Navigating multiple systems is time consuming and complex. Associates have had extensive training on the systems to make them more efficient.

Or how to route them to other systems

Often the service associates do not have the answer and need to contact someone else in the organization (or forward the call from the customer) who has a different set of systems at his or her disposal to process the customer's request.

There's no person available who knows all the systems and how to navigate and use them

While extending each stovepipe application makes the functions available, they cannot navigate and manage outside their bounds.

EXHIBIT 3.2   Traditional Systems Leave Holes in the Process

they need and helping them get it done intuitively and seamlessly. This is absolutely essential for providing them a positive experience that they will tap into again and again.

Traditional business applications and the approach used to build them in the past do not work anymore. They were designed to support a different time and a different space. There is a different world out there, and it represents a whole new world to which companies must adapt.

Business Applications Need to Start with a Business Architecture

If business applications are a reflection of the business functions and processes, a *business architecture* should be a reflection of the business model that uses those functions and processes. An enterprise SOA business architecture would be a reflection of the enterprise business model (i.e., a compilation of everything a company does, how they do it, and whom they do it with). While many companies may not have documented or formally considered an enterprise SOA business architecture, most would readily agree that this model would reflect a world where consumers (whether internal employees or external customers, vendors, or partners) use different channels (the Web, their cell phones, intelligent voice recognition, or the old-fashioned telephone call to service or support employees) to get access to the information or processes they need to conduct business whenever they need to do so. This can be conceptually represented as shown in Exhibit 3.3.

From a high-level (enterprise) business perspective, Exhibit 3.3 truly represents how the business wants to think about its world. It does not want to think in terms of a particular server running a particular application using a specific user interface.

Want to Use...

To Gain Access to...

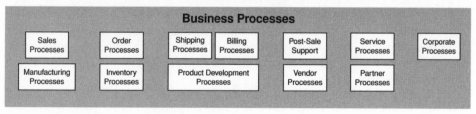

EXHIBIT 3.3 Business Architecture Example

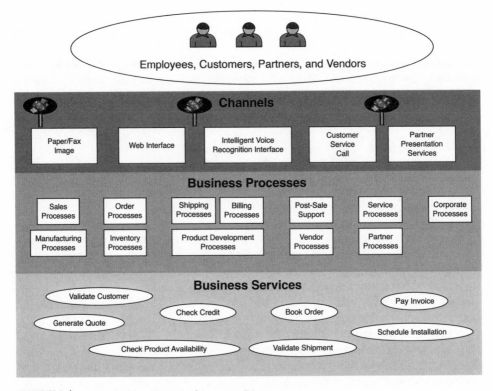

EXHIBIT 3.4   Extended Business Architecture Diagram

Therefore, this exhibit can be generically thought of as a high-level enterprise SOA business architecture. It should represent all the processes of the company, who uses those processes, and how they use them. We can extend this model down even lower to convey more detail. (See Exhibit 3.4.)

A company's enterprise SOA business architecture will show not only that the tens or hundreds of business processes provided by the company needed to be consumed by multiple constituents using multiple channels, but also that these processes are made up of hundreds or even thousands of business services. Just as the processes need to support their use through multiple channels and by multiple consumers, the services need to support their use by multiple business processes.

A "check customer credit" business *service* needs to support an order *process*, a billing and collection *process,* and a customer credit increase *process*.

The order *process* needs to support orders submitted by customers on paper, through the Web, or through an application they use provided by a partner that is an authorized seller of the company's products. The order *process* also needs to support orders submitted by sales representatives sent via fax, overnight paper, direct data entry into a Web order application, or the file transfer protocol (FTP) transmission of an order file from a laptop.

From this enterprise SOA business architecture, the company can readily see that if each one of these variations of business services within business processes, channels, and constituents was a separate business application, one of two things would exist. Either the exhibit would be very small with very few of these permutations of the variations physically implemented or the company would be bankrupt, having spent every available dollar on these applications.

When we present this exhibit *conceptually,* we are representing the *business model* of the corporation. When we present it *logically*, we are representing the *reference architecture model* that parallels the business model. When we present it *physically*, we are representing the *platform architecture model* of what has physically been placed into production to support the logical pieces that support the conceptual model.

It is not by coincidence that the structure of this exhibit used to conceptually represent the business architecture model is the same high-level structure used to logically represent the reference architecture model and to physically represent the physical architecture model. If an effective business application is a direct reflection of the business functions and processes it automates, then would an effective business architecture be a reflection of the business model that represents all these functions and processes? Would the physical implementations of these applications be physical reflections of the logical components in the reference architecture? They would if you had a strong architecture practice in place with strong architectural principles within that practice.

It is also not by coincidence that the structure of this exhibit represents the top layers of the SOA framework defined in this book. This framework is defined and presented in detail in Chapter 5. It is a beautiful thing when the business evolution based on all the influences around it and the evolution of application architecture based on that business evolution end up in a perfectly harmonious and synergistic place.

This business architecture has many values, not the least of which is as a tool to communicate to the business by overlaying specific implementations that have been delivered (see Exhibit 3.5) or planned projects scheduled to be delivered using this framework (see Exhibit 3.6).

Using the business architecture as the high-level representation of any implementation or enhancement of business functionality provides the answers to these questions:

- Which (internal and external) constituents will use the functionality?
- For each of those constituents, how will they access the functionality?
- How will that functionality fit in with the other processes they have access to?

A key point to recognize is that the answer to these questions may present a very large set of requirements that may not be able to be implemented within a single project or within the dollars in the current budget. That is okay. This exercise can be followed up immediately by a prioritization by the enterprise SOA Portfolio Plan Governance Committee slotting the set of requirements across a portfolio and technology roadmap for future initiatives.

One of my favorite tenets is:

Architect to the end state (as best you can) then implement in phases, but never architect and implement in phases.

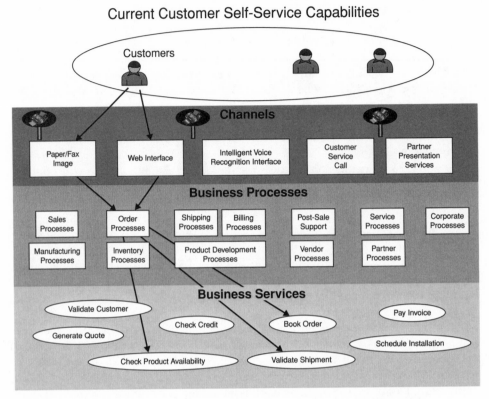

EXHIBIT 3.5   Business Architecture Representation of Customer Current Capabilities

Following this tenet helps the governance process to consider all the current and long-term opportunities for use of functionality being delivered. This allows each implementation phase to consider the best way to take advantage of these opportunities and realize them in the future by promoting architectural design patterns, development frameworks, and design standards in each implementation that can be leveraged toward the next. This results in a high probability that the ultimate implementation of all the requirements over their projected roadmap timeline will occur cheaper and faster. It also helps to ensure that capabilities added in the future can be leveraged by SOA components being built today. This concept will become more evident as you progress through this book.

There is a second advantage to this approach. It allows you to line up and consider your business application portfolio from a top-down, consumer-centric perspective rather than from a bottom-up, system implementation perspective. When new SOA initiatives using this business architecture template are laid out on the enterprise SOA portfolio plan, many commonalties and synergistic opportunities become apparent. Instead of an application portfolio plan that shows system implementations over time, you now have a SOA portfolio plan that shows what functionality is being delivered to each constituent, and which channels are delivering that functionality and over what time period. Being able to see, for example, that three separate IT projects want to deliver new or enhanced functionality to

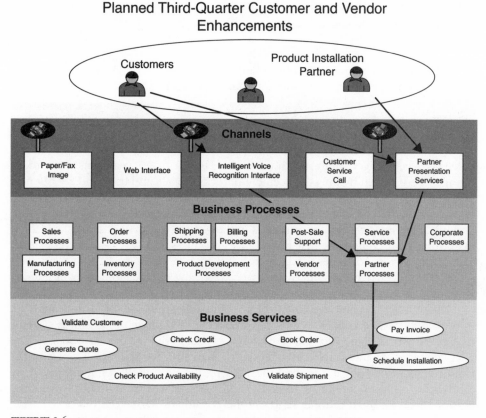

EXHIBIT 3.6 Business Architecture Representation of Future Capabilities

the customer constituent, with each delivering that functionality in three successive quarters, provides the enterprise SOA Portfolio Plan Governance Committee with an opportunity to package the three into one event and save significant money just on training, regression testing, and user acceptance testing alone.

Throughout the remainder of this book, this concept of a top-down approach will be continuously expanded and evolved. I felt it was important to introduce it early and let you evolve toward its full understanding. As you advance through the book, you will see that its evolution will impact everything your business and IT organizations do. As you learn more, you will see that a top-down approach impacts:

- How an architecture practice is organized and functions.
- How governance needs to be restructured.
- How policies and procedures to perform the entire system life cycle need to change.
- How funding of projects and monitoring of IT spending must change.
- What new relationships you must build with your IT vendors and what new influences on *their* strategic direction you must establish.

- How you build partnerships with other complementary businesses to leverage each other's capabilities and increase the competitive advantages you both can achieve.

In other words, you will see how it helps you achieve an organizational, cultural, and operational paradigm shift through your entire corporation.

Summary

Business has changed dramatically over the last 10 to 20 years. Many of these changes were driven by the advancement of technologies and the rapid adoption of these technologies. This is true not only with business but with people in general. In today's world, people do not expect to use just one technology but several options of technologies to perform tasks in their everyday lives. These tasks include interacting with companies that provide the products and services they consume. They want access to these products and services to be immediate and on *their* terms. They do not necessarily want to go to a physical location or even interact with another human being.

This is truly a whole new world that companies must adapt to and thrive in to remain in existence. SOA is the only architectural approach to business systems that is actually designed to take advantage of and thrive in this new world. The SOA model is actually a reflection of this new world. Even though I can buy the latest number-one song at the local music store, through my PC on the Internet, or through my cell phone, the actual song is the same. The artist did not record three versions, one for each channel used. As the consumer, I have the option of using any or all of these channels to get music. If I used the word "service" in this example instead of the word "music," this example would be a description of SOA. SOA truly is a new architecture for a new world.

CHAPTER 4

SOA and Channels

When defining services from a business perspective, we need to take the top-down perspective and answer the questions outlined in Chapter 3:

1. Who else can use the service?
2. How will they use the service?
3. When will they use the service?

When we look at questions 2 and 3, we discover that, in today's world, there is a demand to provide more than one way to provide access to services. Think about a customer that is looking to make travel arrangements. They can use any of these channels:

- They can call or visit a travel agency.
- They can call an airline directly (which may offer to provide their other travel needs as well, like car rental and hotel).
- They can go to the airline's web site.
- They can go to an online travel agency web site, such as Expedia® or Orbitz®.

Regardless of which channel they choose, there is an expectation that the service offerings they receive are consistent and accurate. Users expect that the same flights and hotel rooms are reflected with the same up-to-date information regarding availability, regardless of the channel they use. They expect that they can shop these various sites for sales and promotions providing lower rates on a particular flight or hotel and get the best deal.

For purposes of this book, and the SOA framework defined within, a *channel* is defined as:

Any type of access medium used between two parties for delivering and consuming SOA services.

A channel is not the payload (the specific data or information being communicated) but the mechanism for delivering that payload.

A *party* can be a person or a system. Therefore, an interaction can be between two people, a person and a system, or two systems.

Value of Channels

For companies to be competitively successful in today's world, they absolutely must take advantage of as many of these channels as they possibly can. Each channel in today's world is equivalent to each of the channels in the old physical world. Starbucks increases the sales of its coffee not only by selling it at its own locations but also through retail chains and branded food service outlets where "We proudly serve Starbucks Coffee" is advertised. All three contribute to the volume of coffee sales.

Airlines, car rental companies, and hotels have their own web sites. Travel agencies and online travel sites serve as additional sales channels for their products and services beyond the traditional telephone channel. The early prediction that the World Wide Web would forge new business partnerships and opportunities has become a reality.

I use the travel industry as an example because it represents one of the first industries to recognize the value of multichannel marketing and sales. It was one of the first industries to invest in and leverage an industry-wide network of services. Starting with Sabre (Semi-automated Business Research Environment) in 1964 and evolving to today's interconnected network of global distribution systems (GDS), the travel industry has effectively constructed an industry-wide ubiquitous service network. It is this service network, not the Web, that has allowed the proliferation and expansion of the travel industries' sale channels. The Web is just another channel delivering those services.

I am sure that, initially, many in these industries were reluctant to back and adopt such an undertaking. It could easily be perceived as turning their products and services into commodities. Time has proven this not to be the case. Starbucks selling its coffee through grocery stores did not make its product a commodity or diminish its value. New companies like Expedia, Orbitz, and Priceline® wrapped additional value-added services on top of the travel industry's service network to provide a whole new experience to millions of people. The lesson to be learned is that, with few exceptions, exposing your product or service through as many channels as possible does not diminish its value or make it a commodity. Failure to differentiate your product or service from the competition diminishes its value or makes it a commodity, not the delivery channel.

As stated in Chapter 3, consumers are driving the use of channels and are demanding that the companies they buy products and services from support these channels as well. The SOA approach defined in this book sees channels as advantages and treats them as opportunities. The framework of the SOA reference architecture is designed to specifically position you to take advantage of channel opportunities. In other application architectural approaches, a new channel is seen potentially as a heavy erosion of IT dollars spent on duplication and complexity. Under SOA, a new channel is seen as an opportunity to leverage past investments, to extend market share and increase competitive advantages.

Hence channels represent a key component and opportunity within an SOA. Leveraging these investments, however, will not happen automatically. The architectural framework and the architecture practice must be designed to explicitly ensure that services are designed and implemented to take advantage of these channels as efficiently and effectively as possible. They must be designed so they can adapt to new channels introduced in the future.

Traditional (Non-SOA) Approach to Channels

Most companies not following a service *architecture* philosophy have supported expansion to additional channels by:

- Providing the capability at a tactical project level with no or limited potential for future reuse.
- Duplicating a significant portion of the existing business logic contained in the back-end legacy application.
- Creating another stovepipe solution that added to the overall support and maintenance costs of the portfolio.

If they did adopt some service practices and developed the application with some service components, they have the opportunity to leverage those in the future. However, the cost of leveraging them will be significantly higher if they were not built following a SOA enterprise architecture framework (SOA~EAF™). This is because they probably were not built to leverage, for example, an enterprise service invocation and service authorization framework. They were probably not constructed with an isolated service stub invocation framework allowing additional service stubs to be added in the future to support different deployment standards and protocols. Probably none of the capabilities for invocation or authorization was built using an enterprise service provisioning framework that allows new authentication and invocation mechanisms to be added through configuration changes rather than coding.

SOA Channels Are a Major Paradigm Shift to Traditional Application Development

Channels as adopted by SOA following the architectural approach defined in this book change the entire perspective of a business application. The stovepipe approach where each business application has its own proprietary (to the application) user interface is replaced with an approach that can utilize one or more channels and channel adapters to deliver the functionality of the application to the intended users. (Channel adapters are defined later in this chapter and in the reference architecture section in Chapter 5.) The user interface is the ubiquitous channel adapter that can provide access to any business service in any SOA service component. In fact, the concept of a business application as a monolithic set of code to provide a defined, static set of capabilities is replaced with a set of independent or combined (through orchestration) services that can be dynamically delivered.

Channels Must Apply Architecture Principles to be Effective

While any service has the potential to be reused through any channel, the costs of enhancing that service to be delivered securely through additional channels is significantly higher if the developers did not follow an architecture approach from the beginning. This does not mean that every service built must be build initially to support every type of channel. It does, however, mean that knowing that the service will need to be secured and delivered through different types of channels in the future allows architecture to define the development frameworks and design patterns for constructing services that ensure that their delivery in the future to other channels can be accomplished as quickly as possible and at the lowest possible price.

To have a truly effective SOA approach (i.e., to be able to maximize the flexibility and reuse benefits of SOA), channels must be an integral part of that approach. In fact, it is so important that it has its own distinct layer in the SOA~EAF. Answer this question:

Which has a higher business value or higher return: a service that can be used by two different constituents (e.g., a health insurance claim status service used by a doctor and the member) or a service that can be used by the same constituent using a different channel (e.g., the doctor being able to get a claim status in the office using the insurer's portal, using an intermediary like WebMD, or using the hospital's internal health network portal when at the hospital)?

Obviously the answer would depend on many factors, but there is nothing inherent to any of these options that would preclude it from being more or less valuable than the other option. The point is that making the same service available on additional channels, even if it is to the same target audience, increases its exposure and, it is hoped, its utilization. The target audience for a particular music genre does not change if the channel is online versus in store. The demographics of that audience may be distinguishable, but the genres they prefer do not change.

Thus, SOA initiatives developed from an architectural perspective require the development frameworks, design patterns, and design standards that apply at the channel layer of the framework to be fully incorporated into those solutions. Whenever any business service or business process is constructed, the invocation mechanism is loosely coupled through an independent service stub. This allows the same service to be evoked through a different channel using a service stub designed for that channel. Hence, a service stub is created when the service is created and deployed through its first channel because the development framework specified by the enterprise SOA architects required that the service be built with a loosely coupled channel invocation stub. What the code in the service stub does is specified by the design pattern created by the enterprise SOA architects for that particular channel. How the stub operates is based on the design standards specified by the enterprise SOA architects for that particular channel. Development frameworks, design patterns, and design standards are defined and explained in Chapter 5.

If the most fundamental tenet of SOA is the belief that it allows for reuse and leveraging of investments, then not having to duplicate functionality to deliver the same service through multiple channels is just as cost effective as using that service for other business purposes.

An SOA strategy based on an architecture designed to support and leverage today's multichannel world has the potential to be the single most significant contributor to increased market share, higher customer satisfaction, faster time to (channel) market, and significant costs savings.

What Are the Different Types of Channels?

We defined a channel as any type of access medium used between two parties for delivering and consuming services. Under this definition, virtually any form of communication medium used to convey something from one party to another is a channel.

As humankind has evolved, the communication channels used have grown and expanded. Channels existed even before television and radio. Speech was one of the first forms of communication, and its channel was your voice. Variations or adaptations of this channel were called languages. Writing and print were another early form of communication. Their media was any physical material on which a symbol or character could be drawn or etched. Languages are also the variations of this channel with graphic representation of physical objects and alphabets being the "software" used and "handheld devices," such as sharp stones, sticks, quills, and colored fluids being the "hardware" used. This channel has evolved to include the electronic forms of this medium as well. Hence the medium has expanded not only to include any physical material on which a symbol or character could be drawn or etched but also any electronic medium on which a graphic or character can be entered and retained.

These are examples of human advances that extend or broaden the capabilities of the base core channel. Many technological advances have occurred to expand the capabilities of all electronic channels. In fact, if new or enhanced variations of a channel do not evolve over time, then it probably is not a channel. More than likely it is a variation of another channel. Initially voice interaction between two parties could be utilized only if the two parties were within hearing distance. Today we can voice communicate around the world using the telephone. We can voice communicate face-to-face using tele-video and Webcam technologies.

What is critical to understand is the fact that the voice message one party wants to tell the other or the written message one wants another to read does not change when a different channel is used. The payload is the same.

From an SOA perspective, the software components for capturing, packaging, and delivering the payload must always be separate from each other. The architecture practice needs to specify these requirements within the standards, design patterns, and development frameworks that govern development within the channel layer of the SOA architecture. This includes the components that unpack the payload and process the replies as well. The architecture must also clearly define the interoperability standards and specifications for each component as it relates to each variation of the other components. For example, which packaging components can be used by each capturing component, and how is it used? Which packaging formats are supported by each transport component?

From an IT systems and an SOA framework perspective, the channels in the next lists are the most common ones used within a company. Also note the technologies that have been developed to extend or enhance the channels. These extensions are referred to as *channel adapters* throughout the remainder of this book.

Your company may be using all or some of these channels. You may be using all or some of the channel adapters within a particular channel. The two things that I ask you to remember are:

1. If you are using one of the technologies listed and have not thought of it as a channel, you need to do so as you adopt SOA.
2. If you are not using a channel (i.e., not using any of the technologies within that channel), you need to ask yourself why you are not using it. Are there any strategic values and/or operational efficiencies that the channel could provide?

The four common channels found in a typical company's infrastructure are presented next. Below each channel are some of the common adapters within that channel. The most recent variations are italicized.

Physical Channel
- Paper documents
- Printouts
- Forms
- Correspondence
- Literature
- Electronic data interchange (EDI)
- FTP/SFTP
- Bulletin Board services (BBSs)
- Clearinghouse
- EDI Web services

Telephony Channel
- Phone
- Fax
- Intelligent voice recognition (IVR)
- Computer telephony integration (CTI)
- *Text messaging*

World Wide Web/Internet Channel
- Static Web pages
- Dynamic Web pages
- Web applications
- Web portals
- Web services
- *Web 2.0*
- E-mail
- Instant messaging
- Chat
- Online meeting

Proprietary Client Channel
- Legacy clients
- Windows client
- 3270/TN3270
- Virtual terminal

Applying SOA to Channels

In the 1980s, when I was working for Wang Laboratories (a major supplier of word processing and imaging technologies), the buzz phrase in the industry was "the paperless office." Now, more than 20 years later, paper is *still* a major corporate channel. Some of your customers will continue to mail in correspondence. Some of your vendors will continue to send paper invoices. Paper forms for everything, from magazine subscriptions, to rebates, to taxes, will continue to exist.

Knowing that paper is not going away, several technologies were developed to improve the processing of paper. The most significant technology was the scanner. This allowed for capturing an image of the physical item containing the payload. While there was value to capturing an image of the payload, the image was unable to extract or understand the payload. Intelligent character recognition/optical character recognition (ICR/OCR) software solved this problem by being able to recognize the graphical representation of the payload produced by the scanner and convert (more like translate) it into electronically recognizable characters and graphics. This made the information more valuable because it could now be electronically interpreted. Other technologies, such as bar coding, provided the capability for additional electronic processing, including indexing and routing.

Today's technologies provide us with the capability to convert paper-based information into a machine-readable form that can be electronically processed through the system. Many companies use these capabilities today. Very few, however, have implemented these technologies as an enterprise architecture solution.

In the case of correspondence or other nonformatted documents, how many companies have an enterprise solution for scanning, indexing, storing, and retrieving this information? How many of these solutions allow for the retrieval and processing of the stored information through enterprise retrieval services? From an SOA perspective, the technology needs to provide the ability to treat these capabilities as a channel with supportive services to:

- Scan, transform, index, and store all types of paper documents.
- Create mechanisms for searching and retrieving the documents including mechanisms for retrieving and embedding the documents in other business services and business processes.
- Establish and enforce policies for access and modification of those documents.
- Provide capabilities for archive and retrieval of the documents.

In the case of a health insurer, correspondence from members, providers, and accounts could all be scanned, transformed (ICR/OCR), and indexed through a central enterprise scanning solution in the corporate mail facility. Indexes and search keys would be entered through another set of services that contained the templates that identified the indexes and keys for each type of correspondence (provider, member, account). It may be possible to automatically identify many of these indexes and keys and prepopulate the fields, depending on the sophistication of the ICR/OCR technology and the presence of identifiable index and key data through the use of bar codes.

Another set of services could be built on top of the application programming interfaces (APIs) exposed by the underlying storage and retrieval system (i.e., an enterprise document management or imaging solution). These services would be integrated into the same enterprise SOA security framework utilized across all the other channels, thereby restricting access to the service or restricting what they can access through the service based on their roles in the security framework. For example, a provider service representative would be allowed access to all provider correspondence, but only member correspondence cross-referenced to that provider. Member service representatives may have a role that restricts them from accessing member correspondence from members who are also employees of the insurer.

Other applications, such as the provider services application, could consume these services and embed them into the application so that once a provider's ID is entered, the representative would not only see transactional information, such as pending claims but also a summary list of all correspondence documents received from that provider. Just as the system allows a representative to select and drill down into the details of a specific claim, it also would provide the selection and drill down into any piece of correspondence.

You may wonder why you would go through all the expense of building these custom services and channel capabilities instead of using the out-of-the-box user interface of the document management system. The answer is that you have adopted a strategy to "service-enable" your IT assets so they can be reused and leveraged elsewhere. We invested in building these capabilities as services and integrating them into our channel framework so they could be leveraged through other channels or the same channel for other purposes. The first implementation discussed created a new set of services and a set of service stubs for these services in the form of new and enhanced data link layers (DLLs) in the legacy customer relationship management system (CRMS) application Windows client code. If the client had been a .net application, it could have been stubbed out as Web services. Clearly this integration was driven by a defined business need to provide access to this correspondence to the three service areas using the CRMS (member, provider, and account) system. This could have been accomplished by utilizing the underlying APIs directly. Doing so, however, would have tightly coupled the underlying technology and forced the added functionality (such as role authorization) into the physical code of the application (the DLLs) instead of the enterprise SOA security framework.

Since we isolated the functionality into a service tied to the enterprise SOA security framework, these services can be utilized elsewhere for significantly less cost. For example, a new service stub in the form of a Web service can be constructed for these same services. Since the service is invoked through the enterprise authorization module within the channel layer, the same existing authorization-challenge policy enforcement point within the service will be invoked. A new policy is entered into the configuration file for these services stating:

For *"Role"* **equal to** *"Provider"* **Deny Access to All Records where** *"IndexedID"* **Is not equal to** *"ProviderID"*.
For *"Role"* **equal to** *"Provider"* **Allow access** to *"Provider_Correspondence_Records"* **where** *"IndexedID"* **Is equal to** *"ProviderID"*.

Note: **bold** = policy key words, *italic* = user variable.

All we have to do now is deploy a new link (*"To view correspondence submitted to us click here"*) to the new Web service stub out to the "provider self-service web site," and providers will now have the capability to search, retrieve, and view all the correspondence they have sent into the company.

By making the next policy entries through the configuration tool of the service security module...

```
For "Role" equal to "Member" Deny Access to All Records where
"IndexedID" Is not equal to "MemberID".
For "Role" equal to "Member" Allow Access to "Member_
Correspondence_Records" where "IndexedID" Is equal to "MemberID".

For "Role" equal to "Account" Deny Access to All Records where
"IndexedID" Is not equal to "AccountID".
For "Role" equal to "Account" Allow Access to "Account_
Correspondence_Records" where "IndexedID" Is equal to "AccountID".
```

and deploying links to the same Web service, both members and accounts will be able to view their correspondence through the Web channel as well.

Yes, we invested some additional time and money to build services around a paper channel, but that initial investment was leveraged with minimal effort (development of a second service stub) to a second channel (the Web) and reused by three constituents (members, providers, and accounts).

The SOA implementation just described specifies a framework where user authentication and service privileges are controlled and invoked at the channel invocation layer, but the service authorization happens at the service invocation layer. Having a common enterprise SOA security framework that provides these authentication and authorization services to the channel and the business services through loosely coupled components of the security framework allows any channel and any service to use them. Using these framework components leverages a single enterprise SOA user profile mechanism that all channels and services can share. This approach not only streamlines security administration but improves control as well. Deactivating an individual's profile eliminates their access to all services through all channels.

This is an excellent example of how an architectural approach to SOA is so valuable and so important to maximizing SOA's value.

Intermediary Channels

Having multiple internal channels to service your constituents is valuable. Customer options to use your web site, a voice recognition system, or personal contact through your customer service employees improve the services delivered to those customers. Vendors using an EDI channel or your vendor web site have options as well. Sometimes, however, partnering with other businesses that interact with your constituents is beneficial. These interactions can be exclusive to your business, but in most instances they extend the services of other companies, including your competition.

Revisiting the travel example, customers can go directly to an airline's web site to book a flight or they can go to one of the many online travel sites that offer a host of travel services in addition to flights. Sites like Expedia, Orbitz, and Priceline can book not only airline flights but hotels and rental cars as well. These sites also offer competing flights so customers can choose the best times and prices to suit their needs.

In Massachusetts, doctors can go directly to the health insurance carriers' web sites to process transactions, or they can use a site like Emdeon (a subsidiary of WebMD) that lets them process transactions for all the insurance carriers that they deal with.

These are two examples of *intermediary* sites. They are intermediaries in the sense that your customer invokes the intermediary's application on the intermediary's channel running on its servers, not your application on your channels. These intermediaries provide a value-added service that you alone cannot provide. They facilitate efficiency and decision-making processes needed by the user to make a more effective decision. They can expedite the process, thereby reducing the users' work effort and time commitment.

Online travel sites allow consumers to:

- Enter in their departure and return dates and cities once, instead of on the airline site, the hotel site, and the car rental site.
- Review multiple options for each travel service including competitive pricing for those services.
- Enter in their payment information once and pay for all the services together.
- Get an itinerary that includes all their travel services and set up notifications if any changes occur in the itinerary.

Similarly, Emdeon handles the routing of medical requests or transactions to the appropriate insurance carriers and eliminates the need for a doctor to log onto each carrier's system and split transactions or inquiries by carrier.

Intermediaries provide value-added services that are very compelling to consumers. Intermediaries leverage this value to convince more businesses to partner with them and participate in their sites. Businesses recognize that failure to participate in intermediary sites can be a competitive disadvantage and result in lost sales or higher costs.

Using an intermediary, however, does not mean that you abandon all the architectural principles and philosophies of SOA. It is absolutely critical that SOA principles are applied to intermediaries and that intermediaries commit to them. Using an intermediary that recodes all the business logic needed to process your transaction in its application so it can be deployed as a new channel is just the same as building another legacy stovepipe application. The only difference is that it is deployed on the intermediary's hardware instead of yours. There is no way this logic can be reused in another channel.

In these cases, the companies are not channel intermediaries. They are application service providers. They often sell their applications under the guise of providing a quicker and cheaper entry into a channel like the Web or wireless-enabled personal digital assistants. What you usually end up with is another legacy system with a very specific purpose that has significant redundancy and increased support overhead. Even worse, companies are often convinced to duplicate more of their capabilities on these platforms. If you follow this model to the extreme, you end up with these vendors becoming your IT shop with all your business applications running on their platforms. Once again, this is good for the vendors but bad for the customer—especially if the customer wants to achieve the efficiencies and synergies of SOA as described in this book. For more information on how to handle application service providers and integrate their offerings into your SOA environment, see Chapter 7.

This is not to say that intermediaries have no business logic. It means the business logic is additive and complementary to your business logic. The travel sites mentioned earlier did not rewrite or duplicate the logic to book a flight or hotel room. This logic is supplied in the service provided through the travel service network. The travel sites did, however, write business logic that can use travel information entered once to get availability of all flights, hotels, and so forth and display the retrieved information in an efficient decision-making framework. They also wrote business logic to let the consumer pay for all the services once, thereby streamlining the payment process as well.

Building intermediary partnerships can have tremendous value to your corporation. Building partner relationships with application service providers under the guise of channel relationships can be tremendously detrimental to your company.

SOA Security Framework for Channels

As stated, authenticating users of your internally controlled channels and authorization to the services provided through those channels is controlled by your internal security framework. For external channels, in most cases, it is the intermediary that authenticates the user and authorizes access to services including your services. In some cases there is no need to authenticate the end user into your systems that are tied into the intermediary's site. In the case of Emdeon, this integrated authentication is absolutely required because of the sensitivity of the information and the regulations (e.g., the Health Insurance Portability and Accountability Act [HIPAA]) that govern that access.

There is no regulatory need to authenticate a traveler to an airline, hotel, or car rental company, and initially the travel site intermediaries did not do so. However, there was a business driver to do so. Airlines offer frequent flyer rewards. Hotels offer rewards. Some travelers use contracted rates established by their employers with specific hotels or car rental companies. Most of the intermediaries now allow for the pass-through of the appropriate information to allow back-end partner services to handle these conditions.

Regardless of who performs the user authentication and service authorization, the key aspect of the channel layer in the SOA framework is that it is the layer where authentication is performed and where service privileges are determined. I use the term *service privileges* for explicit reasons to distinguish this process from the transaction or information authorization associated with a service. Service privileges are identified when the user authenticates so the landing page displayed immediately after authentication knows what services to show on that page. Transaction or information authorization is a security detection and enforcement mechanism used when the service listed on the page is invoked.

User authentication and service privilege identification are processes and standards that are specified in terms of their design and utilization in the *channel layer* of the SOA enterprise architecture framework. Transaction or information authorization are SOA components and standards that are specified in terms of their design and utilization in the business process, business service, and integration service layers of the SOA enterprise architecture framework. The enterprise SOA security framework provides all the security services required by these SOA components to manage these services across all the layers.

This security authentication and authorization framework represents another key shift under the SOA paradigm. In the traditional stovepipe approach, each application was built with its own embedded security. These applications required the user to sign in to gain access (authentication). These applications also controlled what the authenticated user could do within the application by limiting the functionality exposed to that user through various mechanisms including screen masks, database record locks, and defined roles.

Two problems arose from this approach. First, users were required to authenticate to each application they used. Because these systems were built at different times using different technologies, each authentication sign-on was usually different, requiring multiple IDs and passwords. This spawned many new products to address this issue by offering single-sign-on (SSO) capabilities, allowing users to maintain a single ID and password for all the applications they use. While SSO helped to alleviate user authentication complexities, it did nothing to eliminate the overhead associated with the redundancies and complexities of the multiple underlying security systems. A second set of products providing provisioning capabilities was developed to address this administrative overhead issue.

The second problem with these approaches was that many of these security systems were designed around controls:

- At the data level (too low).
- At the presentation level (too high).
- Through grouped sets of capabilities at the business logic level (too rigid: i.e., not granular enough to isolate individual capabilities; and too inflexible: i.e., incapable of dynamically exposing granular capabilities independently).

As a result of these conditions, integrating these applications with other applications or exposing their functionality outside of the application's user interface was achieved in one of four ways:

1. Removing data-level restrictions by creating super-user IDs with access to the full database and all the business logic.
2. Bypassing presentation layer security by building business logic layer APIs.
3. Exposing the larger sets of functionality defined by the applications logic level controls and programmatically eliminating or isolating the capability in the security logic of the consuming application.
4. Any combination of the three.

As we build our SOA channel approach, we need to understand and resolve the implications just discussed. We need to understand and document how security is going to be performed going forward. We need to understand and document how we are going to handle the issues of our many and multiple legacy security systems while they still exist in our portfolio. Finally, for each channel in our SOA environment, we need to define and document from a security perspective what that security is and what it needs to capture to integrate with the SOA layers below it. This applies not only to our internal channels but to our external intermediary channels as well. In some cases you will be able to dictate these conditions to the intermediary. In other cases you will not be able to do so. For those that you cannot dictate, you need to understand how you will handle the intermediary's approaches.

Architecture for SOA Channels and Their Security Frameworks

Under an SOA approach, there are no monolithic, self-contained applications. There is no unique, isolated, and separately managed block of code that represents an application. The portal code for the authentication of the user and presentation layer services is the same code for all the services used by that user. The individual services consumed by that portal may be the same services consumed by another portal or channel interface. The legacy application integration components of the individual services may be used by several services.

Thus, when describing an SOA application to a business owner, we are describing a logical or conceptual view of a subset of shared capabilities, platforms, and networks that make up the "system" components that perform the specific business capability being requested.

Getting the business to grasp this concept will be one of the most difficult challenges you will face, especially in companies where the culture believes they own their business applications in their totality (i.e., they believe they own the business data, the business logic, the servers, the embedded security system, etc.). After you read this book, you will understand what it will take to change this perspective. The mechanisms needed to change the business's perspective and mind-set are embedded in every aspect of the SOA model being implemented. The changes that will be made to the way IT projects are structured and approved will help this transformation, as will the changes that will be made to the way business requirements are structured and documented. The conversion from individual system production implementations to scheduled releases of business capabilities involving multiple systems will epitomize this cultural transformation.

Under an architectural approach to SOA, how we build and secure channels needs to be considered very carefully and defined before the first SOA application is developed.

If you have not thought of these considerations, such as security, and developed the architectural frameworks for building them before you start building services and deploying them out through a channel, you will probably not achieve the synergy to deploy them across multiple channels. Even if you followed design patterns documented in some of the better SOA development books that specify the use of enterprise security components, you still need the architecture development framework that defines how they are reused. The technical design patterns define how you code for the use of these security services. The development framework defines exactly what that code needs to do so that all the requirements for horizontal layer reuse and vertical layer leveraging are achieved.

Value-Added Extensions to an Enterprise Security Framework

When an enterprise security framework is applied to SOA, additional value-added capabilities can be incorporated into or facilitated by that framework. These value-added capabilities are *profiling* and *personalization*. Profiling involves the identification of specific characteristics associated to a group for which the authenticated user participates in or has been categorized into. Profiling may be the identification of the authenticated user as a preferred or "platinum" customer to whom special services are offered. These profile attributes may be passed from the framework to lower layers of the architecture in order to be interpreted by lower-layer business processes or business services to customize the way they operate.

Personalization involves the identification of specific characteristics associated uniquely to the authenticated individual. Personalized characteristics may include specifying a language preference, the automatic invocation of specific services the user has subscribed to, or preferred mechanisms for delivering notifications and other communications.

The enterprise SOA security framework authenticates the logon to the channel through a logon service provided by the framework, not the channel. The initial user registration process and user maintenance of the security profile are also services of the framework. The user profile records for each registered user are managed and maintained through services provided by the enterprise SOA security framework. This profile database can be extended to contain profile and personalization attributes as well. These attributes can be maintained by the user through the registration and maintenance services, by administrators within the company, or provisioned from other systems, such as the customer contract application (which provides the customer status classification) automatically.

The advantage of incorporating these into an enterprise SOA framework is they can be made available to and used by any service delivered through any channel. Under the traditional stovepipe approach, the logic to maintain and use these characteristics, and in many cases the data itself, had to be duplicated in every application that wanted to use them. Under SOA, profiling and personalization are just another set of loosely coupled services available to every business service and every channel.

Channel Governance

The decision to establish a new channel should be made at the highest SOA governance level (i.e., the SOA domain governance level). Channels are expensive to build and implement properly. The strategic value for establishing a new channel should be more than one specific business need in one specific area. Channels implemented at the tactical project level or through business application purchases or leases are not SOA channels. They are stovepipe applications that happen to use channel technology.

The value of building a new channel should be the ability to flood that channel with existing, as well as new, services to expand a market, improve competitiveness or increase efficiency. The executives need to recognize that three new stovepipe Web applications, regardless of whether they are built, purchased, or leased, represent three separate channels with all the duplication and wasted overhead associated with stovepipe applications. They must also recognize that three new applications that expose services, controlled by an enterprise security framework, initially deployed through the Web channel, have no duplication and no wasted operational or administrative overhead. See Chapter 8 for more on governance of channels. Also see Appendix C for more information on security, profiling, and personalization under SOA.

Summary

Channels are a major component of the SOA enterprise architecture framework, so important that they have their own layer in the architecture. Channels with a correct architecture to support the SOA paradigm have more potential for delivering SOA adaptability, flexibility, and reusability value than any other layer of the architecture.

Partnerships with channel intermediaries can add tremendous value and competitive advantages. Make sure that the companies are truly intermediaries providing value-added capabilities and business process extensions, not another duplicated stovepipe solution.

Channel technologies embedded in custom-built, purchased, or leased business applications will not achieve the desired adaptability, flexibility, and reusability. Instead, they will ultimately just add to the complexity, duplication, and business paralysis within the company.

Architecture development frameworks for capabilities such as security, profiling, and personalization need to be developed and published before any channels are developed and deployed.

PART II

Architecture Framework and Methodology

CHAPTER 5

Service-Oriented Architecture Enterprise Architecture Framework and Methodology

Developing under a service-oriented architecture (SOA) approach requires that the artifacts within the enterprise architecture documentation library be structured to support the business evaluation and understanding of:

- What exists in terms of services and composite business processes.
- How those services are currently consumed in terms of both the channels and the constituents.
- What it would take to extend existing services to other channels and/or other constituents.
- What are the core, or foundational, capabilities that must be in place to support a service and its deployment.

Developing under an SOA approach also requires a methodology that defines and enforces a top-down approach to SOA providing direct identifiable linkages from the top-level corporate strategy down to the physical implementation of each SOA component. The methodology also needs to drive the process to ensure that leveraged and reused SOA components are maximized in the context of:

- Being designed to be leveraged and reused.
- Continuous evaluation throughout the process to assess their leveragability and reuse.

The first part of this chapter defines the SOA enterprise architecture framework (SOA~EAF™) columns (subframeworks) and the layers common across the subframeworks. The second part provides an overview of the methodology that utilizes and maximizes the SOA~EAF. The content of this book from this chapter forward defines the specifics of the methodology in detail.

SOA Enterprise Architecture Framework

SOA~EAF is the framework used to capture and manage all the documentation and metadata needed to support, manage, and maximize an SOA enterprise architecture practice. The framework is also the mechanism that provides traceable linkages from the highest corporate strategic level down to the physical SOA implementations.

The framework is comprised of five columns and seven rows (or layers). The five columns represent the individual frameworks applied to each of the focus areas of the SOA practice. These frameworks are the:

1. Corporate strategy SOA assessment framework
2. Business unit operational plan SOA assessment framework
3. SOA Business Architecture framework
4. SOA Reference Architecture framework
5. SOA Platform Architecture framework

While the architecture practice facilitates and manages all five of these frameworks, the first three are owned and driven by the business. Architecture also manages the direct correlation and linkages of the artifacts and metadata across the five columns at each layer.

The seven layers that are the same for each of the individual frameworks are the:

1. Constituent Domain layer
2. Business Channel Domain layer
3. Business Process Domain layer
4. Business Service Domain layer
5. Integration Service Domain layer
6. Legacy Application Domain layer
7. Legacy Platform Domain layer

Note

Everything in this book assumes that you have an existing enterprise architecture practice and are looking to adapt this practice to support the SOA paradigm. If you do not have an EA practice, you need to establish one quickly. The first step will be to hire a chief architect and establish at least one of each of the architecture types defined in Chapter 11. These resources are needed to develop your *SOA business strategy and roadmap*, defined in Chapter 14. This document is the basis for initiating the implementation of everything defined in this book. Without an enterprise architecture team and this document you will not succeed at implementing the practice defined in this book.

The corporate strategy SOA assessment framework, business unit operational plan SOA assessment framework, SOA Business Architecture framework, enterprise SOA Reference Architecture framework, and the enterprise SOA Platform Architecture framework make up the *SOA enterprise architecture framework*. This trademarked framework is referred to as the SOA~EAF in this book and other publications. Exhibit 5.1 shows this framework.

SOA Enterprise Architecture Framework™

	Corporate Goal/Strategy Cross-Reference	Business Unit Plans Cross-Reference	Business Architecture (Conceptual)	Enterprise SOA Reference Architecture (Logical)	Enterprise SOA Platform Architecture (Physical)
Constituent Domain					
Business Channel Domain (Enterprise)					
Business Process Domain (Composite)					
Business Service Domain (Unit)					
Service Integration Domain (Isolation)					
Legacy Application Domain (Encapsulation)					
Legacy Platform Domain (Migration)					

EXHIBIT 5.1   SOA~EAF Framework

Corporate Goal/Strategy Cross-Reference Column

One of the major reasons for adopting an SOA approach to business systems is to have the entire IT process for communicating, designing, and implementing those systems structured in terms that are understood by the business and therefore can be driven by the business. We want the business to drive not only the tactical implementations of its projects through its business requirements structured to support the business architecture, but also the strategic evolution of the SOA environment as well. If the goal is to leverage and reuse as many of the SOA components in the SOA infrastructure as possible to maximize the investment we make, the best way to achieve this goal is to have a business strategy for doing so. In other words, there is value in finding time and money savings on each initiative through the leverage and reuse of SOA assets, but there is an even greater value if the business strategically plans for those advantages: a strategic value that not only results in cost and time to market savings, but also in expanding a competitive advantage and finding new market opportunities and business efficiencies.

The purpose of the Corporate Goal/Strategy Cross-Reference column of the SOA~EAF is twofold. First is to identify all the strategic objectives of the company. These include strategies to enter new markets, expand existing markets, and expand product lines or reduce production costs. Second is to identify how the company envisions what role each constituent plays in helping it achieve those strategies. What capabilities are needed to help achieve the strategy, and what is the best way to deliver those capabilities? Hence, we translate corporate strategies and goals into strategies and goals that relate to:

1. Our constituencies and how we strategically value their experiences and interactions with our company.
2. Our channel strategy and how we maximize our investment in each channel for each constituent type.
3. Identification of our highest value services and how they can be leveraged to achieve the company's strategic goals.
4. Finding efficiencies and improvements in the services we deliver.
5. Maximizing the value of the legacy system investment by supporting a strategy to augment them with capabilities that remove or minimize their rigidity in terms of adaptability and flexibility.
6. Providing a strategy to replace or modernize those legacy systems that cannot be augmented.

The conduct of this analysis and the incorporation of the results into the framework should occur as an extension of the corporate strategic planning process. This should not be a separate process or an IT process. The participants evaluating and approving the corporate strategy are the top executives of the company and should be the same representatives who make up the SOA Business Domain Governance Committee defined in Chapter 8.

While the business may clearly see its role as a driver for layers 1 through 4, it may not see itself as the driver of layers 5 and 6. It may see these as IT responsibilities. The problem with IT driving these layers is that if they are not addressed and promoted at a strategic level, IT will not be able to address them at a tactical level. There just will not be the money and time to do so. If they are packaged and addressed as IT strategies at the strategic planning level, the business will see them as competing strategies when it comes to assessing their priority and approving funding for them. In most cases, the IT initiatives will lose this fight.

These are not IT strategic requirements. They are the business strategic requirements so that IT can effectively deliver the capabilities and flexibility the business requires. They are not separate competing strategies but intricate components of the business strategies. Keeping these separate as IT responsibilities is equivalent to sales not recognizing that improvements in customer service impact repeat sales or that reduction in unit manufacturing costs has no impact on competitive pricing or margins. Clearly this is not the case. There is a direct impact to the business units and their strategic goals. Therefore, the business, not IT, needs to take ownership for driving the improvements to the flexibility, adaptability, and efficiency of legacy systems as these result in direct improvements needed to achieve its strategies.

Clearly there are two sides to the coin. One side is establishing the strategy and documenting its components as they relate to the layers of the framework. The other side is how to use the information to drive the tactical decisions we will make to achieve the strategies.

Part of the SOA transformation we are effecting is to change the approach so that we are evaluating and justifying each project at a more strategic level using more consistent metrics. Traditionally we would justify a project by referencing the goals and strategies in general terms (i.e., "This new system will reduce the administrative costs of the order processing department by 10 percent") as a justification against a corporate goal to reduce costs. The reality is that any headcount savings in the order department may be completely offset by the (unpredicted) increase in operational and administration costs associated with running the application. Was the cost of the allocation of 50 percent of an order department resource's time to administer the security and user configuration management of the application factored into the ROI? It probably was not.

The point is there is nothing in the business evaluation and justification process that evaluates whether the solution is the most effective and efficient use of IT assets and investments. There is nothing to evaluate if the solution positively or negatively impacts the work flow or workload of the employees, customers, or vendors that use it. There is nothing to ensure that the solution reuses existing capabilities instead of duplicating them.

In addition to the business need to drive the modernization of the legacy systems, we also need the business to drive the process for ensuring that we are making our IT investments efficiently and wisely. We need the business to address these issues at the enterprise and strategic level, not at a tactical level. As with legacy systems, attempting to incorporate and enforce development of reusable and leveraged SOA components at the project level is doomed to fail. In most cases, the cost and time to do so were not factored into the project. Even if there is no impact to the cost and delivery time, there will be resistance to the unknown. Even worse, components may be accepted and then later used as a scapegoat for other delays or cost increases in the project.

The process of incorporating these strategies into the IT planning process and governing their enforcement is the responsibility of the *enterprise SOA Portfolio Plan Governance Committee*. This governance committee is comprised mostly of business leaders. They focus on both the corporate-wide horizontal strategy of the constituency (service consumers) and the vertical strategy for managing and leveraging capabilities (service providers). Hence this committee has the responsibility to establish these strategies and validate each initiative submitted to it for approval and funding for support of those strategies. The enterprise SOA Portfolio Plan Governance Committee is defined in Chapter 8.

From a horizontal (service consumer) perspective, some of the strategic issues addressed by this committee include:

- Who are our constituents? How many constituent types are there? Are their different variations of constituents within each type? Do our strategies require establishing new constituencies or new variations of existing constituencies?
- How do those constituents interact with us? How do we want them to interact with us? How do *they* want to interact with us?
- How effective is the interaction? How satisfied are they with the interaction? How would *they* improve the interaction? Do our strategies require any of these interactions to change? Expand or contract? Apply different regulations or support different cultures (e.g., a national to global strategy)?
- How effective are the services being provided to these constituents? How much are they using these services, and through what mechanisms? Are there any services not being provided, or not being provided through a particular channel, that would increase their value if they were? Do our strategies require new

services currently not provided or changes to existing services to meet new requirements (e.g., multilingual support or foreign regulatory compliance)?

- Do any services being used by one constituency have value to another constituency?

The answers to these questions are translated into strategic objectives and added to the Constituency, Channel, Business Process, and Business Service domain cells in the Corporate Goal/Strategy Cross-Reference column of the SOA~EAF.

From a vertical (service provider) perspective some of the strategic issues addressed include:

- Are the services provided flexible and adaptable? Are they designed to support the widest audience of potential users? Are the services capable of supporting the needs of the corporate strategy, or will enhancements to existing services or acquisition of new capabilities for new services be required?
- Are the services controlled and accurate? Are they secured with proper authorization policies? Are they compliant with all legal and regulatory requirements? Are they traceable? Auditable? Are all retention and archive requirements supported? Do strategies implicate any of these requirements in terms of new controls, regulations, translations, certifications required by those strategies (e.g., requirements to meet new regulations when entering a new foreign market)?
- Are any services duplicate or redundant in any way? How do we eliminate any duplication or redundancy?
- Are there different versions of the service? If yes, how many and how long are they supported? How do we ensure that compliance with these policies is enforced and funded? Will anything in our strategic plan impact our ability to enforce this, and how do we handle these exceptions?
- What organization or group is the custodian of the service and manages its use and life cycle? (I use the term *custodian* rather than *owner* consciously.) Are any new custodians required to support new capabilities?
- How do the legacy business applications support our services? How effective is that support? Will this effectiveness impact the ability of these services to meet the requirements of our strategies (e.g., going global requiring 24/7 availability)?
- Are any of these legacy systems being strained from a business capability, performance, or capacity perspective? Will the strategy increase this strain?
- Are any of the technologies or platforms used in these applications unsupported or significantly behind in their version currency? What risk does this pose to the business, and how do we mitigate that risk?
- Are their major enhancements or upgrades scheduled or requested for these legacy applications, and do they have strategic value or make sense from a SOA business model perspective? Are their alternatives that have higher value to the business going forward (alternatives such as implementing a rules engine to build an insurance rating system rather than spending as much or more money to implement a major upgrade of a vendor's rating application that still will not interoperate with channel and process layers or the security framework)?
- What are the plans to modernize, replace, or sunset these systems? How are these plans funded and incorporated into the portfolio plan?

The answers to these questions are translated into strategic objectives and placed in the Business Service, Service Integration, Legacy Application, and Legacy Platform Domain cells in the Corporate Goal/Strategy Cross-Reference column of the SOA~EAF.

This process provides the strategic measures and metrics that can be applied to each SOA initiative. How they are applied is discussed in the next section.

Business Unit Plans Cross-Reference Column

The Business Domain Governance Committee establishes the strategic direction for each layer of the SOA architecture, and the SOA Portfolio Plan Governance Committee translates these into identifiable and measurable metrics that can be applied against each SOA initiative. They do so at an enterprise level. Each business unit also needs to evaluate the corporate strategies, what the strategic statements mean to their specific business units, and what they need to do to support the strategy. For example, the impact of going global on constituents, channels, and services is assessed and captured in the strategic column from an overall corporate perspective. But what does going global mean specifically to sales, support, or distribution? Sales may have to expand its sales force into each country by acquiring space, hiring sales associates, and so forth. Distribution's strategy may be to partner with carriers in each country to extend the channel. Support may be building its own staff in some countries and partnering with an outsource vendor for support in other countries. Each business unit's plan for how it would support the strategy would be documented in each of the cells in the Business Unit Plans Cross-Reference column of the SOA~EAF.

Hence, the Business Unit Plans column defines the capabilities needed by each business unit to support the strategy and when those capabilities need to be there. This information is as critical as the strategy itself to structure, evaluate, and prioritize SOA initiatives. The corporate strategy may have identified expansion into seven countries where seven different languages are spoken. Knowing that distribution is going to partner with carriers that will handle the language issues means that the service integration with these carriers will not require language translation capabilities. However, all the sales services and the channel adapters used to deliver those services will require language translation capabilities. The business unit plans may also determine that only three languages need to be supported for the support services with the other four languages supported through the outsource vendor.

Not all strategies will affect all constituents. Not all channels will support each strategy. Not all business units support all constituents. Not all business units support all channels. The information documented in the Corporate Strategy and Business Unit Plans columns of the framework will explicitly identify the presence or lack of these relationships. This provides a mechanism to ensure that tactical implementations are consistent with the corporate strategy and business plans. The information also helps to identify inconsistencies or required changes to the business plans and corporate strategy at the implementation level. Perhaps a capability that was not identified in the business unit plans is determined to be necessary when implementing the solution, or partnering with oversees outsource support partner is determined to be cost prohibitive when negotiations occur. The framework allows these issues to be pushed back up into the business plan and corporate strategic levels where they can be addressed by the right leaders.

An example of a nonapplicable business unit to constituent strategy is a business unit that has no relationship with a particular constituent (e.g., the human resources department may not have any direct relationship with the customers). In this case, human resources would not have any business plan entries under the external customer constituent. An example of a nonapplicable channel strategy is a business unit that has no transactions for a particular constituent supported by a particular channel. For example, electronic data interchange (EDI) may be a strategic channel of value to the company, and providing this channel option to customers and vendors is a stated strategic direction. The sales and finance business units may specify a strategy to provide support for purchase orders (POs) through this channel (Sales = POs in from customers: Finance = POs out to vendors). Finance may also specify support for invoices and "payment remittance" transactions between customers and vendors through this channel as well. The customer training business unit, however, has no defined EDI transactions for the services it provides. Therefore, it would have no plans to support this channel. Each business unit should map its plans on how its unit would or could support each of the applicable corporate strategies.

The corporate strategy may also define specific strategic goals aimed at directing the increased use of specific technologies that have economic and/or competitive value to the corporation in general. These will include strategies to expand the self-service capabilities of customers and vendors through the Web, EDI, and intelligent voice recognition (IVR) channels to reduce service costs. Each business unit would identify the customer and vendor services it provides (it may not provide any) and how it would support customers' and vendors' use of those services through these three channels.

Business units will almost always be comprised of both service consumers and service providers. A business unit will have services that are used by internal and/or external constituents outside the business unit. The business unit will also use services that are provided by other internal (business unit) entities or external (vendor and partner) entities. Therefore, most business units should have mappings to every layer within the Business Plan Cross-Reference column in the architectural framework. However, the business unit needs to be very clear and diligent about making and enforcing this distinction between consumers and providers when building its plans.

Service providers within the unit should map their support plans only as they relate to the Business Service Domain layer or lower. Service consumers within the unit should map only their support plans as they relate to the Business Service Domain layer or higher. The common ground between service consumers and service providers is the Business Service Domain layer.

These are very subtle statements but they represent a *significant cultural and political shift* in the traditional process. We are no longer asking the *owners* of the business applications to define how they are used. We are asking them to define each service provided by the legacy systems of record that they own and the requirements for authorization, accuracy, and control. We are not asking the *users* of the legacy systems to define how they are used either. Instead, we are asking the *people for whom the service is being rendered* to define how the service is used. This is the new dynamic of SOA. This is a top-down, consumer-centric approach to business systems versus the bottom-up development approach to systems. This is the outside-looking-in approach versus the inside-looking-out approach.

CHANNEL INTERMEDIARIES REVISITED   Employees who consume services to support interactions with other constituents should be treated as channel intermediaries, and their requirements should be no different from those expressed by the constituent they interact with. See Chapter 4 for a full description of intermediaries. If a customer calls a service representative to process a transaction rather than using a self-service mechanism, the transaction itself should be exactly the same. The business process may be streamlined in one instance (the service rep) and more detailed in the other (self-service) instance, but, if done correctly, these are just dynamic modifications to the same business process.

JUSTIFICATION CRITERIA   The business justification of the value of a specific business service or process within an initiative is still evaluated through the traditional business metrics. These business metrics include evaluating the service or process in the context of:

- Its ability to improve operational efficiency, reduce costs, or increase revenue.
- Automating a manual business process.
- Meeting a legal, audit, or regulatory requirement.
- Supporting a new market, line of business, or business offering.

The delivery and use of those services, however, is now evaluated on:

- Their support of the documented constituent, channel and Business Process Domain strategies in the Corporate Goal/Strategy Cross-Reference column of the SOA~EAF.
- Their alignment with the business unit plans in the Business Unit Plans Cross-Reference column of the SOA~EAF.

Their technical value assessment is based on their compliance with all the domains of the Reference Architecture framework and the rationalization of that architecture against both the corporate and business unit columns of the framework.

As this approach implies, the decision on what an SOA initiative does and how it does it is no longer a single department or traditional "application owner" decision. This makes sense because the solution is no longer a self-contained stovepipe application. The solution will involve the reuse of SOA components that already exist. The solution will share and leverage existing common SOA components, such as security, and the channel adapter framework established for each constituent. The days of each business unit replicating and duplicating these capabilities are gone. The cost and time savings realized by eliminating these redundancies results in getting new stuff done faster, doing it cheaper, and making more money available to do more.

More information on the corporate strategy and business plan columns of this framework is provided in the "Business Domain Governance Committee" and "Portfolio Governance Committee" sections of Chapter 8.

SOA Business Architecture Framework

The business architecture depicted in Chapter 3 reflects some of the same basic components of traditional enterprise architecture frameworks. In other words:

- Who is doing something?
- Where are they doing it?
- What are they doing?
- And how are they doing it?

The business architecture picture from Chapter 3 is revisited in Exhibit 5.2 to highlight these characteristics.

The reflection of these concepts in the business architecture is 100 percent *conceptual*. There are no physical or logical representations in the exhibit. The exhibit does not depict any servers or other hardware components. There are no database models or defined system interfaces present. This business architecture is simply a conceptual framework that both the business and IT can understand and agree to. The existence of this document is critically important as it represents the baseline of common understanding and agreement between the business and IT. It represents the diagram that is the new communication language between the

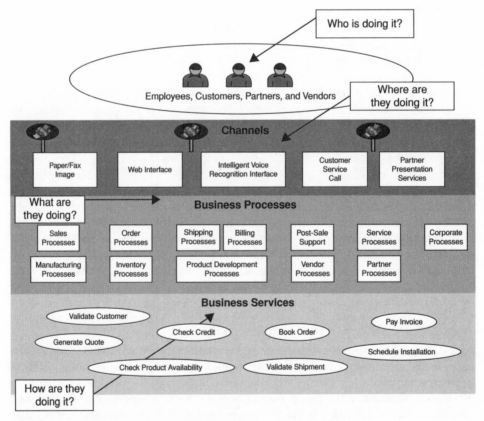

EXHIBIT 5.2   Business Architecture Revisited

business and IT. Everything specified by the business and everything delivered by IT should be able to be mapped to the business architecture. If you cannot map the business specification or an implementation to the diagram, one of two conditions has occurred. Either you are missing something in your business architecture (an undefined constituent or a missing channel), or what you cannot map is not a business process or service (i.e., it is not a business application).

The business architecture diagrams are the conceptual representations of the required capabilities defined in the business unit plans in the Business Unit Plans Cross-Reference column of the framework. In the strategic example given earlier, where support in certain countries was provided by an outsource partner, we would expect to see a business architecture diagram for those countries where a customer accesses a partner's channel to use services that have been integrated into that partner's channel.

So far the business architecture diagram only relates to service consumers. The complete business architecture diagram extends through the remaining layers of the framework to reflect the conceptual views of the service providers as well. A complete business architecture diagram is presented in Exhibit 5.3.

Like the top layers, the three lower layers show no logical design or physical implementation characteristics. They are just conceptual representations. Even though the Legacy Platforms layer contains specific technical terminology, the terminology is conceptual as well. It does not tell us how many COBOL programs, virtual storage access method (VSAM) files, and Customer Information Control System (CICS) regions there are, how they relate to each other, and where they physically reside. They are represented to show that the service providers are, for example, supporting the "Book Order" business services with order system integration services like the "Create Customer Order" integration service, which creates a new order record in the order system running on the mainframe.

Every SOA initiative should have an associated business architecture diagram that reflects all the conceptual SOA business components needed to meet the specified requirements of the initiative. The metadata and artifacts associated with the enterprise SOA Business Architecture framework are managed and maintained by the business architects. They have the custodial responsibility for maintaining the currency and accuracy of the artifacts. Any changes to them must be made by the business architects. The business architects are also responsible for maintaining the horizontal integrity of these artifacts with the SOA reference architecture and the SOA platform architecture, ensuring that any business definitions or concepts impacted by a change to the reference or platform architectures are identified and reflected in the business architecture.

Enterprise SOA Reference Architecture Framework

The enterprise SOA reference architecture is the framework that translates the business architecture conceptual components into components within a logical SOA reference architecture. It represents the next layer of specificity about the SOA Enterprise Architecture Domain. It represents the *logical* view of the SOA architecture. It is the bridge between how the business sees SOA (the business architecture) and how those business needs are logically implemented (the enterprise SOA

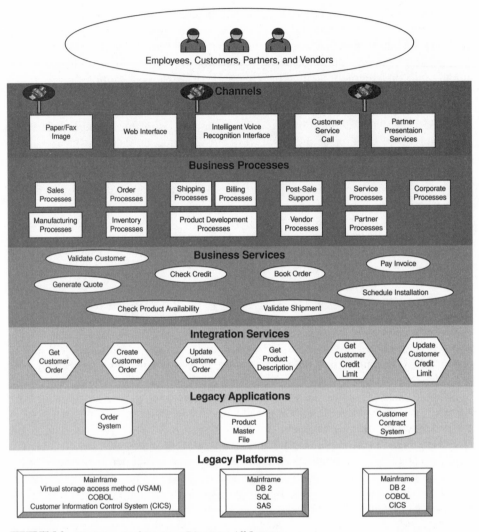

EXHIBIT 5.3 Business Architecture Diagram: All Layers

reference architecture). Exhibit 5.4 represents the enterprise SOA Reference Architecture framework.

Each domain layer in the Enterprise SOA Reference Architecture framework (with the exception of the Legacy Application Domain) is split into sublayers. These sublayers isolate the functionality provided by the component from its integration specifications with the layer below and its invocation specifications with the layer above. The only exception to this is in the Channel layer, where certain layer-specific functionality is embedded in the channel adapter (i.e., a browser contains the functionality to interpret and display hypertext markup language [HTML]; a portal contains the functionality to interpret and display portlets).

The added descriptor of Domain is included in the description of each row. This is done to reflect that specific resources may be dedicated to a specific horizontal

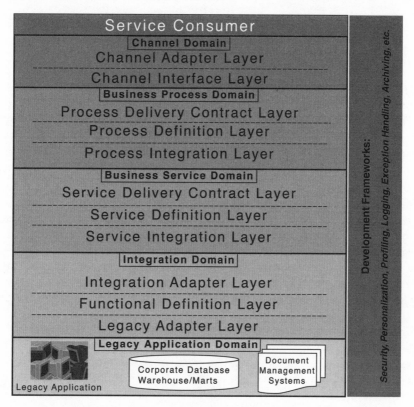

EXHIBIT 5.4   Enterprise SOA Reference Architecture Framework

plane. It is also added to further enforce the demarcation of accountability and responsibility of the layers. As stated at the beginning of this book, SOA will force a paradigm shift in everything IT does. Part of this shift will result in certain groups relinquishing some accountability and ownership while others will add to their domain of accountability.

The establishment of these domains and the isolation of responsibilities within them will help to break the traditional mind-set of application ownership associated with a non-SOA approach. The vertical mind-set belief that a particular department or organization owns the entire application, from the user interface to the data, needs to disappear. It will be difficult to convince departments to let go. They will resist. However, if you can show that the process and practice provides them with these benefits, you have a good chance of winning them over:

- A tightly controlled and transparent mechanism to ensure that they still have visibility and input into the vertical view.
- A new, added responsibility that is more strategic than tactical.
- Measurable improvements in the flexibility and adaptability of the systems supporting their business.

An SOA business architecture diagram may show a customer using a customer portal through the Web channel to consume the listed processes and services. The

SOA Reference Architecture diagram would show the role of customer logging on to the Web using a portal adapter, authenticating and exposing privileges to access the listed services being delivered as JSR 168 portlets.

DEVELOPMENT FRAMEWORKS, DESIGN PATTERNS, AND DESIGN STANDARDS   In addition to the logical representation of all the implemented SOA components in the portfolio, the enterprise SOA reference architecture also includes all the development frameworks, design patterns, and design standards that are applied when developing under SOA. These are the architectural components of an SOA development. Development frameworks, design patterns, and design standards are the *A* in SOA.

Development Frameworks   A development framework has a larger scope than a design pattern and is less specific and rigid in its implementation (i.e., one or more options on how to apply a specific component of the framework may be allowed). An example of a development framework is the framework for the enterprise security module. This development framework transcends from the Channel layer of the architecture all the way into the Legacy Application layer. The framework defines how each business component within each layer interfaces and interoperates with the framework and how the framework's modules in one layer interface and interoperate with the frameworks modules in the layers above and below.

A development framework encompasses many components and interfaces. An SOA enterprise architecture development framework can transcend multiple layers of the architecture, like the three just mentioned, or be specific to a single layer of the architecture. An example of a single-layer framework is one for transforming and orchestrating different message formats at the integration layer.

Components of one development framework may interact with components of another. For example, frameworks for performing personalization or user profiling may also be defined. Components implemented under these frameworks may be required to interact with each other or components of the enterprise security framework. In those instances, the documentation of each framework includes the framework-to-framework integration and operation specifications.

You should have all your development frameworks defined and documented before you start to develop your first SOA-based architecture solution. These frameworks are critical to the consistency, leveragability, and reusability of your SOA components. Failure to do so will result in:

- Components that will not be reusable or leveraged.
- Rewrite and replacement of these SOA components after these frameworks are defined.

How many frameworks you will need to support your SOA environment will depend on your unique environment. The architects need to perform a comprehensive assessment of their environment (e.g., tools, platforms, channels, etc.) to determine the frameworks needed. At a minimum, most companies will need the four just mentioned (security, personalization, profiling, orchestration) as well as frameworks for nonfunctional capabilities (e.g., logging, auditing, exception handling, archiving, etc.).

Design Patterns   Design patterns apply to the specific design of individual components. More than one design pattern may exist for a single component. For example, multiple design patterns will exist for each of the service stubs needed by each of the channels and channel formats that invoke the services. The design pattern for invoking a service through a Windows client will be different from the pattern for invoking the service through a browser client. Within the Web channel, the design for invoking the service as a JSR 168 portlet by a portal will be different from the design for invoking the service through an MVC or Spring-based Web application. However, the design pattern for invoking all JSR 168 portlets from all portals should be exactly the same. Multiple design patterns for the same purpose should not be allowed.

A design pattern tells the developer exactly how to technically code the component. The architect should use examples of previously coded SOA components compliant with those patterns when explaining the requirement to the developer. Design patterns ensure that each installation of a component is consistent (i.e., coded exactly the same way). This ensures that subsequent users of the component will understand exactly how to use the component. The design patterns also ensure that solutions architects will be consistent and more accurate in their initiative estimations.

There will be many design patterns documented within your SOA reference architecture—perhaps as many as 100 or more components, types of components, and variations of components exist. Unlike development frameworks, you can develop your design patterns as you need them. As more SOA components are built, more design patterns will exist.

This puts a significant weight and pressure on your team of architects, especially during the first few initiatives in the early stages of SOA adoption. For these first early initiatives, the team of architects should be addressing and resolving as many of these design pattern requirements as early as possible. They should start addressing them even before the initiative begins if possible.

One way to accomplish this is for the architecture team to review and assess all the approved SOA initiatives that have not started yet. Through this process they can determine what patterns will need to be developed to support the initiatives, how many individual patterns are needed for multiple initiatives, and which design patterns will be needed first based on projected project start dates.

It is absolutely essential that the architects have a center of excellence (COE) at their disposal to conduct proofs of concepts to test out their pattern designs and prove their viability in terms of accuracy and abilities (reliability, scalability, interoperability, adaptability, flexibility, etc.). The COE should include versions of all the technology platforms used in production and development tools used by the developers. It can also be used to recertify existing deployed components on newer versions of the technology platforms before they are upgraded. Components for development frameworks should be developed, tested, and certified in the COE as well.

Architects will often find flaws in how a technology actually works versus how it was documented. Or architects find that features that would make the technology more effective or easier to use are missing. This may initiate many discussions with the vendors' engineers and product development teams. New patches may be delivered by vendors to fix these problems or accommodate the capability identified.

The *last place* you want to discover these flaws is during the development phase of a real project. Flaws discovered at this stage will more than likely jeopardize delivery of the project. It is critical to find and resolve flaws in a certification environment as early as possible.

Design Standards   Unlike development frameworks and design patterns, your architects do not write design standards. They already exist. There are many standards and many standards bodies that govern them. In many cases, there are choices or alternatives for standards to use for the same purpose. In most cases, multiple versions of the standards are available and supported. You need to determine which standards you will adopt in your architecture and which versions you will support.

The decisions on which design standards to support, however, may not be 100 percent at the discretion of the architects. Support for these standards may or may not be embedded in the technologies you use. If you have a lot of business partners and a lot of system interaction with those business partners, you need to understand what standards they support or will be willing to support. (This is especially important for standards like security assertion markup language [SAML].)

Like design patterns, you will not need to have all your design standards defined before you start your first initiative. Very much like patterns, however, you need to have them defined and documented before they are needed by an SOA initiative. It is hoped that many of these standards have already been adopted. Documentation for support of the SOA reference architecture for adopted standards should be easy to determine.

The same process used when assessing design patterns should be used to identify what standards will be needed. The COE should also be used to test out these standards and their versions for the same evaluation and certification reasons that were applied to design patterns.

CONDUCTING CODE REVIEWS AND IDENTIFYING VARIANCES   Code reviews are conducted by project architects during development to validate that artifacts were applied correctly to the code produced. One of three conditions can come out of a code review:

1. The code was written accurately and compliant with the architecture requirements.
2. For some reason (either technical or nontechnical), the architecture standard, pattern, or framework needs to be altered or violated.
3. A unique or first-time condition arises where no previously established standard, pattern, or framework exists.

All other instances of noncompliant code should be rewritten to make them compliant. As more coding experience is gained, the percentage of compliant code should increase.

Approval for a variance to an architectural framework, pattern, or standard must be obtained from the SOA Technology Governance Committee. This may occur, for example, when a partner's technology or the technology used for a purchased business application cannot support an enterprise framework, design pattern, or standard.

MAINTAINING THE REFERENCE ARCHITECTURE DOCUMENTATION   The metadata and artifacts associated with the development frameworks, design patterns, and design standards in the enterprise SOA Reference Architecture framework are managed and maintained by the enterprise architects. These architects have the custodial responsibility for maintaining framework and design pattern and standard currency and accuracy, and any changes to them must be made by the enterprise architects. The enterprise architects are also responsible for maintaining the horizontal integrity of these artifacts with the SOA business architecture and the SOA platform architecture, ensuring that changes to the logical reference model are reflected in the conceptual (business) and physical (platform) architectures as well. The reference architecture metadata and artifacts associated with the logical views of implemented SOA components are produced by the solutions and project architects, who also maintain their currency and accuracy. In other words, the enterprise architects maintain the overall SOA Reference Architecture framework and all the development frameworks, design patterns, and design standards associated with it. The solutions and project architects maintain all the logical views of the specific implemented instances of the SOA components in the environment.

Enterprise SOA Platform Architecture Framework

We discussed that the Business Architecture framework was the conceptual view of SOA and the enterprise SOA Reference Architecture framework was the logical view. The enterprise SOA Platform Architecture framework represents the *physical* view of SOA.

The enterprise SOA platform architecture identifies the specific products and technologies that exist at each layer of the architecture. It maintains all the physical aspects of the deployed SOA components, including the source and compiled code associated with the SOA components and the physical platforms where the deployed code operates. It also contains the artifacts associated with the monitoring and management of the SOA components in production as well as the service-level agreements (SLAs) for the SOA components in the production environment.

The artifacts also include the physical representations of the physical connections and platforms between interoperating components. While the enterprise SOA reference architecture tells developers exactly how to code for each platform and how to design and code the integration with the specific technology platforms above it and below it, the enterprise SOA platform architecture describes the physically implemented instances of those developments in production.

The enterprise SOA platform architecture is focused on the physical attributes of the IT infrastructure that are important to SOA. The intent is not to clutter the physical architecture framework with the entire portfolio of IT physical assets such that it merely duplicates the documentation maintained in the existing enterprise architecture framework. It is recommended that physical artifacts around the company's networks, server farms, storage area networks, and so on be maintained and managed through the traditional framework. The physical platforms captured and managed through the SOA Platform Architecture framework are the technologies used to support the production SOA applications. These platforms include the:

- Channel platforms (e.g., the Web server product, the IVR technology, the Windows and browser clients supported, etc.).

- Business process/composite application platforms (business process management system [BPMS] technology, orchestration technology, work flow technology, application server technology, etc.).
- Business services platforms (enterprise service bus technology, service registry technology, service repository technology, etc.).
- Legacy integration platforms (enterprise application integration [EAI] messaging technology, including message transport and message broker, and data management technologies, including extract-translate-load [ETL] tools and data "hub" tools).

In addition, the platforms for the enterprise development framework components should be captures here as well. These include:

- Security authentication and authorization technologies including supporting technologies, such as directory services and the lightweight directory access protocol (LDAP).
- Provisioning technologies.
- Logging, audit, and tracking technologies, including analytical and reporting tools.
- Archive, retention, and retrieval technologies.
- Document management and database management technologies.
- Business analytical, business intelligence, and business reporting technologies.

To continue our previous example, a customer using a customer portal as described on business architecture diagram translates to a constituent with the role customer using a portal framework invoking JSR 168 portlets and enterprise SOA security components in the enterprise SOA reference architecture. This in turn, would be reflected in the SOA platform architecture as a user accessing, for example, a SunOne portal server where the customer portal application code has been deployed and, after being authenticated by the SOA security services on top of a SunOne access manager application, invokes deployed orchestrated services on a BEA AquaLogic service bus through a portlet service stub.

STRUCTURING YOUR ENTERPRISE SOA PLATFORM ARCHITECTURE   The graphical representation of the enterprise SOA platform architecture for your company will be unique to your company. All the layers within the SOA~EAF should be represented in the platform architecture, but the technology components that you have deployed to perform those capabilities will be unique. For this reason, showing you an implementation example may be more confusing then valuable. Some companies may use multiple products with capabilities focused on a single layer of the architecture framework. Other companies may use a single product or a single vendor's product suite to support multiple layers of the architecture.

The Application Integration layer and the Business Service layer together may be referred to as the enterprise service bus and supported by one product or suite of products from a single vendor. In some cases, the Integration layer may include a legacy investment in a traditional middleware infrastructure like IBM WebSphere MQ series, a collection of integration capabilities built on open messaging technologies like JMS, or off-the-shelf integration drivers such as Java database connectivity (JDBC) and open database connectivity (ODBC).

There are positives and negatives to whatever options you choose. Presenting an example of one approach may put an inappropriate (positive or negative) perception of that implementation in your mind. What is more important is that you are able to map support for each layer and sublayer of the enterprise SOA reference architecture to the capabilities of the technologies in the enterprise SOA platform architecture and the design patterns and design standards have been vetted and certified on those technologies.

PURPOSE OF THE ENTERPRISE SOA PLATFORM ARCHITECTURE FRAMEWORK   In addition to the enterprise SOA reference architecture, the enterprise SOA platform architecture is the other tool used by the architects and developers to design and develop the detail physical specifications of the solution. For each SOA component design specification, the architect describes to the development team the specific platform used to code, test, deploy, and manage the component. This information, along with the specific development frameworks, design patterns, and design standards specified within the enterprise SOA reference architecture, provides project architects and project developers with everything they need to technically develop architectural compliant solutions.

The enterprise SOA Platform Architecture framework is also used by the solutions architect to validate the capabilities and quality of service for existing SOA components that may be targeted for reuse or leverage in their new initiative. Project architects can extract the code and configurations of deployed SOA components as examples to provide to developers coding similar SOA components using the same design patterns and standards. These provide the developer with a real-life example of how a similar component was developed and physically deployed in the past. The artifacts in the SOA reference architecture can provide examples of how previously developed SOA components were *designed*. The artifacts of the SOA platform architecture can provide examples of how previously developed SOA components were *deployed* into production and how they are maintained *and supported* in production.

The enterprise SOA platform architecture is also the primary tool used by the enterprise SOA infrastructure and capacity architect to manage the SOA infrastructure and capacity. The enterprise SOA infrastructure and capacity architect uses these artifacts; the network, server, and direct access storage device (DASD) artifacts from the EA framework; and the IT management and monitoring tools used in the company to analyze, simulate, and project capacity issues and needs. At a global level, this analysis is conducted on an ongoing iterative basis to proactively manage the capacity requirements of the production environment. At a portfolio level, this analysis is also conducted for each SOA initiative to ensure that any added capacity to support the initiative will be there when needed and that funding for that capacity is covered. Finally, at a development level, this analysis is conducted to validate that the component as designed and the capacity as planned will support the capacities and SLAs specified in the requirements.

The metadata and artifacts associated with the Enterprise SOA Platform Architecture framework are managed and maintained by the enterprise SOA infrastructure and capacity architect in conjunction with the IT operations and data center teams. They have the custodial responsibility for maintaining metadata and artifact currency and accuracy; any changes to them must be approved by the enterprise infrastructure and capacity architect. The enterprise SOA infrastructure and capacity architect is also responsible for maintaining the horizontal integrity of these artifacts with the SOA reference architecture and the SOA platform architecture, ensuring that any business definitions or concepts impacted by a change to the reference or platform architecture are identified and reflected in the business architecture.

Leveraging the Artifacts from All the SOA Frameworks

From an architecture practice perspective, you need to pull together and manage all the SOA frameworks. You need to be able to track and manage all the metadata and artifacts vertically through the layers of each framework and horizontally across the frameworks within each layer. The artifacts also need to be identifiable to the specific domain layer they support and structured so that each sublayer in the domain is isolated and can be identified easily and readily. The architects also need a way to identify the relationships among all the interrelated SOA components supporting the applications in the production SOA environment. For example, they must be able to identify all the SOA components that make up the capabilities provided by the customer portal application, from the channel down to the integrated legacy applications that integrate into the customer business services. They need to be able to show these relationships *conceptually* to the business, *logically* to the developers, and *physically* to IT operations.

In order to facilitate an SOA approach, we need a framework that can quickly show all the leveraged and reusable assets in our portfolio. We need a framework with artifacts that can tell us how those assets have been leveraged and reused in the past and how they can be leveraged and reused to support new requirements. In other words, we need a way to quickly understand all the *logical* and *physical* capabilities that exist (or need to exist) in our environment to support their *conceptual* business needs. The business architecture of an initiative is a *conceptual* representation of *what* the business wants. The enterprise SOA reference architecture is the *logical* representation of *how* to deliver those needs, and the enterprise SOA physical architecture is the *physical* representation of what was built and *where* they exist in production.

The business architecture for a new SOA initiative may reflect a desire to provide the capability for customer constituents to use the IVR to check order status using the "GetOrderStatus" service that they were told already exists. The enterprise SOA reference and platform architectures will reflect that, yes, the "GetOrderStatus" service exists, but it is currently deployed only through the legacy client channel of the CRMS desktop application. The enterprise SOA reference architecture could also be used to represent the logical capabilities that would be needed to provide this service to the IVR channel. These capabilities would reflect:

- The requirement to build a new service delivery contract stub for the "GetOrder-Status" service using the invocation format and protocol supported by the IVR technology.
- The need to develop the IVR scripting necessary to add the new touch tone and voice recognition logic to handle and process the order status request, including converting the service reply from text to voice.

- The need to script the authentication and authorization security requirements and integrate to the enterprise channel security module if needed (i.e., the first customer service delivered through the IVR that requires an authentication).

The SOA platform architecture would be used to identify:

- Any additional technology platforms needed to support the initiative (e.g., the purchase of a channel technology like an IVR or portal server platform).
- Any increases needed in the physical infrastructure (servers, CPU, memory, disk, hub, blade, etc.).
- Any increases in licensing fees for the platforms (e.g., database management systems licenses, Web application server licenses, etc.).

Hence the business can leverage its business architects to lay out a need or an opportunity using the Business Architecture framework, and the solutions architect can respond back quickly with IT's ability to meet that need using the information from the enterprise SOA reference and platform architectures.

This can and should be an iterative process. The business should constantly be questioning and looking for new opportunities to leverage the IT assets to improve, expand, or enhance their business. Business architects should be constantly working with the solutions architects to understand what exists and what is new in the SOA asset portfolio. They should be evaluating these assets in terms of their knowledge of the business functions, capabilities, and strategies of the business unit they support. They should be drafting straw-man business architecture diagrams of those opportunities and reviewing them regularly with their business unit, coming back with new or modified opportunities based on feedback and input.

When you are able to conduct this iterative process with your business, you are achieving the ultimate benefit of SOA. The architecture practice is leveraging SOA~EAF as a tool to work hand in hand with the business to help it take advantage of as many opportunities as possible as quick as possible. The IT assets are not seen as a bunch of applications and databases locked in a room somewhere. They are seen as business enablers and business opportunities. This is the transformation from a reactive process of looking at the IT portfolio for potential opportunities and efficiencies to a proactive one that identifies the opportunities and efficiencies already built into the portfolio.

This is yet another example of achieving SOA value through an architectural approach. No technical book on SOA or technical implementation approach to SOA will tell you to set up these frameworks and conduct these activities with your business.

The view we want to take of our IT assets from an SOA perspective is twofold. On one hand, we want to know which assets we have leveraged to take advantage of SOA, how that leveraging was accomplished, and how they can be further leveraged. On the other hand, we want to be able to view our assets from the perspective of those that have not been leveraged to take advantage of SOA. Is there an opportunity to do so, and, if so, is there value in doing so? We want to be able to view these assets from both a top-down and bottom-up perspective, regardless of which layer we start at and which layer we drill up or down to.

Thus, from a top-down representation, we need the ability to extract and present:

- Which channels have been deployed in support of each constituent, and what deployed adapters they use.
- What business processes and business services are available through those channels.
- What legacy systems are integrated into those services, and how they are integrated.

We also may want to represent:

- What channels have been deployed to other constituents but not to this constituent.
- What processes and services are deployed through one channel but not the others available to that constituency.
- What business processes and services have been deployed to other constituents but not this one.

From a bottom-up perspective, we may want to extract and represent:

- What integration services support each business service.
- What business services are embedded in a business process.
- What channels are a specific business process or business service deployed through.
- Who the constituents are who use a specific business process or business service.

We may also want to represent:

- Which legacy applications have no or partial integration capabilities.
- Which integration assets have not been integrated with the Business Service layer.

Understanding these assets in this format is critical to the business architect and solutions architects when evaluating a business requirement. They are also critical for identifying potential opportunities to leverage these assets with their business units. Being able to communicate these capabilities back to the business in terms users can understand is also critical.

Thus, there is no rigid format or structure for storing, analyzing, and presenting the SOA metadata. Just as SOA applications are loosely coupled, SOA metadata needs to be loosely coupled, allowing for an infinite number of dynamically constructed views of that metadata to address a specific business requirement and solution.

The entire purpose of everything we have discussed so far is to facilitate the representation of the system universe from a top-down, consumer-centric view. It also helps to focus the strategy and planning of systems based on the holistic view and needs of the consuming users rather than the individual systems in the portfolio. This is a critical characteristic that results in a model that is a true reflection of the real world, especially when it comes to external consumers.

The good news is that we have the capabilities to allow our customers, vendors, and partners to interact directly with our systems instead of via phone interaction with our employees. The bad news is that how we deliver that interaction can be perceived as effective and efficient or complex and difficult. If the latter happens, the chances of that external consumer using the capability again are almost nil. There is a real risk that you will lose them as customers if your competition provides a more enjoyable experience.

Pulling It All Together

This capability to manage all the artifacts from all the frameworks is facilitated through the SOA enterprise architecture framework (SOA~EAF) and the associated SOA~EAF methodology. This framework integrates the SOA business architecture, the enterprise SOA reference architecture, and the enterprise SOA platform architecture into one model. The model also incorporates the business unit business plans and corporate strategy. Exhibit 5.1 depicts this SOA enterprise architecture framework. It is the overarching tool used by the enterprise architecture SOA team to manage the SOA practice.

From an SOA enterprise architecture practice perspective, we need to know the entire legacy systems of record. We want to promote the isolation of those legacy systems to the largest degree possible by encapsulating their functionality at the lowest functional level possible. We want to isolate that encapsulated functionality from its physical characteristics by providing logical access at the integration layer. We want to use this logical functionality to build services that perform discrete units of work. We want to be able to provide access to these units of work individually or incorporate them into higher-level business processes that use several of these services to perform more complex business activities. We want these services and processes to be accessible through as many channels as possible to any constituent that needs to use them.

We need to explain all of this to the business in terms understood by the business. We need to explain what is required of the SOA application designers in terms that the designers understand. Finally, we need to explain the requirements to the application developers in terms that they understand. We also have to justify the approach to the business unit leaders and the corporate executives.

A DYNAMIC AND MULTIDIMENSIONAL FRAMEWORK   The model should be able to be sliced not only horizontally and vertically, but also dimensionally. You should have the ability to create a view that reflects the specific pieces that make up an initiative that is in production or in development. The Horizontal Constituent Strategy Subcommittee of the SOA Portfolio Plan Governance Committee (defined in Chapter 8) may request a view of all the capabilities in production for a specific constituent and metrics around their utilization of those capabilities. Other examples of dimensional slices of the frameworks metadata include:

- All capabilities delivered through a specific channel.
- Services being delivered to multiple constituents.
- Services being delivered through multiple channels.

The more flexibility you build in, the greater the value it returns.

As architects with years of systems experience, we readily see the value in our technical artifacts and metadata. What we often fail to realize is that the business does not have our technical expertise and experience and does not view them the same way. This framework gives us the capability to cross-reference all our technical capabilities to the business need, the corporate strategic value, and, most important, the business description of those capabilities.

Through this framework and methodology, the architecture practice and IT in general will learn a new way to leverage this technical data by repackaging the information into dynamic, business-friendly models with business-friendly terminology that the business can easily understand and act on.

Layers of the SOA~EAF Framework

The previous section described the columns of the SOA~EAF. The next sections will define the rows of the SOA~EAF.

CONSTITUENT DOMAIN   Referring back to Exhibit 5.1, the highest layer of the SOA framework is the Constituent Domain. Under SOA, the plan or scope always starts with the service consumer (i.e., the constituent). The best technical solution will fail if it does not give service consumers what they want, how they want it, and when they want it. This is one of the major cultural paradigm shifts we are attempting to achieve to support an SOA enterprise architecture approach. This is the cultural transformation from inside looking out to outside looking in.

If you think about it, most of the legacy business applications were built to be used exclusively by employees. In fact, most were designed to be used by a limited number of employees. If anyone else, internally or externally, needs information from those systems or processes a transaction against those systems, they did so through the individual authorized to use the system. This is why the dilemma depicted back in Exhibit 3.2 exists.

The whole intent of SOA is to create an environment where anyone potentially has the authority and ability to get the information or process the transaction directly, eliminating the "facilitating employee" as quickly as possible at the lowest cost possible. As explained in Chapter 4, once the investment is made to build a channel for a constituency, the ability to quickly deploy new services over that channel has tremendous value from a competitive and financial perspective.

To go back to the Starbucks example, once it established the shipping, billing, and collections capabilities to ship the coffee to retail outlets, it can sell any of its other products (e.g., coffee cups and travel mugs) through that channel. Similarly, once you have built the framework to deliver secured services to your customers over the Web channel, the ability to give them access to a new service can be as simple as adding the service to their defined role privileges and exposing the URL for the service on their authenticated landing page. Because you have adopted an architectural approach to SOA, this process can be as simple as a configuration file change to the role and policy files of the authentication and authorization service and a redeployment of the landing page.

The corporate strategy identifies all the constituents and their relationships. Each business unit defines its business model, specifying the relationships it has with those

Constituent Domain	Corporate Business Exposure Strategy	Business Model	Constituents	Roles	Users
	Corporate Goal/ Strategy Cross-Reference	Business Unit Plans Cross-Reference	Business Architecture (Conceptual)	Enterprise SOA Reference Architecture (Logical)	Enterprise SOA Platform Architecture (Physical)

EXHIBIT 5.5 SOA~EAF Constituent Domain Layer

constituents. The business models drive the definition of the constituents in terms of what they are allowed to do when interacting with the company.

These business rules for access authorization to the services of the company translate into roles and privileges logically applied within a security authentication and authorization framework. These are implemented as user security profiles on the security platforms. The cells of the Constituent Domain layer are depicted in Exhibit 5.5.

BUSINESS CHANNEL DOMAIN The Business Channel Domain layer is included in the SOA~EAF to reflect the importance of managing channels as a distinct set of SOA assets. Referring back to the Starbucks example, when the company decided to sell its coffee to retail outlets, the coffee did not magically appear on the shelves the next day. Starbucks did not sign a contract with a shipping company to ship it to one specific retail outlet in one specific location. When it decided to use these outlets, Starbucks planned and built out the entire delivery channel to do so.

Yet when companies decided to use the Web as a channel, they treated each application as its own delivery channel and kept throwing "stuff" out there until frustration and rejection reached such a level that they were forced to rethink their strategy. Users internally and externally did not want to log on to multiple systems and remember multiple user IDs and passwords. To users, it seemed that the systems were dictating their work flow rather than their work flow dictating the systems.

This spawned a new set of products designed to provide single sign-on across multiple applications. In reality, this was treating the symptom rather than the problem. Single sign-on eliminated the need to remember multiple passwords but did nothing to solve the complexities and inefficiencies placed on the user's work flow.

Another set of technologies that tried to get at solving these problems was portal technologies. Unlike single sign-on, portal technologies required a complete rewrite of the Web applications. Portal technologies were a way to bring all the functionality provided by the separate applications under one umbrella, allowing the entire user experience to be managed and maintained through a single user session.

Portals are an excellent solution to the problem because they incorporate some of the very capabilities we have identified as channel capabilities. They provide a way to authenticate the user, set up and manage the session while the user employs the channel, and restrict and authenticate access to individual services within the portal. Hence a portal can be thought of as a Web channel adapter technology that works well with authentication, authorization, and personalization frameworks for delivering services to a constituent through the Web.

The strategies for channels and their use should be established at the highest strategic level of the corporation. Channels designed to support SOA are expensive

Business Channel Domain (Enterprise)	Horizontal Constituent Experience	Business Distribution Mechanisms and Partnerships	Contract/ Interaction Mechanisms	Channel Models	Production Channel Connections
	Corporate Goal/ Strategy Cross-Reference	Business Unit Plans Cross-Reference	Business Architecture (Conceptual)	Enterprise SOA Reference Architecture (Logical)	Enterprise SOA Platform Architecture (Physical)

EXHIBIT 5.6   SOA~EAF Business Channel Domain Layer

to implement, but the value they provide by allowing you to flood them with all existing services results in a high ROI. They have to have this strategic value to warrant the investment. Developing an EDI channel to support one EDI transaction is not a wise investment. In the early stages of SOA adoption, strategic decisions for focusing limited spending on less services and more channels versus more services and less channels will need to be made. *Line managers at a tactical project level should not make these decisions.*

These decisions drive the business unit's plans for supporting the channels with high strategic value to the corporation. Specific requirements for use of these channels are documented and used to develop the logical models and frameworks for implementing them. The cells of the Business Channel Domain layer are depicted in Exhibit 5.6.

BUSINESS PROCESS DOMAIN   The Business Process Domain layer is the layer that aggregates business services and business flows into complex business processes. These are represented by composite applications within a specific business domain. Hence the Sales Domain can have quoting services, ordering services, payment services, and shipping services all part of its composite application service. While this layer, on the surface, looks very much like the old Legacy Application layer, it is distinct in many ways.

Within the Legacy Application layer of our architecture, we identify that quoting and ordering are part of one legacy application. Payment is a second legacy application, and shipping is a third. Under the old legacy model, an employee, trained and authorized in all three of these applications, navigated the customer order process from quote to shipment using these three applications and their three separate user interfaces. The complexities of understanding and navigating all of these systems were hidden from view of the customer on the phone.

Under the new model, the composite application hides the existence of these three systems and manages the "quote to ship" process utilizing a set of discrete logical services in a work flow. Under the old model, the payment application was *owned* by finance and the shipping application was *owned* by distribution. They had to approve the access privileges of every sales employee who used these systems and often required that they had training on how to use the entire application even though they used only one small function.

Under the new model, the "CheckPaymentStaus" service has been defined with the roles that are allowed to use the service as specified by Finance. One of those roles is "Sales_Order_Administrator." Similarly, the "CheckShippingStatus" service has been defined with the roles that are allowed to use this service as specified by distribution. One of those roles is "Sales_Order_Administrator." Under the new model, a Sales_Order_Administrator automatically gets access to the payment and shipping services he or she needs, but only the services needed, not the entire payment or shipping application. Nobody in finance or shipping has to train a new user and set up security.

Under the old model, three different logons and user interfaces were required to do the job. Under the new model, a single logon and user interface is used. Under the old model, the only way to access each of the user interfaces was through the proprietary presentation layer of each application. Under the new model, the user can use a telephone voice recognition interface, a Web portal, or a customer services Windows client to access and use the same business process.

This is a different approach from the model that builds a new monolithic stovepipe application that duplicates the business logic. Even new Web applications that use the integration layer assets to get the underlying business functionality but do not follow an SOA architectural approach will have their own mechanism for controlling the presentation and flow of the business process. The application will have its own mechanism for structuring, presenting, and managing the display of the process. The application will probably duplicate some of the field validation logic associated with those displays. Under the SOA approach, these functions are handled once by the business process within the composite application.

The corporate strategy for the business practice and business operational model that represents how the company operates in the future is documented in the corporate strategy cell. The "Service Consumer" horizontal strategy leaders within the business units document their responsibilities for delivering the processes within the business practice that delivers the new operational model capabilities. The detailed requirements of specific business processes, many of which will transcend multiple business units, will be defined. These will be translated into logical process models to be developed and deployed into production. The cells of the Business Process Domain layer are depicted in Exhibit 5.7.

BUSINESS SERVICE DOMAIN   The Business Service Domain is the next layer in the framework. This layer will ultimately become the most critical layer of the framework. It represents the lowest layer of assets designed to be fully compliant and supportive of the SOA. This layer represents the base portfolio of assets with the highest level of reusability. It also is the common shared demarcation point between the service providers and the service consumers.

The ultimate goal is to get those in the business who were traditionally seen as the owners and maintainers of the legacy business applications to focus on everything from this layer down. In other words, their accountability is to manage the plan for enabling the legacy application assets to support a full set of granular services

Business Process Domain (Composite)	Corporate Business Practices	Business Unit Responsibilities	Business Processes	Process Models	Process Implementations
	Corporate Goal/ Strategy Cross-Reference	Business Unit Plans Cross-Reference	Business Architecture (Conceptual)	Enterprise SOA Reference Architecture (Logical)	Enterprise SOA Platform Architecture (Physical)

EXHIBIT 5.7   SOA~EAF Business Process Domain Layer

that can be leveraged across the enterprise. They are no longer focused on the user interface or defining one specific, rigid, and hard-coded way to process those services. Instead, they recognize that lower-level, more granular capabilities embedded in their hard-coded application have value to other business entities and business processes. After all, it usually can be proven that these other business entities have acquired this capability through back-door data extraction and duplicated business logic embedded in applications that they now own.

The architects can show these individuals that this new model will actually *increase* their control over the data in their domain, not decrease it. If they look at all the places the data from the system they think they own, which they believe to be the system of record, has been replicated and all the duplicate business logic that has been written to process that data, do they really think they are in control? They have no visibility or control over the accuracy of the replicated data and duplicated business logic.

They may have authorized the extraction of data from their system from a particular business area for a specific purpose at some point in time, but do they know who is accessing that data? Are they sure that the other business unit did not give the extraction ability to someone else or allow the data to be pulled from its data store with a new extract? In most companies, the path of data from its system of record is almost untraceable.

If you change the business rules within your application (the system of record) to, for example, require the capture of a nine-digit zip code for all customers, are you then guaranteed that all other applications that extracted that customer data will follow suit? Most likely they will not. Even if they were made aware of the change, they might not have the funding needed to make the change in their copy of the data. So when a major customer complains that it continues to get mail with a five-digit zip code when you contractually agreed to send all mail with a nine-digit zip code, it will be traced to some obscure individual in some other department who, with all good intentions, generated mailing labels from a department application that stores only a five-digit zip.

Under the SOA paradigm, the goal is to have everybody use the same service regardless of where and how they use it. Thus if an "Extract Customer Addresses" service existed and those addresses were extracted directly from the system of record, everyone would have a nine-digit zip extract. The older version that produced a five-digit zip could be shut down for applications consuming the service's presentation layer or allowed to exist for a limited period of time until the applications consuming the service at the business logic layer could adapt to the field change. For those applications and services that were built correctly, if the XML structure and the presentation layer handling of that structure is dynamic, there may not be any modification needed.

While the service providers are not concerned with the delivery and presentation of the service, that does not mean they do not own or control the service. They are accountable to ensure that the service functions, properly and accurately, including all validation and audit requirements associated with the back-end system. They also set the policies for who can use the service and how. Thus while they may not know any specific person using the service, they will know that every person will be authenticated and have a valid role that authorizes the use of the service. The role may also limit how or when people use the service. The role may result in only some of the options for using the service being exposed. These are all controls that can be specified by the service provider and coded within the Business Service layer and enterprise SOA security framework.

The businesspeople responsible for providing the service actually have a lot to gain by adopting and supporting this approach. They can be much more confident about the use, accuracy, and exposure of the data and functions within their domain. The business as a whole benefits by:

- Improving overall accuracy as more people use the same service with a single set of business rules and a single data source.
- Reduction in physical and human resources as more and more of the old redundant solutions are decommissioned.

The Integration Domain and the Business Service Domain layers combined can be referred to as the enterprise service bus (ESB). Ideally architects would like a single ESB platform to maximize efficiency and cost. This is not always a reality. What is important is that a preferred platform is identified and that all in-house development leverages that platform. Whatever platforms exist or are preferred, a good SOA architecture will specify a platform architecture and framework that adds layers of abstraction and isolation from the physical attributes of the underlying technology. A good architecture will ensure that any changes to technologies above, below, or inside the ESB will have little or no impact on the deployed set of services, the applications that use them, or the applications that feed them. Enforcing the same development frameworks, design patterns, and design standards to services built on other ESB technologies (e.g., services embedded in a purchased or leased application) ensures their interoperability with your services and frameworks. It also allows these services to be ported to your ESB if the need arises. Replacing the customer credit system should have no impact on any application consuming the "Get Customer Credit" service. Replacing the ESB used to build and deploy the "Get Customer Credit" service should not impact the service for consumers who use the "Get Customer Credit" service.

The amount of success you have in achieving the promoted values of SOA will be directly impacted by how effectively you manage these two layers. That is why they are pulled out and so prominently represented in the framework. Their management from an architecture practice perspective is as important as any other aspect of the architecture portfolio when it comes to SOA.

The corporate strategy identifies the key service capabilities needed to achieve the strategy. The business units define their requirements for participating in or supporting those services. This drives the definition of each of the business services, which in turn drives the architectural model for developing those services that are then deployed into production. The cells of the Business Service Domain layer are depicted in Exhibit 5.8.

INTEGRATION SERVICE DOMAIN   Like most companies, yours probably has millions of dollars invested in legacy applications. Also like most companies, the belief is that these applications do a (relatively) good job at supporting the core business capabilities they were purposed for. The less favorable perception of these systems lies in their flexibility and adaptability. They lack flexibility to participate and add

Business Service Domain (Unit)	Corporate Business Capabilities	Business Unit Activities	Business Services	Service Models	Service Implementations
	Corporate Goal/ Strategy Cross-Reference	Business Unit Plans Cross-Reference	Business Architecture (Conceptual)	Enterprise SOA Reference Architecture (Logical)	Enterprise SOA Platform Architecture (Physical)

EXHIBIT 5.8   SOA~EAF Business Service Domain Layer

value to larger, more complex business activities without the intervention of a highly trained human to manually bridge their capabilities to those of other systems. They are also not very adaptable to changes in business rules or processes; major funding for IT resource involvement is required to effect the changes. Once again, these are the very constraints highlighted in the introduction of this book that are driving us to a new and better way of doing what we do.

The architecture approach to SOA involves a conscious and concerted effort to relegate the legacy applications to a level where their rigid and restrictive capabilities around adaptability and flexibility are mitigated but their competency to perform the core business functions they support is leveraged. Any SOA strategy that expects to succeed has to leverage the legacy applications. The cost and time it would take to holistically replace the total functionality of these applications is so large that we do not even go there in our discussions. How effective an approach you take architecturally to this integration is also key to how successful you will be. Attempting SOA without an architectural approach to legacy integration may have some short-term early successes, but this approach will eventually fall under the unmanageable and unsustainable weight of traditional approaches.

What we do not want to leverage in a legacy application is the proprietary custom user interface. What we do want to leverage in the legacy application is the data it contains and manages and the business rules and conditions that are applied when creating, reading, updating, or deleting the data. This includes what data must change together, in what order the data changes must occur, and what changes are required based on other changes. So, we need an approach to expose the data and business logic outside of the proprietary user interface framework. We cannot, however, violate any of the authorization, validation, logging, and auditing requirements maintained and enforced by the legacy application. We also want to make sure that the approach we take for exposing these capabilities and maintaining the integrity is consistent, not only within a specific legacy application but across all legacy applications. We want to make sure that while each legacy application and the payload in each integration may be different, the format of that integration mechanism and the naming conventions and standards used are consistent for every integration. What we are specifying here is an architectural approach to integration, one where development frameworks, design patterns, and design standards exist to govern and enforce these characteristics. This helps to make future reuse of these integration assets easier and the development of new integration assets faster.

Thus, under SOA, the legacy application integration strategy and architecture is critical to effective SOA development. As you move up the architectural framework (from integration to channel), the physical number of assets, especially reusable ones, will decrease. You may have hundreds of integration assets but only four channel alternatives. Therefore, the less architectural focus you have on developing the lower layer assets, the less reuse and leveragability you will have on the biggest population of assets. Under SOA, integration must have its own domain and be a prominent, recognizable layer within the framework with heavy focus on its strategy and management. This is true for all horizontal views of the integration layer (conceptual, logical, physical, and strategic).

As a final point, it is vital to recognize that, while this layer will have high visibility and have critical importance as you embark on the SOA path, its visibility (especially to the business) will diminish over time. That is because these assets, while leveraged, were not constructed as business service assets. They were constructed as application integration (AI) assets. Eventually one of two things will happen to these assets:

- They will be wrapped in a higher-layer business service technology with this layer taking over the visibility and focus.
- They will be decommissioned by new replacement components built with the higher-layer business service technology integrated directly to the underlying legacy applications.

When this happens, most of the business and reference architecture focus will shift up to the Business Service Domain layer. Ultimately this is the lowest layer that you want the business to focus on. This is the layer where all the discussions are around a conceptual and logical service rather than a physical representation of a legacy connection point. This is the layer where semantic data models and structures based on industry standards, when available, have replaced the proprietary and application bounded data sets of the integration layer.

The business-represented community that is set up under the governance model defined in Chapter 8 to help the architecture practice strategically govern this layer is the vertical *provider*-centric subcommittee within the SOA Portfolio Plan Governance Committee. The horizontal *consumer*-centric subcommittee assists the architects with the strategic governance of the channel, process, and service layers of the architecture. The vertical *provider*-centric subcommittee helps the architects strategically manage the integration service layer of the architecture. Governance at this level will be more likely to support the development of sharable and reusable integration assets using an integration technology and framework rather than a quicker and cheaper custom-built one-off interface.

Integration Layer Development Frameworks   Another key component of the integration layer architecture is the presence of development frameworks to define the integration approaches. These frameworks can include definitions around:

- Using a common shared set of code translation tables to augment the request and reply data sets with user-understandable translations of data codes stored in the legacy applications.
- How to handle aggregation when the population of a specific set of data is split across multiple systems of record.
- Mechanisms to support synchronous and asynchronous communications.

■ Queuing and latency support for integration with legacy applications that do not support 24/7 availability.

■ Security framework for pass-through of authentication and authorization credentials required by the embedded security system of legacy systems.

These are a few of the architectural considerations that should be defined and applied to all the integration components developed.

Integration Service Domain Cells   The corporate strategy should provide direction on how legacy applications need to support the SOA approach and which of these systems have the highest strategic value to the company. The corporate strategy also establishes the policy for adoption of industry standard transaction and data formats at this layer. This includes the semantic models published by standards bodies (e.g., EDI), industry regulatory bodies (e.g., HIPAA),[1] or industry-specific consortiums (e.g., ACORD).[2]

The business units augment this strategy by defining the data and transactional capabilities embedded in these systems and their weight in terms of their business value. They also define the specific business requirements for the integration layer, including the rules for mapping and managing their proprietary formats to the standard models and the priority for exposing and isolating these capabilities.

Architects develop the logical approach for developing integration assets to meet these business requirements, including the development frameworks, design patterns, and design standards applied when building these capabilities. Ultimately these integration assets are deployed into production utilizing the integration technologies and platforms. The individual cells of the Integration layer of the framework are depicted in Exhibit 5.9.

LEGACY APPLICATION DOMAIN   The Legacy Application Domain layer is where all the artifacts associated with the legacy applications that are integrated with or need to be integrated with the SOA applications. From a corporate strategy view, the framework needs to identify the strategic direction for modernization of these applications. For those on platforms identified as at risk by the corporation and documented at the Legacy Platform Domain layer, the strategy for replacement of these applications should be defined at this layer. For those on platforms that are not at risk, the strategy for how those applications need to support the business going forward needs to be documented. This is not a technical strategy; it is a business strategy. Strategic statements, such as "The application needs to be more flexible and adaptable to business changes" or "Reduce the amount of money and time it takes to change the application," are examples of the contents of this cell.

Service Integration Domain (Isolation)	Legacy Application Leveraging Strategy	Data and Transaction Source Plans	Integration/ Isolation Requirements	Integration/ Isolation Approach	Integration/ Isolation Implementations
	Corporate Goal/ Strategy Cross-Reference	Business Unit Plans Cross-Reference	Business Architecture (Conceptual)	Enterprise SOA Reference Architecture (Logical)	Enterprise SOA Platform Architecture (Physical)

EXHIBIT 5.9   SOA~EAF Service Integration Domain Layer

Legacy Application Domain (Encapsulation)	Legacy Application Modernization Strategy	Utilization Plans	Conceptual Legacy Application Usage	Logical Legacy Application Usage	Physical Legacy Application Usage
	Corporate Goal/ Strategy Cross-Reference	Business Unit Plans Cross-Reference	Business Architecture (Conceptual)	Enterprise SOA Reference Architecture (Logical)	Enterprise SOA Platform Architecture (Physical)

EXHIBIT 5.10 SOA~EAF Legacy Application Domain Layer

Based on the stated strategies, the business units should develop their plans for how they will utilize (or not utilize) these applications in the future and how they will prioritize the efforts to modernize them. The business architects should assist in this process by extracting conceptual models of the legacy applications' monolithic capabilities into a business architecture diagram.

Logical approaches to these modernization views can be developed and ultimately implemented as enhancements to the application or displacement of the functionality through the use of a newer technology.

The cells of the Legacy Application Domain layer are depicted in Exhibit 5.10.

LEGACY PLATFORM DOMAIN The Legacy Platform Domain is the layer where all the artifacts associated with the infrastructure supporting the legacy non-SOA applications are captured and maintained. The documentation maintained in this layer should be for only those legacy applications that have been or will be integrated into the SOA architecture. If there is no plan or need for the application to be extended or leveraged by SOA, keep any architectural documentation you have on the application in your EA framework where they already exist. This will eliminate clutter and confusion by both the business and IT as these assets are addressed and modernized or migrated.

From the corporate strategic perspective, the business focus should be on providing direction for an obsolescence mitigation strategy. Many legacy systems, especially core mission-critical applications, are extremely large and took many years and lots of money to get to where they are today. Every business application, however, will eventually need to be replaced. Most often this will be driven by obsolescence or by ever-increasing maintenance and support costs of the platforms underlying those applications. Eventually all platforms will reach an obsolete status, and the cost of maintaining these applications on these platforms coupled with the cost of keeping these applications current with the business needs will force a change. The corporation needs to set forth a strategy that explicitly addresses the modernization of these platforms, no matter how expensive their replacements will be or how long it will take to replace them.

The business units must then develop support plans to replace these legacy platforms over time as the applications that run on them are modernized or replaced. The business units will also need to provide conceptual migration plans on how each system under their control will be replaced.

The architects will need to develop logical approaches for migrating these platforms so that minimal impact to the business occurs. They will need to determine if the replacement strategy can be evolutionary, like the examples given in Chapter 12, or require an all-at-once, big-bang approach.

Legacy Platform Domain (Migration)	Obsolescence Mitigation Strategy	Support Plans	Conceptual Migration Plan	Logical Replacement Strategy	Infrastructure Modernization
	Corporate Goal/ Strategy Cross-Reference	Business Unit Plans Cross-Reference	Business Architecture (Conceptual)	Enterprise SOA Reference Architecture (Logical)	Enterprise SOA Platform Architecture (Physical)

EXHIBIT 5.11   SOA~EAF Legacy Platform Domain Layer

Ultimately these migration activities will result in the old physical infrastructure being replaced with new, modern technologies and platforms. The cells of the Legacy Platform Domain layer are depicted in Exhibit 5.11.

SOA~EAF LAYER SUMMARY   The exhibit at the end of each section provides a summary description of the focus of each cell in the framework for that layer. Exhibit 5.12 provides the complete table of all the entries in each cell. These entries help to highlight that the framework is used, not only to reflect current state of the environment but to reflect future states as well. The framework facilitates extracting views to represent any desired state that is, past, present, or future.

Overview of the SOA~EAF Methodology

A framework like the one just described is used to capture data in a structured consistent format so it can be managed and leveraged. It represents the *what* in terms of our SOA management practice. The methodology tells us the *how* in terms of our practice. Exhibit I.1, presented in the introduction of this book, is a high-level overview of the SOA~EAF methodology.

The flow of the methodology is represented in the center of the diagram. It starts with the corporate strategy. From there the process moves to the business units' strategic plans to support the corporate strategy. This information is used to drive the definition of SOA initiatives that provide the system capabilities needed to achieve those business plans. The initiatives in turn define the SOA projects that develop those capabilities culminating with their production implementation.

Some key points about the methodology are:

- While the corporate strategy drives the business unit plans that in turn drive the SOA initiatives, SOA projects are driven by SOA initiatives but can also influence them.
- Similarly, SOA implementations are driven by SOA projects but can also influence SOA projects and even SOA initiatives.

Both of these conditions are due to the fact that the entire SOA value proposition is based on leveragability and reuse. Therefore, work being performed in an SOA project may not only benefit the initiative that funded the work but may present opportunities for additional capabilities for other initiatives as well. Existing SOA components already implemented and in production will not only influence the cost and effort of projects that are leveraging and reusing them but can drastically reduce

	Corporate Goal/Strategy Cross-Reference	Business Unit Plans Cross-Reference	Business Architecture (Conceptual)	Enterprise SOA Reference Architecture (Logical)	Enterprise SOA Platform Architecture (Physical)
Constituent Domain	Corporate Business Exposure Strategy	Business Model	Constituents	Roles	Users
Business Channel Domain (Enterprise)	Horizontal Constituent Experience	Business Distribution Mechanisms and Partnerships	Contact/Interaction Mechanisms	Channel Models	Production Channel Connections
Business Process Domain (Composite)	Corporate Business Practices	Business Unit Responsibilities	Business Processes	Process Models	Process Implementations
Business Service Domain (Unit)	Corporate Business Capabilities	Business Unit Activities	Business Services	Service Models	Service Implementations
Service Integration Domain (Isolation)	Legacy Application Leveraging Strategy	Data and Transaction Source Plans	Integration/ Isolation Requirements	Integration/ Isolation Approach	Integration Isolation Implementations
Legacy Application Domain (Encapsulation)	Legacy Application Modernization Strategy	Utilization Plans	Conceptual Legacy Application Usage	Logical Legacy Application Usage	Physical Legacy Application Usage
Legacy Platform Domain (Migration)	Obsolescence Mitigation Strategy	Support Plans	Conceptual Migration Plan	Logical Replacement Strategy	Infrastructure Modernization

EXHIBIT 5.12 All Layers of the SOA~EAF

the cost and time of delivering entire initiatives. These will potentially influence future submitted and approved initiatives. An initiative that provides significant value to the business by leveraging and reusing a significant amount of existing SOA components will be much cheaper and faster to implement than a similar-valued initiative where fewer SOA components are reused and more new SOA components are required.

Managing and controlling this process flow is the SOA enterprise architecture *practice*. The architects manage and control this process through the publication and enforcement of the policies, procedures, and standards defined within this book.

The *policies* that need to be developed to transform the company to the SOA paradigm will be created by and enforced through the governance bodies defined in Chapter 8. The top two committees (SOA business domain and enterprise SOA portfolio plan) are focused on business strategic policies, and the remaining bodies are focused on technical and operational (tactical) policies. These policies will provide the criteria that will be the basis for governing how:

- SOA initiatives are structured and evaluated.
- SOA initiatives are approved and funded.
- SOA initiatives are implemented.
- Those implementations are monitored and supported.

The policies will also provide the basis for enforcing reuse and leveraging of SOA components.

The *procedures* represent the detail activities that make up the high-level methodology pictured in Exhibit I.1. These procedures are defined throughout the other chapters of this book. These procedures include the:

- Governance process
- Development life cycle
- Vendor application evaluation process
- Capacity planning and monitoring process
- Legacy application modernization and sunset process

In addition to the policies and procedures, specific *standards* need to be identified to support the SOA architecture. The governance bodies are also responsible for the identification, adoption, and enforcement of these standards. These include not just technology standards but also industry business standards, regulatory standards, legal standards, and so forth.

As you adopt the SOA enterprise architecture model defined in this book, you will be transforming all the processes associated with business application development. All the standards that apply to business application development will be transformed as well. The basis for these transformed procedures will be the new policies and standards developed to support SOA. These policies and standards will be developed and enforced by the governance committees and governance bodies.

If we look at the model from a side view perspective (Exhibit 5.13), we can see that the SOA EA Practice is the foundation that encapsulates all the other layers of the methodology. This practice is responsible for making everything in the layers above happen. The SOA EA Practice facilitates the development, publication, and enforcement of the policies and standards that drive the SOA enterprise architecture processes. They facilitate setting up all the new processes, educating participants in their roles and responsibilities regarding the processes, and manage their smooth

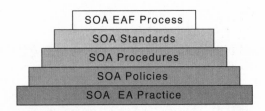

EXHIBIT 5.13   SOA~EAF Methodology: Side View

ongoing operation. Finally, they capture all the documentation and artifacts produced out of these processes; structure and categorize them within the SOA~EAF; and produce dynamic, adaptable views of the framework information to support processes going forward.

Summary

This chapter defined the SOA~EAF and all its individual components. It defined the purpose of each of the individual SOA architectural frameworks and their relationship to the other architecture frameworks. It showed how all these are pulled together and managed from an SOA enterprise architecture practice perspective. It also showed how the framework supports and facilitates the business involvement in the strategic direction and value of the IT investments to support their needs and how this strategic involvement plays a critical role in maximizing the return on those investments across the enterprise.

This chapter also provided a high-level overview of the methodology that manages and leverages the framework. The remaining chapters provide the information necessary to implement both.

The framework and the methodology are living, evolving entities. This should be obvious, but I will state it to make sure it is consciously understood and enforced. The contents of the framework will change constantly. The use of the content happens continuously. The methodology is constantly operating. The processes defined by the methodology occur over and over. This means that both the framework and the methodology are operational assets that must be managed and maintained daily by operational people; likewise, the outputs and deliverables must be reissued continuously to maintain currency throughout the company. Failure to keep the framework current and the methodology operational will quickly make the process useless and bring a slow death to the SOA enterprise architecture practice. Do not invest all the time and money to get this process up and running if you are not going to invest in keeping it going.

Finally, I hope this chapter begins to show that this new approach and this transformation of how the business and IT communicate and operate with each other results in a more effective, more efficient, and more dynamic company,

In the next chapter, we define how this framework relates to traditional enterprise architecture frameworks and what is necessary to translate artifacts from these other frameworks into the SOA~EAF.

Notes

1. From the cdc.gov web site:
   The Health Insurance Portability and Accountability Act of 1996 (HIPAA) was adopted to ensure health insurance coverage after leaving an employer and also to provide standards for facilitating health-care–related electronic transactions. To improve the efficiency and effectiveness of the health-care system, HIPAA included administrative simplification provisions that required DHHS to adopt national standards for electronic health-care transactions. At the same time, Congress recognized that advances in electronic technology

could erode the privacy of health information. Consequently, Congress incorporated into HIPAA provisions that mandated adoption of federal privacy protections for certain individually identifiable health information.

2. From the official ACORD web site (www.acord.org):

ACORD (Association for Cooperative Operations Research and Development) is a global, nonprofit standards development organization serving the insurance industry and related financial services industries. ACORD's mission is to facilitate the development of open consensus data standards and standard forms. ACORD members include hundreds of insurance and reinsurance companies, agents and brokers, software providers, and industry associations worldwide. ACORD works with these organizations towards a goal of improved data communication across diverse platforms through implementation of standards.

CHAPTER 6

Incorporating Existing Enterprise Architecture Documents and Artifacts into the SOA~EAF

This chapter focuses on how to modify and incorporate the enterprise architecture frameworks used within your current EA practice to support the SOA enterprise architecture framework (SOA~EAF™). How this is done will depend on what framework your EA practice currently uses. This chapter presents a specific example of how to transform and integrate documents within a Zachman Framework™ into the SOA~EAF.

For those of you using other frameworks, such as The Open Group Architecture Framework or Scott Bernard's Enterprise Architecture Cube (EA³)™, this chapter provides a general approach and analytical technique for assessing these artifacts and adapting them to the SOA~EAF. This chapter provides a direct mapping of the Zachman Framework cells to the SOA~EAF cells. The discussion of each layer of the Zachman Framework, however, includes general concepts and analysis that can be used when evaluating the artifacts of other frameworks.

If you use these frameworks, or variations of them, this section explains how to leverage them to support SOA~EAF. If your EA practice does not have a tool for capturing and maintaining EA metadata and artifacts, you need to think about getting one or building a homegrown solution. If you have a document management system with a work flow management capability or a team management capability, you may be able to put something together relatively quickly. Even tools like MS Access can be used and can add value if no other alternatives exist. A tool that lets you create dimensions of the data into different views or facilitates a process to do this will have the greatest value.

Relationship of the SOA Enterprise Architecture Framework to Other EA Frameworks

Many EA frameworks manage the artifacts from an organization or functional perspective. Frameworks like the EA³ track and manage the assets across the corporate domain but slice and categorize those assets by line of business domains as well. This approach tends to put a silo perspective on the assets even if, in fact, that may not be the case. For example, a corporate system (e.g., general ledger) may be shared by all the lines of business, or a single data center may house all the systems for all the business units. These shared assets need to be recognizable and distinguishable from assets dedicated to the line of business when taking the SOA view.

Other traditional EA frameworks like Zachman focus on compiling the IT assets and capabilities horizontally from an IT system development perspective (i.e., planner, owner, designer, etc.) and vertically from a traditional IT implementation perspective (i.e., what data, logic, connectivity, user, availability, etc.)

These frameworks, however, were not designed to facilitate an evolutionary and migratory transformation from traditional legacy systems to an enterprise SOA system. As stated earlier, you need to think of SOA as one system, not many systems. Every component has the potential to be shared. Every component has the potential to be leveraged for different business purposes. Even capabilities like security, personalization, logging, auditing, and archiving may be shared. Nothing is built in a (stovepipe) vacuum anymore.

The metadata compiled through traditional EA models is valuable for finding opportunities for efficiencies, especially while we are in a mixed architectural mode of traditional and SOA-driven solutions. However, the format of the frameworks and the artifacts within are not structured to support the *representation* of *opportunities* and *efficiencies* of the defined SOA~EAF.

It is important to note that I am not advocating that any investment previously made in compiling EA artifacts and metadata be thrown away. In fact, the more you have, the better off you are. I am suggesting, however, that we are going to restructure and reorganize this information in a different way and leverage this new format to communicate and assess our portfolio from a very different perspective. We are embarking on a journey to evolve architecture to a model where the business readily understands and adopts the ability to make better decisions about IT and present new ways and opportunities to think about IT.

To accomplish this, we need to evaluate the artifacts of our existing enterprise architecture framework and determine how we can cross-reference their content from within the SOA~EAF and vice versa. The two frameworks initially can be populated and maintained separately, but they need to be linked so that changes in one model can be reflected in the other model. When you first start out, the existing architectural framework will still be the dominant one since most documentation will exist under this framework and most development will still be under the traditional model. As more SOA initiatives are completed and more SOA initiatives are funded, there will be a tipping point where the SOA~EAF will become the dominant one. This tipping point will come from the business that, as it becomes more comfortable with the SOA business architecture approach, will understand more and more of its value and ask, or even demand, that all initiatives and discussions around the IT capabilities are structured this way. This demand will be natural because the framework communicates the information from the business's conceptual perspective.

Certain aspects of the traditional frameworks, especially as they relate to the legacy applications, can and probably should continue to exist in those frameworks until those legacy systems are decommissioned, replaced, or modernized. (See Chapter 12 for more information on decommissioning, replacing, and modernizing legacy applications.) The management of the legacy application code, the platforms those applications run on, and the physical data models of their data stores all can be maintained and managed within the traditional framework. Links to this information would be provided within the SOA~EAF. The *integration layer* documentation associated with those applications, however, should be tracked and managed by the SOA~EAF.

As we build more SOA capabilities, we will be consciously weaning users off the proprietary user interfaces of the legacy applications. (The capability they need is now being delivered as services through a channel interface.) The goal is to eliminate the use of these proprietary interfaces completely. Any remaining users of these interfaces should be managed through the old framework as well. The enterprise SOA Technology Governance Committee should be seeking opportunities to eliminate the use of these interfaces as part of its strategic governance agenda. The user interaction defined in these traditional stovepipe interfaces may be helpful in defining the presentation logic for some exposed services. The logic may not be valuable, however, if the new interface adopts a standard semantic model and the old interface uses a proprietary format. These interfaces may not have value at the process level either. Many of the new processes will transcend the functionality of multiple systems and provide a work flow very different from the old interfaces. Tracking these interfaces in the EA framework will enable you to identify opportunities to transform these interfaces to SOA solutions. As this occurs, these interfaces should be decommissioned and flagged as such in the EA documentation.

Value of Mapped EA Artifacts

When mapping information from existing EA artifacts into the SOA~EAF, you need to classify the information into one of two categories:

1. Information about applications that can be readily leveraged by an SOA initiative
2. Information that cannot be leveraged but can assist in assessing the functionality of the application and identify opportunities and approaches for modernization of the application

Within an existing legacy stovepipe application, information about the data stores and any established mechanisms used to access those stores directly is valuable and can be leveraged. Information about any application programming interfaces (APIs) or embedded messaging capabilities is also valuable and potentially can be leveraged.

Information that explains the functional capabilities of the application and how the application authenticates users and controls their access to the functionality cannot be leveraged in an SOA development. The information is, however, valuable when defining constituent authentication and authorization requirements in an enterprise SOA security system. This information is also helpful for identifying high-value functional capabilities that become high targets for service developments.

These distinctions should be clearly identified within the newly structured artifacts. Thus the framework will include six categories of artifacts:

1. SOA component artifacts for all SOA components created to date
2. Various stages of artifacts for SOA components under development on active SOA initiatives

3. Legacy artifacts that can be leveraged and used in their current state
4. Future SOA strategic documents
5. Legacy artifacts that cannot be leveraged but document characteristics and capabilities of those applications that can be assessed for modernization/migration opportunities
6. Strategic legacy modernization, migration, and decommission documentation

Having this information available and classified this way is valuable to every aspect of the SOA enterprise practice. The first four categories contain artifacts that are heavily used by business and solutions architects when describing and analyzing business needs. They are also used by project architects during the SOA development process. The documents in categories 5 and 6 are used by enterprise architects to support and drive the legacy modernization/migration process. Documents in any or all of the categories can be used by the governance committees and governance bodies to assist them in the governance process.

Incorporating Zachman Framework Artifacts into the SOA~EAF

The Zachman Framework consists of six columns and five rows. The columns represent:

1. **D**ata (What)
2. **F**unction (How)
3. **N**etwork (Where)
4. **P**eople (Who)
5. **T**ime (When)
6. **M**otivation (Why)

The rows have these labels:

1. **S**cope (Contextual)
2. **E**nterprise Model (Conceptual)
3. **S**ystem Model (Logical)
4. **T**echnology Model (Physical)
5. **D**etailed **R**epresentations (Out of Context)

The SOA~EAF with the description of each cell is repeated in Exhibit 6.1. It can serve as a reference in understanding the Zachman cell mappings to the SOA~EAF depicted in Exhibit 6.2 as well as the comparison paragraphs that follow.

This cross-referencing of the Zachman Framework cells to the SOA~EAF cells should be used as a guide when reviewing and assessing your Zachman documentation. Many documents will contain information that relates to several of the SOA~EAF cells. This is because the traditional documents represent traditional applications that were designed using traditional stovepipe and tightly coupled, monolithic methods.

	Corporate Goal/Strategy Cross-Reference	Business Unit Plans Cross-Reference	Business Architecture (Conceptual)	Enterprise SOA Reference Architecture (Logical)	Enterprise SOA Platform Architecture (Physical)
Constituent Domain	Corporate Business Exposure Strategy	Business Model	Constituents	Roles	Users
Business Channel Domain (Enterprise)	Horizontal Constituent Experience	Business Distribution Mechanisms and Partnerships	Contact/Interaction Mechanisms	Channel Models	Production Channel Connections
Business Process Domain (Composite)	Corporate Business Practices	Business Unit Responsibilities	Business Processes	Process Models	Process Implementations
Business Service Domain (Unit)	Corporate Business Capabilities	Business Unit Activities	Business Services	Service Models	Service Implementations
Service Integration Domain (Isolation)	Legacy Application Leveraging Strategy	Data and Transaction Source Plans	Integration/ Isolation Requirements	Integration/ Isolation Approach	Integration Isolation Implementations
Legacy Application Domain (Encapsulation)	Legacy Application Modernization Strategy	Utilization Plans	Conceptual Legacy Application Usage	Logical Legacy Application Usage	Physical Legacy Application Usage
Legacy Platform Domain (Migration)	Obsolescence Mitigation Strategy	Support Plans	Conceptual Migration Plan	Logical Replacement Strategy	Infrastructure Modernization

EXHIBIT 6.1   SOA~EAF Cell Descriptions

Key Considerations When Conducting the Cross-Reference Assessment

ZACHMAN "WHERE" COLUMN   The Where column of the Zachman Framework is concerned with the Network as it relates to the location of the application and the location of the application users. Under the SOA~EAF, the Where is really a concern for what channels exist, what services are provided over those channels, and what is the overall performance and reliability of the SOA components required to deliver those services to the consumer through those channels. Channels, as defined in Chapter 4, now play a more dominant role in the architectural framework. This is to reflect the fact that there is no longer a single access node for services. Knowing which channels exist by constituency indicates the level of effort required to deploy new or other services to those constituents. Hence, the conceptual concerns around the network, from a business architecture perspective, focus around the constituents and the channels they use. The logical concerns around the network, from a reference architecture perspective, focus on the relationship between the user and the

	Corporate Goal/Strategy Cross-Reference	Business Unit Plans Cross-Reference	Business Architecture (Conceptual)	Enterprise SOA Reference Architecture (Logical)	Enterprise SOA Platform Architecture (Physical)
Constituent Domain	People and Motivation Scope	People and Time Scope and Enterprise	People and Enterprise	People System	People Technology
Business Channel Domain (Enterprise)	Network and Motivation Scope	Network and Time Scope and Enterprise	Network Enterprise	Network System	Network Technology
Business Process Domain (Composite)	Function and Motivation Scope	Function and Time Scope and Enterprise	Function Enterprise	Function System	Function Technology
Business Service Domain (Unit)	Function and Motivation Scope	Function and Time Scope and Enterprise	Function Enterprise	Function System	Function Technology
Service Integration Domain (Isolation)	Data and Motivation Scope	Data and Time Scope and Enterprise	Data Enterprise	Data System	Data Technology
Legacy Application Domain (Encapsulation)	Detailed Representations	Detailed Representations	Detailed Representations	Detailed Representations	Detailed Representations
Legacy Platform Domain (Migration)	Detailed Representations	Detailed Representations	Detailed Representations	Detailed Representations	Detailed Representations

EXHIBIT 6.2   Zachman to SOA~EAF Cross-Reference

channel and the standardized invocation of the underlying business processes and business services to the channel itself. The physical concerns around the network, from a physical architecture perspective, focus on the node-to node interconnectivity within the infrastructure and the bandwidth and performance across the nodes of the network.

ZACHMAN (LOGICAL) SYSTEMS MODEL ROW   The artifacts within the (logical) system model row of the Zachman Framework are more than likely structured around a single business application. Even though they may be logical representations with no physical reference to the system itself, they will contain logical representations of a traditional self-contained application. The logical application architecture will more than likely reflect a grouped set of business capabilities controlled by a central application controller, not a set of discrete and isolated services independently callable and consumable outside a central controller mechanism. The logical human interface architecture will probably reflect a self-contained, self-secured structure directly tied to and controlled by the underlying application rather than a logical description of how each service exposes its capabilities and interacts back and forth with the consumer, and the role the channel plays in delivering the service.

Therefore, the documentation around the core application itself is less valuable than the documentation around any APIs exposed by the application and/or any custom built integration capabilities associated with the application. The legacy framework artifacts and metadata around the core application have two values:

1. Necessary for maintaining the application until it is replaced
2. Necessary when developing new integration capabilities on top of the application to support new SOA initiatives

This documentation should remain within the legacy framework to be maintained by maintenance and enhancement developers as necessary. The information on the APIs and integration assets, however, should be maintained by the new SOA framework in order to reflect that the portfolio of existing applications must be considered as legacy assets. The applications represent investments that will continue to exist, but their legacy status sets an expectation that they represent the old way, and how we deal with them going forward will change. The key transformation at this layer is to capture information about the legacy applications, not in the context of the traditional modus operandi but rather their capability to support the Integration Service Domain layer of the SOA~EAF.

While all the traditional information about the application needs to be retained and managed, additional metadata around the integration capabilities of the application needs to be captured or, if already captured, restructured to a consistent format across all applications. Depending on the age of the application and the underlying technologies, integration capabilities may have been added at any or all of the application layers. Integration may have occurred at the data layer by allowing other applications or data access tools to go directly against the application's data store. Alternatively, all or part of the data may have been replicated to a secondary store utilized by other reporting and analytical tools or applications. This replication may involve bidirectional synchronization. The key is to understand the data, where it has been integrated, and what the system of record is for the data.

Integration may also occur at the business logic layer. This could include subroutines and remote procedures that were added to the code to allow access to the business logic outside the core application. The integration may be through APIs that were provided by the software vendor or custom built in house to expose the logic. All business logic integration capabilities need to be documented and evaluated in the context of their ability to be leveraged by the SOA enabling technologies employed at the higher layers. Those that can be leveraged should be left alone for now. Those that cannot be leveraged should be targeted for replacement as part of the legacy application migration/modernization strategy.

Finally, integration can occur at the presentation layer. This was traditionally done with *screen-scrapping* technologies, a common approach in the 1980s and 1990s used for mainframe applications based on 3270 and CICS. The shortcomings of this approach are well documented, and screen scrapping is hardly ever used today. Screen-scrapping approaches exist for Windows and browser-based applications as well. These are equally bad and should not be used. All existing screen-scrapping capabilities should be replaced when their underlying functionality is needed to support an SOA initiative.

There is a fundamental tenet to application layers that will forever hold true. Data is the most static and least volatile in terms of its structure and use. How often do companies redefine the "order" data element in their databases, or any data element for that matter? Data element changes do not happen often, if ever. Usually it is a catastrophic event (e.g., expand the size of the field) that forces changes to data.

Business logic is the next least volatile, although it is much more volatile than data. The need to change business logic occurs frequently. (Changes in tax rules or volume discounts are two common examples.) When these changes are required, you must assess the impact across the entire continuum, including other applications using replicated copies of the data and duplicate instances of the business logic. This can be a costly and time-consuming exercise when the business logic has been duplicated in multiple applications.

Finally, presentation layer logic is the most volatile. Presentation logic can change often and drastically. Any integration approach that scrapped the presentation layer of legacy applications is either:

- Constantly being changed as well
- Constantly being versioned
- No longer used
- Very expensive
- Any combination of the above

Some applications may be completely isolated in that they have never been integrated at any layer. Very few of these types of applications should exist. If your company is like most, most of the integration will consist of direct access to the applications data store or replicated copies of the data store. This type of integration is usually a point-to-point solution where very little leveragability exists for reuse. The key is to identify which of those point-to-point solutions have leveragability across other applications. The assessment may identify that several solutions have a significant amount of common data among them. These solutions should be assessed for an SOA opportunity. The strategy should be to migrate these point-to-point solutions to a common data service based on a semantic data model tied to a single source representing the system of record for the data. This will allow each existing application to migrate its interface to the semantic service and structure over time and eventually eliminate the multiple point-to-point code sets.

MANAGING INTEGRATION GOING FORWARD   Since integration started out as point-to-point data interfaces or data replication mechanisms, these were traditionally documented as embedded components of the application architecture of the respective systems. They were not perceived, designed, and deployed as reusable integration assets; therefore, there was no need to separately identify them. Companies that adopted a middleware technology and approach in the 1980s and 1990s began to develop leveraged and reusable integration components within their portfolios. The presence of these technologies allowed architects to add this layer to their EA framework or at least maintain its metadata separately. Some of these architects infused this documentation below the System Model (logical) layer and above the Technology Model (physical) layer of the framework, making it subservient to the application

architecture. While this approach was correct under a traditional stovepipe application development paradigm, it is not appropriate under an SOA paradigm.

Under SOA, the integration points of the application are promoted to a higher
level of importance than the applications themselves. The monolithic user interface
and application-specific security components of the application are not important to
SOA. The embedded business logic and data are important. Hence, any integration
assets associated with the application are the assets we want to identify, analyze,
and modernize. We also want to explicitly establish development frameworks, standards, and design patterns for the construction of any integration capabilities going
forward. By inserting an architectural framework layer specifically for integration,
we can promote the level of importance and infuse domain-specific criteria for all
integrations across the enterprise.

This layer also allows us to more quickly identify and structure these assets at a
much more granular level and categorize them with more specificity. For example, a
company may have a large monolithic back-end legacy system that is the processing
system of record for customers, orders, products, and prices. Over the years, a series
of middleware messages were developed to provide this granular information:

- Several customer messages providing customer address, account number, territory, sales volume, and volume discount.
- Several order messages providing orders by territory; orders by week, month,
  quarter, and year; orders by customer; and orders by product line.
- Product messages providing product prices, product discounts, and product
  descriptions.

Each of these messages is captured and documented at the Integration Domain
layer of the framework along with all the other messages that have been built on top
of other applications. While these are physically mapped to the specific applications
with which they integrate, they can be logically categorized many different ways.
In fact, the documentation (and a tool used to capture and store the metadata)
should be designed so that any one of multiple views of available messages can be
constructed depending on the business need and/or audience.

I use messaging as an example, but any integration artifact—whether an ODBC
driver, a stored procedure and trigger, or whatever—should be documented.

In some instances, the integration layer may contain the documentation of specific custom APIs that were provided as part of the business application itself. These
APIs may be 100 percent custom code built in house or supplied by the application
vendor or built on top of the foundational class APIs of the underlying platform.

Whatever technology is used, the intent of this layer is to provide the first layer
of abstraction of data and business functions from the underlying applications. If the
integration is achieved through the construction of a Web service, it is important to
separate data access layer objects from the business logic layer objects and business
logic layer objects from presentation layer objects. This is necessary to ensure a
level of loose coupling that allows other services to utilize existing data access and
business logic assets.

Whether any of these documented integration assets are reused to support a
future need is an entirely different matter. We have to document that they exist so
we can assess their value. That value assessment includes determining if the asset

complies with the strategic direction of the architecture and if it is stable and reliable. Some integrations may not have been built by IT. They may not have been fully vetted and tested. Even worse, they may not even be maintained and supported by IT operations. They may be based on old technologies that have a high maintenance cost or a known obsolescence horizon.

Some of these assets will be directly leveraged without modification. Others may be leveraged with some effort to modernize them or make them more compliant with the architectural standards. Finally, some will be explicitly identified as risky, obsolete, or highly noncompliant and be targeted for replacement if a new need to use or enhance them arises.

This documentation, especially for this last type of asset, is critically important to the governance team and process. The governance teams will facilitate and drive the replacement and elimination of these "bad" assets. If, however, they are unaware that they exist, do not understand the risk of continuing their use, and have not been presented with a pragmatic alternative for dealing with them, you have no hope of eliminating these assets.

ZACHMAN ENTERPRISE MODEL LAYER   The Enterprise Model layer of the Zachman Framework will relate mostly to the Business Process Domain layer of the SOA~EAF. While almost all the artifacts at this layer can be utilized within the Business Process Domain, several key distinctions should be understood and a few changes must be incorporated.

First, not all the assets will be considered enterprise. Some assets, which will clearly be recognized as never having an enterprise purpose, may still have value to be captured and managed at this level. For example, even though there may never be more than five people allowed to enter journal entries directly into the general ledger system, there may be a reasonable business justification for building a service to do this. An example might be to allow work-at-home employees to input the entries through a secured service without giving them access to the entire general ledger system. From an architecture audit and control perspective, it is important to know this service exists and how it is used.

Second, many of the artifacts will more readily map to the Business Service Domain rather than the Business Process Domain. Some business services may be very granular; some may be very coarse. Coarse ones may encapsulate significant and complex portions of the higher-layer business process in a single business process. They are in themselves miniprocesses that contain their own semantic data documents and process steps. In these cases, the Business Process layer may add little more than choreographic capabilities to orchestrate one process to another.

Unlike the Integration Domain layer, where the strategic approach is to have all the Integration Domain assets flow through the Service Domain layer, some of the Business Service Domain layer assets will flow directly to the Channel Domain layer, bypassing the Business Process Domain layer. In these instances, the Business Process Domain layer may include a notation referencing a business service that can flow directly to a channel. The artifacts of the lower layer would be referenced, not replicated.

Finally, in the traditional EA model, artifacts at this layer do not represent top-down conceptual representations of a business process but rather fully functional production versions of those business processes as monolithic implementations.

This includes business models developed in languages such as business process execution language (BPEL) and deployed using a BPMS technology platform. There is nothing in these tools or platforms that forces the recognition and isolation of channels and constituents. There is nothing that identifies constituents or channels as enterprise assets. Therefore, most of these artifacts will reflect these very similar to traditional monolithic applications. BPMS solutions built compliant with the development frameworks and design patterns of an SOA reference architecture are very different from traditional monolithic approaches.

ZACHMAN SCOPE LAYER   Most of the documents captured at the Scope layer of the Zachman Framework will map to the Constituent, Channel, and Business Process layer cells under the Corporate Goals/Strategy Cross-Reference and Business Unit Plans columns of the SOA~EAF. Additionally, these artifacts may map to these three layers within the Business Architecture column of the SOA~EAF. The business architects should be heavily involved in evaluating these artifacts and reconstituting their structure to reflect concepts around constituents, channels, and services. Once they are reconstituted, they should be evaluated horizontally across the three layers to identify common business themes and conditions. One way to achieve this is to lay out all the documentation in a spreadsheet format with each column representing a scope artifact and the artifact contents split among three rows representing constituents, channels, and services. Once this is done, the business architect can look horizontally across all the scope documents for constituent commonalties, service-sharing opportunities, and channel expansion opportunities. This analysis will also show the amount of waste and duplicity that exists in the current applications and provide a compelling argument for adopting an SOA approach.

General Approach for Integrating and Leveraging EA Artifacts into the SOA~EAF

Regardless of what framework you currently use to capture EA artifacts, these principles should apply:

- The artifacts should be decomposed so they can be restructured to reflect a top-down constituent-centric view of the application. The presentation layer user interface should be called a proprietary legacy channel. If multiple constituents use the user interface, it should be identified under each constituent using it. If functionality delivered through that user interface is restricted to specific constituents, the functionality should be identified as a service development opportunity only under those constituents authorized to use it. Duplicated functionality used by multiple constituents should be listed under all those constituents. This provides architects the ability to identify high-value, multiconstituent service opportunities within each application.
- Assets that can be leveraged immediately should be classified as such so they can be identified by the solutions and project architects who are estimating, designing, and developing the new SOA applications.

- Integration and API capabilities of the application are the most valuable pieces of documentation, but only if those APIs and integration capabilities are below the presentation layer and built with technologies that can interoperate with the technologies deployed at the SOA Integration Service layer of the Enterprise SOA Platform Architecture.
- Information about the functionality provided by the application and who uses that functionality can be noted at the Business Service, Business Process, and Constituent layers of the Business Architecture column of the SOA~EAF to facilitate evaluating modernization and migration opportunities.
- Information about authentication and functional authorization mechanisms within the application can be helpful for providing a broader picture of security roles and privileges when setting up the enterprise security profiles of the constituents in the Enterprise SOA Security Framework modules.
- Information about the underlying technologies and platforms that the application runs on is valuable to determine if those technologies and platforms contain any inherent capabilities that can be used to extend or expand the application's interoperability characteristics or capabilities.
- Information about any standards or semantic models embedded in or supported by the application is important for assessing the openness of the application.

Summary

This chapter identified approaches and techniques for evaluating existing application artifacts and leveraging their information into the SOA~EAF. The chapter also provided a specific example using the Zachman enterprise architecture model. It identified the different categories used to classify artifacts stored within the SOA~EAF and the usage distinctions of these categories.

The key point to remember is that you should incorporate only those existing artifacts that provide one or more of these values:

- Identifies assets that are readily usable by SOA initiatives.
- Documents information that allows SOA architects to assess the modernization and migration opportunities for those applications.
- Provides strategic information about the modernization and migration plans for these applications.

All other artifacts should continue to be maintained in the EA framework already in place until a tipping point is reached where most of the artifacts are now being generated through the SOA~EAF. The old framework should be shut down after a majority of the legacy applications have been modernized or migrated and decommissioned.

PART III

The SOA~EAF Methodology Processes and Considerations

CHAPTER 7

Dealing with Purchased or Leased Business Applications

There are two realities we must face that have implications for our service-oriented architecture (SOA).

1. We will always have to deal with a portfolio of legacy applications that were not designed as SOA applications.
2. There will always be vendors selling or leasing (i.e., application service providers [ASPs]) business applications that conflict not only with the SOA application architecture but in many cases with your platform standards as well. We must recognize that there will be a compelling business argument on many occasions to acquire these business capabilities rather than building them. We also must recognize that many of these purchases will be the result of vendors reaching out and negotiating with the business directly.

From an SOA architectural perspective, we must accomplish two objectives.

1. We must put a process in place that does not restrict the business from learning and evaluating what is out there but provides proactive mechanisms to ensure that architectural considerations are included in the evaluation process.
2. We must ensure that any agreements or contracts signed with these vendors include commitments to achieve a common interoperability architecture.

The business has to be committed to the SOA approach and its value proposition. If the business is allowed to replace the building of stovepipe applications with the ability to purchase or lease them at any level of scale, then do not bother following an SOA strategy. We know that not every application will be an SOA application, but we want these to be the exception rather than the rule.

The following activities describe what we must do to manage purchased or ASP application vendors:

1. We need to document and publish our vendor compliance architecture standards.
2. We have to factor this evaluation into the decision-making process.

3. If we decide to *partner* with the vendor, we need to incorporate requirements to eliminate critical gaps in the architecture over specified periods of time and incorporate those requirements into the contract. I use the word "partner" deliberately. We cannot treat suppliers of business applications as vendors. We cannot deliver the flexibility, adaptability or the cost-saving efficiencies required by our business leaders if some of our business applications do not comply with or support the architecture. The suppliers of business applications need to know this and agree to be our partners in this mission.

A Future Vision of Vendor Participation in SOA

Before we discuss how to deal with vendors today, let us first discuss how we think SOA will impact how vendors develop their business applications in the future. You may ask, "Why do we even care?" The answer is twofold:

1. If you believe that your company will continue to procure a fair share of already developed vendor-supplied business applications, not trying to have as many of those solutions aligned and consistent with your architecture will result in a major gap and shortfall in your architecture.
2. If the vendors accelerate their movement in the SOA direction, your business will recognize these values and seek out these types of solutions.

So let us assume that tomorrow's vendor business application is not a self-contained stovepipe application but an SOA architectural solution—a solution that exposes its capabilities from the lowest functional level up to the complex process level if desired. It is an application that does not include an embedded proprietary security framework but rather a standards-based security integration system incorporating configurable trusted relationships and roles. The application does not force the users into proprietary interfaces but allows the functionality to be integrated with and consumed not only through channel interfaces but through business processes and business services as well. In other words, the application looks just like the applications you are building under SOA.

Vendors are realizing that a combination of the SOA approach and the ever-increasing standardization of industry transaction sets and semantic models present a unique opportunity for their products. That opportunity is the ability for their business application offerings to integrate and interoperate with their customer's business applications at a service-to-service business level instead of a data-to-data duplication level. This means that the services provided by vendors' applications will plug into your service delivery framework and do so out of the box. If your internal systems process transaction uses industry-standard formats and transaction sets, and vendors' products do the same, then integration of the vendors' systems becomes more a configuration issue than a coding issue. If vendors support the same security and SOA standards as you do, the setup may be completely based on configurations with no coding needed at all.

Let us look at a health industry example. Assume that a health insurer requires its members to get authorizations and referrals from their primary care physician

(PCP) for services performed by someone other than the PCP. Their legacy system processes these transactions based on three factors:

1. The benefit coverages of the member
2. The network providing the service
3. The diagnosis code associated with the service request

Authorizations and referrals can be approved or denied based on these three factors.

Now assume that the insurer wants to base its authorization and referral decisions on a much larger set of data and analytical rules. It wants to be able to approve or reject based on:

- The past treatment history of the patients with the same medical condition and the outcomes of those treatments (evidence-based medicine).
- The service requested as it relates to a preferred medical protocol for treating the diagnosed condition based on clinical evidence of success.
- The quality and performance ranking of the provider entity performing the requested service as it relates to the prescribed protocol.

The details of what these additional conditions mean are not important for this example. What is important is to recognize that they pose these problems:

- The data needed to apply these new rules is not fully contained within the legacy membership and claims adjudication systems but contained in a multitude of additional internal and external applications.
- Getting all this data replicated into the legacy membership and adjudication systems and writing the new rules to support these new conditions would be a massive undertaking, potentially absorbing a significant portion of the IT budget for several years.
- The rules governing these conditions need to be flexible and dynamic and require constant ongoing modifications based on analytical changes to the underlying data.

This last issue poses a significant problem for the legacy system. This is not how the legacy systems operate. Maintaining these changes would require either ongoing code modifications to the legacy systems or a complete re-architecture or replacement of those legacy systems to support the flexibility needed through rule configuration rather than coding.

Following the traditional application architecture approach, however, there are very few options available other than the modification of the legacy applications.

The good news for the health insurer is that the government HIPAA regulation established a standard transaction specification for processing referrals and authorizations between providers and insurers and required their adoption throughout the industry. There is now a well-defined and globally adopted specification for processing the transaction (i.e., a semantic model).

Health insurers that adopted and followed an SOA strategy when implementing these regulated transaction sets did so by:

- Restructuring all the channels where these services were submitted by the providers to consume (process) a single SOA business service to process these transactions.
- Leveraging integration services within the business service to handle the proprietary-to-standard back-and-forth mappings of the legacy data.

Those health insurers that did not adopt an SOA strategy probably embedded duplicate presentation and business logic in each application used by providers to accommodate the change. The result of this multiple application duplication approach is that these health insurers are not positioned to take advantage of a vendor solution to provide the new capabilities; to do so, they would have to incur the cost to integrate that vendor capability into each application containing the duplicated transaction logic.

Now assume that several vendors have developed business applications with an underlying user-configurable rules engine to provide the approve or disapprove decision rules for the new conditions just described. If the mechanism for receiving input into these applications and the mechanism to providing the output from them is the HIPAA referral/authorization-compliant format exposed through a Web service or other standard interface like Java Message Service (JMS), then the mechanism for *accessing* the functionality in these systems (at least for the transaction itself) is simple and straightforward.

If, however, some of those vendors supported the processing of those transactions only through the proprietary user interface provided by their application or through a batch file process, then the *integration* of their capability into an existing and complementary process is not simple and straightforward. This is a representation of the exact model identified at the start of this book as the flaw we are trying to eliminate. Requiring users to go to one system for one step of the process and another system for the next step is the "human" process management approach to stovepipe systems that we are trying to eliminate. It is the same situation where the black hole is created when exposing these services externally.

Our analysis eventually leads us to one vendor whose solution in its application exposes a referral/authorization approval or denial service that accepts as input a standard HIPAA 278 (request for authorization and service review) request and provides its output as a standard HIPAA 278 reply.

Joining this SOA-philosophy vendor to our SOA-philosophy health insurer creates the perfect match. The current internal SOA referral/authorization service (a composite representation of the referral/authorization business process) is enhanced to consume the newly purchased or leased vendor referral/authorization approval or denial service. Since all our referral/authorization requests are being handled by the single internal service, regardless of which channel they are received on, every transaction will now be subject to the new rules of the new service as well. We also have flexibility in how we process the rules. We could process the old legacy rules first and then process the new rules before we return the response, or we could do them in reverse. We could do them in one order for certain patient profiles or conditions and the other way for others.

Vendors that recognize the competitive advantage of building their solutions as SOA solutions that can plug and play at any level of their customers' architecture will become more prominent. The additive and synergetic value that their solutions provide above those of their competition will be readily recognized by those following the same philosophy.

In fact, these vendors will be much more able to take advantage of a lease model for their business services in addition to the traditional purchase model. For example, a vendor may offer a software product that you can purchase and install internally that will calculate the price charged by the U.S. Postal Service and three independent shipping companies based on the destination, size, and weight of the package and schedule pickup by the chosen carrier. The vendor may alternatively provide you with a secured link to a service that your internal applications (services) can consume to process these requests. Under the lease service, there is no application to install or hardware to buy, and the product is available and supported 24/7. Your ability to use the leased capability is immediate. Thus the concept of an ASP is really a business service provider (BSP) relationship. BSPs will offer much more granular capabilities and alternatives than the alternatives possible under a purchase or ASP arrangement. A BSP is to an ASP as iTunes is to a record store. With iTunes, you have an option to buy only the song you want. With the record store, you buy the whole CD.

Software as a Service and SOA

More and more vendors are providing their business application software as a service (SaaS). SaaS, however, is not the same as SOA. SaaS is a concept where you pay for usage only when you use it. In the shipping calculation example, an example of SaaS is a contractual arrangement where you incurred no up-front investment to gain access to the service but would be charged a set amount each time you use it. The same contractual arrangement can exist for applications that you log in to and use. In the preceding example, instead of your system consuming a service, the solution may have been for your shipping associates to log in to the vendor's application and enter the information to generate the shipping costs. The contract would be to charge a usage fee each time your associates logged on and submitted a transaction.

Both of these are examples of SaaS solutions. Only the first one is an example of an SOA SaaS solution. You need to seek out and partner with vendors that are providing SOA-based SaaS solutions and avoid those that are not. If you have to use a non-SOA SaaS solution (if a compelling business reason exists to do so), make sure that you contractually establish the architectural relationship and requirements to move the vendor in the SOA direction going forward.

Are You Backing the Right Horse?

Vendors that hold onto the belief that locking their customers into their solution increases future revenue (by requiring the vendor to provide any flexibility or adaptability that will inevitably be needed) will slowly disappear. You want to align your company with vendors heading in the business service provider direction and be a key partner with them as they head in that direction.

Adopting SOA Partnerships with Vendors Supplying Leased or Purchased Business Applications

Based on the discussion and examples just provided, we can surmise these facts:

- The vendors we choose to partner with who allow us to acquire business capabilities rather than build them have a tremendous business value, but their approach to delivering that capability can have an equally devastating and negative impact on our ability to deliver that value effectively over time.
- Ignoring this fact by not proactively working with vendors to help make their solutions SOA compliant will have just as significant a negative impact on your success as ignoring SOA for your internal systems.
- The more purchased or leased applications you have, the bigger the impact will be.

Hence, as architects, we need to engage our vendors early and often and turn those relationships from vendor to partner relationships. We need to engage our business community and make them be aware of and appreciate that the values these vendor solutions bring to the business at a *tactical* level can turn out to be barriers or obstacles to the business at a *strategic* level. We need to ensure that we negotiate architectural requirements and commitments into any business application contracts we sign.

When we are evaluating the architectural capabilities of a vendor's business application, we are looking for:

- Architectural capabilities that comply with SOA principles, such as Web services exposing underlying business capabilities.
- Architectural capabilities that would facilitate the encapsulation of underlying capabilities into architecture-compliant capabilities (e.g., application program interfaces [APIs] that expose underlying functionality that can be encapsulated into integration services).
- Standards like SAML that are consistent with your environment.
- Deployment on platforms supported in your environment if purchased rather than leased.

When evaluating the vendors themselves rather than their application, we are looking for:

- Knowledge, competencies, and capabilities of the vendor's resources as they relate to SOA.
- Vendor's executive-level understanding and commitment to the SOA philosophy.
- Documented business plans and future release requirements that support their stated SOA commitment.
- The divergence and gap in their current solutions and platforms from an SOA architecture and an estimation of the commitment needed to transform those solutions and platforms.

We need to recognize that vendors offering traditional architecture solutions will continue to be in the majority for some time. We also need to be able to recognize which of those vendors are moving away from the traditional approach and how far along they are in that transformation.

This vendor transformation and paradigm shift to the SOA architectural approach is no less daunting or complex for vendors than it is for us effecting our own internal transformation. It is difficult and risky for them as well. They will have to balance the demand and drive to move toward the future approach with the resistance and lack of comfort of their customers who are not moving in this direction. These customers will not see the same value of vendors moving in this direction, as they will be less capable of taking advantage of these changes. Those who are pursuing SOA, however, will be very open and accommodating to vendors that are pursuing it as well.

This presents an opportunity for your company to influence these vendors toward solutions that are much more aligned with the strategic needs of your business, including the adoption of the same standards and versions that you have adopted. It can include influencing their designs to take advantage of the foundational framework capabilities that you have built into your architecture, such as providing hooks to use your enterprise logging and archiving capabilities or access images from your image retrieval services. Contractually agreeing to address these issues with vendors and obtaining their commitment to incorporate these capabilities into future releases of their products significantly increases your chances of them actually happening.

You need to recognize that many vendors will claim they are offering an SOA solution because their products provide some Web services. Having Web services does not make an application an SOA application. An application that has Web services that integrate with an industry-standard security framework for federated authentication and authorization makes an application more SOA compliant from an architecture perspective. Recognizing that its services will need to be incorporated with different service contracts and service invocation stubs so it can be deployed to different channels and different users in an SOA enterprise architecture solution makes an application more SOA compliant too. These are the kinds of influences you need to have over your vendors.

SOA Considerations for Requests for Proposals and Requests for Information

In most companies, the first point of establishing a formal relationship with a vendor is through a *Request for Information* (RFI) or *Request for Proposal* (RFP) process. These are traditional mechanisms for soliciting formal responses from vendors on the ability of their products and services to meet a specified business need. These documents need to incorporate the architectural needs and requirements of the company as well. Architectural needs go beyond identifying the tools and platforms used by the vendor. They must address the architectural strategy of the company and the key design aspects that business applications must have to support the architectural strategy. This does not mean that every vendor business application has to be built exactly like your internally built SOA applications. It does, however, mean that they should be designed to work with that architecture as effectively and efficiently as possible.

Architecture should incorporate verbiage similar to the next example of a company's boilerplate RFP/RFI documents. By using such terminology in requests for solicitations, vendors are explicitly aware of requirements before they respond.

Some boilerplate RFP/RFI text for inclusion in an architecture requirements section is presented next:

COMPANY ABC has adopted a service-oriented architecture (SOA) strategy. The intent of this strategy is to move away from monolithic or stovepipe business applications that involve multiple presentation layers and security mechanisms that complicate user experiences. Our model is to provide business functionality that can be decomposed if necessary for some purposes and aggregated if necessary for other purposes to provide our internal and external users with a holistic and seamless user experience. We want to be able to provide these capabilities through multiple channels and to different constituents without incurring excessive costs on redundant and duplicate capabilities. We want to manage and control all our services through a common enterprise framework for authentication and authorization using industry-standard federated capabilities. We want the flexibility and adaptability within purchased applications to isolate the inherent business capabilities and target them for consumption in other business services and business processes built and maintained outside the vendor's application.

All future custom developed applications within COMPANY ABC must comply with this strategy. Vendors that provide business applications for purchase through an ASP model or a SaaS model that comply with and complement this strategy are given significant preference in this RFI/RFP application selection process. **To this end we place a high value on the following:**

- *Applications constructed to provide consumption of the underlying functionality through discrete, presentation-layer agnostic services*
- *Applications that expose those services through an industry-standard federated authentication and authorization framework*
- *Applications that use industry-standard formats and semantic data models within those services*
- *Applications that are highly user configurable with business rules supported with technologies like rule engines*
- *Applications that can integrate not only at the business logic level but also at the data logic level through data service mechanisms rather than data replication or data duplication mechanisms*

Vendors that incorporate these capabilities in their current product will be given the highest technical preference. Vendors that contractually commit to provide these capabilities in releases over the next specified number of months will be given a higher technical preference over vendors that make no such commitment.

Vendor Contracting

The architects are responsible for the analysis and assessment of these criteria during the RFP/RFI gap analysis and vendor ranking processes. This would include conversation with and assessment of the vendors' development resources and technical management team. Specific discussions and agreements between the architects and the vendors would be documented and factored into the decision-making process. These vendor discussions and commitments would be explicitly documented in the contract signed with a vendor before the acquisition or lease of the application occurs. Statements similar to the next ones represent examples of commitments that would be included in the contract to legally bind a vendor to the architectural requirements going forward:

Vendor Contract Architectural Commitments:

The vendor agrees to have all the application functionality listed under Phase I in "Attachment X" redesigned and recoded as consumable Web services using the SAML federated model provided by COMPANY ABC in version X.X of the application being purchased under this contract scheduled for general release on XX/XX/XXXX.

The remaining application functionality listed under Phase II in "Attachment X" will be redesigned and recoded as consumable Web services using the SAML federated model provided by COMPANY ABC in version Y.X of the application being purchased under this contract scheduled for general release on XX/XX/XXXX.

The vendor also agrees to provide the capability within its application to consume the benefit and claims data currently replicated in its application database through real-time services provided by our benefit and claims databases utilizing ASC X-12 HIPAA-compliant formats (270/271 for Benefits and 837 for Claims).

All costs for developing testing and certifying these capabilities in the vendor's application will be incurred by the vendor. The vendor retains all rights of ownership and usage relating to these capabilities.

A signed attachment to the contract (labeled "Attachment X" in the example), which identifies all the specific detailed requirements of the enhancements and the delivery schedule of those enhancements, would be incorporated into the signed contract with the vendor.

In some cases, you may require the vendor to incur all the costs of the specified enhancements. You can argue that its investment will be returned through future revenues by being able to offer a more flexible solution to a wider audience of users over a shorter period of time. If vendors balk or resist the commitment, you can assess whether there is value in sharing the cost of these enhancements. The answer will depend on the strategic value of the functionality a vendor is providing and the benefits you will realize through these enhancements. Clearly, if these enhancements improve the user's work flow, especially if it is an external user; if the value of extending the functionality to other processes is high; and if the vendor can deliver them faster and cheaper than you can develop them in house, the investment may be worth it.

The architects, especially the business architects, need to facilitate the documentation and assessment of these potential values with the business. The strategic documentation contained within the SOA enterprise architecture framework (SOA~EAF™) can be used to identify and evaluate these values. This evaluation process will include assessing if any of the functionality provided by the vendor's application is identified as capabilities within the Business Service and/or Business Process layers of the Corporate Strategy, Business Unit Plans, or Business Architecture columns of the framework.

Some considerations to assess when conducting this evaluation include:

- If these capabilities are needed, do the capabilities also have strategic value for being deployed through multiple channels and/or to multiple constituents?
- Have the capabilities been identified by the constituent horizontal experience governance committee within the SOA Portfolio Plan Governance Committee as ones that need to be seamlessly integrated and delivered to constituents holistically?
- Are the capabilities provided by the vendor's application part of a higher-level business process that must be aggregated into a single process flow?

If the answer to any of these questions is yes, there is a high probability that investing to SOA-enable the vendor application is worth it. The architects, leveraging the information provided by the SOA~EAF, can show the business how not enhancing the vendor's application will impact the strategy and business plans. They can help the business recognize that it has only three options:

1. It can invest in enhancing the vendor's application so it can support the business's strategy and plans.
2. It can find another vendor solution that already has these capabilities, if one exists.
3. It can change its strategy and business plans.

This process helps the business understand up front the implications of the application on its business needs and strategic direction. If the business purchases the application without enhancing it, the company is committing to change its strategy and plans. These changes should be approved and incorporated into the SOA~EAF. Thus there will be no surprises later on when the strategic objectives cannot be supported.

This process will ensure that a major strategic decision like the one in this scenario will be elevated at the right level within the corporation. The decision will not be made by the project team that was set up within the business unit to evaluate vendor applications. Many of the strategic values of the functionality identified through the SOA~EAF documentation may be associated with other business units that are not involved in this current vendor product evaluation. Beyond this, it is highly unlikely that all the key business leaders who initially established the strategies and business plans are participants in this evaluation process.

If the path to pay for these enhancements is chosen, you should also pursue your right to receive additional value in the future for the investment you are making. This could include:

- Reduced prices on future releases.
- Revenue sharing on future releases that incorporate the enhancements.
- In the worst case, future exclusivity of use for the enhanced functionality that you are paying for.

This last option should be pursued only if there is a perceived competitive advantage over competitors that use or may use the vendor's application by retaining exclusivity. Exclusivity may put support for these capabilities at risk, requiring you to also fund the incorporation and certification of the capabilities in future releases as well.

Value of Architectural Management of Vendor Business Applications

Many of the values of the process outlined in this chapter have already been stated. The most significant advantage, however, is that it allows architecture to be flexible and pragmatic in its support of the business and the business advantages that buying or leasing business applications have, but does not compromise the ability to support the strategic needs of the business in the future. Knowing that the vendor agrees to add the architectural capabilities in future releases helps the architecture practice to provide short-term relief for an immediate need but not at the expense of long-term value to the business.

Under this approach, the architects can be pragmatic and supportive of the business to help it get needed functionality quickly but also ensure the long-term strategic value and return on that commitment. The agreement may be to immediately bring in the vendor application in its current state, replicate the necessary data to support the application, and allow the proprietary user interface with its proprietary security module to be used by the business. This would be done with the understanding that as the future releases become available, the new services would be integrated into the existing Business Service and Channel layer components deployed in your SOA environment. This will allow the eventual shutdown of the proprietary user interface and the data replication approach used in the vendor's original product. This provides the capability to manage and plan the capabilities of purchased solutions from an enterprise perspective. It allows users to maximize the value of the functionality and minimize the impact on the consumers of that functionality by leveraging it throughout your enterprise architecture model. It also provides the capability to plan for these enhancements in your enterprise SOA portfolio plan, incorporating future releases of the vendor's application into your internal release process.

IT will have to live with and support another stovepipe solution for a period of time. The business will need to hold off advancing some of its strategic plans until the vendor delivers supporting capabilities. Ultimately, however, both will get what they want.

Special Considerations when Business Applications Are Hosted or Located in Multiple Data Centers

All of the evaluations and assessments just listed apply to both purchased and leased business applications. Leased (hosted) applications from ASPs (which we will now call BSPs through our vendor partner relationships) require additional architectural considerations. These applications will run in a data center operated by the vendor or the vendor's agent. In some cases, your connectivity to these applications will be exclusively over the Internet using an open or secured (virtual private network [VPN]) connection. These connections are becoming more and more the norm. Alternatively, there may be a requirement to establish a private physical connection between the vendor and your company. These are commonly supported today through frame relay, analog transmission (T) level or digital signal transmission (DS) level connections (e.g., T1, T3, DS1, DS3, etc.). In cases where both exist, the Internet channel will typically be used by those using the application and the private channel will be used for system-to-system activities, such as service invocations and message processing. As the vendor application becomes compliant with the SOA architecture, users of the application will migrate from the vendor application's proprietary user interface to the user interfaces of your channels. When this occurs, the access to the underlying capabilities that the vendor application provides will be through your infrastructure across the network to the vendor's infrastructure. The connection between you and the vendor may be either public or private. Regardless of whether the connection is public or private, it is a wide area connection and inherently has lower bandwidth and latency than servers in your data center with gigabit or higher bandwidth connections. This latency must be taken into consideration when integrating applications hosted in different locations.

> **Note**
>
> The latency issue will exist if any of your other business applications reside in two or more data centers with wide area connections between them. The architects need to consider the state from front to back to ensure proper performance capabilities are built into the solution.

You need to work with the vendor to ensure that the implemented solution will meet the performance service-level agreements (SLAs) for constituents established by your company. Performance improvements may include more public or private bandwidth, depending on which is used. It may also require that the services be based on more efficient technologies. Web services are great, but they have larger network footprints and more complex processing requirements. Delivering Web services through SOAP has more overhead than delivering them through a message transport like MQ.

This gets back to a point made earlier in this book. SOA is not just about Web services. SOA is about leveragability and reusability. The best solution may or may not be a Web service. In some cases, it may be a vendor message service utilized at a federated system-to-system level that manages the data pass-through and back-end business logic invocation. The back-end message would be used by a local Web service in the company's environment that handles the security and presentation layer logic. Another option is for the vendor to deploy some of the application's core functionality on its infrastructure but deploy its Web service on the customers' platforms in their data centers.

Once again, the center of excellence (COE) should be leveraged to assist in this process. As partners, the vendors should be willing to expose their development and test environments to the COE to performance-test prototypes and alternatives. The other side of this equation is the projected volume and frequency of the service utilization by the business. Low-volume, infrequently used services have less of an impact on the business, and a lower performance SLA may be acceptable. If, however, a service involves a high-volume, mission-critical service, meeting performance SLAs is absolutely required.

If you determine that the performance levels would be more achievable if the application was local to the other SOA platforms, you should consider hosting them on-site. Even if there is no need to host them locally, initially your contract with the vendor should explicitly state what your options and alternatives are for doing so in the future. If the vendor offers only a hosted solution and you contractually want it to move toward the SOA modernization of their application, you should require a proof of technology and a proof of concept pilot before you sign a contract, if you are concerned about the solution's ability to meet your performance requirements.

Performance Techniques for SOA

There are many ways to architect technically efficient solutions to the geographically disbursed, distributed platform application architecture. These have existed and evolved ever since distributed computing began. The distinction with SOA is that we need to build solutions that involve many more of these distributed interactions and more frequently. These interactions are at the logic layer, not the data layer; therefore, traditional performance techniques, such as data caching, do not apply. Techniques like precaching and reply caching of integration services and process fine-tuning, however, do apply.

For example, when a constituent authenticates to a channel and invokes a process or service, most likely many steps need to be performed to complete that service or process. In many cases, we can predict what services may be needed based on the process the user selected. For example, after authenticating to the channel, the customer invokes the "Check Order Status" service. The first step in this service is to provide a presentation layer display of the selection criteria for status. This could include options for status on a specific order based on the order number or the customer purchase order number. Alternatively, it could give status on orders within a specified order placement date range. What the customer does not realize is the service already knew who the customer was from profile credentials passed from the service authorization framework. The "Check Order Status" service used this information to invoke another lower-level service called "Get Customer Orders" to get all the orders starting with the most recent status change date or orders that have been open the longest as soon as the user invoked the "Check Order Status" service. The "Check Order Status" process did this because the order records and the status on those records reside on the corporate mainframe in a different data center from the platform where the "Check Order Status" service resides. This is an example of precaching business logic–level services. The architect of the service leveraged business knowledge to help solve a technical performance problem. The business knowledge was knowing immediately on the invocation of the "Check Order Status" service that information about order status is going to be requested and orders that have been open the longest or had their status recently changed are the most likely ones to be viewed. Additional business knowledge has provided guidance that past order status statistics through all channels reflect that customers checking order status check on the status of more than one order more than 80 percent of the time. Half the users look up multiple orders by specifying individual orders one at a time. The other half select multiple orders using the date range option.

The performance problem was not necessarily that the order mainframe is located on the other side of the country (or the globe), although this does add some latency. The performance problem was that the processing overhead of the order system's APIs and the message transport delivering the results to the local data center ESB affect performance. The architect took advantage of these business facts and the knowledge of who the customer was from the authentication profiles to initiate this process while the customer was entering an order number, a purchase order number, or a date range. While the time it takes the customer to enter this information may seem minimal, it is massive in terms of CPU processing cycles and network packet delivery.

The architect also had business knowledge that many customers had many orders and technical knowledge that waiting for the order program to extract all the customer's orders and sort them in the right order could take a significant amount of time. Therefore, the reply from the order system was structured to select and return the first 20 order records, then the next 20, until there are no more orders or the count of 60 orders has been reached. If the last reply received by the service was flagged as end of orders, the service knows not to request any more orders. If not flagged as end of orders, the service can continue to request orders, only this time the request specifies a specific order number, purchase order number, or date range. This request will be sent only if the individual order or date range of orders was not included in the initial replies. This is an example of reply caching, in which process-intensive activities on large volumes of data are broken up and delivered in chunks to improve performance.

The third thing the architect did was to not modify the order system API or the "Get Customer Orders" integration service on the ESB to sort the data being returned. The responsibility for doing this was coded into the higher process layer "Check Order Status" service. This was done because there is no need to sort the orders if the customer enters an order number or purchase order number, which happens 50 percent of the time. Therefore, orders will be sorted only when necessary.

At this point, you should recognize that the "Check Order Status" service is a Business Service layer SOA component that is exposed to the customer through one or more channels, either directly or through a higher-layer business process. It handles most or all of the presentation layer logic used by the customer. The amount controlled by the service depends on the channel. In an IVR system, the platform will handle the conversion of the "Check Order Status" service text to speech.

You should also recognize that "Get Customer Orders" service is an Integration Service layer SOA component that provides a logical service that isolates the physical legacy order application. I could have described an example where there were three separate legacy order systems and the integration service needed to pull orders from all of them (order systems are for products, services, and parts) or from one of them (separate order systems for national accounts, government accounts, and local accounts). To the actual consuming customer or the "Check Order Status" service itself, none of this matters. These physical complexities and any future changes to them are completely hidden from both.

Finally, you should recognize that these two services are loosely coupled; there is nothing physically hard-coded that stops either of them from consuming or being consumed by a different service. The "Cancel Customer Order" Business Service layer service also invokes (uses) the "Get Customer Order" Integration layer service. When the "Check Order Status" service, the "Cancel Customer Order" service, and several other Business Service layer services are deployed out to the customer service's customer relationship management system (CRMS) workstation to support the customer telephone channel, they are encapsulated in a higher-level Business Process layer service called "Manage Customer Account."

The example of performance techniques just mentioned and how these techniques are implemented at the different layers of the SOA enterprise architecture need to be applied to all applications, including internally built ones. I purposely presented them in this chapter to highlight the fact that it is even more critical that they are applied to purchased and leased applications. If you did not apply these techniques when you built these capabilities internally and you run into performance problems, you can always go back and re-architect them to improve performance. If, however, they were built by the vendor and delivered as part of its product, you are now at the vendor's mercy to correct and improve the product. It is better to address performance considerations holistically, up front, before anything is delivered than it is to have them appear after a product is in production.

This is why it is so critical to establish a partnership with your vendors that supply your business applications. Having them and their product developers participate with your architects in your COE is critical to your business. When the relationship is a partnership, vendors have as much interest in your environment and how you need to support your business's strategy as you have in their solutions and how they support your technical strategy.

I hope you see the value of building these relationships and investing in these efforts, especially if your company acquires a portion of its business application capabilities. If, however, you are thinking, "Why would I even begin to think about doing this?" I suggest that the real question you should be asking yourself is, "Am I really committed to achieving the SOA vision and delivering all the business capabilities and synergies that it has to offer?" Being able to deliver on 80 or 90 percent of a vision may not be enough to achieve the value needed or to gain an advantage. If you were a car manufacturer, would you agree to build a totally electric car and accept only 80 percent of it being delivered? I think a statement like "It has everything except a way to steer and stop it!" would scare you as much as it does me.

The bank where I do my online business would be less valuable to me if I could manage my bank accounts, certificates of deposit, loans, and brokerage account all on one web site that holistically managed my interactions across all these lines of business but forced me to a different web site to manage my bank credit card because an ASP vendor provided this service. Even if single sign-on was provided, some of the capabilities that customers may want, such as merging their credit card's rewards with their debit card's rewards, may not be possible.

Delivering a holistic process that provides a mostly positive and rewarding customer experience, except for one little piece that is missing because it is buried in a vendor's application and not accessible, can have a devastating effect on your strategy. You cannot do SOA halfway. If you do not force purchased or leased applications to comply, that is exactly what you are doing.

Summary

In this chapter we discussed how purchased and leased business applications are different but in almost every way need to be treated no differently from how we deal with internally developed applications. The business's ability to purchase or lease business capabilities plays a critical role in supporting it. Validating business requirements against existing business application software and finding a significant match absolutely accelerates the delivery of those capabilities. However, once the application is implemented and being used by the business, in reality it is no different from any other application from the business's perspective. The business should not be forced to compromise on its strategy because a decision to purchase business capabilities rather than build them was made. Often, however, a business does not realize that it has made this compromise until it is too late. The money is already spent, the vendor is under no contractual agreement to fix the problem, and the business is frustrated. If we truly want to achieve our SOA vision, which in reality is how IT will be able to support the business achieving its vision, we can no longer treat vendors as vendors. We need to treat them, and they need to treat us, as partners.

This chapter discussed how the SOA architects need to be proactively involved with the business application vendor evaluation and selection process right from the start. The process starts with the implementation of a formal RFI/RFP process that incorporates the SOA architecture requirements and considerations and a top-down business-driven governance commitment to validate those requirements and considerations. The process includes an in-depth analysis of the vendor's technical capabilities and its ability to deliver the right solution in the future. This may include the requirement for the vendor to participate in a proof of technology or proof of concept prototype exercise to validate its capabilities and competencies. Next the process involves documenting and contracting the specific detailed architecture and coding enhancements that the vendor needs to deliver and when it needs to deliver them. This agreement also includes the right for your architects to participate in the design specifications for these enhancements as they are being developed. Finally, it involves the vendor participating in your COE so your architects can validate and certify the architectural compliance of those enhancements.

CHAPTER 8

Transforming Governance to Support SOA

Without a doubt, the largest barrier to achieving a successful enterprise SOA strategy will be the entrenched practices and culture of the corporation as it relates to how the business perceives, supports, and funds IT systems and what they expect IT to deliver. While dealing with the political aspects of changing the process will be significant, moving the entire business community out of their comfort zone and getting them to understand and adopt a whole new way of doing things when it comes to their business applications will be even more significant. After all, the business is focused on doing its business. It is, by nature (and by incentive), myopic in its views (i.e., shipping is focused on improving shipping, not increasing sales). The entire cultural and political process of how it fights for *its* needs when it comes to IT are well established and well understood. Asking business users to throw this all away and start over is not going to be easy. Changing those who understand the existing process the best and who tend to get more than their share of the pie is most challenging.

For these reasons, you must deploy a strategy that effectively forces a top-down approach to SOA. Ensuring that the top executive management of the company actively participates in the process and drives the transformation is critical. The architects, however, have to invest significant effort and commitment to ensure the involvement of the executives is efficient and effective. What they are asked to do and how often they are asked to do it must be well thought out and efficiently managed. If the process becomes burdensome or if the activities and their purpose are unclear, the entire strategy will come to a screeching halt. The quickest path to failure will be to have the executives think you are wasting their time.

Enterprise SOA Portfolio Plan and the Release Approach to Application Delivery

Before we begin our discussion of governance, we need to define what we are governing: the enterprise SOA portfolio plan and the delivery of the contents of that plan. The governance processes documented in this chapter define how to perform this governance from the highest strategic level to the lowest tactical level. As you will see throughout this book, the SOA~EAF™ and methodology are structured not only to improve the process of building SOA applications but to support the full governance of those processes as well. As stated in the introduction, the framework and methodology have been designed to provide a traceable and accountable path from corporate strategy, to business plan, to business IT initiatives, to SOA projects, to production. They have also been designed to govern this path efficiently and accurately. Thus, the governance processes described in this chapter cover everything from establishing what is in the SOA portfolio plan, the priority of delivering its content, and ensuring compliance with the SLAs established for these systems when they are placed into production.

The structure and process around the enterprise SOA portfolio plan and the release approach to delivering the initiatives in that plan are two of the most significant transformations we are trying to accomplish to adopt SOA and achieve all its benefits.

Getting commitment at all levels of the company to adopt this new planning structure and the release approach to business software delivery is critical to your SOA success. Obtaining these commitments will be some of the earliest activities identified in your *SOA enterprise architecture strategy and roadmap*. This document will represent IT's business unit plan. Just as sales and manufacturing have business plans that define what they are going to do to achieve the corporate strategies and what capabilities and resources they need to achieve those objectives, the SOA enterprise architecture strategy and roadmap is IT's business unit plan for how to deliver the business applications needed by the business units to achieve the corporate strategy. This document is explained in Chapter 14.

The enterprise SOA portfolio plan and the release process are explained in this chapter to support the understanding and rationale of each of the governance committees. The enterprise SOA portfolio plan and the release process are further described and referenced throughout this book.

Enterprise SOA Portfolio Plan

The enterprise SOA portfolio plan is the most central and most used *business* document within the SOA governance process. This document is the driver for a key paradigm shift within the company. That paradigm shift is a business-driven process at the enterprise level that sets the direction of IT and IT projects by managing a series of SOA *initiatives* through *releases* over the next one or more years. The paradigm shift is that SOA initiatives are enterprise-owned initiatives. They are not business unit system projects. Prioritization and release of funds for IT purchases and developments are occurring at the enterprise portfolio level, not the project level.

Because many SOA initiatives will have capabilities delivered that will be shared with other SOA initiatives that use the same components, deliverables can no longer be prioritized individually. A decision to accelerate the development of a channel to support one constituent group and delay the delivery of a channel supporting a different constituency could have significant impact on the development and delivery of the underlying business processes and business services scheduled in the plan.

You may argue that making such a drastic change to the portfolio plan is highly disruptive and should be avoided at all costs. While I agree that it is disruptive, avoiding or resisting change may be detrimental to the business. Sometimes things change. In fact, they change more often than we would like. Sometimes competition forces us to rethink our plan and adjust to counteract what it is doing.

The good news is that we have now structured a process and built a framework to better manage and adjust for these changes and minimize the loss of time and money involved. Remember, the second major value of SOA is flexibility. Flexibility not only means the ability to quickly adapt services to changing conditions; it also means the ability adapt and change at a much coarser portfolio level. Because the process allows the portfolio governance team to quickly identify and assess the impact of any changes made to the plan, team members can quickly determine the feasibility and loss associated with those changes. Because an SOA by its nature requires the development of loosely coupled components, you can conduct a more granular determination of what needs to change and when it needs to change.

This is significantly more beneficial than the traditional "waterfall" approach of monolithic systems. For example, shutting down a monolithic stovepipe project for an extended period of time usually means that most, if not all, of the work done to the point of shutdown will have to be revisited and reevaluated if and when the project starts up again. In many cases, the individuals who worked on the project initially may not be the same ones when it restarts. This is true for business resources as well as IT resources.

When an SOA approach is being used, some or all of the services being developed to deploy over the channel that needs to be delayed may continue their development to completion. They simply will be tested, certified, and "published" but not yet placed into production. The entire production cycle associated with those services from requirements to testing will be completed. This will eliminate the need for any restart learning curve to complete them later on. A decision may be made to construct a second or alternative service wrapper around them so they can be deployed to an alternative, existing channel until the new channel comes online. Similarly, any constituent roles or access policies that were developed could be completed and registered in a nonproduction state as well. Ultimately, once this process is established and running efficiently, little or no wasted time or money should be associated with portfolio changes. This is truly a different world! When you reach this maturity level, the business will see the portfolio management process as a key strategic differentiation. It will see the process as tool that significantly enhances its ability to adapt and compete.

The enterprise SOA portfolio plan maps out the SOA initiatives for the next N number of periods. A plan can be mapped out in months or quarters, depending on how granularly you want to manage the process at the portfolio governance level. If you map and manage it by quarter, lower-level governance bodies will still need to prioritize and micromanage each day in each quarter. The enterprise SOA portfolio plan can encompass from one to N number of years, depending on the organization's structure and level of comfort. I highly recommend that it cover at least two years with the annual project prioritization and budget process mapping each subsequent year.

This is not to say that everything mapped to year 2 on the plan automatically becomes the next year's prioritized and budgeted SOA initiatives. In fact, the process that I describe creates a proactive rolling management of the portfolio that allows additions, deletions, or reshuffling to occur on an ongoing basis. The key is that modifications and changes are made in the context of a holistic, previously established plan from an enterprise impact perspective, not a project versus project impact assessment. A new plan is not built from scratch each year, but a new plan may exist after each time the top two governance committees meet.

Note

As you begin to adopt an SOA approach to IT systems, you will have a mix of existing non-SOA projects and new SOA initiatives active at the same time. You may not be able to have every new project structured as an SOA initiative. You may be forced to start slow with a small percentage of the projects as SOA initiatives until a successful track record builds business confidence in the process. Under these circumstances, you will need to evolve your enterprise SOA portfolio plan and the governance associated with it gradually over time. It is critically important, however, that this enterprise SOA portfolio plan and its governance be separate and distinct from the existing processes. The goal is to establish an enterprise SOA portfolio plan and governance process designed to operate under an SOA paradigm and maximize the SOA return. Mixing and managing SOA initiatives within the old legacy process will put every SOA initiative at a disadvantage. That is because the "rules" of the old process will be stacked against the SOA initiatives. The traditional processes, including their cultural and political impacts, will occur, and these will all favor the traditional project approach. Remember, this book does not tell you how to technically implement SOA. It shows you how to create a cultural, organizational and political paradigm shift in how your company operates in order to make SOA successful. The key is not how many of the initiatives are SOA; it is how effective you are at establishing and institutionalizing the new SOA management and governance processes to accurately and efficiently manage and govern them.

Obviously, the more successful you are in obtaining complete top-down commitment to the SOA paradigm from the company's executive management, the greater percentage of projects will be structured as SOA initiatives and the faster you will reach the point where every initiative is being structured and managed by the enterprise SOA portfolio plan. If you must start out slower, seek to achieve a tipping point that leads all others to follow as soon as possible. In other words, the SOA architects must take the added responsibility (and work) to make sure that every SOA initiative is perceived business as better, more favorable, and more valuable than the non-SOA projects. This will occur when those participating in the SOA governance processes (especially business participants) recognize that this new process:

- Provides them with better insight to the overall IT spending.
- Shows them exactly how that spending maps to their business plans and the corporate strategy.
- Gives them more valuable information about how to support their business.
- Delivers more capabilities and delivers them faster than the old projects could.
- Benefits all the business units in the enterprise.

- Provides a much stronger understanding of how reprioritizing affects the portfolio and a much more cost-effective way to handle these changes.

They will also recognize that the new process, which promotes decision making at an enterprise level for solutions beyond individual business units, results in:

- New business alliances being formed across multiple business units to serve mutual causes.
- Each business unit recognizing that it is getting more for less and faster than it did under the old process.

What I hope I was successful in communicating is that you have enhanced your architectural framework and practice to provide you with the capability to identify, design, and leverage as many of your IT assets up the layers of the architecture (i.e., leveraging integration components, business service components, business process components, and business channel components). Therefore, the expectation is that each and every initiative will, in fact, contain and leverage some of these components. Over time, as more and more of these SOA components are funded and built, the cost of subsequent initiatives will be less and less because the number of reusable SOA components will continue to increase. It should become readily apparent that the approved initiatives represent the most efficient and effective utilization of the approved IT spending.

Adopting a Release Strategy for SOA Initiatives

The SOA paradigm shift requires a transformation from *business system implementations* to *business service releases*. This, in turn, requires a transformation from the delivery of traditional self-contained business applications using a one-off or standalone approach to the deployment of highly leveraged enterprise SOA components using an enterprise release approach.

As more initiatives contain a larger percentage of reused SOA components, the number of common SOA components used in multiple initiatives will increase. As the number of common SOA components in initiatives increases, management of the delivery of those initiatives needs to be more tightly coupled. The best way to manage this is through the adoption of a *release strategy* for delivery of SOA business software.

If you think about it, a release strategy is not only the best way to maximize the return on SOA initiatives; it is the most efficient as well. Think about a traditional project process, where three projects submitted by three different business units were approved and funded. All three were projects to improve how the different business units service or support the customer. The initiative submitted by the sales department improved the way customers place orders so they can be booked faster. The initiative submitted by the finance department improved the details and accuracy of the invoices and increased customer visibility into how payments were being applied. The initiative submitted by shipping was to implement radio-frequency identification (RFID) tagging of the products to allow for automatic tracking of inventory levels, expedite the inventory-pulling and truck-loading processes, and provide customers with better product tracking information all the way to the final shipping destination.

Here are some key observations.

- Any one of these projects could be completed on its own. None was linked to the others.
- All of them were focused on building or enhancing self-contained stovepipe systems.
- They were all "inward looking out" in that each business unit was attempting to improve how it services customers, but doing so based on how it (internally) supports customers and only from the limited perspective of the functions within a specific business unit.

If, however, the process was designed to look at these projects from a top-down SOA perspective (i.e., following the business architecture presented in Chapter 3), it would provide the capability to look horizontally across these vertical initiatives and readily see the commonalities. This SOA perspective is shown in Exhibit 8.1.

If the company already has a customer portal and an employee portal that were built as part of earlier SOA initiatives, Exhibit 8.1 would be enhanced to reflect the channels.

Exhibit 8.2 shows the three initiatives and the channels required to support those initiatives.

We now have visibility into the fact that three separate business units have projects that will impact the customer next year. We also learn that all three had separate plans to communicate these changes to the customer and none was aware of the other business units' plans to do so. All three wanted to give the customer access

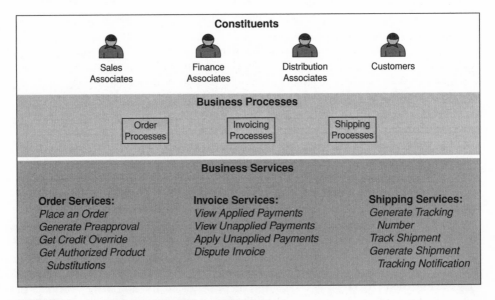

EXHIBIT 8.1   Aggregation of Three Separate IT Projects

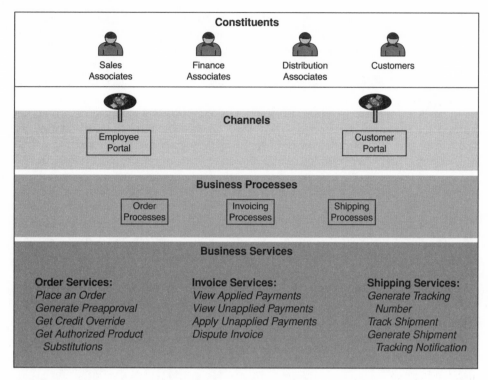

EXHIBIT 8.2   Three IT Projects in the SOA Initiative Business Architecture

to the functions through the Web. All three independently specified requirements to authenticate and authorize customer access to the functionality without consideration of the other business units' requirements.

While this preceding example may seem obvious and you may argue that your company would have seen these commonalities and resolved them, I am using this example simply to make a point. When the situation is obvious, the issues become apparent and get resolved. However, the countless number of commonalities that are not so obvious do not necessarily get resolved. Even if the obvious ones do become apparent and get resolved, you need to have a methodology and process in place that can identify those that are not obvious. Today's process is more after the fact; this analysis is performed by looking across all the projects after they have been funded and started. Tomorrow's process proactively structures initiatives from a top-down, constituent-centric perspective so that potential synergies are immediately visible and understood.

Our SOA objective is to leverage as much as possible and be as efficient as possible. For the three projects just discussed, we will have to design and build new services that let customers:

1. Enter orders more efficiently.
2. Review their payments and outstanding balances.
3. Track and follow the status of their shipments.

We want to be able to deploy these services through the existing customer portal framework using the existing customer authentication and authorization capabilities.

We fully expect that each subsequent SOA initiative will use more and more previously constructed channel, business process, and business service components. In addition, at any point in time, more and more initiatives will be using the same shared components.

Under an SOA release approach to system delivery, each initiative no longer defines, plans, and implements on its own. Each initiative is delivering not a monolithic stovepipe solution but rather a set of new capabilities leveraging existing capabilities. Savings can occur when the same shared SOA components are cycled through the process together. The release approach also ensures that separate projects looking to utilize some of the same shared or leveraged SOA components will not step on each other.

As stated throughout this book, the new paradigm is a top-down, not a bottom-up, approach. We have defined a business architecture framework that not only allows us to specify our requirements from an SOA perspective using a consistent and standard model but also helps us to plan and manage our portfolio on an ongoing basis. Not coincidentally, the release schedule for our SOA initiatives will map directly to that SOA portfolio plan. In fact, a planned release date for each component in Exhibit 8.2 could be listed next to each component as shown in Exhibit 8.3.

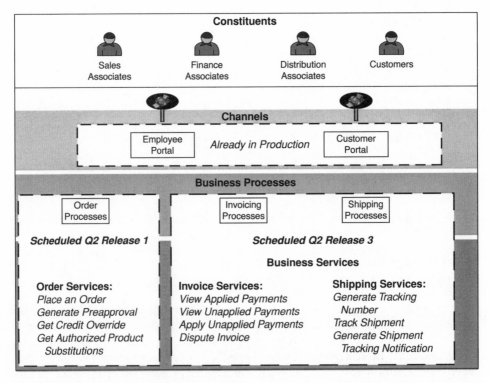

EXHIBIT 8.3   SOA Initiative with Release Overlay

If these SOA components were reflected on a document that showed them by the month or quarter they were planned to be completed and placed into production, along with all the other component delivery dates of all the other approved initiatives, the resulting document would be the enterprise SOA portfolio plan, and these buckets of delivered functionality into production would be the releases.

Enterprise SOA Portfolio Plan Impact and Opportunity Assessment Process

When this enterprise SOA portfolio plan document containing all the delivery dates of all the SOA components of all the SOA initiatives is completed, it provides us with a new tool that quickly shows:

- What is being delivered to each constituent and when.
- If new channels are being built and when.
- Which services are being deployed over each channel and when.
- How many different channels and/or constituents will be using the same business processes or the same business services and when.

In other words, the document gives us visibility into business decisions and impacts to constituents that we never considered before. We can now look at what we are planning to deliver going forward and assess its impact in terms of:

- *The consuming constituent.* For example, is it better to deliver all the new functionality to the customer at once or over, perhaps, three months because of complex training issues?
- *Deployment costs.* For example, if the same business process or business service is being deployed over a different channel or to a different constituent over two consecutive months, can we reduce testing, training, and other deployment costs by scheduling them to be released together in the same month?
- *Additional opportunities.* There may exist additional opportunities for leveraging and reuse with the potential for:
  - Increasing the business functionality being delivered. For example, can other business services already in existence be incorporated into this business process to make it more flexible, comprehensive, or accurate?
  - Expanding the audience for that functionality with no or minimal incremental cost and time. For example, if the channel exists for both customers and sales reps, what would it take to deliver a new functionality being delivered to the sales force to the customer as well?

This analysis is called the enterprise SOA portfolio plan impact and opportunity assessment process.

The enterprise SOA Portfolio Plan Governance Committee conducts this assessment process at a macro and conceptual level. The results of this analysis and the subsequent changes to delivery dates and scope are made to the plan, creating a new official enterprise SOA portfolio plan. In some cases, these changes will need to be approved by the SOA Business Domain Governance Committee. If so, the enterprise SOA portfolio plan becomes official after it is reviewed, approved, and funded by this committee.

Any changes that were made to the dates and/or scope of the deliverables as a result of this analysis and process need to be reflected back into the individual business SOA initiatives that were affected. This is an example of the iterative process that will occur to manage the enterprise SOA portfolio plan on an ongoing basis. The business and solutions architects also conduct this process when documenting the original SOA initiative proposal and developing the scope estimates for those initiatives.

Each submitted SOA initiative must initially supply estimates for costs and a projected delivery time frame. These estimates, produced by the business and solutions architects, are based on the:

- Requested business delivery date.
- Availability of SOA components that can be leveraged.
- Complexity and estimated effort to build new components.
- Prerequisites and dependencies associated with other SOA components being built that are needed by this initiative.

All of this information is produced when the initiative is first documented and submitted for approval. These initial estimates will contain assumptions.

Once the estimates of cost and delivery time are determined, the enterprise SOA portfolio plan impact and opportunity assessment process just described can occur. This time, however, it occurs at a micro, individual project level. This assessment is based more on the logical and physical architecture considerations rather than the conceptual considerations used at the macro level. This assessment may result in changes to dates or costs of the initiative if opportunities were found in other scheduled initiatives for sharing or combining capabilities.

Once the initiative is analyzed against the plan, many of the assumptions made in that initiative may change. Some capabilities or components may have been identified in several initiatives, as each was unaware of the existence of the other initiatives. Some initiatives may request the same or similar business services but for different constituents. This assessment process helps to identify these conditions and take advantage of them.

Managing the Impact on Architecture Resources

Many initiatives will be submitted by the business each year—many more than the budget will support. The bulk of these initiatives traditionally are submitted annually during the next year's budgeting process. This also means that many initiatives will not be approved. The architects and the governance bodies cannot afford to provide the same amount of analysis, detail, and due diligence for every submitted initiative. In the early stages of rolling out the enterprise SOA portfolio plan process, this annual bombardment will occur. As we move to higher layers of maturity in the process, it will disappear. It will disappear because the identification and compilation of each business unit's initiatives is part of an ongoing process between the business unit and its business architects. The annual budget process will become a prioritization exercise, not a documentation exercise. See the business architecture roles and responsibilities defined in Chapter 11 for more information on the initiative assessment process.

In the meantime, there has to be some process for preliminary prioritization and ranking of the initiatives before they are evaluated and estimated to minimize the number that are carried through the full detailed assessment. This is required because the current legacy process in most companies makes this assessment process an annual, one-time event rather than an ongoing business process.

Thus the need to perform a large annual assessment will be required until the cultural and process transformation occurs. This transformation will occur when the details and artifacts associated with the enterprise SOA portfolio plan become *the* tool for the business to define, structure, and submit its new initiatives. At this point, each submitted initiative is reflected in the context of the business architecture framework with full understanding and knowledge of how it fits into the plan. The business's understanding of available and planned business services, business processes, and infrastructure components, such as channels, is fully matured and well understood. In other words, IT and the business are on the same page and speak the same language. The business is realizing the value proposition that was promised. When you have reached this point, the transformation will be complete. The paradigm shift will have occurred. You will have achieved implementing SOA as an architecture.

Five Levels of SOA Governance

Exhibit 8.4 depicts the SOA governance bodies and their relationships to one another. The highest and most strategic governance body is the SOA Business Domain Governance Committee. The next is the Portfolio Governance Committee, followed by Technology Governance, Project Governance, and SLA Governance. All of these bodies are described in detail in this chapter. For now it is important to understand two aspects represented by Exhibit 8.4.

First, recognize that each governance committee encapsulates the governance bodies below it and provides higher-level guidance and direction to those lower layers. The initiatives within the portfolio and how they are managed and prioritized are directly dictated by the higher-level strategic plans of the business domains. The implementation of the technologies and infrastructure investments and the leveraging of those investments through architecture compliance are directly driven by

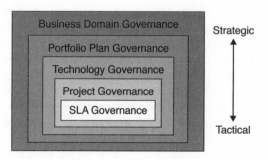

EXHIBIT 8.4 Five Levels of SOA Governance

what is contained in the enterprise SOA portfolio plan. The technology platforms, development tools, and development methodologies (including design specifications, testing methods, and deployment models of each release) are dictated by the Technology Governance team. The synchronization of all the SOA projects and their readiness for deployment into production is managed by the Project Governance team. Finally, the production-readiness criteria specified in the functional and non-functional requirements of the release, along with the defined SLAs that must be met and maintained by operations once the process is placed into production, are managed by the SLA Governance team.

Second, as you move from the highest (Business Domain) governance level to the lowest (SLA) governance level, the activities and decisions move from a more strategic focus to a more tactical focus. The frequency at which the committees meet increases as you move from a strategic to a tactical focus. The SOA Business Domain Governance Committee may meet as rarely as twice a year. The Project and SLA Governance teams may meet daily if necessary.

That is not to say that there are no tactical activities at the highest layer or strategic activities at the lowest layer. There will be. Each governance layer requires strategic and tactical activities to function and operate. In general, the higher domains are concerned more with the strategic aspects of those investments; for example, questioning how much we should spend and on what. The lower layers, however, are more concerned with the tactical aspects of those investments; for example, reporting what was spent and what the company got for that spend.

SOA Business Domain Governance Committee

Business executives from all the business units are the representatives on the SOA Business Domain Governance Committee. The committee is chaired by the president or chief executive officer (CEO). The executives' responsibilities while participating in this committee are to:

- Set the strategic direction and objectives for the enterprise SOA Portfolio Plan Governance Committee.
- Approve the IT budget for the enterprise SOA Portfolio Plan Governance Committee.
- Resolve any issues that cannot be resolved at the enterprise SOA Portfolio Plan Governance Committee level.

The SOA Business Domain Governance Committee is chaired by the CEO or president of the company but should be facilitated by the chief information officer (CIO). This means the office of the CIO is responsible for setting up the meetings, creating the agenda, documenting the meetings, communicating the results, and making sure that all follow-up tasks, activities, and deliverables are completed. Other participants on the team (with the exception of board-level participants) should be the same participants responsible for carrying out the company's strategic business plan. This is usually the president's direct reports represented by the executive vice presidents (EVPs) and senior vice presidents (SVPs) of the company. It should not, however, be extended to include the EVPs' or SVPs' direct reports. This could quickly create too large a committee that will collapse under its own weight or, even more dangerous, an imbalance of power and partiality by larger organizational units. While it is true that larger organizations should get a bigger piece of the pie, this does not always happen. A better way to look at the situation under this new model is to view larger units as having more responsibilities and bigger commitments to achieve the business strategy. Therefore, they will have bigger commitments to the enterprise SOA portfolio plan as well.

Multi-subsidiary companies or conglomerates may manage their IT budgets globally at the corporate level or independently within each subsidiary or company. If the subsidiaries or companies share common customers, partners, or vendors and see strategic value in presenting one face to these constituents, the best way is to adopt the SOA strategy defined in this book and manage IT investments through a central corporate process. If these constituent relationships do not exist or if there is no strategic value to creating them, then each entity can maintain and manage initiatives separately. The architects within each entity, however, should be linked and managed holistically. Refer to Chapter 13 for more information on this subject.

The chief technology officer (CTO) and/or chief architect should be members of this governance committee as well. The level of their involvement will depend on the IT savvy of the executives on the committee. Since the CTO and/or chief architect will be responsible for facilitating the next two lower governance committees (Portfolio Plan Governance and Technology Governance), they will be aware of all activities of these committees if any questions or issues arise. Their presence may help facilitate and expedite the SOA Business Domain Governance meetings because they can answer any questions or issues raised by those committees.

The enterprise SOA Portfolio Plan Governance Committee needs to make decisions on which initiatives to approve based on the corporate strategy and the business unit plans developed to support it. The committee needs to determine the priority of these initiatives using the same strategies and plans. The enterprise SOA Portfolio Governance Committee also needs funding to accomplish the initiatives in the enterprise SOA portfolio plan. Finally, it needs authority to make final and absolute decisions when lower governance committees are stalemated. The SOA Business Domain Governance Committee provides all the direction, funding, and authority to the enterprise SOA Portfolio Plan Governance Committee to accomplish these activities.

SETTING THE STRATEGIC DIRECTION AND OBJECTIVES FOR THE ENTERPRISE SOA PORTFOLIO PLAN Executives do get involved in the IT process today. In the traditional non-SOA approach, this involvement is usually associated with the annual budgeting process. In most cases, each executive has been supplied with a list of initiatives compiled within his or her business unit that are seeking funding. These lists can be compiled in many ways, and there are many approaches to how they are funded, including multiyear funding.

Whatever the process, the fundamental underlying premise is that each project is structured from a bottom-up systems perspective and almost always owned and controlled within the submitting business unit domain. However, once prioritization is made or the final cut is achieved, most of the initiatives are totally (technically) independent of the others. Projects that are approved are fully contained with funding sufficient to deliver the entire system. There are exceptions, but, for the most part, this is how they are structured: as monolithic stovepipe solutions (i.e., representations of the traditional way of building systems). Some may be labeled SOA projects or specify the use of some SOA-like design components. However, if these projects have not been mapped to an enterprise SOA and do not specifically identify which parts of the funded initiative are leveraging existing SOA components or which parts are investments mapped to future leveraging, then these projects have minimal incremental value beyond a traditional design approach. For the most part, the level of detail needed to make these determinations is usually nonexistent.

Typically, the project identifies the need for a system or enhancements to systems to provide some business capabilities that the organization believes will help it achieve goals specified in the (formal or informal) business plan. These goals can be as simple as references to the requested capabilities to help achieve the corporate strategy statements or specific measurable improvements specified in the strategic business plan.

What is missing in this process is a holistic view to determine if there is any duplication of effort or overlapping capabilities within the approved projects. What is also missing is a traceable and measurable linkage to the corporate strategy and the corporation's strategic business plans. The initiative may reference the plans and strategy. It may associate some measure to those references, but in reality, the structure of a traditional IT project is not designed for, nor does it lend itself to, a clear, understandable, and measurable link to the strategies and plans. Traditional IT projects are structured as silo projects from the bottom-up, technical system perspective. Consequently, they are viewed and assessed that way. Corporate strategies and business unit plans are usually structured from an enterprise or divisional top-down perspective and are viewed and assessed from that perspective. The two opposite perspectives make it difficult to align one with the other.

Our goal is to get the top-level business executives out of this operational and tactical role. Instead of putting the executives into a position where they are reacting to a plethora of projects with no real traceable tie to the corporate strategy, we want to position them to be proactively setting the vision and strategy and providing top-down criteria and metrics that each initiative must trace to. Instead of asking the executives to be the judge and jury that make the tough decisions that the unit leaders are unable to make, we are asking them to be the definers of the criteria for those unit leaders to use. Hence, these decisions are pushed back down to the unit leaders. The SOA~EAF provides the traceable mechanism for mapping the initiative to the business plans and corporate strategy.

The executives need to document their strategic direction over the next three to five years and communicate their ideas and thoughts on how each business unit plans to achieve that strategy. If the business strategy is to expand their market, for example, by going global or entering into new markets by selling a complementary product, the executives need to communicate those intentions. They need to communicate if these expansions will be through internal growth, acquisition, or both. They need to give their views on how they will support these expansions (i.e., how sales will support them, how distribution will support them, etc.).

What I have just described should sound familiar. It should be a description of your current strategic planning process. This process, however, has to be carried to another level. It needs to add the business architecture vision that is needed to support the strategy and the business plan. Each business unit leader, armed with business plan, attends the Business Domain Governance strategic planning sessions for this purpose. Each will discuss the business plan that he or she has developed to support the corporate strategy in terms of:

- Internal and external constituents involved in the plans.
- How he or she believes those constituents will need to interact with the business to implement the plan.
- The existing or new capabilities required to support those interactions.

These are high-level vision statements rather than specific details. There may be specific references to channel technologies, but there are few or no references to legacy systems. The capabilities are described as high-level conceptual business processes and business functions, not in reference to detailed business requirements or technical implementations.

The business architect supporting each business unit leader will have worked with the unit leader's staff to extract this information from the business plan and compile it into a business architecture representation. The leader has reviewed and approved this documentation and now meets with the rest of his or her peers to discuss all the plans from each unit together. The process involves reaching consensus and agreement as to which parts of the models stay and which parts go. It also involves prioritizing and/or ranking the importance of the capabilities described in the model and the ranking order of each delivery channel that will deliver those capabilities for each constituent.

This output is plugged into the Business Unit Plans Cross-Reference column of the SOA~EAF. The documentation within each SOA initiative can now be linked directly to the entries in this column on the framework. The more the initiative lines up to these entries and the higher priority of those linkages, the higher the probability that the initiative will be approved. Since this strategic and business plan data provided by the executives is documented, the decisions around funding and priority can be made more readily at the portfolio planning level.

SOA BUSINESS DOMAIN APPROVAL OF THE ANNUAL PORTFOLIO PLAN The next step in the process is to submit all the initiatives that have not yet been approved to the SOA Portfolio Plan Governance Committee so its members can merge them with the prior year's approved initiative already in the portfolio plan. This newly updated enterprise SOA portfolio plan containing all initiatives being recommended for the next year is next presented to the SOA Business Domain Governance Committee for approval and funding. The process of creating the updated portfolio plan is explained in the section titled "Enterprise SOA Portfolio Governance Committee Alignment from a Business Service Delivery Model Perspective" later in this chapter.

In the context of the prior year's submitted portfolio plan, the SOA Business Domain Governance Committee would be presented with a new enterprise SOA portfolio plan recommendation that has:

- All the initiatives that were completed removed from the plan.
- All the remaining initiatives that were on last year's plan, whether they have been started or not, reflected in the year 1 and year 2 sections of the plan.

- The newly recommended initiatives that have not been approved inserted into one of the three years on the plan.

This new plan also includes supporting documentation that shows initiatives that:

- Were supposed to be completed in the current year but are now pushed to next year.
- Had their release delivery schedule altered to accommodate the priorities and commitments of new initiatives.
- Were dropped from the plan because of a change in strategy or a lower prioritization.

The SOA Business Domain Governance Committee may question:

- The reasonableness or rationality of the initiatives and their timing for delivery based on their alignment with the corporate strategy and business unit plans.
- Whether certain initiatives can be phased in faster or slower by making larger, smaller, or more instances of the releases containing the initiatives' capabilities.
- The estimated cost of the initiatives or identify which ones are leveraging and reusing the most resources versus those that have a high percentage of new components.

Ultimately a budget will be set to cover the initiatives that will be started or completed in the upcoming year. Some of the initiatives so scheduled may be shifted into the subsequent year if a funding amount less than the total of the year 1 initiatives is established.

There will be instances during the year when new initiatives may need to be added to the enterprise SOA portfolio plan. These can be because of legal or regulatory requirements or a change in strategy or any other type of commitment. In these instances, the enterprise SOA Portfolio Plan Governance Committee will attempt to accommodate the timing and cost of these changes within the plan by reprioritizing the approved initiatives. If the committee cannot do so at the portfolio plan level, a special meeting of the SOA Business Domain Governance Committee will be called. In this meeting, the executives can either make their own reprioritization decision of the approved initiatives in the plan or approve a budget override to cover the initiative.

ONGOING EXECUTIVE OVERSIGHT   The Program Management Office (PMO) provides status to the enterprise SOA Portfolio Plan Governance Committee on an ongoing basis to inform members of the plan's progress. This includes informing them of any budget overruns or delivery delays in the initiatives under way. The PMO also informs committee members of the planned activities for the upcoming quarter. An executive-level summary of this information is provided to SOA Business Domain Governance Committee executives on a periodic basis. The enterprise SOA Portfolio Plan Governance Committee or any of its members may be asked by one or more of the SOA Business Domain Governance Committee executives to meet and discuss this information at their discretion.

SOA BUSINESS DOMAIN GOVERNANCE COMMITTEE SUMMARY   Under the executive governance model just described, the executives are not reviewing and funding specific projects submitted by individual business units. They are reviewing and approving a plan for future capabilities to be delivered over specified periods. Each future period in the plan, depending on the desire of the business domain (monthly, quarterly, or even weekly), reflects the delivery of one or more sets of business capabilities communicated from a top-down perspective. Instead of each deliverable being a project delivering a specific system within a specific business unit, each deliverable is a set of business capabilities being delivered to a set of (consuming) constituents through releases. Many business domains and the associated systems within those domains may be involved in any one of these deliverables.

An enterprise SOA portfolio plan for a health insurance company, for example, may depict business capabilities being delivered to each of its external and internal constituents for each quarter of the plan. With this model, it is readily understood what capabilities are being delivered to members by quarter, to providers by quarter, and so forth. This is a totally different perspective from the old model, which showed which projects owned by the sales department were being delivered by quarter, which by claims operations were being delivered by quarter, and so on.

The old model was a bottom-up approach focused on the systems owned by the service providers. The new model is a top-down approach focused on the business capabilities needed by service consumers. Under the old model, delivery of the project was managed based on the interests of the business unit providing the service without regard to how many different constituents were impacted, when they would be impacted, and what impact other projects might have on those same constituents.

This new model provides executive management with a more strategic view of the enterprise SOA portfolio plan because it is a top-down approach. It provides a view of the plan that is much more aligned to the business plan. For example, if the business strategy is looking to enter into a new line of business (LOB) next year, it is much easier to understand and communicate when the capability will exist with a portfolio plan that shows when functionality needed to support the new LOB comes online for customers, vendors, internal sales, distribution, and others than with one that shows when the order system modifications are completed, when the customer service modifications are completed, and so forth. Hence, the executive-level SOA Business Domain Governance Committee is really focused on setting up and monitoring how IT is supporting the business strategy from a top-down perspective.

The SOA Business Domain Governance Committee should convene at least twice a year to review and add input to the enterprise SOA portfolio plan; the committee will convene once when the annual budget is being approved and midyear from that point. I use the word "convene" to reflect the fact that more than one meeting may be involved when the committee meets, especially during the annual budget process. The SOA Business Domain Governance Committee should also be amenable to convene on an emergency basis to deal with major strategic changes or other business conditions that may occur at any time. If, in the last example, the decision to enter a new LOB was made during the year after the annual plans and budgets were established, the enterprise SOA Portfolio Governance Committee will request a special meeting of the SOA Business Domain Governance team to review and approve the new enterprise SOA portfolio plan that reflects:

- The initiatives to support the new LOB.
- Any priority modifications to SOA components of the prior plan that need to occur to support the new initiatives.

The plan may also reflect initiatives that are recommended to be deferred to supply funding and other resources for the new initiatives being added. Alternatively, the plan may reflect requests for additional funding or budget overrides to pay for the new initiatives.

As a final note, the SOA Business Domain Governance Committee should be the body that approves any decisions to create new channels. As stated in Chapter 4, channels are expensive to implement. Also, any new channel within a constituency must be ready to fully support all the capabilities and services provided by the other channels used by that constituency, if required. This may incrementally add more cost as well.

Channels are strategic, not tactical, decisions. The process should never allow strategic decisions to be made at a project level or any tactical level, for that matter. The need for a new channel should be clearly documented in the Corporate Goal/Strategy Cross-Reference column of the SOA~EAF and placed there as a result of the strategic direction set by the SOA Business Domain Governance Committee. The business units that have plans to use this new channel should already be documented in the Business Unit Plans Cross-Reference column of the framework. Any initiative submitted by any business unit that has a requirement to build a new channel that cannot be cross-referenced to these two columns should be immediately flagged and resolved. In most cases, however, the business and solutions architects would have caught this problem and resolved it before it reaches any business governance committee.

Enterprise SOA Portfolio Plan Governance Committee

The enterprise SOA Portfolio Plan Governance Committee is the hub of the SOA governance process. This committee is responsible for approving and managing all the initiatives in the enterprise SOA portfolio plan. It is also responsible for governing when those initiatives start and when they need to be completed. The responsibilities of this committee include:

1. Developing the proposed enterprise SOA portfolio plan each year and submitting the proposal to the SOA Business Domain Governance Committee for review and approval.
2. Structuring and publishing the approved enterprise SOA portfolio plan.
3. Releasing funds to the SOA projects under the approved initiatives.
4. Reviewing and approving the results of any enterprise SOA portfolio plan impact and opportunity assessments conducted.
5. Monitoring progress and schedules of the approved initiatives to ensure that all deliverables are delivered on time and within budget.
6. Communicating any changes or adjustments to the plan during the year as new business conditions arise.

7. Packaging and presenting to the SOA Business Domain Governance Committee any enterprise SOA portfolio plan changes or adjustments identified in responsibilities 1 through 6 that cannot be resolved at the enterprise SOA Portfolio Plan Governance level.

8. Establishing and governing the corporate strategy and business unit plan linkages used to justify, rank, and prioritize the initiatives in the plan.

The enterprise SOA Portfolio Plan Governance Committee should be comprised of senior management directly below the business unit executives. It should also include the IT leaders from all the IT organizations, such as operations, development, project/program management, and so on. The committee should, if possible, also have representation for all the major external constituents who will be using the systems developed in the enterprise SOA portfolio plan. This can be accomplished most efficiently by having internal ombudsmen who represent these constituencies and can conduct periodic information and feedback sessions with representatives of these communities on an ongoing basis. If your strategy is to expose services to customers, vendors, or partners over one or more channels, then you need to make sure that they are involved. You need to make sure that they are aware of what you are doing, how it will impact them directly, and that they are represented and have input into the process.

If your company has any major business or IT partnerships that play a critical role in the delivery of services, these should be represented on the enterprise SOA Portfolio Plan Governance Committee as well. A business partner example would be an outsource partner that provides all your customer service support for customers using the telephone channel and integrates with your business applications to provide those services. This is an example of a major channel intermediary partner that has to support and adopt the SOA enterprise architecture strategy you are implementing as much, if not more, than the internal business units have to.

An IT partner example would be an outsource partner that contractually develops all the business applications for your company. The availability of its resources and its commitment to the planned delivery schedules of the releases in the enterprise SOA portfolio plan is critical for managing the plan.

The highest-level associate you interact with within these partner companies should be the participant on the enterprise SOA Portfolio Plan Governance Committee. This is usually the business partner executive or account executive, whoever is on-site the most.

Note

If you have outsourced all or a major portion of your IT development shop, you need to treat these vendors as partners, and you need to manage and govern them no differently than if they were an internal development shop. They need to take all their development direction from your SOA enterprise architecture team and be accountable to the team for what they deliver.

Also, do not assume that you can outsource your architecture practice and the SOA implementation and management strategy defined in this book. I firmly believe that doing so is a recipe for disaster. Although the outside company is a partner, it is still a different company with its own set of goals and objectives that are very different from yours. Another major risk of this approach is that, even though the company is a partner, many within your business will still perceive it to be a vendor and may try to influence directions and decisions as the "customer." This can and will happen at every level of management. There is no bigger barrier to effecting a cultural paradigm shift then to give those being affected real or perceived power and influence over those that are trying to make the cultural change.

The other disadvantage of this approach is that you have no direct control and influence over the careers of the partner's associates and no ability to apply retention policies to them. Architects represent a significant amount of intellectual capital that is very expensive and time consuming to replace. If they were internal associates, you would have many more options at your disposal to retain the good ones.

As I stated earlier, the good news is that your external constituents are interacting more and more with your systems directly (without internal employee involvement). The bad news is that, if you do not ask them how these changes impact them or how you could improve these interactions to reduce the impact or improve their work flow, you run the risk of negatively impacting the adoption rate and continued use of the services.

It is a well-documented fact that, if customers find their first dealings with a company difficult and frustrating, there is a very high probability that the company will lose them as customers for life. Unless you have the luxury of providing a product or service that nobody else offers, which I doubt, customers will always have a more pleasant alternative to choose from.

Companies have spent significant money training all associates who interact with customers to be kind, courteous, and positive and to always strive to make customers' experience pleasurable. Although most companies understand this, many have exposed their customers to multiple systems with distinct and sometimes radical differences that provide a very complex, disjointed, and confusing set of capabilities that are frustrating and difficult to understand.

The message here is that if you invest heavily in one channel to ensure your customers have the best experience possible and totally ignore providing them the same experience on other channels they use or will use, you might as well not bother at all. One bad experience can easily destroy the memory of numerous pleasurable experiences.

ALIGNING THE RESOURCES THAT PARTICIPATE ON THE ENTERPRISE SOA PORTFOLIO GOVERNANCE COMMITTEE TO SUPPORT A SERVICE MODEL   The participants of the enterprise SOA Portfolio Plan Governance Committee should be members of one of the two groups:

1. Those who represent or support the needs and requirements of the *consumers* of the services

2. Those who represent or support the needs and requirements of the *providers* of the services

HORIZONTAL *CONSUMER*-CENTRIC GOVERNANCE BODY In terms of the SOA~EAF architecture framework, the service consumer representatives are focused on the top four layers:

1. Constituent Domain
2. Channel Domain
3. Business Process Domain
4. Business Service Domain

This group is responsible for governing compliance with the horizontal consumer-centric aspects of the corporate strategy and business unit plans (i.e., what capabilities are delivered to [consuming] constituents over time and how are they delivered). Their authority gives them exclusive governance of the top three layers (constituent, channel, and business process) and shared governance of the Business Service Domain layer with service provider representatives.

The horizontal consumer-centric governance body makes sure that:

- All the capabilities are delivered to the constituents when required, in the priority they established.
- These capabilities are developed to support all the channels identified in the corporate strategy and the business unit plans.
- They are delivered in a way that is the least disruptive to the constituents.
- They provide improvements to the constituents' work flow and efficiencies, or at least no impact to their work flow and efficiency.
- Capabilities are delivered through a highly pleasurable user experience.

VERTICAL *PROVIDER*-CENTRIC GOVERNANCE BODY The service provider representatives, in addition to their shared governance of the Business Service Domain layer, have exclusive governance over the remaining lower layers. These layers are:

1. Integration Service Domain
2. Legacy Application Domain
3. Physical Platform Domain

This group is responsible for governing compliance with the vertical provider-centric aspects of the corporate strategy and business unit plans. They govern what the services they provide do and how they do it (i.e., how the services are secured to ensure they are used only by those authorized to use them and controlled to ensure they are accurate, recorded properly, and can be traced and audited if required).

The vertical provider-centric governance body makes sure that:

- The maximum amount of efficiency and reuse of services is achieved.
- Non-SOA legacy capabilities are isolated, and standard formats and semantic models are adopted and used.

- All aspects of security, reliability, accuracy, and audit trail of the underlying business operations are met and enforced.

SHARED GOVERNANCE AND SPLIT GOVERNANCE DISTINCTIONS   The Business Service Domain is the layer that bridges the service provider and the service consumer. It is the layer that must provide both the flexibility and adaptability required by the consumers and all the controls and validations required by the service providers. Both parties have a vested interest in this layer.

If you think about it, do the service providers really have to be concerned with who consumes the service and what channels they use to consume it? As long as all the authentication, authorization, validation, and delivery protection (i.e., secured channel, Secure Sockets Layer [SSL] encrypted payload, etc.) requirements specified by the service provider are enforced by all the layers of the architecture, it should not matter to them.

Similarly, does it really matter to the service *consumers* that the rates provided by the "Get Rates" business service are processed through IBM WebSphere MQ messages linked to three back-end legacy rating applications and the data from the three applications is mapped and normalized to an insurance industry standard semantic model for rating? As long as the rates are provided accurately within the specified user response time window, how it is done should not matter.

What is interesting is that these two paragraphs look very similar to paragraphs that define a Web service. How the Web service performs its embedded functionality is completely hidden from the consumer. Similarly, the Web service has no idea of the consumer's reason for using the service, nor does it know what the consumer will do next once he or she receives the reply from the service. The Web service only knows that the consumer correctly invoked the service and passed the authorization challenges required and enforced by the service before processing the request.

It is not coincidental that we are transforming our entire corporate culture, including the culture of governance, to think and act this same way. We are creating a corporate culture that thinks in terms of services and defines how they think about them in terms of those who use them and those who provide them. In other words, we are transforming the company culture to a corporate SOA culture.

ENTERPRISE SOA PORTFOLIO PLAN GOVERNANCE COMMITTEE ALIGNMENT FROM A BUSINESS SERVICE DELIVERY MODEL PERSPECTIVE   Exhibit 8.5 shows an example of how an SOA portfolio plan governance strategy is split between service consumers and service providers for the health insurance industry.

Remember you are trying to transform a culturally entrenched legacy process of governance based in traditional stovepipe application design to a process that achieves the benefits of SOA.

What do I mean by a horizontal and vertical governance process? Let me start by putting forth the statement of one of the most key and critical objectives of the SOA Portfolio Plan Governance Committee:

To never let how we process *business dictate how we* conduct *business.*

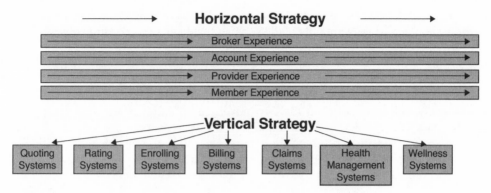

EXHIBIT 8.5   Health Insurer Example of Horizontal and Vertical SOA Strategy

This key objective can be further clarified with this governance scope statement:

How we process *business is the governance responsibility of the* service provider domain. *How we* conduct *business is the governance responsibility of the* service consumer domain.

Thus, the vertical governance body is the group comprised of business unit leaders responsible for the underlying systems that provide the transactional and informational services. The horizontal group is one comprised of business leaders who consume the services or represent the (external) consumers of the services.

The vertical (service provider) governance is focused on building services that accurately and efficiently maintain the logical-to-physical relationship between each constructed service and the physical legacy applications and data stores supporting the service. In other words, its responsibility is to ensure that every service developed is accurately and efficiently tied to the underlying systems of record with full audit and compliance tractability. This governance body understands how a transaction is *processed* and guarantees the accuracy and accountability of those transactions. It has the final decision authority to resolve any conflicts relating to authorization, validation, standardization, and repudiation as well as service source system of record and transaction retention.

This body also manages the legacy systems migration and sunsetting activities. As more components are built providing services based on ubiquitous semantic capabilities, the use of old redundant capabilities in the underlying stovepipe legacy systems can be shut off, allowing the entire system to be eventually retired. This governance body can and should be used as a strong advocate for transitioning these point-to-point legacy integration solutions into shared and standardized SOA integration solutions. Chapter 12 provides more information on the process of transforming legacy systems to support SOA.

The *horizontal* constituent-centric governance body does not have direct governance over the underlying physical systems that process the business but does have an influence on how the SOA business services logically perform those services. Since this governance body represents the users of the services, they should be the ones to validate that the service provides what they need and how they need it.

Therefore, this body governs these aspects and has the final decision authority to resolve conflicts. It is aware only of the services that have been constructed exposing its specific business capabilities, not how the service accomplishes those capabilities. This body is, however, responsible for defining the roadmap for when those services need to be delivered, whom they will be delivered to (consumers), and how they will be delivered (channels).

Finally, the glue between the two governance bodies is the SOA enterprise architecture team. The role of this team is to ensure that the needs of both service providers and service consumers are understood and met. It also is responsible for validating that all nonfunctional requirements, such as security and SLAs, are met.

This model provides a way to organizationally and culturally retool the company away from a traditional system delivery mentality toward a service provider and service consumer mentality. It also promotes the development of services that are enterprise oriented (i.e., services designed on semantic data models, channel agnostic and compliant with enterprise security and service-level policies).

The SOA enterprise architecture team facilitates both of these governance subcommittees and synchronizes their efforts. It also manages the process for resolving conflicts between the subcommittees.

The *horizontal* governance subgroup also drives the contents of the enterprise SOA technology roadmap for the acquisition of technologies and platforms associated with channels, business processes, and business services. The *vertical* governance subgroup drives the contents of the enterprise SOA technology roadmap for the acquisition of technologies and platforms associated with business services and integration services and for the replacement and/or modernization of legacy applications.

It is important to recognize that business unit leaders (and their subordinates) will find it difficult to retool their thinking and beliefs along these lines. Many will believe that they should continue to own both the consumer and provider responsibilities, especially when most of the legacy systems and the employees who use them in support of the constituents are within their business unit's domain. These business leaders need to understand that even though their employees are the biggest users of the applications they "own," in most cases, these employees are using these systems as intermediaries between another (internal or external) constituent and their business unit. They are using the systems to support customers and vendors that are not allowed to access them or choose not to use other channels that make the services available to them. In this example, even though employees are the system users, the ultimate consumer of the services within those applications is the customer or vendor.

These employees tend to think of the capabilities of the application in the context of how *they* use the system and how it improves or restricts *their* work flow and efficiencies. They do not necessarily think of how the *constituents* would use those applications and how they would improve or restrict the constituents' work flow and efficiencies. This view is one of the biggest reasons there tends to be an inside-looking-out approach rather than an outside-looking-in approach.

Over time, the value of splitting service consumers from service providers will become more and more evident to committee members. What was traditionally a group of business leaders each attempting to own and justify a narrow vertical slice of the IT systems is now two groups of leaders focusing their best skills and leadership qualities at an enterprise level on the domains where they have the most strength and knowledge.

Each had to give up something, but each also got something in return. The service consumers gave up their perceived right to define how the back-end systems supplying services are constructed and operate. In return, they are no longer at the mercy of those applications and their owners to define how and when those services are consumed. The service providers gave up their perceived right to own the user interface and control who used it, how they used it, and when they used it. In return, they gained a much tighter control over the accuracy, consistency, and tractability of the data and business rules they have custodial responsibilities for.

The enterprise SOA Portfolio Plan Governance Committee should meet at least twice a month. It should meet more often when the business begins to use more of the competitive advantages that the new process offers and the understanding and comfort level with the process increases. Ultimately, these meetings will revolve less around managing the enterprise SOA portfolio plan and more around maximizing the strategic business value of the plan. This will include the strategic management of future portfolio releases in terms of any competitive advantages identified by analyzing the plan. In the early stages of rolling out this SOA enterprise architecture strategy, these meetings should also be used by the SOA enterprise architecture team to work with the business to:

- Continue the education of the business leaders about the strategy being implemented and the progress on that strategy.
- Help them understand how they can leverage what is being implemented to achieve a more strategic and competitive advantage with their IT investments.

The enterprise SOA Portfolio Plan Governance Committee should be chaired by the CIO and CTO, if both exist, along with the chief operating officer (COO) of the company. If a COO does not exist, the chief financial officer should be the co-chair. The CIO/CTO will also be responsible for facilitating the process that requires their organizations to set up the meetings, create the agendas, document the meetings, communicate the results, and make sure that all follow-up tasks, activities, and deliverables are completed.

ACTIVITIES PERFORMED BY THE ENTERPRISE SOA PORTFOLIO PLAN GOVERNANCE COMMITTEE
As stated at the beginning of this section, the enterprise SOA Portfolio Plan Governance Committee is responsible for:

- Developing the proposed enterprise SOA portfolio plan each year and submitting the proposal to the SOA Business Domain Governance Committee for review and approval.
- Structuring and publishing the approved SOA portfolio plan.
- Releasing funds to the SOA projects under the approved initiatives.
- Reviewing and approving the results of any enterprise SOA portfolio impact and opportunity assessments conducted.
- Monitoring progress and schedules of the plan initiatives, ensuring that initiative deliverables are delivered on time and within budget.

- Communicating any changes or adjustments to the plan during the year as new business conditions arise.
- Packaging and presenting to the SOA Business Domain Governance Committee any enterprise SOA portfolio plan changes or adjustments identified in the bullet points above that cannot be resolved at the portfolio plan governance level.
- Establishing and governing the corporate strategy and business unit plan linkages used to justify, rank, and prioritize the initiatives in the plan.

Each of these is described in the next subsections.

Annual Portfolio Planning Process   The enterprise SOA Portfolio Plan Governance Committee reviews and approves initiatives during the annual enterprise SOA portfolio plan reset and funding approval process and whenever new initiatives need to be evaluated due to changing conditions (i.e., strategic, legal, financial, etc.). The purpose of the annual reset process is to reconfigure and adjust the year-over-year SOA initiatives within the enterprise SOA portfolio plan and present the updated version with the recommended changes to the SOA Business Domain Governance Committee for review and approval. Once approved by the SOA Business Domain Governance Committee, the output deliverable of this process is the new N year enterprise SOA portfolio plan, which includes the budget approval to cover the cost of implementing everything listed in year 1 of the new plan.

Each business unit is responsible for providing its annual list of proposed SOA initiatives to the enterprise SOA Portfolio Plan Governance Committee for review and inclusion into the next year's plan. The business and solutions architects have worked with the business unit *throughout the year* to create the new SOA initiatives that the business wants considered for the next year. Refer to the business architecture and solutions architect roles and responsibilities sections in Chapter 11 for more information on producing these documents.

The list of submitted initiatives may not represent all the initiatives that have been created. You may decide to direct each business unit to submit a limited number of initiatives based on criteria established by the enterprise SOA Portfolio Plan Governance Committee. These criteria could be based on a total dollar amount, a quantity, or one or more corporate strategy statements from the Corporate Strategy Cross-Reference column of the SOA~EAF. The enterprise SOA Portfolio Plan Governance Committee may also allow the business units to submit SOA initiatives with sponsorships across multiple business units. Alternatively, they could be directed to submit initiatives that meet or exceed a certain baseline of ranking based on their alignment with all corporate strategies. There are many ways to approach the criteria for submitting initiatives, and often some leeway is allowed in those approaches. The key is to limit the number of initiatives that the enterprise SOA Portfolio Plan Governance Committee has to review to come up with the final list of recommended initiatives. Since the individual business unit leaders submitting the SOA initiatives are the same people who sit on the committee that approves the initiatives, they will control the breadth and depth of the analysis undertaken. If they decide to review more initiatives, they are committing more time to the review process as well.

The objective of this governance activity is to reach consensus on the revised enterprise SOA portfolio plan to be implemented over the next N years and to obtain funding approval for this new plan from the SOA Business Domain Governance Committee. Doing this will require a series of give-and-take exercises among the business leaders on the enterprise SOA Portfolio Plan Governance Committee. Unlike the old approach, however, these exercises are not battles to justify one business unit's applications versus the others. It will be more of a compromise between the consumers of the capabilities being delivered by the initiatives and the providers of those capabilities over the ability to deliver them in the requested time frames. The enterprise SOA architects and the business and solutions architects will be called on frequently to help the enterprise SOA Portfolio Plan Governance Committee members resolve these issues. The issue of which initiatives have the higher strategic value should already be resolved based on the information in the Corporate Goal/Strategy column of the SOA~EAF and the process that was used to rank and set the priority of the initiatives.

It will help if the enterprise SOA Portfolio Plan Governance Committee has been given an estimate of what the next year's budget will be from the SOA Business Domain Governance Committee. This will help it to build a reasonable proposal of initiatives. If for any reason the total funding for the recommended initiatives is not approved, the plan will need to be revisited by the enterprise SOA Portfolio Plan Governance Committee and resubmitted to the SOA Business Domain Governance Committee for final approval.

This is a very different approach for determining the IT initiatives for the company. It is a top-down enterprise approach driven by the corporate strategy. It is an enterprise architectural approach for achieving SOA.

The final revised plan with all the consensus changes is presented to the SOA Business Domain Governance Committee for approval and funding. Any changes to the proposed plan as a result of this review and approval process are incorporated into the proposed plan to produce the final approved enterprise SAO portfolio plan.

Structuring and Publishing the Approved SOA Portfolio Plan   After the SOA Business Domain Governance Committee approves the new enterprise SOA portfolio plan, the committee communicates the approved plan to all the leaders in the corporation. This new plan includes:

- The formal start dates for all SOA initiatives to be kicked off next year.
- The SOA components of each initiative included in each production release scheduled next year.
- The formal end dates for initiatives completed next year (including any current- and prior-year initiatives scheduled to complete next year).

This information may be communicated in phases since it will take time to formally structure all the start and finish dates and the contents of the releases.

The Program Management Office is responsible for compiling the SOA resource utilization and scheduling plan for the next year. Doing this includes the scheduling and synchronization of all the resources on all the SOA initiatives for the upcoming year. This resource utilization plan maps to each month on the enterprise SOA portfolio plan as a support document, just like the enterprise SOA technology plan. Hence the three documents are published and synchronized in unison.

1. The enterprise SOA portfolio plan communicates:
   - All the initiatives that have been approved and funded.
   - Their estimated start date, cost, and timeline.

- The specific release or releases that deliver the capabilities into production.
- Any inter- or intra-initiative prerequisites or dependencies.
2. The SOA resource utilization and scheduling plan communicates:
   - What resources are needed for each initiative on the SOA portfolio plan.
   - When those resources will be needed.
   - How long they will be needed.
3. The SOA technology plan communicates:
   - What new technologies need to be acquired to support the initiatives on the SOA portfolio plan.
   - When the evaluation, recommendation, acquisition, implementation, and certification of those technologies needs to be completed in order to meet the availability requirements of the initiatives.
   - What estimated capacity enhancements to platforms or infrastructure are needed to support the initiatives.
   - When these capacity enhancements need to be available.

Releasing Funds to the SOA Projects under the Approved Initiatives   The entire cost for each SOA initiative was estimated by the solutions architect when the initiative proposal was created. These estimates included the costs needed for the resources identified on the SOA resource utilization and scheduling plan as well as the costs of the technology and infrastructure capacity enhancements identified in the enterprise SOA technology plan.

As each initiative moves closer to making the final approved list, these cost estimates may have increased or decreased, depending on:

- How much overlap in shared capability development exists with the other approved initiatives.
- How quickly or slowly the capabilities are delivered and over how many releases.
- Any increase or decrease in business scope.
- More accurate estimates of the acquisition costs of new technologies and/or capacity.[1]

Ultimately, however, there is a budget amount associated with the initiative, and this is the amount that is tracked and reported to financial management. As each project under the initiative starts and resources begin to be consumed, their costs are tracked against the budget for the project. These may be "real" costs, such as paying vendor resources working on the project, or "memo" costs, such as charge-backs for infrastructure or other internal resources.

It is important to note that resources working on a project may not be 100 percent dedicated to that project. Also, work they are doing (such as implementing a channel) may be supporting several initiatives. An analogy comparing SOA development to the concept of modular home building is described in Chapter 9. In a modular development model, only one plumbing crew may plumb all the houses. This plumbing crew is dedicated to one house only while it is plumbing that house; only the labor expended on that house is charged to that house. The forklift crew, however, may be delivering pallets of plumbing materials for the next four houses.

This labor would be charged to overhead that would be allocated back to the four houses using a standard rate.

Note

If you require very stringent cost management controls over your IT projects, as is often the case when outsource resources are involved, you need to define and set up this cost tracking and allocation process as part of your SOA strategy rollout plan. The need to develop this process should be clearly identified in your SOA business strategy and roadmap. (See Chapter 14.)

It is the responsibility of the program manager (who is responsible for the overall initiative) to track, monitor, and report these expenditures and obtain approval for their consumption from the enterprise SOA Portfolio Plan Governance Committee. This can be done many different ways so I will provide just a few examples.

You can decide to monitor and approve only real costs or both real and memo costs. My recommendation is the latter, since it gives the most accurate reflection of the true costs incurred. Even if you do not require such a stringent cost tracking process, this information can be very valuable to the solutions architects for estimating the cost of future initiatives. A system of *standard costs* similar to the ones used in manufacturing can be used to come up with standard prices for each resource consumed. This approach also helps to smooth out actual price variances and apply more consistent metrics to each initiative.

You can approve and release funds in as coarse or granular a manner as you like. Where detailed accuracy is important, the best approach is one where funds are released at the SOA project level, not the SOA initiative level, to support each of the development phases of the SOA system development life cycle (SDLC). Under this process, approvals for funds for the next phases of the project would be contingent on sign-off of the current phase by all parties required to do so. Remember, we are not applying a waterfall approach. In some cases, each component at each layer of the SOA enterprise architecture can progress from requirements to prerelease certification independent of the SOA components in the other layers and perhaps even in the same layer. Thus, a process exists where sign-off of each subset of business requirements, such as the defined business requirement for a specific business service or integration service, can get approval and funding to move to the design phase, coding phase, and so on. While the process can be this granular, I do not recommend it. In this example, if the requirements for the business service need to change because requirements somewhere else (e.g., at the Business Process layer) are just now being completed, all downstream work has to be revisited and potentially redone.

Pragmatically, you will probably structure a process where all the SOA components within a specific SOA layer are funded and completed through the phases as a group. The only exception to this is the costs of business requirements gathering on the front end. The release costs on the back end (i.e., integration testing, release testing, and release deployment) would be treated as overhead and charged back directly to the initiative.

The real importance of this process is to make sure the funds being released are mapping reasonably and justifiably back to the estimates that were the basis for the initiative's original funding amount. Slippage in the delivery schedules of any activity on any project and excessive expenditures or unjustifiable costs should raise a flag of concern. Cost and time overruns are best dealt with early and often. The longer you wait to deal with them, the less likely they will be corrected and resolved. You may be able to make up a delay in completion of business requirements by utilizing a few more resources in the design and development phases. Allowing this delay to push out the design and development dates almost guarantees a missed production delivery date. Since the planned delivery of the initiative was through a release process, these delays will impact the release schedule and potentially other initiatives in the same or subsequent releases.

Reviewing and Approving Recommendations from Any Enterprise SOA Portfolio Plan Impact and Opportunity Assessment   The enterprise SOA portfolio plan impact and opportunity assessment was described earlier in this chapter. This assessment is conducted at a micro level by solutions architects when assessing new SOA initiative proposals to:

- Identify any synergistic opportunities with the other approved SOA initiatives in the pipeline.
- Ensure that the requirements of the new SOA initiative being evaluated do not impact or are not impacted by other initiatives in the pipeline.

This assessment should also be conducted at a macro level by the SOA Portfolio Governance Committee on an ongoing basis. The purpose of these assessments is to provide an ongoing reevaluation of the enterprise SOA portfolio plan in relation to any new impacts or opportunities that may arise.

Impacts that may occur include:

- Slippage in schedules or cost overruns on initiatives under way.
- New SOA initiatives that need to be added to the plan or reprioritization of existing initiatives due to changing business conditions.
- Adjustments for a budget reduction in the enterprise SOA portfolio plan annual budgeted amount.

Opportunities include:

- Reallocating resources and savings from initiatives delivered under budget and earlier than projected.
- Adjustments to take advantage of synergistic leveraging or sharing opportunities across SOA initiatives that were not identified or known in their earlier phases.
- The identification of a new tool or technology by the enterprise SOA Technology Governance Committee that could reduce the implementation costs and/or accelerate the delivery of the initiatives on the plan.

This assessment should be coordinated and scheduled with the enterprise SOA Portfolio Plan Governance Committee by the PMO. It should be conducted at least once a quarter and more often if necessary to address any of the opportunities or impacts that occur.

An updated or revised enterprise SOA portfolio plan incorporating the resolution of any impacts or the inclusion of new opportunities will be delivered out of these assessments. These changes will also include changes to the release schedules and the content of the releases.

Monitoring Progress and Schedules of Plan Initiatives to Ensure that Initiative Deliverables Are Delivered on Time and within Budget As described, impact assessments can be triggered when cost overruns or delivery slippages occur on initiatives. However, if initiatives reach the point where they are impacting the schedules and costs at the portfolio plan level, the cost and effort to resolve them increase, and they may not be able to be put back on track at that stage. The reason for initiatives to reach the impact stage should be unknown or unforeseen circumstance, not poor estimates or bad project management. Therefore, the progress and status of every initiative as it relates to the budgeted estimates and project milestone delivery dates should be monitored and reviewed by the enterprise SOA Portfolio Plan Governance Committee on an ongoing basis. Reviewing the initiatives milestones early and often allows the business (through the enterprise SOA Portfolio Plan Governance Committee) to take action to get the costs back in line and/or the schedule back on track. These actions can include:

- Reallocation of resources from other projects.
- Pressure on resource vendors' SLA commitments.
- Resolution of an issue that could not be resolved at the project level and has been impacting the schedule of an SOA project.

The PMO should also be responsible for monitoring all the SOA project resources and schedules and any status reports for the enterprise SOA Portfolio Plan Governance Committee.

Communicating Changes or Adjustments to the SOA Portfolio Plan Any and all changes to the enterprise SOA portfolio plan should be communicated by the enterprise SOA Portfolio Plan Governance Committee. These communications should be across the entire company and to all levels of management. They may also be to vendors and partners heavily involved with and supporting the delivery of the portfolio initiatives.

These communications may be structured differently and contain more or less information, depending on the audience. For example, communications to vendors and partners may not contain any estimated or actual financial information about the portfolio. Some communications (especially those containing financial information) should clearly be marked as "internal use only" or "do not copy or distribute to anyone other than the authorized names on the distribution list." All communications, even those shared with partners and vendors, should be marked "Confidential." No partner or vendor should receive any communication if it has not signed a nondisclosure agreement with your company. Lower-level leaders may receive plans and updates that reflect only the initiatives within their business unit. Alternatively, some sensitive initiatives may be removed, such as an initiative that involves the use of a new channel intermediary partner that will displace in-house personnel.

Confidentiality of the Enterprise SOA Portfolio Plan Is Critical   The content of the enterprise SOA portfolio plan is very strategic and should be held in the highest level of confidence. You must be very conscious of the need to protect its strategic value but also recognize the value of the information it contains to the internal and external resources delivering the plan. Allowing vendors or partners to see what you have estimated for costs and time frames to deliver initiatives gives them a price negotiation advantage. Having a competitor who somehow, in some way, got a copy of your portfolio plan that was not marked "Confidential" will give the competitor insight into the capabilities delivered by the initiatives and the potential to counteract any competitive advantage you may have hoped to achieve. Remember, your old portfolio plan just had a bunch of IT projects to build, buy, or enhance systems. Competitors would find some value in this information but would find much more in knowing what capabilities you are delivering to your constituents and when you plan to deliver them.

Obtaining SOA Business Domain Governance Committee Decisions for Issues, Changes, or Adjustments Associated with the Enterprise SOA Portfolio Plan that Cannot Be Resolved at the Enterprise SOA Portfolio Plan Governance Committee Level   Occasionally, members of the SOA Portfolio Governance Committee will not be able to resolve issues. Most of the time, these are financial issues. Try as they might, committee members may not be able to justify shutting down or pushing out the delivery of an initiative. A major legal or regulatory requirement that becomes known during the year may require such a financial commitment that a significant amount of the SOA portfolio budget needs to be reallocated. These events may put the company's strategic objectives in jeopardy and require the executive leadership to reorder or revalidate the priority of those strategic objectives.

In these cases, the SOA Business Domain Governance Committee is responsible for resolving these issues. Their decisions can delay or shut down specific initiatives and/or increase the portfolio budget.

The enterprise SOA Portfolio Plan Governance Committee is responsible for scheduling the meeting with the SOA Business Domain Governance Committee to resolve these issues and for carrying out the results of their decisions.

Establishing and Governing the Corporate Strategy and Business Unit Plan Linkages   Finally, the most important strategic role performed by the enterprise SOA Portfolio Plan Governance Committee is to establish and govern the corporate strategy and business unit plan linkages used to justify, rank, and prioritize plan initiatives. Aligning the corporate strategic objectives to the SOA~EAF and assigning rank and weight values to them provides a consistent and measurable basis for prioritizing initiatives submitted for approval and funding. Alignment of the business unit plans to the SOA~EAF enables the committee to verify that the SOA initiative being reviewed was identified and ranked by the proposing business unit(s).

This information is critical not only for consistency and fairness when approving and prioritizing initiatives but also for validating that the initiative truly reflects those strategies and plans. For example, a proposed initiative seeking to support a constituent through a new channel that was not identified as a strategic channel in the corporate strategy will be immediately identified and questioned. An initiative that requests the ability to deliver services to a constituent that the sponsoring business unit has no defined or identified relationship with would also raise a flag.

The information captured in these two columns of the SOA~EAF needs to be updated and republished if any changes occur during the year. Implications to the enterprise SOA portfolio plan as a result of these changes would be addressed and resolved through one or more of the other activities performed by the enterprise Portfolio Plan Governance Committee.

Enterprise SOA Technology Governance Committee

The role of the enterprise SOA Technology Governance Committee is to ensure that all the initiatives identified in the portfolio plan are implemented in a manner that is compliant with all the SOA standards, design patterns, and frameworks defined by the SOA enterprise architecture team.

Thus, the enterprise SOA Technology Governance Committee serves as the "arms and legs" of the enterprise SOA Portfolio Plan Governance Committee. The Technology Governance Committee assists the business to package up and structure all the initiatives that are submitted to it for review. It manages the resolution of any issues, questions, or concerns that its members may have about the initiative, helping members to understand why an initiative is structured the way it is. It explains why an initiative is slotted into a specific release or releases within the enterprise SOA portfolio plan and whether there are any strategic implications to any architectural concessions made and why they were made.

The enterprise SOA Technology Governance Committee may also be solicited by the enterprise SOA Portfolio Plan Governance Committee when changes to the plan need to be assessed based on a strategic change or a change to a business condition. An example of the process to assess a changer by a competitor is presented next.

A change by a competitor has resulted in that company getting a much more favorable price with an overseas parts supplier that you both use. The competitor received the pricing discount by taking on the responsibility of performing any warranty repair work on the parts in house, rather than shipping them back to the supplier for repair. This resulted in a small but significant price reduction of the competitor's product, allowing it to price under your pricing levels. In order to remain competitive, your company is looking to negotiate a similar deal with the supplier and wants to know what it would cost to add the capability to allow field service reps to use an internal part return and repair process rather than the current supplier's process.

Upon notification, the enterprise SOA Technology Governance Committee assigns a business architect and a solutions architect to work with the head of the current internal refurbishment department to assess these questions:

What would it take to enhance the existing legacy applications to receive and track refurbishment of the new part?

What would it take to build new services on top of those applications to be deployed out to the field and on the floor to manage the new process?

Knowing that the current systems used by the refurbishment department are old, the committee also instructs the architects to assess how complex the changes would be and if it would make sense to replace or modernize these applications to a more flexible and adaptable solution.

The architects are also asked to review the existing channels available to the field support team and the refurbishing team and to identify if any new channels or enhancements affecting these constituents are in the SOA portfolio plan.

The business architect developed a business architecture diagram and use cases, on which the solutions architect performed a technical analysis. The findings included:

- The data and business logic modifications to the existing legacy refurbishment applications would be relatively minor, would incur a relatively low cost, and could be completed in three months, which would make them available by the end of the second quarter if they were started immediately.
- An integration and service bus framework and capability was already in place for the existing legacy refurbishment applications so the new services could be developed at relatively low cost in the same three-month time frame.
- There is currently no channel in place to support the delivery of services to the field support associates, but there is a project on the enterprise SOA portfolio plan to deliver a Web-based secured channel to the field in the fourth quarter.
- The refurbish department personnel currently use the legacy user interface of their department's applications but also have access to the internal corporate intranet web site for authenticated access to other services. Modifications to the existing legacy user interfaces would be substantial and result in the same disjointed and manually intensive stovepipe approach as the existing process. For this reason, two alternative solutions were developed:
  1. The refurbish process for the new part is developed and delivered through the corporate intranet channel. This alternative would take approximately two months.
  2. New services are built to replace all the refurbish user interfaces with a new business process service interface. While this would add time and money to the initiative, it was well received and supported by the department. This alternative is estimated to take five months.

This process has allowed an assessment that can leverage the existing and planned SOA assets to structure several alternatives. It also gives the enterprise SOA Portfolio Plan Governance Committee more detailed specifics around how the changes will impact what is already planned. By presenting the solution in terms of what already exists and what is already in the enterprise SOA portfolio plan, the committee gains a more detailed and accurate basis for making a decision. Its members may, for example, ask the enterprise SOA Technology Governance Committee to assess whether the planned fourth-quarter delivery of the field support channel can be accelerated and delivered earlier. They may ask for recommendations on how to shift other deliverables scheduled in earlier releases to accommodate the accelerated release of the field support channel.

Whatever decisions are made, whether they are for technical or business reasons, the details around those changes and the impact they have on the rest of the portfolio is much clearer under this process. The artifacts in the SOA~EAF and the process itself have been specifically structured to facilitate this type of analysis and decision making. Most important, these decisions are being made from an enterprise strategic level, from a top-down perspective, rather than at a tactical project or department level.

In addition to supporting the requests and directives of the enterprise SOA Portfolio Plan Governance Committee, the enterprise SOA Technology Governance Committee is also responsible for:

- Reviewing and approving the high-level technical approach described in each SOA initiative submitted to the enterprise SOA Portfolio Plan Governance Committee for funding approval.
- Assessing and recommending new tools and technologies to be utilized and deployed to support the SOA environment.
- Managing the acquisition, implementation, and certification of approved tools and technologies and ensuring their availability when needed through the enterprise SOA technology plan.
- Reviewing and approving all development frameworks, design patterns, and design standards employed in the SOA environment.
- Granting or denying variances from the development frameworks, design patterns, and design standards that may arise during the design or development phases of the SOA projects.
- Evaluating traditional IT projects not being developed as SOA initiatives to assess their implications to the SOA environment and make recommendations to minimize those implications.
- Establishing and reviewing the architectural and contractual requirements of any purchased or leased business applications.

Note

Adopting an SOA enterprise architecture approach significantly changes the way legacy systems are enhanced going forward. It also significantly impacts how new core business applications, whether purchased or built internally, are implemented. The implications of purchased or leased business applications are discussed in Chapter 7. Building new core business applications and modernizing existing legacy applications are discussed in Chapter 12.

REVIEWING AND APPROVING THE HIGH-LEVEL TECHNICAL APPROACH DESCRIBED IN EACH SOA INITIATIVE In the early stages of adopting the SOA enterprise architecture approach defined in this book, it is critical that every component developed be designed from an enterprise perspective. That is, every component should be designed not just to support the immediate needs of the initiative building them but also to maximize the ability of those SOA components to be leveraged or reused in future initiatives as quickly and cost effectively as possible. Achieving this objective at a project level after the traditional non-SOA approach is difficult if not impossible. Pressures to deliver less flexible but simpler-to-implement solutions will have a high probability of occurring on traditional projects due to much tighter delivery time frames and smaller budget allocations. There will also be more pressure from the project business sponsors, who may feel the money and time would be better spent on their specific needs versus enterprise needs.

This is one of the major reasons why we are structuring the SOA business activities at more of an enterprise initiative level and the technical implementation activities at a project level with multiple SOA projects to complete each initiative. This approach helps to remove the "ownership" factor that occurs under traditional project approaches. While each business unit submits SOA initiatives, individually or with other business units, the ownership of these initiatives resides with the enterprise SOA Portfolio Plan Governance Committee that governs their delivery. The ownership of every initiative is shared between the committee representatives responsible for the horizontal consumer needs and the committee representatives responsible for the vertical provider requirements. Hence, the commitment to develop shareable and leveraged SOA components is not the decision of the one or two business units getting immediate value from the component but of all the other business units that see future value to those SOA components as well.

While the enterprise SOA Portfolio Plan Governance Committee owns and governs *what* is delivered and *when* it is delivered, the enterprise SOA Technology Governance Committee owns *how* it is delivered. Each SOA initiative defines what is being delivered, and the releases of the enterprise SOA portfolio plan defines when it is delivered. These are the key documents used by the enterprise SOA Portfolio Plan Governance Committee.

The SOA projects established to deliver the capabilities specified in the SOA initiatives, as well as any technology or infrastructure capacity acquisitions identified in the enterprise SOA technology plan, define how the technology is being delivered. These are the key documents used by the enterprise SOA Technology Governance Committee.

The last thing you want to do after spending all the effort to organizationally and culturally structure our governance processes to facilitate this enterprise approach is not take advantage of it. Therefore, the enterprise SOA Technology Governance Committee must make sure that all SOA initiatives are supported by SOA projects that are structured and managed to accomplish this objective.

As the process matures and more previously developed SOA components are leveraged and reused, the value of this approach will become more evident to the business and will be fully supported.

Solutions Architects and Business Architects: A Brief Discussion   Before delving into the enterprise SOA Technology Governance Committee structure and process, I want to briefly discuss the roles of solutions architects and business architects. The roles and responsibilities of these individuals are discussed in great detail in Chapter 11. For now, I only want to discuss their roles as they relate to their support of the enterprise SOA Technology Governance Committee.

The solutions architects and business architects play a crucial role in the day-to-day operations of the business by assisting it in defining, setting scope, and packaging IT initiatives for approval and funding. Their duties include:

- Helping the business define and document its portfolio initiatives.
- Structuring and compiling multiple initiatives into enterprise initiatives that incorporate and synchronize all the common, shared SOA components among

the initiatives as well as synchronize all other activities planned or under way in the SOA portfolio plan.

- Facilitating multi–business unit partnerships and sponsorships.
- Establishing dependencies and prerequisites for these components.
- Establishing cost estimates and validating delivery timelines.

Objectives of Review of SOA Initiatives by the Technology Governance Committee All SOA initiatives are reviewed by the enterprise SOA Technology Governance Committee. This committee does not evaluate the business value or business justification of the initiative; that evaluation is the responsibility of the enterprise SOA Portfolio Plan Governance Committee. The enterprise SOA Technology Governance Committee evaluates the compliance of the proposed solution with the SOA architecture policies, standards, guidelines, and frameworks. In other words, it validates that the proposed solution complies with the architecture and to what degree it does so. The enterprise SOA Technology Governance Committee also reviews the submitted initiatives in terms of:

- The accuracy or reasonableness of the costs and delivery timelines specified in the SOA initiative proposal.
- Validating that there is maximum reuse and leveraging of sharable and reusable components.
- Validating the slotting of the initiative into the enterprise SOA portfolio plan releases.
- The accuracy and compliance of purchased business application capabilities specified in the initiative.
- Validating proposed solutions for bringing noncompliant SOA components of the initiative into compliance in the future.

It is important to recognize that any one of the next items may end up as the solution presented in an IT project, especially in the early years of SOA adoption:

- An ideal initiative with an SOA solution that is fully compliant with the architecture.
- An initiative with some SOA compliant components and some non–SOA compliant components that are necessary because of:
  - Restrictions within current legacy environment.
  - Market commit dates that do not leave enough time to enhance or replace the non-SOA compliant components to comply.
- Some or all of the capability is being purchased from a software vendor whose product does not comply with your SOA standards. Refer to the discussion in Chapter 7 for reasons why noncompliant purchases may make sense.

It is important to ensure that there is a process whereby initiatives that fall into any one of these categories are reviewed and vetted by both the business and the solutions architects prior to submission. It is critical that any issues or decisions presented to the higher-layer strategic governance bodies made up primarily of business leaders are *business* issues or decisions, not *technical* issues or decisions.

This process ensures that all initiatives that reach the enterprise SOA Portfolio Plan Governance Committee have the full backing and support of both the business sponsors and the enterprise SOA Technology Governance Committee. The enterprise SOA Portfolio Governance Committee readily understands that any architectural compromises embedded in the initiatives have been vetted and agreed on by the business and IT communities; thus, the committee can focus on the business value proposition of the initiative.

This is not to say that the enterprise SOA Portfolio Plan Governance Committee will not question the validity of the business rationale or what caused the technical compromise. In fact, just the opposite is true. Since this committee is the one that validates the business value of the initiatives and makes the recommendation to fund them to the SOA Business Domain Governance Committee based on that business value, it should question all aspects of the business justification, including why a certain delivery date is absolutely essential and firm, if the ROI presented seems realistic, and so forth.

If any of these issues or justifications are deemed unrealistic or based on bad assumptions, the enterprise SOA Portfolio Plan Governance Committee may bounce the initiative back to the enterprise SOA Technology Governance Committee along with instructions for reassessment, alternative assessments, or revalidation based on documented concerns or findings. Initiatives requiring revalidation will be handed back to the business and solutions architects identified on the initiative for revalidation who, in turn, will work with the business sponsor(s) to resolve the issues raised by the committee.

This is not to say that these higher-level committees will never be asked to address technical issues or make technical decisions. They will be. But that should be the exception, not the norm. The issues these committees address regarding technology should be strategic, not tactical. Therefore, the only time these committees should get involved in tactical decisions or issues is when they cannot be resolved at the enterprise SOA Technology Governance level. With the right participants and the right process, there should be few technical decisions that need to go beyond the enterprise SOA Technology Governance Committee, but there will be some.

A good strategy is to try to resolve these issues outside of the formal committee process with the sponsoring members of those committees. Often a rigid stance on an issue at one layer of the organization can be softened by more powerful leaders at a higher layer. Allowing that leader to do so without publicizing the issue builds relationships and trust with all participants in the process.

Finally, this process allows for trade-offs and concessions between the business needs and the architectural compliance to be brokered through a proactive presubmission process rather than a reactionary and contentious confrontation at the executive level or after it is funded and started. Architects understand that the business needs capabilities as fast as possible and want all the money to be used on business functionality rather than architecture compliance. The business, for its part, needs to take ownership of the full cost and true ROI of an initiative. Business leaders need to be educated so they understand that the true cost of any IT solution is not simply the cost of the vendor software and the hardware to run it on. They must recognize that solutions that do not comply with the architecture are less flexible and less adaptable to future changes and needs. The SOA approach has shown them that the architecture does not exist to serve IT but rather exists to serve the business. Hence, they will recognize that compromises on the architecture will restrict their capabilities in the future and, it is hoped, will readily support and commit to incorporating the future resolution of any architectural compromises into their initiative proposals. In other words, the initiative is structured so that any architectural compliance issues can be deferred and addressed in a specified subsequent release; and the initiative spells out exactly how issues will be resolved in that future release.

ASSESSING AND RECOMMENDING NEW TOOLS AND TECHNOLOGIES TO BE UTILIZED AND DEPLOYED TO SUPPORT SOA   Technology is constantly changing and advancing. Tools to improve our ability to design, build, deploy, monitor, and manage our applications are constantly being introduced. Some technologies may capture the imagination of the public and be thrust into the must-have list of every company. There will always be technologies looking for a business need, just as much, if not more, than business needs looking for a technology.

A key role of the enterprise SOA Technology Governance Committee is to make sure that every technology acquired by the company maps to an initiative on the portfolio plan or directly supports the IT development or production infrastructure.

This does not mean that the business is prevented from investigating and evaluating new technologies. It is critical that it continues to do so. The enterprise SOA Technology Governance Committee can simply be viewed as a protection mechanism to make sure there is "steak behind the sizzle."

The fact that a technology is new or "sexy" does not make it more valuable to the company. It does not mean that it has a higher ROI or lower cost of ownership.

The other reality is that the cost to implement a technology as presented by the vendors to your business leaders is almost always nowhere near the actual cost incurred when all is said and done. Many of these technologies represent just another stovepipe solution that adds to the incremental year-over-year erosion of IT dollars for support and maintenance.

It is not the technology that has the value. It is the business application embedded in (or enhanced by) the technology that has the value. It all boils down to the fact that it is just another business application on a different platform or channel. Vendors usually erroneously say that, magically, this new platform or channel will be the foundation for almost everything you do in the future. Nothing could be further from the truth. They usually do not mention the significant up-front and ongoing costs associated with maintaining and integrating a limited use platform or channel.

The purpose of the enterprise SOA Technology Governance Committee is not to say "no" to the business when evaluating new technologies. The purpose of the committee is to make sure that the *true* costs and *accurate* ROI of the investment is known *before* a decision is made. The committee is responsible for providing the right information so all the facts are known and to ensure the decision is made through the standard due diligence process. This is necessary to provide the opportunity for the business governance committees to evaluate the solution in relation to the other initiatives seeking limited IT dollars. Refer back to Chapter 7 for more information on this process.

MANAGING THE ACQUISITION, IMPLEMENTATION, AND CERTIFICATION OF APPROVED TOOLS AND TECHNOLOGIES   Once the decision is made to bring in a new tool or technology based on evaluation of all the costs and benefits, the enterprise SOA Technology

Governance Committee should oversee acquiring and implementing the technology. Many of the issues and decisions revolving around these projects will be technical ones. A PMO-driven SOA project governance process or the business leader–driven enterprise SOA Portfolio Plan Governance Committee does not have the right participants to resolve these issues.

These projects are captured and managed on a plan separate from the SOA portfolio plan. They are managed through the *enterprise SOA technology plan*. The SOA technology plan contains:

- All technologies and platforms needed to support the initiatives on the SOA portfolio plan.
- Any technologies needed to support the SOA development and production environments.
- Technology and platform enhancements and expansions to support projected SOA capacity requirements.
- Upgrades to existing tools and platforms as new versions are released by vendors.

The enterprise SOA technology plan is the mechanism used to ensure that all these technical projects are completed when needed. If possible, the enterprise SOA technology plan should have its own budget separate from the enterprise SOA portfolio plan budget. Since many of these projects will require commitments from external vendors, shutting down these initiatives after they start will result in large sunk costs that, in all probability, will not be recovered.

Keeping the tool and platform versions current is critically important to the SOA environment. Unlike stovepipe applications, where the underlying platform can be maintained exclusively for that application for an extended period of time, SOA components are disbursed over many platforms and shared by many applications. Failure to upgrade leveraged or shared SOA components means that each new share or leveraging adds more work when the upgrade eventually occurs. Most of this rework will be minimal if the SOA components were developed properly, but there will be some rework at least for regression testing and certification. Some rework may be significant (i.e., when the vendor does not support full backward compatibility). Having the underlying platform of a shared component go into unsupported status may impact tens or even hundreds of applications.

The enterprise SOA Technology Governance Committee (supported by the SOA architects) is responsible for proactively identifying these conditions and developing and managing the plans for their resolution. This process may include the adoption and support of new standards embedded in vendor upgrades. The process for standards is explained further in the next section.

It is the responsibility of the enterprise SOA Technology Governance Committee to adjust the enterprise SOA technology plan to reflect any impacts from changes to the enterprise SOA portfolio plan.

REVIEWING AND APPROVING ALL DEVELOPMENT FRAMEWORKS, DESIGN PATTERNS, AND DESIGN STANDARDS EMPLOYED IN THE SOA ENVIRONMENT The most critical technical role performed by the enterprise SOA Technology Governance Committee is to ensure that all SOA components delivered into production comply with the SOA enterprise architecture framework. The mechanisms to ensure this compliance are the development frameworks, design patterns, and design standards established by the enterprise architects and approved by the Technology Governance Committee. More information on these development frameworks, design patterns, and design standards can be found in Chapters 5, 9, and 11. As a reference for this section, examples of the development frameworks that ensure that all SOA components are constructed using all the enterprise and foundational services defined within the architecture are listed next.

- The enterprise security framework provides authentication and authorization challenges and enforcement on all deployed channels and services.
- The foundational frameworks provide exception handling, logging, and auditing of all services.
- The global session management frameworks provide transaction persistence, session recovery and full transaction rollback from the service to the back-end legacy application.

The individual enterprise architects are responsible for defining and documenting these development frameworks, design patterns, and design standards within their domain area of expertise. Once compiled, these documents are reviewed by the enterprise SOA Technology Governance Committee where they can be assessed and validated by all the enterprise architects from an enterprise perspective. Upon approval, they are incorporated into the SOA Reference Architecture column of the SOA~EAF. Additionally, these development frameworks, design patterns, and design standards can be extracted from the Reference Architecture column; compiled into the SOA Reference Architecture Policies, Procedures, and Standards Document; and distributed to all external development vendors participating in the SOA development process. These extracts can be tailored to provide each vendor the specific development frameworks, design patterns, and design standards needed to complete the development they are assigned. This has two benefits.

1. It allows vendors to focus directly on the pertinent documentation, which expedites their learning curve.
2. It can protect proprietary information not pertinent to their efforts from being exposed to vendors.

Development frameworks are identified, defined, tested, and validated by the enterprise SOA architects as part of their ongoing responsibilities. This process is supported by the center of excellence (COE), which is used by the architects to define, test, and certify new development frameworks.

Design patterns are identified by the SOA solution and SOA project architects under the guidance and direction of the enterprise SOA architects and are also defined, tested, and certified through the COE.

Standards are established by the various standard bodies in the public or private (e.g., Microsoft) domain. This includes newer versions of the standards. Many of these standards are supported via their inclusion in the technologies and tools supplied by vendors. The enterprise SOA Technology Governance Committee is the body that decides:

- What new standards or new version of standards the company will adopt and when that adoption will occur.
- Which technologies and tools used by the company need to support these standards and what is needed to get them incorporated and supported by the vendors.
- Which standards or older versions of standards will no longer be supported and when will their support stop.

Vendor support for older standards or older versions of standards is usually limited. Vendors will publish their unsupported status date well in advance to allow their customers time to adjust. The enterprise SOA Technology Governance Committee works with all vendors to understand these milestones and effect the necessary changes to ensure that all production SOA components are upgraded to current standards.

The enterprise SOA Technology Governance Committee ensures that all the development frameworks, design patterns, and design standards documented in the SOA~EAF Reference Architecture column remain current and accurate.

GRANTING OR DENYING ARCHITECTURE VARIANCES DURING THE DESIGN OR DEVELOPMENT PHASES OF SOA PROJECTS   As with all architectures, situations may arise where the physical implementation cannot comply with the architecture. Examples include:

- Standards interoperability failure at the tool or platform layer, even though those tools and platforms were certified on those standards.
- Bugs or incompatibilities in the tools or platforms that were not uncovered in the COE.
- An acceleration of the delivery date of the application due to a changed business condition.

The enterprise SOA Technology Governance Committee should oversee and drive a process to resolve the first two conditions with the vendor if at all possible. If, however, pursuing this path impacts the delivery schedule of the initiative, the scenario for condition 3 should be followed.

For condition 3, the SOA solutions and project architects working with the enterprise architects will develop alternative solutions to allow the implementation to proceed to meet the required delivery date. Included in this process, however, is the action plan for bringing the component into compliance as a day 2 item. Thus, the proposed deliverable includes a compromise approach and an action plan to remove that compromise at a future date. The proposed alternative moves forward if it is accepted by the enterprise SOA Technology Governance Committee. If the impact of the proposal has several implications to the architecture or significant cost to correct later on, the enterprise SOA Technology Governance Committee will forward the proposal to the enterprise SOA Portfolio Plan Governance Committee for approval or rejection. Approval at this level includes approving the necessary incremental funding to correct the variance in day 2.

The enterprise SOA Portfolio Plan Governance Committee, as a business-owned committee, has the authority to push out the business requirement date to allow time to resolve the variance. It also has the authority to allow the compromise to move forward and not fund the day 2 correction. In this event, the SOA components when certified for deployment will be marked as "noncompliant" and will not be available for assessment for reuse or leveraging in other initiatives unless those initiatives include the funding to correct the variance and retrofit the production application using the noncompliant component(s).

EVALUATING TRADITIONAL IT PROJECTS NOT BEING DEVELOPED AS SOA INITIATIVES TO MINIMIZE THEIR IMPLICATIONS In the early stages of the SOA practice adoption, many of the IT projects will still be traditional ones. Some say there will *always* be some projects that will not be SOA. I believe that ultimately every project will have some SOA flavor to it. From a business management perspective, every project will benefit by following the top-down and consumer versus provider management model described in this book. As the portfolio of core legacy applications gets modernized or displaced by SOA-enabled core applications, the number of non-SOA initiatives will dwindle.

Also remember that pure technical projects have not been interwoven and integrated into the enterprise SOA portfolio plan. These projects are included in and managed through the enterprise SOA technology plan. This was done consciously. Therefore, every initiative on the enterprise SOA portfolio plan should have consumers and providers involved.

As long as non-SOA projects continue, there needs to be a mechanism to assess the implications of these projects as they relate to the SOA architecture and a mechanism to influence these projects to minimize those implications. This role is also performed by the enterprise SOA Technology Governance Committee.

This assessment process is facilitated by the SOA solutions architects and the enterprise architects. The assessment addresses the impact of these projects to each layer of the SOA enterprise architecture and looks for opportunities to incorporate SOA components or capabilities (frameworks, patterns, and standards) into the design of these initiatives. These recommendations can be as simple as leveraging integration layer services instead of proprietary one-off integrations. However, they can be as complex as removing the embedded proprietary security within the application and replacing it with integration to the enterprise SOA security framework. Recommendations may also include building new business logic as services that get orchestrated by a proprietary control framework within the application but can also be consumed and orchestrated by the SOA service and orchestration technologies. Finally, these recommendations may include replacing embedded proprietary foundational services such as logging and exception handling with integration to the enterprise SOA foundational frameworks.

All the recommendations coming out of this process help the entire portfolio of legacy applications to evolve and migrate toward the SOA paradigm. The actions, in and of themselves, result in the modernization of the legacy portfolio. Each of these actions results in more openness, flexibility, adaptability, and reusability that would have been completely overlooked under the traditional approach.

ESTABLISHING AND REVIEWING THE ARCHITECTURAL AND CONTRACTUAL REQUIREMENTS OF ANY PURCHASED OR LEASED BUSINESS APPLICATIONS Architecture recognizes that opportunities to acquire business application capabilities, instead of building the capability, will occur. The acquisition can be the purchase and installation of the capability on-site or leasing the capability by using an application hosted in the vendor's data center. Without proactive participation by architecture, these applications can have a significant impact on the ability to achieve all the benefits of SOA.

The process for addressing purchased or leased applications was described in detail in Chapter 7. This section addresses the strategic role the enterprise SOA Technology Governance Committee plays in this process.

The goal of the enterprise SOA Technology Governance Committee is to establish partnership relationships with these vendors to establish a common and consistent vision that leverages their products to the same extent as the internally built applications.

As a company, you want to align yourself with vendors that have the same vision and expectations. Companies have done this for years with non-IT vendors. Manufacturers have aligned themselves with suppliers that support just-in-time inventory delivery. Hewlett-Packard built a strategic alliance with UPS that uses UPS not only to pick up and return personal computer repairs but to perform the warranty repair work as well.

We need to take the same approach with vendors supplying business applications. The enterprise SOA Technology Governance Committee:

- Directs the enterprise architects to work with vendors before a relationship is established to identify the architectural gaps in their business application offerings and to document all vendor agreements and commitments to close or eliminate these gaps.
- Ensures that these agreements and commitments are incorporated into the contract with the vendor.
- Monitors the vendor's progress toward those agreements and takes action when those commitments slide.

In addition, the CTO and the chief architect should meet periodically with their vendor's counterparts in order to revalidate the common strategies and identify new issues and opportunities that may exist between the two entities.

Beyond the tremendous value that SOA can provide when applied to internally built applications is the value that can be achieved if the same approach is used by your external vendors. SOA provides a level of flexibility, adaptability, and interoperability that simply cannot be achieved in other architectural approaches. Vendors that participate in this process truly can achieve rapid plug and play in their customers' environments. The results will be faster time to market, lower implementation costs, and lower total cost of ownership.

This will not happen automatically. Just because a vendor adopts an SOA approach does not mean that its application will plug and play with your environment. Vendors need to understand your reference architecture and all the design frameworks, design patterns, and design standards applied; and they must commit to interoperability at this level to achieve true plug-and-play interoperability.

You may think that no vendor would agree to customize its application to your specific architecture. You are right, but that is not what we are asking. Remember, your architecture is loosely coupled and based on standards. We are asking vendors to develop their applications following the same philosophies and approach. For example, if the services exposed by their application have policy challenge points and policy enforcement points exposed through application programming interfaces that support standards security frameworks like SAML, those services can be readily configured to the roles in your security module that get exposed through your enterprise security framework. Having a loosely coupled service stub layer on top of the services in their application allows you to build new service stubs on top to allow their consumption through other layers of the architecture.

Vendors that take this approach will have products that are more flexible and adaptable in your environment and in other customers' environments as well.

TECHNOLOGY GOVERNANCE COMMITTEE REPRESENTATIVES Thus, the role of the enterprise SOA Technology Governance Committee is to facilitate the portfolio planning and management process from a technical and architectural impact analysis perspective. For this reason, the committee is comprised of the enterprise architecture team and the leaders from the other IT departments. It is chaired and managed by the CTO and the chief architect. It may also have representatives from key IT vendor partners if they are involved in the day-to-day systems delivery process. For example, if some of the application development is done by an outsource partner, the lead architect and development team manager supplied by that vendor should participate as well.

There should be limited business representation to avoid the committee from becoming so large that it cannot make quorums and reach decisions. However, the business may feel uncomfortable or excluded if it is not allowed to participate. One recommendation is to have two or three business representatives participate for a limited period, say a month or a quarter; and then replace them with business representatives from other areas, repeating the cycle as time goes on. This will not only quell the participation concerns that the business may have, but it can also be used to educate a wider audience of businesspeople about the technical values of the architecture and give them insights into the complexities of managing and maintaining it. Another long-term value of this approach is the probability that some of these participants will advance in the company and one day sit on the higher-level enterprise SOA Portfolio Plan and SOA Business Domain Governance committees. As this occurs, their knowledge and appreciation of the enterprise SOA technology governance process will be invaluable.

Project and Service-Level Agreement Governance

The remaining two governance bodies do not meet periodically as the ones already described do. They are operational committees that meet and operate on a daily basis. They are embedded participants in the SDLC and monitor and manage this cycle on a daily basis. They are responsible for the tactical delivery of the portfolio. In other words, the governance committees described earlier determine what should be done and how to do it. Project and SLA governance are responsible for making sure that what should be done is, in fact, done and that how it was done meets all the requirements and conditions that it was supposed to meet.

PROJECT GOVERNANCE   Project governance is the responsibility of the Project Management Office or whatever organization in which the project management resources reside. The governance activities should be documented in and enforced by the PMO or the body responsible for quality assurance and on-time, within-budget delivery of the initiatives on the enterprise SOA portfolio plan. The distinction between the traditional stovepipe development life cycle and the associated project management process from the SOA system development life cycle is that the latter is an enterprise release model and the project management responsibilities are a matrix structure under SOA.

Under the SOA enterprise release model described earlier in this chapter, any one project may have deliverables and implementations that span multiple releases. In fact, most will. If the goal is to leverage and share reusable components, then the implementation and delivery of those SOA components have to stand on their own and be available when needed by the first application needing them is released.

This means that any one project may have several project managers involved with each accountable for a piece of the delivery. A project no longer represents a stovepipe or monolithic application that gets delivered. A project may be reliant on other initiatives to deliver functionality it needs or vice versa. This requires that the project managers work closely with all the other project managers and become intimately aware what deliverables impact their initiatives. Each delivery milestone of each component within each project must meet the delivery timelines specified for that component in the project plan. (See Chapter 9, Phases VI and VII, for more information on this process.)

The PMO meets with the project managers on a daily basis, if necessary, to ensure that all these delivery milestones are met. If the delivery of a component or the completion of a phase turns from green (on schedule) to yellow (risk of schedule delay) or yellow to red (behind schedule), the PMO governance takes immediate action. There can be many reasons why a slippage occurs; the resolution to get it back on track will be based on those reasons. If it is a development resource issue, the PMO can work with IT to potentially shift workload to make up the gap. This would include stopping work on a future release and shifting those resources to an earlier release. If it is a technical issue with a vendor, the PMO can leverage its financial influence over that vendor to get the issue resolved.

The PMO needs to take whatever action is required to get the deliverable back on track so it can meet its target release date. This does not, however, give the PMO the authority to compromise on the business or architectural requirements of the deliverable. If the only solution is a technical compromise, this needs to be approved by the (higher-level) enterprise SOA Technology Governance Committee. If the only solution is a business compromise, this compromise needs to be approved by the (even higher-level) enterprise SOA Portfolio Plan Governance Committee.

It is important to emphasize that the project governance process does not govern the release. The daily operational management of releases is the responsibility of the release management team. This team resides in the production delivery team within IT operations and is governed by the enterprise SOA Portfolio Plan Governance Committee, not the PMO. The PMO may have representatives on the release team to support quality assurance certification, but the release team is run by and mostly staffed with IT technical resources.

How you structure the project monitoring and reporting process will depend on how much initiative overlap exists in the projects. Clearly, from a business perspective, the desired approach is to understand the project statuses from an initiative perspective. The business wants to know that everything within its sponsored initiatives will be delivered on time and within budget. From a resource management perspective, however, the desired focus may be from an architectural perspective. Understanding where the pool of resources at a specific layer is, in terms of where it stands on delivering all that is needed at that layer, for all the active and starting initiatives is key as well. Finally, the projects need to be managed and monitored in relationship to the specific releases on the SOA portfolio plan. The PMO needs to monitor and manage all the projects to support these different perspectives.

From an overall portfolio plan and SOA SDLC, the focus starts at an initiative level for the initiation through business requirements phases. The focus shifts to an architectural layers perspective during the design and development phases. A release focus is used through the test, certification, and deployment phases. Finally, the focus shifts back to the initiative level for postproduction assessment and initiative shutdown.

This last phase is often overlooked or ignored, but it is the most critical phase to facilitate quality improvements to the SOA process. It is in this phase that the "lessons learned" assessment is conducted. The results of this analysis help to fine-tune and improve all aspects of the SOA SDLC going forward. This is especially critical and helpful in the early adoption of the SOA model. Some of the assessments conducted and the improvements made from them are:

- Cost and time—actual versus estimates.
- Project plan completeness and accuracy.
- Resource utilization management.
- Governance support and effectiveness.
- Phase-by-phase quality assessment.

The results of these assessments are used to improve the overall process. Each of the examples in this list is described in more detail in the next subsections. It is important to understand that these are not the only assessments that need to be made. Others include completeness and accuracy of documentation (including architecture documentation), number of bugs and testing errors encountered, and the general efficiency of the process itself (i.e., too bureaucratic and lengthy, well understood or poorly understood by participants, etc.). Applying quality assessment and improvement techniques (whose definitions are beyond the scope of this book) will help the PMO identify additional measures and metrics to monitor to help improve the process.

COST AND TIME: ACTUAL VERSUS ESTIMATES   One of the most critical metrics of the SOA process is the accuracy of the initial cost and delivery timeline estimates of the SOA initiatives as compiled by the SOA business and solutions architects. The accuracy of these estimations has implications to the:

- Number of approved initiatives on the portfolio plan.
- Number of times needed to seek additional funding.

- Success of the release schedule.
- Management of resource schedules.

The more accurate these estimates are going into the initiative, the more efficient the overall process will be. The PMO defines the SOA project management process so that actual costs and timelines are captured to the level required so that they can be compared to the original initiative estimates. Discrepancies can be the result of many factors, including invalid scope estimates, underestimated complexity of SOA components, or improper resource planning due to poor estimates. This assessment includes comparing the actual costs and timelines of developing each component to the actual cost and timelines to deliver similar SOA components in the past and how close or far those SOA components were from their estimates. Questions to ask are:

- Why did the transaction service built for this initiative cost $XXXX when the average transaction service developed in the past cost $X? Was it the complexity or something else, such as the experience and knowledge of the resources that developed it or defined it?
- Similarly, why was the delivery time frame underestimated so badly? Can the actual reasons be identified?
- Was the original scope used to develop the estimates insufficient? What needs to be done to improve the scope-setting process?

The results of this analysis are used to improve the up-front estimating process.

PROJECT PLAN COMPLETENESS AND ACCURACY   From a PMO perspective, the most critical metric for the process improvement is the completeness and accuracy of the project plans. This includes the:

- Project plans used to manage individual SOA projects.
- Project plans used to manage release project plans.
- Project plans used to implement projects on the enterprise SOA technology plan.
- High-level SOA initiative project plan used to matrix manage the individual SOA project plans.

The accuracy and completeness of these plans is also critical to ensure accurate up-front estimates and on-time, within-budget delivery. More important, incomplete or inaccurate project plans can be extremely disruptive to the resource planning process. The reliance on the availability of resources on the specified start date on one project is almost always based on the accuracy of the completion date of assignments on a previous project.

Any changes to the project plans from their initial compilation to their final completion should be clearly identified and traceable throughout the project. The causes and impacts of these changes should be evaluated at the end of the initiative. The project templates should be updated and new versions published to incorporate any of the project plan improvements recommendations coming out of this process. Other process improvement changes may be recommended as well.

RESOURCE UTILIZATION MANAGEMENT   Project managers are responsible for coordinating and managing the schedules of all the resources assigned to projects. This does not just include human resources. It includes:

- Getting their physical and systems access privileges set up.
- Scheduling meeting rooms for the project.
- Scheduling time for use of COE, development, test, and all other preproduction environments needed by the project.
- Managing the schedules of project participants to the line items on the project plan, including the scheduling of business resources for requirements gathering and user acceptance activities.

GOVERNANCE SUPPORT AND PROJECT EFFECTIVENESS   The SOA project governance team and the PMO support the activities of the enterprise SOA Technology Governance Committee to resolve technical issues they encounter at the project level and the activities of the enterprise SOA Portfolio Plan Governance Committee to resolve business issues that arise at the project level. Examples of these issues were given earlier in the description of these two governance committees. To revisit an example of each:

- A project-level technical issue would be the request for an SOA compliance variance due to a technical flaw with a development tool.
- A project-level business issue would be a request for a scope increase due to a previously undocumented business requirement.

The PMO also needs to have all the initiative and project status documentation up to date and available for these two committees whenever they request them. This information must be structured to support the multi-initiative activities being performed at the project level so that other projects on those initiatives are aware of the status of any dependencies and prerequisites.

PHASE-BY-PHASE QUALITY ASSESSMENT   The SOA project governance team is responsible for ensuring that everything required for each project phase is completed. This includes the completion and cataloging of all required documentation and the signatures of all the leaders required to approve each phase. The team will audit the results of the project phases on an ongoing basis. These audits are conducted to evaluate the project management effectiveness of the project phases as well as the overall project management effectiveness. The results of these audits are used to make process and program management improvements to the SOA SDLC. These improvements are presented as recommendations to the enterprise SOA Technology Governance and Portfolio Plan Governance Committees for approval to make the changes to the process or policies governing those processes.

PROJECT GOVERNANCE REPRESENTATIVES   The project governance process is chaired by the leader of the PMO. Participants in the process include:

- Program managers and the project managers.
- SOA business, solutions, and project architects.

- Relationship managers for all the SOA vendors and partners who participate at the project level.
- Release managers.
- Business sponsor's business manager assigned to the projects and/or initiatives.

The first three groups participate in every meeting held by the SOA Project Governance Committee. It is important that these resources are aware of the details and status of all the initiatives and projects. The last two participant groups (release manager and business manager) attend as needed. As each release approaches, the release manager for that release will participate more and more. If, however, an issue that would potentially impact a release is encountered before the release manager starts her involvement, the committee will solicit her participation in its resolution.

The business managers on the projects and initiatives will be asked to attend meetings where their initiatives and projects are on the agenda for discussion. Ideally, they will be given a specific time window within the allotted meeting time to help them with their workload and schedule efficiencies. Many SOA projects and the initiative they support will be open and active at the same time. Not every project can be reviewed and discussed in every meeting. Therefore, business participation should be limited to those meetings impacting their projects and initiatives.

SETTING THE PROJECT GOVERNANCE STATUS MEETING AGENDAS Determining which initiatives and projects are discussed in a meeting should be based on these points:

- Any project that has a red or yellow status on any of its activities or deliverables should be on every meeting agenda until problems are resolved and the status turns to green.
- SOA initiatives that are impacted by these red- or yellow-flagged projects should be listed on the agenda as well.
- Any releases that have been switched from green as a result of the flagged projects should be on the agenda.

As the process progresses and matures, the expectation is that these red and yellow flags will occur less frequently.

In addition to these flagged items, the agenda should include status reports on the next releases scheduled for production and the upcoming SOA initiatives scheduled to start. Finally, all initiatives that have been completed, including their postproduction assessment, should be scheduled for a final status presentation.

OTHER ONGOING PROJECT GOVERNANCE MEETINGS In addition to the project governance status meetings, the PMO should conduct ongoing quality assessment and improvement meetings. Most of the time, these meetings should be held with just PMO representation (program and project managers). The purpose of these meetings is to manage the incorporation of all the process improvements that have been identified from the postproduction assessments and accepted for adoption. Once these improvements have been identified and the plan for incorporating them is documented by this internal team, the rest of the committee members should participate in the implementation of the improvements.

SLA GOVERNANCE BODIES   The SLA governance bodies are the entities that guarantee that all SOA components and the applications they produce meet or exceed all the functional and nonfunctional requirements of the initiative when they are placed into production. Unlike the other governance groups described earlier, there is not one single SLA governance body. There are several, with each addressing a specific subset of the production and operations environments. All the SLA governance bodies, however, should roll up under the head of IT production and operations. The chairs of each of these bodies should meet with each other on an ongoing basis and with the vice president of production and operations periodically for ongoing status and strategic direction.

The SLA governance bodies are:

- Production certification and release governance body
- Change management governance body
- SOA application management and monitoring governance body
- Vendor application, platform and technology SLA governance body
- Business continuity governance body

Production Certification and Release Governance Body   This body ensures that everything that needs to be completed before the SOA components are released into production is in fact completed. This process includes confirmation that:

- All SOA components have been certified by architecture and properly published.
- All technical and business testing was successfully completed.
- The specific SLAs required have been documented, including the analysis conducted and criteria specified to achieve those SLAs. This includes vendor SLAs for purchased or leased applications.
- All associated technology and capacity requirements needed for the release as defined and delivered through the enterprise SOA technology plan have been completed.
- All the necessary change control requests to the production environment and the configuration modules within this environment have been submitted and scheduled with change management.
- All applicable user and support training has been completed.
- All operational and monitoring specifications have been submitted to and accepted by the impacted operations personnel.
- All help desk and escalation mechanisms and procedures have been documented and accepted by operations.
- All business continuity requirements for availability and disaster recovery of the SOA components have been specified and incorporated into the release.
- The PMO has received all sign-offs on all phases of the projects in the release.
- The release plan, including the back-out and restoration recovery plan (in the event of a deployment failure), is completed and signed off.

These confirmations become the basis of the go/no-go decision on the release. This confirmation process should not be treated as a single event conducted close to the release date. The release plan should specify the completion dates for each of these activities, and their completion should be formally reported to and accepted by the production certification and release governance body. Under this approach, the final go/no-go meeting should be a confirmation of completion of all the deliverables.

The production certification and release governance body should be immediately notified if any of these activities turn yellow or red on the release plan so immediate action can be taken. This action can be as minor as issuing a waiver for small, low-risk issues to, if possible, a repackaging of the release into a smaller set of deliverables or ultimately a delay in the release date if necessary.

Delaying a release can have severe and significant impact on the remaining scheduled releases. It also presents a high probability that an expected or (even worse) legally bound delivery date will be missed. Therefore, it is critical to identify and resolve any issues or problems anywhere in the process as early and quickly as possible.

Change Management Governance Body   The change management governance body oversees all the administrative and configuration changes within each environment. It also manages all code deployment and instantiation of that code within the environments as well as all necessary environmental, configuration, and code rollbacks and image reinstatements. The environments managed by this body include the common code prerelease environment, the test environments, the preproduction staging environments, and production.

This governance body manages the schedules for these environments and allocates the necessary time slots to each project and release based on project plans. Resources within the change management department help the projects identify, document, and submit all their environmental, configuration, and code deploy change control requests for the common code prerelease and test environments. The project architect oversees this activity and validates the accuracy and completeness of the change control requests.

The release manager is responsible for packaging and submitting the change control requests for the preproduction staging and production environments. The release manager works with the change management department and project architects from all the projects involved in the release to identify document and submit the changes for these environments.

It is highly recommended that all the changes and deployments are physically made by a central change management group. This will ensure that every change made will have a documented and logged change request behind it. It also allows for the changes to be consistently and accurately applied. I once came upon a situation where environmental entries entered using the platform's command line placed the new or changed variables at the end of the string, but the same entry through the management console utility placed the new or changed variables at the beginning of the string. A variable that was expected at the end of the string was placed at the beginning because the console was used, and several existing components abended because they tried to use the new variable instead of the old one. Having limited resources in a centralized group manage the physical changes creates a knowledge base of experience to minimize these types of risks and exposures.

SOA Application Management and Monitoring Governance Body   The SOA application management and monitoring governance body is the group that oversees the "wellness" of the applications in the production environment. It represents the resources that maintain and use the management and monitoring tools implemented in the production environment. These include:

- Network monitoring tools
- Application monitoring tools
- Server management and performance monitoring tools
- SLA monitoring and reporting tools

These tools are used to monitor the availability and performance of all the application code in production. In terms of an SOA environment, this application code is not a single or majority block of code deployed on a single platform or cluster. The SOA "application" is represented by multiple, discrete, and loosely coupled code sets deployed on multiple servers and clusters potentially across multiple physical data centers. The approach and mechanisms for monitoring and managing applications in this environment are very different. Monitoring and assessing availability and performance of an application in this environment requires knowledge of:

- All the SOA components at every layer of the architecture that are used by the application.
- Where those SOA components reside.
- What other applications are using those same SOA components and to what extent.
- What else is on the servers or clusters where they reside and what their utilization is.
- What the network topology is and the latency between all the nodes where these SOA components reside.

As you can see, attempting to monitor this environment from a (traditional) application-by-application perspective is complex and difficult. What needs to be monitored is each *layer* of the architecture and the platforms and components within those layers. We can use information from the Enterprise SOA Platform Architecture column of the SOA~EAF and from our network monitoring tools to create an application topology overlay identifying the location and connectivity of all the SOA components used by the application. We can then use this information to drill down into the monitoring statistics of the servers at each layer where those SOA components reside.

The SOA application management and monitoring governance body makes sure all the documentation needed to conduct this application-level analysis is complete, accurate, and up to date. It works with the SOA enterprise architecture team and network operations to ensure that all parties are current and in sync. It also works with the business continuity team to make sure that its application views, as well as its availability and recovery SLAs, are consistent with the views and SLAs being monitored in production.

The SOA application management and monitoring governance body is responsible for escalating any outages or SLA noncompliance to the appropriate management levels for resolution. This includes escalation to any external application vendors with SLAs in their contracts or external support vendors providing outsource SLA and production support services, for example, an outage and repair support contract with a hardware manufacturer.

SOA component-level SLAs are defined in the functional and nonfunctional requirements of the SOA initiative and are designed into the component's contracts and driven into the development through the design patterns and design standards provided by the project architect. In the case of leveraged or reused SOA components, however, the project architect must revalidate the component-level SLAs against the new requirements. For example, a component when initially deployed to support internal users had an availability SLA of 8 AM to 7 PM, Monday through Friday. As the component is now going to be consumed by an external constituent, the availability SLA now needs to be 24/7. This may require modifications to the component itself, to the way it is deployed (clustered), or to where it is deployed (main data center with 24/7 support). The SOA application management and monitoring governance body makes sure that these changes are reflected in the monitoring and management documentation for this component.

The SOA application management and monitoring governance body is comprised of members from the network and data center operations departments. They work with the enterprise architects, especially the enterprise infrastructure and capacity architect, to define the SOA SLA standards and metrics.

Vendor Application, Platform, and Technology SLA Governance Body   The SOA application management and monitoring governance body is a tactical operational body in that it defines how to monitor the environment and what actions need to be taken when an event occurs. The vendor application, platform, and technology governance body is an administrative management body. By this I mean that it manages the relationship with vendors and make sure that their SLA commitments are being met.

These SLA commitments are not to be confused with the architectural and strategic commitments negotiated and managed by the SOA enterprise architects and the enterprise SOA Technology Governance Committee. The SLAs are specific, measurable, and accountable commitments. For example, the contract with a vendor that is providing the use of a business application hosted at its site on an application service provider arrangement may have explicitly stated in the contract that the system would be available 24/7 with no more than a two-hour maintenance downtime window each month. If an outage occurred, the SOA application management and monitoring governance body would be the entity to detect the outage and contact the vendor's support resources to resolve the problem. The vendor application, platform, and technology SLA governance body would be the entity to document the outage that occurred. It also documents the recovery process and timeline to get back online and to assess the exposure the outage created. Finally it will seek compensation from the vendor based on that exposure assessment and the vendors contractual penalties.

The vendor application, platform, and technology governance body also defines the standard SLA requirements to be incorporated into all request for proposals and for information and ensures that they are included in all vendor contracts.

The vendor application, platform, and technology governance body is comprised of members from the operations administration group. They work with the enterprise architects when defining the standard SLA requirements and when evaluating variations from those standards on a vendor contract-by-contract basis.

Business Continuity Governance Body The business continuity governance body manages all the business continuity plans of the company, including disaster recovery and high-availability plans. Its focus is not just applications. Its focus includes telephones, office workspace, electrical backup, as well as backup data centers and networks.

Every production SOA component needs to be defined in the context of the business continuity model needed to support it. Since many SOA components will be shared and leveraged, the business continuity model associated with the component needs to be reevaluated every time a new shared or leveraged use occurs. For example, a component used internally did not require high availability or "priority one" disaster recovery status since the users still had the option to use the legacy interface if a disaster or application outage occurred. Now that the component is being deployed directly out to the customer and half the current internal staff will be reassigned because of increased use of self-service, the component absolutely needs to have high availability and priority-one disaster recovery status.

The business continuity governance body ensures that the continuity plan is updated to reflect these changes and that the appropriate policies, procedures, and resources are defined to carry out those requirements if necessary. It is also responsible for ensuring that funding exists to support the business continuity of the component.

Summary

This chapter defined the five levels of SOA governance and the roles and responsibilities of those governance bodies. The interactions among the governance bodies and the architecture resources were also defined. The approach facilitates the governance of SOA from the strategic management to the tactical implementation and support. These governance processes are designed to work with the SOA~EAF and SOA SDLC defined in this book. All the supporting documents and information needed by these governance bodies can be extracted and produced from the framework and the SDLC deliverables.

This governance model should be established separate from the existing governance processes used for traditional IT projects, even if the majority of projects are not structured as SOA initiatives. The objective is to move more initiatives to the SOA model over time, eventually eliminating the old approach and associated governance committees. When you have reached the highest level of SOA maturity, every initiative, including core back-end processing systems, will be structured and governed as an SOA initiative.

Note

1. The original estimate may have been based on published list prices of the technologies and platforms. These may have been fine-tuned by procurement through conversations with the vendors or through the issuance of an RFP by the enterprise architecture team.

CHAPTER 9

SOA System Development Life Cycle

What we have discussed so far is the fact that SOA projects are very different from traditional IT projects. Traditional IT projects were the development and implementation of fully self-contained business applications. Under the new process, SOA projects are the development and implementation of a set of fully functional SOA components needed by one or more SOA initiatives. Each individual component represents only a portion of the total capabilities needed by the initiatives.

Traditional projects are also comprised of fully self-contained project teams. In other words, all the resources, funding, and management to complete the project is within a single project. Note that even if portions of the project are subcontracted to different groups, those resources and the work they perform is 100-percent focused on the explicit requirements of the specific project. For example, you may have the integration work associated with building the messages on top of your legacy applications done by a specific set of internal or outsource resources. The funding for that development and the functionality encompassed in those messages is, in most cases, fully determined by the requirements and funding of the specific project.

For those companies that have had an enterprise application integration (EAI) philosophy and approach in place, there has probably been some enterprise focus applied to these developments. They may, for example, develop semantic data models for the message requests and replies rather than using the proprietary structures of the underlying application. They may return more than the required data, allowing the message to be used for different or larger purposes in the future. If you are doing these types of enhancements at the integration layer, then congratulations! You already understand the philosophy and value behind the SOA approach.

I was very specific in labeling representations of SOA activities on the enterprise SOA portfolio plan as initiatives, not projects. This is a subtle but critical distinction that begins the awareness of the paradigm shift in the process. The new approach raises the assessment, approval, and funding of IT developments to a higher layer than the project level. There is no longer a one-to-one relationship between the business initiative on the enterprise SOA portfolio plan that was approved by the SOA Domain Governance Committee and the individual development projects that are defined by the SOA solutions architect to deliver that business initiative. Each of these initiatives, when mapped into the enterprise SOA portfolio plan, reflect the common or shared SOA components that are also in the other initiatives in the plan. Part of the Project Governance Committee's responsibilities is to ensure that these common shared SOA components are synchronized and coordinated into appropriate releases to ensure their availability when needed by the first initiative requiring them.

Paradigm Shift of IT Development Resources, Processes, and Practices to Support SOA

The SOA concept of *loose coupling* allows for the development of SOA components independently. As long as the service contracts or integration requirements are clearly defined, any component can be developed independently of other SOA components that interact with it. Thus, the SOA enterprise architecture framework presented in Chapter 5 allows us to develop integration components separate from business service components, separate from business process components, and separate from channel components.

It is key to recognize that there is a distinction between separate development and development coordination. Even though they are developed independently, the coordination of their delivery for integration, testing, and deployment with other components is still necessary. These are activities defined within the release project plan.

To refer back to the EAI example, even though the development of the integration messages is subcontracted to a different development team from the one developing the rest of the application, those messages have to be available for integration testing with the application when specified on the project plan.

You may ask, "Why would I have a separate development team dedicated to developing my integration messages? Why don't I use the resources on the project team?" You could do so if one of these conditions exists:

- The resource on the team is one of a dedicated set of resources used to develop integration components. (This is the same as using a dedicated team.)
- The development frameworks, design patterns, and design standards artifacts supporting the EAI assets is so well defined and managed that there is confidence that all EAI components will be developed in a consistent manner and use standardized formats and structures.
- The metadata to ensure that message duplication or overlap is avoided is comprehensive and up to date, and the code check-out/check-in mechanisms effectively track any concurrent changes being made.

This very seldom is the case. You would dedicate resources to development within a specific layer of the architecture to ensure that the consistency, standardization, and leveraging of EAI assets occur. In fact, what you are building is a very focused level of expertise and an intellectual capital base that helps to expedite the delivery of SOA components at that layer and in a more cost-effective and consistent manner.

Even if you had the most comprehensive set of documentation and tools around the frameworks, standards, design patterns, and metadata of the existing EAI asset portfolio, any developer who has not developed integration components before or recently will have a significant start-up learning curve even if he or she has extensive experience with the integration development tools. The SOA paradigm shift lets us retool and refocus our development resources into highly knowledgeable and efficient work groups that result in a significant increase in productivity and expediency.

House-Building Analogy

This architectural analogy of house building reflects the type of paradigm shift that modular home building caused within the housing construction industry. There are two ways you can build a house. You can hire a developer or contractor that will come to your lot and build one on-site. Part of the overhead of this approach is the delivery of all materials. The scheduling of all work crews also takes a lot of effort. If the developer has several houses under construction at the same time, this effort is more complex, especially if those locations are not geographically close. The developer may be required to schedule multiple crews for the same job (e.g., multiple plumbing, electrical, and finish carpentry crews) in order to meet the deadlines and schedules. The efficiency of any one of these crews and the quality of workmanship will not be exactly the same.

The second way to build a house is to buy a modular home that is built in a factory, shipped in modular components, and assembled on-site. The advantage of this approach is that, instead of bringing the materials and crews to the home site, the home is built in the factory that also stores all the equipment and materials to build the house. One crew can now do significantly more work because it:

- Does not have to travel to multiple or remote sites.
- Does not have to carry and set up equipment as it moves from one site to another.
- Does not have to wait for materials to arrive and unload/unpack them.
- Almost always receives the right materials in the right quantity.
- Can replace faulty materials in minutes, not days.
- Can receive materials that are precut or prepackaged to the specific requirements of the specific house.
- Can move from one house to the next in a matter of minutes as work on the previous house is completed.
- Can jump from one house to another if something holds up work on one.

As a final benefit, the entire work flow and work space of each crew can be evaluated and made more efficient over time through quality assessment and improvement assessments. And if the on-site builder is going to charge you $400,000 and have the house completed in two months, the modular home manufacturer is going to charge you $300,000 and have it assembled on-site in three weeks.

The SOA development approach creates a similar paradigm shift for application development.

Efficiencies of an Architectural Approach

This scenario begs the question: How can the modular home builder deliver a house of equal or greater value almost 63 percent faster and 25 percent cheaper than the on-site builder? Economies of scale may play a role, but clearly the biggest reason lies in efficiencies. The modular homebuilder can frame, wire, and plumb three houses in the time it takes the on-site builder to do one. Delays due to crew scheduling, material deliveries, and even weather conditions are nonexistent for the modular manufacturer. Work oversight and quality assurance are intricate, visible parts of the process.

The modular manufacturing approach to home building was a major paradigm shift in the home building industry. While this market was initially penetrated by manufacturers of low-end homes that did not compete with higher-end custom-built luxury homes, the market today has many suppliers that are building high-quality, high-end homes that rival the most luxurious custom-built houses out there. Initially buyers were limited to a few designs and layouts. Today buyers can customize almost any design and layout to suit their unique needs and desires. The benefits of this approach were clearly seen by those "builders" that moved into this space and those buyers that chose this route.

But what did these manufacturers have to do to tap this market and gain its competitive advantage over traditional builders? They had to adopt a completely different and radical approach to home building. They had to invest in the "factory" and retool their people and processes to build differently. They had to change the construction model from a waterfall monolithic approach where the entire house is built as one contiguous unit to a model where modular pieces of the house were constructed, but designed and built so they could be quickly integrated and assembled at the site.

This is the same type of paradigm shift we need to adopt for SOA. Developing under SOA versus the traditional monolithic approach is akin to building modular homes versus on-site construction. Remember, the whole intent of this book is to show that adopting SOA from an architecture perspective versus a technology perspective is the only way to achieve and maximize the benefits of SOA. Buying an enterprise service bus (ESB) and developing some services may buy you value in terms of other potential uses for those services, but it will not make your IT shop more efficient. Building and consuming Web services is not a paradigm shift. Totally retooling and redesigning your IT operations and processes is.

If you believe that the EAI approach, where dedicated resources do the development and focus is placed on enterprise values to those developments in terms of semantic data and reuse, returns significant savings and efficiencies, it makes sense to apply this same model to the higher layers of the architecture. Having dedicated resource pools at each of the higher layers will build the same intellectual capital capabilities and development efficiencies attained at the integration layer. What we are doing is retooling and restructuring our development resources to support the development of the various loosely coupled components at each layer of the architecture. In doing so we are specifically limiting the scope and domain of knowledge needed by any one resource to develop efficiently and consistently. Over time, for example, resources focused on building business services will become experts in business services development and have extensive knowledge of the inventory of business service components. They will be the most knowledgeable regarding:

■ What SOA business service components already exist.
■ How the components are related to other existing components.

- What versions of the components are still supported.
- What integration services they use and how they use them.
- What business process or channels consume them and how they consume them.
- What *development frameworks* apply to the components.
- What *design patterns* and *design standards* apply to the business service components.

From a pragmatic perspective, however, you need to balance this approach against the need to balance the resource load. Clearly you do not want to have development resources idle in one area when another area is going full tilt with an increasing backlog. If your development resources are completely from an outsource vendor, you have other issues to deal with, but resource downtime will not be one of them. To avoid this problem, a development resource rotation program should be implemented, allowing developers to switch from one layer's development team to another's. This should be encouraged for all resources but not required. (Some resources are very good at certain things, such as messaging or data modeling, and want to stay where those skills can be leveraged.) This process also helps to strengthen the entire development operation over time. This is a little bit different from the old model where resources were expected to know every layer and all the design patterns and design standards for developing at all those layers. Under the new model, we now have an isolated set of resources in a controlled environment for which we can focus on quality and quality improvement.

Remember the house builder example? The on-site builder has three finish carpentry crews, and you can tell which crew worked on each house by walking through the houses. Just as the homeowner who draws the less skilled carpenters ends up with a lower-quality home, the business that draws the less competent resources may end up with a lower-quality application.

In our modular manufacturer example, there may be three finishing crews per shift and two shifts may run. In this example, however, there is a controlled environment where resources can be isolated and workmanship can be focused on. The quality of work is improved through education and training on improved development techniques and standards. Several of the employees may be trained and certified to work on more than one crew. For example, someone could be trained to work on both the framing crew and the finishing crew. These resources would be more valuable because of their flexibility, but they would absolutely be required to meet all the training, certification, and performance evaluation criteria of both crews.

Under the SOA development process defined in this book, we have the ability to institute the same type of quality improvements with our development crews.

Phases of the SOA System Development Life Cycle

I could devote an entire book to the SOA system development life cycle alone, especially as it relates to the development phase. The intent of the next section is not to provide you with a book's worth of details. Its intent is to show you the steps of the complete cycle at a high level and focus on the differences from the traditional approach and the unique characteristics and considerations that do not show up in a traditional development cycle.

Remember, a key aspect of the changes defined in this book to successfully achieve SOA is the adoption of loosely coupled modular components and a release approach to system development. This presents a different set of issues and considerations that are not encountered in the traditional model of individual implementations of stovepipe applications. Hence, many of the characteristics and differences highlighted are a result of employing a release approach and a modular SOA development model.

The SOA system development life cycle comprises 10 phases:

Phase I: Evaluation
- Defining the initiative
- Setting the scope
- Estimating the cost
- Projecting the delivery dates
- Synchronizing with the enterprise SOA portfolio releases

Phase II: Approval
- Technical review and approval by the enterprise SOA Technology Governance Committee (if necessary)
- Initiative proposal sign-off by the business sponsor(s)
- Review and financial approval by the enterprise SOA Portfolio Plan Governance Committee
- Review and executive approval by the business SOA Domain Governance Committee if the initiative:
  - Contradicts a corporate strategy or objective
  - Requires additional funding beyond the annual development budget approved by the business SOA Domain Governance Committee and administered by the enterprise SOA Portfolio Plan Governance Committee

Phase III: Initiation
- Defining and structuring the projects needed to complete the initiative
- Establishing the project teams and the initiative management team
- Identifying and enrolling the business participants
- Scheduling and conducting the initiative kickoff meeting
- Creating the first draft of the project team structures and initiative project plan

Phase IV: Requirements
- Documenting all the functional and nonfunctional requirements (use cases, business process models [BPMs], swim lanes, etc.)
- Developing the service contracts required to meet those functional and nonfunctional requirements
- Conducting a risk assessment if required and identifying contingencies as necessary
- Reviewing and validating all the business service and service integration component contracts by the business service provider custodians of the impacted business units

- Reviewing and validating all the business process and channel components contracts by the business service delivery custodians of the impacted constituents
- Signing off on the requirements and contracts by the initiative sponsor(s) *and* the solutions architect (to validate that original scope and approved funding estimates are still reasonable)

Phase V: Design
- Identifying and categorizing the components and contracts
- Specifying the development frameworks, design patterns, and design standards to be applied when developing the component and its interfaces
- Identifying the tools and platforms to be used to develop the components
- Extracting and isolating the functional and nonfunctional requirements explicit to the internal business functions within the component

Phase VI: Development
- Code development
- Code review
- Unit test
- Integration test
- Component certification
- Component publication

Phase VII: Prerelease Aggregation and Acceptance
- Aggregating and configuring all the initiative components being deployed in a specific release package
- Technically certifying all the components of the release (pulling all the components together to be tested and certified in a common interoperability and test environment).
- Business certification of the initiative components of the release
- Release manager acceptance and sign-off

Phase VIII: Release Deployment
- Aggregating and integrating all the components from *all the initiatives* being deployed in the release
- Releasing interoperability certification
- Releasing load and stress certification
- Final user acceptance
- SLA certification
- Production readiness assessment
- Production deployment

Phase IX: Production Support
- Release postmortem
- SLA monitoring and compliance

Phase X: Initiative Completion Phase: Assessment, Closure, and Sign-off
- Compiling and publishing all project documentation including the SOA enterprise architecture framework (SOA~EAF™) documentation

- Project assessment and "lessons learned" survey
- Project shutdown, including release of resources and financial closure
- Program Management Office (PMO) sign-off for certification of completion and cataloging of all the project documentation, deliverables and signatures

Three key attributes of the SOA system development life cycle to remember are:

1. Phases I to VII and Phase X are performed by projects within each initiative. Phases VIII and IX are performed by each release manager.
2. Each release may contain components from more than one initiative.
3. Each initiative may be implemented through multiple releases.

Phase I: Evaluation

Obviously, SOA developments do not occur without the SOA initiative first being submitted and approved by the enterprise SOA Portfolio Plan Governance Committee. For most initiatives, this is done as part of the annual portfolio funding and reset process described in the SOA Domain Governance Committee and Enterprise SOA Portfolio Plan Governance Committee sections in Chapter 8. The rest will go through the same enterprise SOA Portfolio Plan Governance Committee approval process but will represent off-cycle additions or changes resulting from top-down changes to strategy or business conditions (e.g., a decision to expand outside the United States or a new regulatory requirement).

Thus, the first question we must answer is: What does an SOA initiative look like, and how do we package it for submission and approval?

Not coincidentally, a graphical representation of an SOA initiative looks very much like the conceptual business architecture diagram from Chapter 3 or, more accurately, a subset of that conceptual architecture.

In the next scenario, assume that sales, customer support, and field technicians all have separate web sites for customers to interact with them. Although a single sign-on and password synchronization mechanism was put in place to ease the customer's use of the web sites, customers complained that navigating the web site was difficult and nonintuitive and often required them to enter redundant information. Sales felt that there were opportunities to up-sell or cross-sell customers when using the support and field technician web sites, but no mechanism to identify those opportunities and trigger the process exists since each web site is separate. Each of the three organizations submitted projects to replace its web site with an integrated portal solution. These projects were merged and packaged as an SOA initiative that was submitted and approved by the SOA Domain Governance Committee at the beginning of the year and placed on the enterprise SOA portfolio plan.

The next scenario provides an example for understanding what the initiative business architecture diagram looks like. In this example, there is only one constituent impacted: the customer constituent. There are, however, three distinct sub-constituencies of the customer:

1. Those that interact with your sales force (i.e., make purchases).
2. Those that use customer service.

3. Those customers that interact with your field technicians (i.e., schedule installs and repairs).

In the current applications, every customer registered to use the sales or field technician Web applications is automatically registered to use the secured services within the customer service Web applications. Customers are supported by the single sign-on process when clicking a link from one application to the other. Customers who register only with the customer service application are not registered on, nor do they have automatic access to, the other two applications. Those customers registering on the sales Web application can register as a procurement agent or a contract agent or both. Each role (procurement agent or contract agent) determines the functions the customers are allowed to perform. Both roles require customer approval by individuals at the customer's company who have been set up as administrators by the internal sales administration department of your company. Thus, an employee of a customer can have from one to five roles established to gain access to the capabilities of the three applications.

There is only one channel impacted: the Web channel. This initiative, however, is proposing the implementation of a new channel adapter. IT is requesting that a portal technology be evaluated. If procured, the development of the customer portal application will be the first implementation using this technology. This is the first step in a business plan to support the corporate channel strategy to have a single Web portal application for all individual customer interactions and services. The customer portal developed in this initiative will ultimately become the preferred channel for Web access by these customers.

Since this is the first portal being developed by the company, there is a requirement to determine if the purchase of a portal technology is necessary. For example, would it be cheaper to build your own portal framework or buy one? If it is determined that buying is the best solution, a process to assess portal products and the acquisition, installation, and certification of this technology needs to be funded, conducted, and completed before the initiative requirements phase begins. This acquisition requirement is reflected on the enterprise SOA technology plan, which is an underlying plan containing the technology acquisition requirements to support the initiatives in the enterprise SOA portfolio plan. The enterprise SOA technology plan is managed and administered by the enterprise SOA Technology Governance Committee, defined in Chapter 8.

The initiative example impacts three areas at the Business Process Domain layer of the architecture:

1. Sales processes
2. Customer service processes
3. Field technician processes

The sales processes for contract agents include:

- Set up and maintain an account.
- Establish a credit line.
- Set up billing and payment terms.
- Generate a pricing and volume discount quote.

- Accept a quote and sign a contract.
- Set up monthly and year-to-date order analysis and reporting.

The sales processes for procurement agents include:

- View products and prices.
- Check product availability.
- Place an order.
- Change or cancel an order.
- Check order status.

The customer service processes include:

- Look up products.
- Compare products.
- Check product availability.
- Request product literature.

The field technician processes include:

- Schedule an installation date.
- Request an installation date change.
- View all scheduled installations.
- Complete a customer installation satisfaction survey.

The initiative has also defined two new business processes that need to be developed. Both relate to creating the ability to trigger additional orders and services for customers using the customer service and field technician processes.

The first new process will determine if the customer using the customer service processes also has the procurement agent role in his or her profile. If the customer does not, we want to insert additional logic into each of the first three processes just listed to see if the person wants to submit an order for the products to their procurement agent. If the customer says yes, we want to expose a customized version of the "Place Order" business process used by procurement agents. The individual will be allowed to enter the order information along with the company e-mail address of the procurement agent. The e-mail address will be validated against the profiles of all the registered procurement agents under the same customer account. If the address is not found, the customer will be asked to revalidate and enter a new e-mail address. Based on input from the Customer Governance Committee, a decision was made not to expose a list of all the valid procurement agent e-mail addresses for control and security reasons.

Instead of processing the order immediately, the customized "Place Order" process will hold the order in suspense in a queue set up under the procurement agent's profile. An e-mail will be sent to that procurement agent notifying him or her of a pending employee order placement. When the procurement agent logs onto the portal, a message banner will say that there are orders in the queue. When the procurement agent invokes the "Place Order" service, he or she will be able to call up the orders in the queue for review and approval. After this is completed, the process will generate a status e-mail back to the individual who entered the original order request, informing him or her whether the order was accepted, partially accepted or rejected by the procurement agent. When the individual logs back onto the portal, a link will take him or her to the specific details of the order, including total amount charged and estimated delivery date(s).

The new customized "Place Order" service will also be modified to provide product alternatives and recommended additional products as part of the order placement work flow. The product alternative service will identify what is being ordered. If there are higher-end products in the same line (i.e., more expensive), this service will inform the user of these products and give them the option to swap the chosen product for a higher-end product.

The "Recommend Additional Products" service will identify what is being ordered and provide a list of complementary products for the customer to order if desired. This is similar to the functionality on many web sites today that tell customers that "other customers who have ordered what you are ordering have also ordered these products."

In the old customer Web applications, procurement agents were the only individuals who had access to the order system. These individuals never changed the ordered items and never ordered additional items because the end consumers who were paying for the order out of their budgets were not involved in the order entry process. Since this capability is now being exposed to any customer service–registered employee, the opportunity to tap these opportunities will now exist.

The second new process involves modifying the "Schedule Installation Date" and "Request an Installation Date Change" processes. The company wants to offer preferred or priority installation services for a fee. Customers will be allowed to move up in the installation schedule by paying a priority installation fee. This fee is based on additional costs to use a faster shipping mechanism as well as the cost to, if necessary, bring in resources from other field locations with schedule availability. The procurement agent must also approve these fees. Once the next available installation date is presented to the customers, they will be presented with an option looking at earlier available priority dates and their incremental costs. If customers choose one of these earlier dates, the similar process to the one discussed earlier will be invoked. They will be asked to supply their procurement agent's e-mail address, an order for priority installation will be placed in that agent's queue, and a notification e-mail will be sent. A status e-mail and portal link will also be sent back to the requesting employees in this process as well. Thus, this initiative involves the enhancement and SOA modernization of 19 existing business processes (6 contract, 5 procurement, 4 customer service, and 4 field technician processes) and the development of 2 new business processes ("Non–Procurement Agent Entered Orders" and "Request, Approve, and Submit Priority Installations").

In addition, these two business processes identified the need for developing four new business services to support them. The first new service will be the "Get Alternative Products" service that will be used by the "Non–Procurement Agent Entered Orders" business process to identify the high-end products. The second is the "Get Suggested Product" service that will be used by this same process to get the list of other products for potential purchase. The new service will extract this data from the order analysis database, which is an online analytical processing (OLAP) dimensional database summarizing order commonalities and tendencies.

Two business services are also needed to support the "Request, Approve, and Submit Priority Installations" business process. The "Schedule Out-of-Territory Technician" service performs two services.

1. It extracts and produces a new version of the field installation calendar that shows availability of out-of-territory field technicians and the adjusted rate for them to perform installations in the specified territory.
2. It creates the scheduling entry in the scheduling system to book the technician.

The final service updates the ship date and ship method in the shipping distribution system. The ability to find the current ship date and ship method of an order already exists in the services already in production; therefore, these are not duplicated. In the past, expedited orders were low in volume and handled by direct data entry into the shipping distribution system by inventory personnel. The new priority installation process is expected to significantly increase the number of expedited orders. The entry and acceptance of those changes need to be returned immediately to the customer using the service on the portal.

The solutions architect also identified that new service stubs may need to be developed for the enterprise security modules' registration and login/logout services if a portal technology is used. This will be the first time these existing services are consumed by a portal product. The services themselves would not have to be modified. The new unique customer data captured at registration, the customer authentication data and mechanism, as well as the role authorization processes for services are all handled through changes in the configuration capabilities of the security module, which processes its payload as XML documents. Therefore, the new service stub (in this case a JSR portlet) simply formats the registration and login services into the portlet container. The registration and login services in this enterprise security module support the capability for end users to perform their own "Forgot_UserID," "Forgot_Password," and "Reset_Password" activities. These services will be used by the customer portal. The single-sign-on (SSO) mechanism used by the current three customer applications will no longer be needed once the portal is implemented and will be decommissioned. This will also eliminate the previous requirement for customers to call into the support center for user ID and password resets. Exhibit 9.1 was developed to represent this proposed business initiative.

All the information about the initiative to this point would be compiled by the business architect working with the business units. At this point, before the initiative has been submitted and approved by the enterprise SOA Portfolio Plan Governance Committee, there is enough information from the business for the solutions architect to begin to scope out and produce a high-level estimate of the cost and time frame to deliver the initiative. Working with the development, enterprise architecture, and operations support teams, the solutions analyst would develop the high-level estimate for the initiative. This would include cost and time estimates for:

- Conducting the portal technology evaluation and acquisition (including licensing, hardware, installation costs and training).
- Developing the customer portal component of the application (including the cost to configure and integrate the security module).

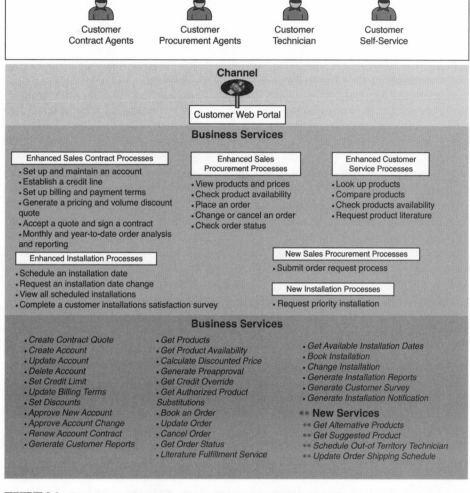

EXHIBIT 9.1   Business Architecture Diagram: Customer Portal Initiative

- Rearchitecting and enhancing the 19 existing business processes.
- Building and incorporating the 2 new business processes.
- The integration layer effort for enhancing the existing integration services and incorporating them into the ESB.
- Enhancing the existing back-end legacy field installation scheduling system to incorporate priority installation pricing and processing as well as out-of-territory scheduling of field resources.
- Enhancing the legacy order and billing system to accept and process priority installations.
- Creating a new integration and business service on top of the legacy shipping and distribution application to change the shipping schedule and distribution priority of an order.

While conducting this scope and estimation exercise, the solutions architect will also conduct an enterprise SOA portfolio opportunity and impact assessment to review all the current releases in the enterprise SOA portfolio plan. Refer to Chapter 8 for more information on this assessment. This evaluation will be conducted to:

- Determine if any of the new components required for this initiative are also required by another scheduled initiative and, if so, when they are scheduled to be released.
- Determine if any other initiatives require enhancements to components also requiring enhancements for this initiative.
- Evaluate which releases contain planned delivery of functionality to the same constituent, and whether it makes sense to deliver all or part of this initiative's functionality to those constituents in a different release to accelerate delivery timelines or reduce the impact on the consuming constituent (i.e., amount of new functionality, training, etc.).
- Determine if there is release capacity to support the delivery of the initiatives functionality within the projected time frames.

The results of this analysis can be valuable for:

- Identifying additional cost reductions in the initiative estimates for components already funded for development.
- Managing and minimizing the impact on the consuming constituents.
- Validating the ability to deliver functionality when needed based on the bandwidth and capacity of the release management and deployment resources.

As stated earlier in this chapter, organizing your development resources around the layers of the architecture builds intellectual capital around the knowledge and expertise of that layer. In the last example, those who manage the integration domain and its development assets know those assets intimately and can quickly identify which ones need to be enhanced and how long it will take to enhance them. The same will be true for the Business Service layer, Business Process layer, and so on. Therefore, the ability of these resources to provide more accurate estimates increases. Over time, as more assets are produced and more experience is gained at developing them, the estimate of future developments becomes more accurate.

All of these estimates are compiled and packaged into a total estimated cost along with the earliest estimated delivery date for the initiative. These estimates are presented by the business and solutions architects to the business sponsors for review and approval. Since this initiative is requesting the potential use of a new technology platform, it must first be submitted and approved by the enterprise SOA Technology Governance Committee before the enterprise SOA Portfolio Plan Governance Committee sees it. The enterprise SOA Technology Governance Committee validates that the technology is necessary to support the *reference* architecture and that the capability is not in any current technology in the *platform* architecture. When a specific platform is recommended, the enterprise SOA Technology Governance Committee will review the recommendation for compliance with the standards and compatibility with the other technologies in the *platform* architecture and approve or deny the selection.

Note

At this stage, there exists only a high-level understanding of the business functional requirements, SOA component requirements, capacity requirements, and others. The business architect only needs to document the requirements of the initiative to a level of detail that allows the solutions architect to estimate the costs and delivery timelines. In some cases, especially when a large or complex initiative is involved, the business architect may have to iterate back to the business more than once until this level of detail is attained.

The template for structuring SOA initiatives for submission to the enterprise SOA Portfolio Plan Governance Committee for review and approval contains:

- An executive overview of the initiative with a brief explanation of what it is and what business values and objectives it achieves.
- The business architecture diagram showing all the components of the initiative.
- The linkage of the conceptual components at each layer of the initiative's business architecture diagram to the business unit plans and corporate strategy cells of the SOA~EAF.
- The technology components that need to be added to support the initiative.
- The cost estimates and delivery timeline.
- A summary of the new, leveraged, and reused SOA components including SOA components funded and being developed by other initiatives and an estimate of the savings from those leveraged and reused components.
- The expected return on investment ROI of the initiative, including expected increase revenue generation and opportunity cost saving for future initiatives.

The next executive overview was developed for the example initiative just discussed.

Customer Portal Initiative Executive Overview

Initiative Background

The customer portal initiative is sponsored by the sales, customer service, and field support organizations. It is a proposal to replace the three current customer-utilized Web applications with a single, integrated customer portal solution. The current applications are completely separate from each other and not very user friendly or intuitive. Many customers have complained that navigating from one application to another is difficult and often requires that they redundantly enter information from one site to another. While a single-sign-on solution was implemented to eliminate the redundant login requirements, customers still find the process cumbersome.

In addition to making the customer experience more intuitive and user friendly, there are two other business objectives needed to support our corporate strategies that cannot be supported efficiently through the current separate systems.

(continued)

(*Continued*)

The first of those business objectives is to potentially generate additional sales by "marketing" higher-end and complementary products to the end consumer. Under the current system, only procurement agents at the accounts can place orders. They very seldom add to these orders since they are not the end consumers. This new solution will still keep the integrity of the procurement agents' approval but will also provide the ability of the non–procurement agent employees to enter and submit order requests to their procurement agent. This will give the end user consumer direct access to the order process, allowing us to take advantage of this to up-sell and cross-sell.

The second of those business objectives is the ability to offer customers priority installation services at an increased fee. This strategy for increased installation revenues has been discussed for several years now, but the necessary enhancements to the systems could never be justified. Because of this customer portal initiative, however, the incremental cost of adding this capability is one-third the amount of the original (stovepipe) proposal. This is due to the fact that, with the exception of the back-end legacy systems modifications and two new product shipping and installation scheduling services, all the other pieces that need to be modified, enhanced, or modernized in the original proposal are being modernized and enhanced by this portal initiative. Therefore, the incremental cost for the modifications of these SOA components is being shared with all the other modifications being made. Thus, this initiative provides an opportunity to support this business objective at one-third the original cost.

Business Justification Summary

This initiative supports business objectives that align with three of your corporate strategic goals. Those goals are:

1. Increase year-over-year revenue.
2. Develop new revenue sources.
3. Increase customer satisfaction

It is projected that the enhanced customer order capabilities of this solution will increase the volume of directly submitted customer orders by 20 percent. This projection was based on direct customer feedback from a customer survey conducted two months ago. It is also projected that up to 10 percent of orders will choose the priority installation option, resulting in a new revenue stream for the company.

This proposed solution also aligns with our corporate strategy (as documented in the constituency and channel layers of the Corporate Strategy column of the SOA~EAF) to:

Increase the customer's satisfaction and expand their utilization of self-service capabilities through the use of a comprehensive and engaging Web portal providing all their services and interactions through an intuitive and user friendly mechanism.

This new portal will significantly increase the number of customers adopting and reusing self-service capabilities and eliminate the previous negative feedback by providing a more holistic and positive experience.

Critical Success Factors

The critical success factors of this initiative are:

Revenue increases directly tied to the new order capabilities of this solution result in at least a 20% increase in Web-submitted orders.

Priority installations are accepted and embraced by field installations.

The trend of reduced customer adoption of the online services is reversed with new customer registration and utilization across at least 60% of the customer accounts within the first six months.

Return on Investment Summary

The detailed cost estimates and ROI of this initiative are provided in the detailed ROI section of this SOA initiative template. The payback period for this initiative is estimated at 24 months. The projected revenue increases from the up-sell, cross-sell, and priority installation fees as well as the internal cost savings resulting from higher customer adoption of the integrated solution are projected to return an annual ROI of 20 to 25 percent over five years.

Alternatives

The alternative to this solution is to continue to maintain and enhance the three current customer Web applications. Clearly, the biggest benefit of this approach is that it will eliminate the need to invest fairly significant dollars to modernize and replace functionality that already exists. This, however, is strictly a short-term benefit. The redundancies and complexities associated with the current applications are resulting in increased maintenance and support costs each year. The cost of adding or enhancing the functionality of these systems is increasing as well.

These applications are also very rigid and disjointed, making them not very user friendly and requiring significant time and money to adapt them to changing business conditions. This is evident in their low adoption rate and decreased utilization by our customers.

We did assess the alternative of building a new customer order capability exclusively within the current customer service Web application where both the non–procurement agent order entry and procurement agent approval processes would occur. This process included the up-sell and cross-sell capabilities but did not include priority installations. The cost of doing this was estimated at 35 to 40% of what this total initiative would cost.

(continued)

(Continued)

This option was presented to the Horizontal Consumer-centric Subcommittee and reviewed by several customer representatives on that committee. It was met with resounding resistance and negativity by those representatives. Clearly, presenting them with another order entry mechanism *in addition to the one they already use* was not their expectation. While they did not see this option as us helping them improve their work flow and efficiencies, they did see these benefits in the option recommended in this proposal.

The remaining sections of the SOA initiative template would be completed by the business and solutions architects, reviewed by the business sponsor, and submitted to the governance bodies for approval. The initiative template format with an explanation of each section is provided in Appendix A. Refer to this appendix for a more detailed description of the template.

As a rule of thumb, the completed initiative document should not exceed ten pages in length, and the executive summary should be no longer than two pages. A one-page executive summary would allow executives to have a single two-sided sheet of paper with the initiative description on one side and the executive summary on the other. Similarly, visual presentation of the materials at the review meetings can consist of the initiative description on one projector and the executive summary on the other or, alternatively, a two-page projection on a single projector.

Remember that the intent of this document is not to provide the full set of requirements or the full detailed specification of the initiative. Its intent is to sell the initiative as a valuable proposal that should be approved when compared to all the other proposals being submitted. Adopting and enforcing a template for the initiatives ensures that proposals are evaluated using an apples-to-apples comparison so that the members of the enterprise SOA Portfolio Plan Governance Committee and the business SOA Domain Governance Committee have a consistent and fair way of conducting their evaluations.

The initiation phase is owned by the business unit leaders and facilitated by the business architects.

Phase II: Approval

The first step in the approval process is the technical review and approval of the proposed initiative by the enterprise SOA Technology Governance Committee. This review and approval is necessary only if the initiative requires the acquisition of a new technology tool or platform. A new technology platform requirement can be for any layer of the architecture, including the acquisition of a purchased or leased business application that needs to be implemented and integrated into the Reference Architecture framework. This evaluation by the enterprise SOA Technology Governance Committee is to ensure that the technology platform complies with the technology standards supported in the architecture and that "effective and reasonable" interoperability of the technology platform can be achieved. In the case of purchased or leased business applications, this may require negotiations with the vendor to enhance or improve the standards and interoperability capabilities of its product and if necessary a compromise (or "variance approval") on compliance and a contractual commitment to resolve the variance at a future date. Refer to Chapter 7 for more details on handling purchased or leased business applications.

The next step in the approval process will be the sign-off on the proposed initiative by the business sponsor(s). This will be the first step if no new business applications or technologies are involved.

The business sponsors' sign-off is their agreement that:

- The high-level scope of the capabilities defined in the initiative is accurate.
- The high-level description of the performance and other SLA requirements are accurate.
- The costs and delivery time frame are reasonable.
- The business justification and alignment to the business unit plans and corporate strategies are accurate.
- The critical success factors, success measures, and ROI are accurate.
- The risk assessment and alternatives are acceptable.

After business sponsors sign off, the proposal can be scheduled for review by the enterprise SOA Portfolio Plan Governance Committee. Any issues impacting the sponsors' sign-off may require all or part of the cycles performed to this point to be reiterated. The next approval step is the approval by the enterprise SOA Portfolio Plan Governance Committee. The role of this committee is to:

- Validate that the business justification, business plan, and corporate strategy alignment and ROI are accurate.
- Rank the importance and priority of the initiative as it relates to the other initiatives in the approved enterprise SOA portfolio plan.
- Agree to fund the initiative if available funding exists in the portfolio budget.
- Agree to the release schedule, including any modifications or shifting of release components in other approved initiatives,

The proposed initiative will be rejected and returned to the sponsor(s), along with the reasons for rejection, if consensus cannot be reached on these criteria. The committee may also include directives, corrections, or any other recommended changes in their rejection response. Once these are resolved, the proposal can be resubmitted. Once again, this may require all or part of the cycles performed to this point to be repeated.

In the event that the enterprise SOA Portfolio Plan Governance Committee agrees that the proposal is valid but (1) the committee does not have the funding to support it or (2) it conflicts with a corporate strategy or objective, the proposal will be submitted to the SOA Domain Governance Committee for review and approval.

The enterprise SOA Business Domain Governance Committee gets involved in initiative proposal approvals only when these last two conditions exist or when it is conducting the annual enterprise SOA portfolio plan budget assessment and approval process. Its role is to approve or deny a budget override to fund the initiative or rescind budget approval for already funded initiative to cover the costs. This alternative to reprioritize the initiative funding may have already taken place at the enterprise SOA Portfolio Plan Governance level but could not get resolved.

The committee also addresses and resolves strategic conflicts. An example of a strategic conflict would be a demand by large customers or vendors to accept and process orders or invoices sent via fax using their own proprietary format when the corporate strategy is to eliminate submission of these transactions through the fax channel by replacing them with electronic data interchange (EDI) or online submissions using X-12 or industry-standard semantic formats. Resolution may require executive involvement with customers or vendors to get them to back off their demand or to approve manual and technical capacity improvements needed to support these customers or vendors.

The approval phase is owned by the enterprise SOA Portfolio Plan Governance Committee and facilitated by the PMO and the architecture leaders.

Phase III: Initiation

The initiation phase is the formal start of the tactical implementation of the initiative. The first step in this process is to decompose the initiative into individual projects that will manage and deliver defined subsets of it. Some of these projects (e.g., requirements gathering, project aggregation, and release management) will be managed globally with all other subprojects coordinated under these efforts. The remaining projects will be more discrete and bounded at a more macro level. The overall initiative management project coordinates and manages all the deliverables dependencies, prerequisites, and timelines of the other projects. These can be structured into one overall project plan or as separate plans with synchronization links to the other plans. It is highly recommended that project templates be established for each of the project types, including a master project plan that includes all the relationships among them. These templates can be used as a starting point for setting up the project plans and modified appropriately to the needs of a specific initiative. Modifications to these templates, however, should be reviewed and approved by the initiative's project management team.

Earlier, we defined how we need to retool and redefine our development resources, processes, and practices to support SOA and how to package and submit SOA initiatives. We can now define what an SOA project is and how it is different from a traditional stovepipe application project.

An SOA project is . . .

- a set of project resources (one or more business analysts, system designers, application developers, testers, architects, etc.) . . .
- and management resources (one or more project managers, initiative coordination and oversight management, release management, etc.) . . .
- dedicated to building and delivering a specific component or set of components . . .
- at a specific layer of the architecture . . .
- to be coordinated and *assembled* with other components that already exist or are being developed in another SOA project . . .
- to be aggregated and tested at the deployable "release" level . . .
- and delivered into production in the specified release defined in the enterprise SOA portfolio plan.

In our customer portal SOA initiative example, the decision is made to deploy the initiative in iterations over three separate enterprise SOA portfolio releases. Each release provides a workable, functional solution of a subset of the defined capabilities with all the capabilities delivered by the third release. These are reflected on the enterprise SOA portfolio plan by a series of SOA projects embedded in the details of the three releases.

The first SOA project defined is to develop the new Web portal channel adapter for customers as a single entry point for all customer interaction with the company. Ultimately, this will be the single conduit for all customer self-services offered over the Web. This portal will eventually replace the separate Web applications currently used by customers. The project will also include documenting the design patterns and design standards used to design and *configure* the security authentication and role-based service authorization mechanisms within the portal by leveraging the enterprise SOA security framework previously built to support authentication in other channels and for other services. The enterprise security component was designed to allow new channels to define the constituent and the authentication mechanism through a configuration module. Similarly, the security framework's policy configuration module defines the roles of those constituents, the services they are authorized to consume (service privileges), and the rules for consuming them (service authorization).

The estimated development time to complete this channel was driven by the business's desire to have the new portal available in the third quarter so that customers would have experience with the portal going into the peak interaction period, which occurs in the fourth quarter.

A second SOA project team is chartered to develop the business services to replace the current stovepipe services offered on the three web sites with SOA services. Most of these services involved leveraging the existing legacy integration components of the existing web sites and reengineering their model view controller (MVC)–controlled business logic into distinct business services. This team was assigned to work only on services that were being ported from the old architecture to the SOA architecture. The existing services that were identified by sales as the services that present opportunities for up-selling or cross-selling were assigned to another project team.

The business services developed by this team will be deployed into production in the same quarter-3 (Q3) release as the portal channel application built by the portal project team. The release that contains the portal and the ported services delivers a fully functional replacement for employees of the current customer Web application whose roles allow them to use the customer service and/or customer relations web sites. These individuals are not authorized and therefore do not use the current sales web site. Approximately 20 percent of a customer's employees have an additional role that allows them to use the sales web site. These employees will continue to use the old sales application until the next release containing the new and enhanced sale services is offered.

A third project team was chartered to develop the new business services and new business processes to support the identification of up-sell and cross-sell opportunities and the integration of existing sales services into a new business process to take advantage of those opportunities.

These new business services and business processes are scheduled to be deployed in the first release of Q1 of next year. Even though they could be delivered in the fourth quarter of the current year, the horizontal Portfolio Plan Governance Committee members, who represent the customer constituent, did not want them to be exposed to such a major change in the portal application during the peak customer utilization period and deferred its delivery to the next quarter.

A fourth project team was established to make enhancements to the enterprise service bus to incorporate the existing integration messages into the ESB and provide the necessary transformations for those messages to be consumed by the new business services. The current messages were directly consumed and managed by the existing individual Web applications. At the time they were built, the ESB platform did not exist. The strategy followed by the enterprise SOA Technology Governance Committee was to not invest in porting messages to the new ESB until a new project based on business needs required them. Since other applications besides these three use the messages in their existing format, they will be allowed to be used in their old format directly as well as through the ESB until all the other applications are enhanced.

Enhancements to several of these messages were already scheduled to support requirements of other projects on the enterprise SOA portfolio plan. These were being delivered in Q1 and Q2 of the current year. Since these enhancements included their assessment at an enterprise level and included semantic data structures, it was quickly determined that these messages would fully support the requirements of the customer portal initiative once their Q1 and Q2 scheduled deployment to the ESB is completed. The remaining messages were slotted to be available for integration testing by the first week of Q3 and deployed into production in the same Q3 release as the portal.

Some of these new integration messages were dependent on enhancements to the legacy order, billing, and field scheduling applications. The scope and complexity of these changes was simple enough to be addressed by the legacy application maintenance team. These enhancements were scheduled with this team so their design specifications and implementation would support the delivery timelines of the integration development team.

Resources from the release management team were assigned to incorporate the steps to aggregate the deliverables from this initiative with the deliverables from the other initiatives scheduled for the same releases. The release project plan will identify and manage all the activities and resources to conduct the aggregated release level testing, sponsor user acceptance, and certification of the release.

In summary, we have taken three applications that were developed under the old stovepipe approach and packaged a new SOA initiative to modernize and replace them with a new, fully integrated customer portal solution. As we have shown, this business initiative does not have a one-to-one mapping to a single IT project. Instead, it will be delivered through the four SOA projects and the release management projects just described.

Phase IV: Requirements Phase

Even though there are several projects under the SOA initiative, they are all based on a single common set of business requirements. In other words:

- Business requirements are gathered and documented at the *initiative* level.
- The system architecture is also defined and documented at the *initiative* level.

- Design specifications and component developments are done at the project level; therefore, they are specified and documented at the *project* level.

Even though SOA promotes the development of loosely coupled components that can be technically isolated from the layers above and below with the technical aspects of how those calls from the layers above or below are invoked, the big picture of the business requirements needs to be understood before components are developed or assessed for reuse. Any data, business logic, or exception handling provided by the component needs to understand the overall business requirement in order to be designed correctly. For example, a business service used to "Get Insurance Coverage" may be required to return:

- Current coverage.
- Coverage as of a certain date.
- A certain type of coverage (i.e., collision versus comprehensive in auto or inpatient versus outpatient for health).
- A combination of date and type.

These requirements can be derived only from the use cases or other form of requirements gathering at the process level. Alternatively, they may be defined, along with the semantic data model, by a standards body, such as the Association for Cooperative Operations Research and Development, (ACORD), or a regulatory act, such as HIPAA, that specify both the data and interaction rules of the transaction. Knowing that the business requirement can be fully supported by these service functions can be determined only by understanding the business requirement.

This does not mean that requirements gathering needs to be done in a waterfall fashion (requiring all business requirements to be documented and signed off before design specification begins). It does mean, however, that requirements for the design of any component needs to include the business context of how it is used by the layer above and how it uses anything from the layer below. Thus, the use case for the "Get Insurance Coverage" service needs to be completed before the "Get Insurance Coverage" service can be designed. The business requirements of the "Authorize Service" use case, which is a composite business process that includes the "Get Insurance Coverage" use case in one of its process steps, does not necessarily have to be fully documented to design and develop the "Get Insurance Coverage" service.

There is, however, no separate set of business requirements or a different use case for the "Get Insurance Coverage" step in the authorize service process defined in the same initiative. The requirement is the same for both. This common requirement definition would be very difficult to validate and maintain if the requirements were gathered multiple times by several projects. Therefore, all requirements, no matter how they are gathered, must be compiled, vetted, and approved at the initiative level.

The use cases, process models, integration, and invocation rules used to define the component all need to be packaged and captured in the service contract developed for the component. Each instance of use of a component, either within the current initiative or in a future initiative, will more than likely be required to have its own service contract. These service contracts do not change the business functionality of the service but can change the service stub invocation mechanism or the SLAs associated with the service (i.e., increase availability of the service to 24/7).

There are many examples of use cases, process models, integration models, invocation models, and service contracts. They exist in the public domain, within standards groups, and within the literature supplied with vendor technologies. It really does not matter which specific ones you use, as long as you understand how to use them to support the SOA model and framework presented in this book. The key is that they allow the representations produced out of the models to be classified and identifiable to the layers and sublayers of the SOA~EAF.

A use case that shows an actor using a service needs to conceptually capture the recognition of one or more channels between the actor and the service as well. The use case should conceptually reflect not only the channel but the channel adapter as well. A business process model reflecting user interaction across an orchestrated set of services should represent those user interactions in a logical, semantic format that is channel and presentation layer agnostic. Use case and business process requirement specifications that are framework components (e.g., security, logging, exception handling, etc.) need to be clearly identified as such and isolated. Incorporating these characteristics into the business requirement documentation will expedite the design and development phases and minimize miscommunication and confusion.

Note

The process for documenting the architecture metadata and production of all the architecture artifacts associated with the initiative is described in the Phase VIII section later in this chapter. While requirements gathering for any initiative occur at the initiative level, sign-off of those requirements will occur at both the initiative (business sponsor[s] of the initiative) and component (architecture) level. The architecture metadata and artifacts are documented at the component layer and in the context of the enterprise reference architecture. In other words, the initiative that funded the initial design and development of the "Get Insurance Coverage" business service and the "Authorize Service" business process defined those SOA components with a set of interrelated and interacting use cases within a single business requirement document for the initiative. The project team, however, extracted out the use case for the "Get Insurance Coverage" business service and structured it as supporting metadata within the documentation for this component in the Business Service Domain layer of the architecture. Similarly, the "Authorize Service" business process swim lanes will be extracted and stored along with other metadata artifacts (e.g., the BPEL for the process) at the Business Process Domain layer of the architecture.

The use cases stored at this level will reference, not duplicate, any business service use cases embedded in the process. Therefore, the step in the "Authorize Service" business process use case that invokes the "Get Insurance Coverage" business service will point to the "Get Insurance Coverage" business service use case stored at the Business Service Domain layer. Use cases will be stored in the business architecture cell at the Business Service Domain layer. The service contract associated with invocation of the service by the use case would be stored in the Reference Architecture cells at the Business Service Invocation sublayer. The design specification for the component would also be stored in the Reference Architecture cell. Ideally, links to a service repository, a Universal Description, Discovery, and Integration (UDDI) repository as well as links to the source code in a code management repository should all be implemented.

The "Get Insurance Coverage" business service over time will be used by several other business processes or be deployed as is directly through one or more channels. This will be reflected in the architecture metadata when those projects are completed. Thus, any component at any layer can be traced and managed in the context of all its usages and interactions with the layers above and below.

The next initiative that uses either the "Get Insurance Coverage" business service directly or uses the "Authorize Service" business process will not define the requirements for these in its business requirement document from scratch. These requirements will be extracted from the architecture documentation stored in the Business Architecture Framework column of the SOA~EAF (e.g., use cases and business process models) and presented to the business analysts on the new project for validation. If the existing business functional requirements do not meet 100 percent of the new initiatives requirements, one of two things can occur:

- The business can change its business requirements and accept the current version as is.
- It can request a new version of the service or process.

As stated, having those use cases reflect the channel and channel adapter used helps to validate that the existing service can provide the functionality required and deliver it through the desired channel. If the initiative requires and implements a new channel or channel adapter for the service, this change will be reflected in the use case so the next initiative evaluating it will see this second option as well.

Approval for new versions of SOA components must come from the enterprise SOA Technology Governance Committee. As you move up the layers of the architecture (closer to the consuming constituent), more and more variations of the SOA components should exist, but the total number of variation instances should be fewer than for the layers below. As you move down the layers of the architecture (toward the back-end, core legacy systems), fewer variations of the SOA components should exist but many more instances of unique SOA components should exist. In other words, you may have several channel adapters for each channel, but you probably have fewer than 10 channels in total. You probably will have hundreds of integration messages built on top of your legacy business applications, but it is not good to have more than one or two variations of an individual message. For example, an "Authorize Service" business process used by a doctor or a hospital may be less complex than one designed to be used directly by the health plan member. The member process may have to explain terminology or options in more detail then the process used by the doctors and hospitals. There is a clear and strong business need to have different processes to support these two different audiences.

If, however, the mismatch in the requirement is a resistance to using a semantic data model or the standards body specifications because the sponsors like the old *proprietary* format and rules, the enterprise SOA Project Governance Committee should have full authority to deny these requests and have the full backing of the enterprise SOA Portfolio Plan Governance Committee to do so.

If your governance bodies have approved the full commitment to standardized transaction sets and your "Get Insurance Coverage" business service semantic data model is based on the ANSI X-12 270/271 HIPAA format, you should not allow a second version of the "Get Insurance Coverage" business service to be built using the old proprietary data format. Remember, you adopted the SOA approach to leverage and reuse capabilities and move away from the old replicate-or-duplicate capabilities model.

IDENTIFYING BUSINESS PARTICIPANTS FOR THE SOA INITIATIVE REQUIREMENTS PHASE   The first step in determining who in the business should participate in the SOA initiative and what projects they should participate in is to define the different roles that you need from the business to develop an SOA initiative. You need business participants who understand the business *needs* and usage requirements of the *consuming* constituencies that will use the capabilities being delivered by the initiative. You also need business participants who understand the business *capabilities* and *control* requirements of the business units that are the *providers* of the services. Both these roles were often played by the same individuals in traditional projects. This worked because there was always one ultimate business owner who was empowered to filter and control the input of the business participants. Traditionally, business participants from outside the business unit that owns the application suggest or request what they want. Ultimately, however, the acceptance or rejection of these suggestions or requests was controlled by the owner participants who have to deliver what *they* need within the budget and time frame allotted.

Traditionally, these compromises have been in the favor of the service provider and to the detriment of the service consumer, since most legacy applications were owned by the business units responsible for providing the capability. This dynamic will appear in your SOA projects if you do not (1) clearly define and articulate these role distinctions and (2) make it clearly understood that the company (enterprise) owns the initiative, not a business unit. This is supported and confirmed by these facts:

- The initiative was approved and is monitored by the enterprise SOA Portfolio Plan Governance Committee (which comprises business representatives from every business unit), the body that:
  - Receives and reviews all status and progress reports.
  - Approves the scope and capabilities of the project and controls any changes to that scope or those capabilities.
  - Controls the completion and dictates the delivery of the initiative into production.
- The initiative is sharing and reusing capabilities that do not belong to the units responsible for or those that use the functionality.

While all of the business representatives will participate together in the requirements-gathering process, specific individuals will be appointed as suppliers of service consumer requirements and others suppliers of service provider requirements. This can be done in-band (during the requirements-gathering sessions) or out of band (after requirements are gathered) by two review groups representing the two views. These roles are explained in the next section.

The SOA model often produces solutions that automate business processes that cross and integrate the services from multiple business units (i.e., integrate the legacy systems from several business units). Business associates who understand the front-to-back (cradle-to-grave) relationships of the activities of a business process are very valuable in SOA requirements gathering and are included on the requirements-gathering team. The advantage of an SOA business process is that it provides the automation of the previously manual process of navigating from system to system and extracting the needed functionality. (See Exhibits 3.2 and 3.4.)

The SOA model extracts the functions from the legacy system through its Integration layer, makes them consumable through the Business Service layer, and combines them into front to back business Processes through the Business Process layer. Understanding the application-to-application navigation and relationships were not part of business requirements gathering in traditional developments.

Business process modeling tools and analysts trained in those process model techniques will be instrumental in helping the business define these processes. Business participants with experience in multiple business units and more midlevel leadership experience will be instrumental in expediting this gathering process.

If the consumers of the processes are external constituents, it is very valuable to have members of those external communities involved in the requirements process. It is highly unlikely that you will be able to get full-time participants from these communities (although it has happened). Your company may be successful in establishing focus groups or relations committees that meet periodically that you can run by or validate the processes they will use to interact with your systems. Ultimately, the ideal situation will be the ability to establish user groups in these communities not just to validate your thoughts on how to support them but actually to drive how you support them.

You might think that this works for software companies that establish user groups to define future capabilities of their software, but you are not a software company. *The reality is, in today's world, any company that allows its external constituents to use its systems to conduct business is just like a software company!* When the customer is using your application, the ability of that application to provide them what they need efficiently, effectively, and pleasantly is no different from what you would expect when you deal with a software vendors supplying a business application to your company. These resources are valuable not only to requirements gathering but to user acceptance testing and user documentation/training as well.

This is different from feedback solicitations on the constituent-used systems. These mechanisms are still valuable and increase the population of respondents, but they are after the fact. *Feedback* on improvements to a process after it is in production will never be cheaper than *input* before it is designed.

The SOA paradigm shift we are creating allows us to be more outside looking in rather than inside looking out. We are now able to realize values we never even thought to address before in terms of not only creating a new and better way for business and IT to work together but also a better way for IT to help the business support its customers, partners, and other external constituents. Finally, targeting and involving representatives from all the constituents provides high-value resources to the project.

FRAMEWORK FOR GATHERING REQUIREMENTS   Not surprisingly, the template for gathering business requirements is the same template used for the business architecture diagram that was included in the initiative's proposal. (See Exhibit 9.1.) The captured requirements represent the drill-down details for every constituent, channel, business process, business service, and legacy function identified in the business architecture. Any business requirement that cannot be mapped at a high level to this diagram will most likely represent a scope change. The only exceptions to this are nonfunctional requirements that were not represented on the business architecture diagram (for visual simplification) by the solutions architect but documented in the component estimation sheet.

BUSINESS PARTICIPANT ROLES AND RESPONSIBILITIES   The consumer-centric participants take a top-down approach and focus on the channel and business process requirements of each constituent. The provider-centric participants take a bottom-up approach and focus on the business services, integration services, and functional capabilities of the underlying legacy applications. The bridge between these two groups will be represented by the business participants who understand the front-to-back multi–business unit relationships of the company. These individuals ensure that the described process is complete and accurate. Consumers know what they want to do and have opinions on how they want to do it, but they will not necessarily understand all the corporate requirements involved in a transaction or even be aware of them. The providers know the capabilities of the legacy systems they control and the capabilities of the integration and business services that have been built on top of those legacy systems but may be unaware of additional rules that are applied to the same data elements in a different legacy system controlled by a different business unit during later steps in the process farther down in the transaction cycle.

Understanding these situations provides the opportunity to merge the back end rules with the other up front rules and process them holistically with the constituent at the same time.

These business participants may also have insight into legal or audit requirements that apply to the transaction in general, not individual steps in the process, and, therefore, would not be known by the individual service providers.

Finally, this group addresses the management and executive needs of the process. Under the traditional stovepipe approach, management and executive requirements for measuring and monitoring business processes were often addressed by extracting data out of several of the back-end legacy systems, conducting analysis, and producing summary measures and metrics for them to review. The SOA approach to business processes creates the opportunity to provide management and executives with more real-time metrics on transactions since the entire process is now controlled by a single process module instead of people and multiple separate legacy applications.

This is another advantage of the SOA enterprise architecture approach to business systems—the ability to make management and leadership more nimble and proactive.

Finally, the business plan and corporate strategic drivers that were used to justify the initiative should be posted at every requirements-gathering session.

ROLE OF ARCHITECTS IN REQUIREMENTS GATHERING The business and solutions architects need to establish and guide the most efficient and effective way to gather requirements. This will depend on the scope, breadth, and depth of the initiative. Requirements gathering should be sliced and prioritized based on:

- The number and timing of releases where the initiative will be deployed.
- The dependencies and prerequisites identified across all the projects.
- The ability to isolate and address a vertical or horizontal path down the initiative (i.e., a specific set of services are being delivered exclusively to one constituent through one channel [vertical] or focusing on all the integration services requirements at once).
- The volume of new versus reused components.

Requirements gathering does not have to be linear or conducted in a single large group session. In fact, this most certainly will not be the case. The best approach is to hold single sessions initially and incorporate into those sessions' discussions around options and alternatives for gathering requirements going forward. Let the business make the decision on how to proceed, but make sure the options and alternatives are defined by the architects.

The architects will extract and compile the business artifacts associated with the reused and leveraged SOA components to be used by the initiative. The documentation about a reused component (e.g., an existing "Check Credit" business service) or a leveraged component (e.g., the existing roles set up for a constituency and the existing services authorized under those roles) would be presented to the business participants for review. If the description meets the requirements of the business, it is added to the requirement documentation for the initiative. If the requirement does not meet the need, a gap analysis is conducted. The architects can use this analysis immediately to determine the best technical approach to meeting the requirement.

If the requirement is met by a subset of the service, existing documentation for that portion of the service should be added to the business requirement document. If the business requirement disconnect is a business request to use the old proprietary format and definitions rather than the semantic definitions and standards–based format of the proposed service, this issue would be taken to the SOA Project Governance Committee for resolution and, if necessary, to the enterprise SOA Portfolio Plan Governance Committee.

The architects should also be evaluating the existing SOA components against all business requirements as they are documented. The initial compilation of new and reused SOA components for the initiative was compiled from very high-level requirements for the purpose of generating the initial initiative cost estimates. As your SOA environment matures, it will be highly probable that some of the new SOA components in the estimate will already exist in full or in part. Also, as requirements become clearer, the opportunity to find more reuse increases.

REQUIREMENT PHASE DELIVERABLES   The deliverable of this phase is the detailed business requirement document. Traditional requirement documents tend to be functionally focused and bottom up in structure. In other words, a function is first described in terms of its data, then the business rules associated with the data are presented, then who uses the function is specified, and finally how and when they use the function is indicated.

SOA requirements are defined in reverse; they describe:

- First, the user constituent.
- Then, the ways users interact with you (channels).
- Next, the roles the constituents play.
- Next, the processes used by the constituent when performing those roles.
- Next, the functions that make up the processes.
- Finally, the data and transactional systems of record that integrate with those functions.

The deliverable should be in the SOA format, not the traditional format. It should start by listing the channel contracts for each constituent, including its authentication and role definitions, followed by the process and service contracts for each service provided to each channel for each constituent, including the supporting process models, use cases, and role definitions.

The service provider representatives add to these requirement definitions by incorporating the requirements for the business function rules and business data definitions, the authorization rules for the functions and data, as well as all the logging, tracking, and retention rules.

All other nonfunctional requirements not specified by the business participants should be added by the architects. Global requirements should be documented in a separate section. Examples of global requirements are:

- An audit record containing the name, date, and timestamp and transaction ID will be logged for each service.
- All services must be available 24/7 for the Web and IVR channels and M–F 8:00 AM to 6:00 PM for all other channels.

An example of a nonfunctional requirement is a requirement that the channel must maintain a state for each user while logged onto the channel and recover that user's state if a connection failure occurs.

Phase V: Design

As stated at the beginning of this book, many publications explain the technical approach for coding SOA components. It is not my intent here to explain these technical approaches. Here I present guidelines to follow and principles to remember when applying those technical approaches. They address more the process of coding rather than the technique.

Every component specification should have three parts at a minimum:

1. The core functionality of the component.
2. The service contract for consuming it.

3. The invocation specification for consuming SOA components from the layer below, if applicable.

The service specification may include the invocation specifications of enterprise framework components such as security, logging, exception handling, and so forth.

In addition to the business requirements for the component that were compiled during the requirements-gathering phase, the architects add:

- The specific design patterns to be followed and design standards to apply when constructing the component.
- The integrated development environment (IDE) tool used to code the component.
- The target platform for the component.

The developer is also directed to the design specifications for the invocation of the development framework components that need to be integrated with or used by the component being built. The design patterns and design standards should also address nonfunctional requirements, such as persistence to support load balancing and session recovery. They should also include specifications for conducting unit tests and certification of the component.

Enterprise consideration should be given to interoperability testing of the components. One approach to interoperability testing is to provide a global framework for testing stubbed-out versions of the component being built and the SOA components it interacts with within a common test environment. This is in effect specifying the creation of a test version of every component built. It is especially valuable for integration components but is also for framework components such as security. It allows for test data sets to be created and used to mimic the data stored in a back-end legacy system or in a security directory to facilitate interoperability testing. You do not want to use production security data or legacy business data when conducting testing, especially if the component creates or updates data in those data stores or if the information in those systems is sensitive. This approach also saves time and money by eliminating the need to set up new test data every time a component is used in an interoperability test.

There are advantages to using these stubbed-out test versions of the SOA components for user acceptance testing as well. For example, if the initiative is delivering a modification to an existing business process to add one additional checkpoint, but all the underlying business services are consumed by the process without modification, then there is no need to retest these business services. Being able to stub out these services so the process can be exercised by the user to test the new process step saves time and money.

Components that have been completed, tested, and certified (through code reviews by the architects) should be deployed to a common component environment and published as available for production release. Once placed in this environment, they become available for use by the other project teams. For example, a new integration service deployed and published to this environment becomes available for the developer building the business service that consumes it to conduct interoperability testing.

> **Note**
>
> Developers building components that consume other components that are under development do not have to wait for those components to be published to begin their coding. The service contract for invoking a component can be used to expedite their coding effort. While changes to the service contracts are rare, they will happen, especially for components in the higher layers of the architecture. An effective check-in/check-out mechanism of all design specifications should be employed to ensure that changes by one developer are captured and made visible to anyone else checking in or out those specifications.

Phase VI: Development

As with the previous phase, I am not going to cover the technical aspects of effective development in this section. The intent is to explain the development process that has been set up for developing SOA components and the management considerations to have this process run efficiently and accurately.

For any given SOA initiative, these development conditions may occur:

- Multiple development groups are established with each group focused on the development within one of these layers:
  - Developers focused on making necessary enhancements to back-end legacy systems or implementing a new purchased or leased legacy system.
  - Developers building or enhancing legacy integration components.
  - Resources building or enhancing business services or business processes.
  - Resources installing and building a new channel.
  - Resources building or enhancing a channel adapter.
- There may be resources working on other initiatives that are building or enhancing SOA components that will also be used by this initiative.
- The developers could be internal developers or external developers (vendor developers for purchased or leased applications, vendor installation and configuration resources for new technologies being implemented, or general outsource developers through an onshore or offshore contract).
- The developers may be on-site, off-site, or both.
- Prerequisites and dependencies among all the teams need to be managed.

All of these activities need to be monitored and coordinated. Any issues or delays anywhere in the process need to be addressed and dealt with globally. This is the responsibility of the SOA Project Governance Committee defined in Chapter 8.

Each project manager is responsible for defining the deliverables of the project and the dates for completing those deliverables. These deliverables include the sign-off dates for the design specification of each component, the date for deployment of the SOA components into the prerelease environment, and the date they are published as certified for release. These are critical delivery dates on the project plans, since other projects on the same initiative or other initiatives may have those SOA components as prerequisites or dependencies. Each project manager is responsible for immediately reporting any changes to the status of these deliverables to the Project Governance Committee. In addition, every project manager should review and validate the green, yellow, or red status of all their deliverables on a weekly basis. While the SOA Project Governance Committee will manage and direct the resolution of the yellow and red deliverables, it is the responsibility of the project managers working with the other project managers impacted by the condition to implement and correct the issues.

The most critical activity under the development phase is the code review conducted by the project architects to validate that the code complies with and properly used the development frameworks, design patterns, and standards from the design specifications. Failure to comply with these requirements will result in components that will not be reusable in the future but also may fail the interoperability testing when integrated with the other components of the release. Code reviews should not begin after all the components are completed. They should occur early and often for each component being developed, especially in the early adoption stage of this new SOA development process. As more components are developed, the code reviews will become easier, and fewer violations will be encountered.

Phase VII: Prerelease Aggregation and Acceptance

We have defined a release as a specific event on the enterprise SOA portfolio plan that delivers a holistic, workable set of capabilities. Within any one of these releases there may be delivery of SOA components resulting in a workable or deployable set of capabilities associated with one or more initiatives. This is similar to the concept of a phased implementation under the old project approach, where subsets of the total functionality (in this case a subset of services) are delivered in phases until the total functionality is completed.

We also defined the different types of projects needed to support a release-based SOA model. A project team must be established within the release management group to be responsible for the aggregation of all SOA components within the release, the final certification and acceptance of those SOA components, and their deployment into production.

A release could be made up 100 percent of a single initiative but more than likely it is comprised of deliverable subsets of multiple initiatives. Remember, the model we are following is not the deliverable of a stand-alone application but of new SOA capabilities across a shared and leveraged environment. Thus, our focus has shifted from a bottom-up delivery of an application to a top-down delivery of constituent capabilities.

In the earlier example of the customer portal initiative, we specifically split the delivery of the initiatives capabilities into three separate releases. This decision was based on the impact to the constituents and the business units that support them, not on the technical restrictions of the old development model.

Therefore, the release management team will specify the delivery date requirements for all the SOA components in all the initiatives targeted for each specific release. This means that the release manager sets the last acceptable date that a project can deploy a component to the prerelease environment and obtain certification and publication sign-off. These dates are determined by the release team based on the scheduled release date and:

- Input from the architects on the amount of time that will be required to compile and certify all the SOA components in the release.
- Estimates from the test team on time needed to conduct user acceptance testing and get final sponsor review and sign-off.
- Estimates from the SLA Governance body on time to conduct final quality assurance analysis and complete production readiness activities.

Different date requirements may be established for certain SOA components or component types being delivered based on input from these groups. For example, the delivery of a new channel or channel adapter technology may be required earlier than the delivery of some integration service components. This would allow more time for operations to set up and simulate the support requirements of the new channel as opposed to the operational support of the integration infrastructure which would already be well established.

Many publications explain the technical aspects of a release management approach to software development. While not many specifically focus on SOA, those that focus on release management of distributed multitiered applications over a shared platform environment are the ones to look for.

How you physically deploy code, and how many environments you deploy to, will vary from company to company, depending on many factors of their unique environments. At a minimum, I suggest you have separate environments for development, test, staging, and production. This may vary depending on the types of components and technologies involved. What I want to stress from a process and management standpoint are:

- You make sure that each project moves all its SOA components into the prerelease environment no later than their planned delivery dates.
- Once all the project SOA components have been placed in this environment, they can be integrated with all the other in-production components, tested, and certified.
- The users are allowed to conduct a final review and approval of the release.
- You have a mechanism to freeze the production environment prior to deployment of the release.
- The deployment refreshes all the reused and leveraged SOA components encapsulated in the release as well as the new SOA components deployed at the *discretion* of the release manager.

Not all releases will require a refresh of the entire deployed environment. Major releases deploying significant functionality to one or more channels more than likely will. Minor releases or release patches, however, may not. An SOA model is different from an object-oriented model in that when we reuse SOA components, we are using existing instances of those SOA components, not deploying new separate physical instances of those components; therefore, there is no need to redeploy these SOA components if no changes have been made. If, however, there was a change to a dynamic linked library in a Windows client application to be able to consume a new service, the entire client code for that application should be refreshed.

The release manager may opt to move some of the SOA components into production through a minor release or a release patch prior to moving the rest of the SOA components through their scheduled release. Again, this will be based on analysis and input from all parties involved.

The project managers and project architects are responsible for ensuring that all change controls needed to move the SOA components developed within their project to the published prerelease environment are documented, approved, submitted, and completed.

The release manager is responsible for ensuring that all change controls needed to move the SOA components in the published prerelease environment to the remaining environments (including the interoperability test environment) are documented, approved, submitted, and completed. Since the release manager (through his or her release project plan) is the only one who knows all the SOA components from all the projects that will be deployed in the release, this person is the one who will define all the interoperability testing requirements for the release.

Phase VIII: Release Deployment

Each release deployment is a scheduled event. Everyone involved should be aware of the release events and what they contain well in advance. This includes business units and constituents. There should be no surprises to the business as to when functionality is being delivered, who it is being delivered to, and how it is being delivered. Therefore, notification of a pending release and the business awareness and support of it should be uneventful.

Every release should have a contingency and rollback plan. In the event that something fails or breaks during the release into production, the entire process needs to be rolled back and the old production environment reinstated if necessary. The old world of deploying completely self-contained code on dedicated servers did have its advantages in terms of risk to the environment. Over time, however, this old approach becomes unsustainable in terms of costs and maintenance. The risk in deploying SOA applications is much higher. That is why everything done by the release manager up to the deployment has focused on mitigating and eliminating these risks. In the event that a release has to be backed out, however, the ability to do so and restore the old environment has been built into the release plan and release timeline.

Some releases will require shutting down old applications and cutting over to the new capabilities. In our customer portal example, two legacy Web applications are replaced by the portal in one release with the third replaced in a different release. The first deployment of the customer portal will replace the domain name system (DNS) URL for these two applications so they redirect to the portal application. Once this is done, the code for those two applications needs to be decommissioned and removed from production. The user profiles in the security modules for these constituents may contain production configuration changes to support this cut-over. If the portal release fails, all these configurations and domain changes need to be reinstated.

The entire release process must be supported by a well-managed and strictly enforced change control process. Every environmental variable change, configuration change, and code change needs to go through change control. Every deployment of these changes through every environment needs to be managed by change control as well. All changes should be performed by a centrally managed group within operations. A process where changes are performed by development or release resources rather than operations increases the risk of something going wrong during the deployment of the release.

The release deployment phase handles everything required to move the release into production, including all the configuration changes and code deployment instructions. The actual deployment of the release, however, is performed by the production support group within IT operations.

Phase IX: Production Support

Production support reviews and supports *releases,* not initiatives or projects. Production support is responsible for ensuring that the applications in production meet all the quality of service and SLA requirements specified by the business. This is accomplished through the SLA governance bodies defined in Chapter 8. Those bodies are repeated here for convenience. They are:

- Production certification and release governance body.
- Change management governance body.
- SOA application management and monitoring governance body.
- Vendor application, platform, and technology SLA governance body.
- Business continuity governance body.

Through these governance bodies, production support validates that everything that needs to be completed before the SOA components are placed into production is, in fact, completed and everything needed to support them once they are in production is documented and approved. Some examples include:

- Help desk support for the constituents who will be using the components.
- Validation of all the names and contact information for everyone identified on any SLA escalation contact lists.
- Updated business continuity plans integrating the new SOA components into the plan.

The activities performed in this phase can be referred to as the production-readiness activities. These activities are the basis for the final go/no-go decision on the release.

After all this, production readiness criteria is validated and the go decision is made, the production support team executes the release deployment plan and places the SOA components and configuration changes into production. The release manager, project architects, and lead developers need to be on-site and work with the production support team to execute the deployment plan.

Phase X: Initiative Completion Phase—Assessment, Closure, and Sign-off

A final postmortem assessment should be conducted after the initiative is completed. This assessment evaluates the delivery of the initiative from cradle to grave and identifies any quality improvements to the process. The assessment includes:

- The completeness and accuracy of the original scope and cost estimates.
- The accuracy of all the delivery dates on all the projects.

- The effectiveness of the interactions of the project teams with each other and with the release manager.
- The sponsor(s)' satisfaction with the process and the delivered functionality.
- The completeness and accuracy of all the delivered documentation.

Feedback from this analysis is used to improve the process going forward. If patterns begin to emerge as multiple initiatives are assessed, this information should be brought to one of the higher governance bodies for resolution. For example, if project teams responsible for designing and developing business process services are consistently missing delivery dates on initiatives, the SOA Project Management Governance Committee should be notified of this pattern. The committee, in turn, may allocate resources to dig further to determine the root cause of the delays. If it is discovered that the root cause is the vendor or the outsource resources responsible for building SOA components at the business process layer are unfamiliar with the business and require significant follow-up with the business subject matter experts to clarify business requirements, then appropriate action with the vendor may be taken. This could include requiring the vendor to send some resources to business training courses offered by the company's training department.

A key assessment conducted at this phase is to evaluate the accuracy and value of the artifacts captured in the SOA~EAF that were used during this initiative's development cycle. This includes how helpful these artifacts were in identifying the reusable and leveraged SOA components that the initiative could potentially use. It also includes the effectiveness of the documented development frameworks, design patterns, and design standards that were used by the developers as well as the examples of previously deployed SOA components that were used as models by the developers. This information is used by the SOA enterprise architecture team to improve the SOA~EAF documentation captured.

All the project managers and architects who participated in the initiative should attend this postmortem session. The release managers and operations associates who participated in the initiative should participate as well. The business sponsor's leaders can participate in these sessions or, alternatively, a separate session between them and the PMO leaders can be conducted to get their feedback.

Summary

In this chapter we defined the SOA system development life cycle. We introduced a model that is very different from the traditional stovepipe application approach. The SOA SDLC process defined in this chapter is designed to facilitate two critical SOA principles needed to maximize the value of SOA:

1. It represents a process that builds and leverages expertise and intellectual capital for building SOA components in the different layers of the architecture.
2. It facilitates the delivery of SOA business capabilities from a top-down, consumer-centric enterprise perspective rather than from a bottom-up, functional perspective.

The SOA SDLC is designed to facilitate a layered approach to the development of SOA components delivered through a release approach to software delivery. The process is designed not only to maximize the reuse and leveraging of existing SOA components but also to maximize the efficiency for deploying shared capabilities to multiple constituents and to minimize the impact of each deployment on those constituents.

This chapter also defined how to leverage the management information to provide ongoing quality improvements to the process.

CHAPTER 10

Capacity Planning under SOA

Under the traditional stovepipe approach, most applications had their own dedicated platforms. Thus, the capacity and performance requirements were physically visible and explicitly defined. Under SOA, however, most new SOA components will be deployed on existing platforms. The delivery of the capacity and performance enhancements needed to support these new SOA components is based more on the volume and order in which those components are deployed, not the specific dedicated platform requirements of the application. Therefore, SOA requires that we not only change the way we assess the capacity and performance requirements for each SOA initiative but that we adopt a proactive enterprise approach to capacity and performance planning and analysis.

Assessing capacity and performance requirements becomes very complex in a distributed environment with highly leveraged and shared infrastructure components. Pieces can often be overlooked or evaluated inaccurately. Since distributed environments are the very nature of an SOA infrastructure, understanding and effective management of these issues is critical. The enterprise SOA infrastructure and capacity architect provides a dedicated focus for capacity management and resolution of these issues as they arise.

Analyzing and effectively managing these issues requires a holistic understanding of:

- All the infrastructure components in all the layers.
- The current capacities, utilization, and performance of those components.
- The estimated increase demand on each layer's SOA components for the developments in the queue.
- The capability of those components to meet the projected demand and the necessary enhancements or additions needed if they cannot meet that demand.

Assuming that a solutions or project architect can accomplish this by himself or herself is a big risk. Assuming that these issues can be addressed at each domain layer independently is also a big risk.

Layered Approach to Monitoring and Managing a Distributed SOA Architecture

The components that make up an SOA application are deployed on multiple platforms at each layer of the architecture. In many cases, the legacy applications are deployed on their own dedicated mainframes or servers. Integration services can be deployed on their own servers or as distributed agents on multiple platforms, including the legacy platforms. For example, IBM Websphere MQ managers can be installed on each legacy mainframe or server to support integration message queuing and persistence. Integration services and orchestrated business services can also be deployed on servers supporting centralized or distributed enterprise service bus (ESB) technologies. Channel technologies (Web servers) and channel adapter technologies (portal servers) can also be deployed on their own dedicated servers or share their platform with other technologies (Web application server). Databases may have their own dedicated clusters. All of these servers and mainframes are interconnected through network devices that could be interconnecting systems thousands of miles apart.

The bottom line is, understanding the performance and capacity requirements of any SOA initiative will call for a comprehensive and complex set of analytical tools and metrics. This analogy will help you understand the difference between evaluating traditional legacy applications and SOA applications.

Assume you are asked to assess how long it will take to move 1,000 gallons of water from a faucet to a holding tank 2,000 yards from the faucet. You have no hoses available to do the job. You are given the choice of having one person using a single faucet and one 20-gallon container to move the water or five people using five faucets and five containers (three that hold 4 gallons and two that hold 5 gallons). The faucet used to fill the 20-gallon container has a flow rate of 4 gallons per minute. Of the five faucets used to fill the five containers, one flows at 4 gallons per minute, two flow at 3 gallons per minute, and the last two flow at 2 gallons per minute.

The average travel time to the holding tank using the 20-gallon container is 2 minutes due to the weight of the container and the need to go slower to avoid more spillage. The return trip averages 45 seconds. The average travel time for the 4- and 5-gallon containers is 1 minute, since they are lighter and have smaller openings that cause less spillage. The average return trip for these containers is also 45 seconds.

The average loss due to spillage on each delivery using the 20-gallon container is 5 percent of the payload. (Think of this as packet drop and recovery.) In the case of the 20-gallon container, this is 1 gallon lost per trip. The average loss due to spillage of the 4- and 5-gallon containers is less than 2 percent of the payload.

Calculating the total number of trips and the total time needed to accomplish the task under the (legacy stovepipe) single 20-gallon container, single-faucet scenario is straightforward and simple. Calculating the total number of trips needed using the five containers and how long it will take to complete the task is much more complex. One unknown that has to be determined is which containers are using which faucets. Given that the travel time is constant, would it be better to use the higher-flow faucets with the smaller containers, allowing them to fill faster but requiring more trips? Or would it be better to use the higher-flow faucets for the larger containers, taking longer to fill but requiring fewer trips, which would reduce overall spillage?

The simplicity of the first alternative versus the complexity of the second alternative is similar to the process of assessing the capacity and performance of a monolithic stovepipe application versus an SOA application. While the complexity of the SOA alternative is significantly greater than that of the legacy stovepipe alternative, the efficiency and performance advantages of this approach are evident through the preceding scenario. Without doing the exact calculations, the second alternative can disperse 12 gallons per minute and make the round trip in 105 seconds. The first alternative can only disburse 4 gallons per minute and takes 165 seconds for a round trip.

SOA Initiative Capacity and Performance Assessment Process

When assessing the capacity and performance requirements of SOA implementations, we need to assess each component in the context of:

- The estimated number of interactions and the processing complexity of those interactions that will be generated by the application.
- The estimated amount of CPU cycles, memory and input/output (I/O) utilization needed to support the estimated peak load processing of the estimated interaction volumes.
- The available compute capacity (CPU, memory, and I/O) of the platform or cluster where the component will be deployed.

After this is completed for all components, the network utilization analysis between all the SOA components would be evaluated. Again, the average and peak bandwidth utilization of those network connections would be used as the baseline for adding the estimated average and peak utilization metrics of the new application.

While understanding the platforms and topology of the infrastructure as it relates to each new SOA initiative is critical to conducting the appropriate analysis, understanding the business utilization metrics associated with the SOA initiative is key to improving the accuracy of these estimates. If the current peak utilization of the servers where two interoperating services are deployed is between 3 PM and 5 PM, Monday through Friday, and the new SOA components being deployed support a interaction where 90 percent of the projected daily volume will occur between 8 AM and 10 AM, Monday through Friday, there is no need to build capacity to support the added peak capacity of the new services to the current peak capacity of the servers and network. For example, deploying new SOA components that support the hospital admission process (of which 90 percent are processed from 8 AM to 10 AM) on servers currently containing components to support the discharge process (of which 90 percent are processed between 3 PM and 5 PM) is an efficient utilization and balance of the infrastructure assets.

Another example of why understanding the business usage of SOA components is so critical is the enrollment process within a health insurance company. Approximately 80 percent of the enrollment transactions processed by a health insurer occur between November and the middle of January. Therefore, the services supporting the enrollment process consume negligible capacity and processing resources from February to October, but their utilization spikes significantly for the November–January period. As new SOA components get deployed during the year, failure to recognize these business conditions can have a devastating impact on performance come November.

Thus, the architecture team plays a critical role in the capacity planning process. The business architects compile and provide the business estimates and metrics for the SOA initiative. The solutions architects provide the list of components that will be reused or developed by the initiative and the projected deployment platforms for those components. As the initiative progresses, the project architects will provide additional information on the data volume and processing complexity of the component to be used to validate or refine the capacity estimates. Unit testing of the individual components and precertification interoperability testing of the components will supply more refined information.

All of this information is compiled and analyzed by the enterprise SOA infrastructure and capacity architect to provide the capacity requirements for the initiative. This information is used by the enterprise SOA infrastructure and capacity architect and the release managers to determine the capacity and performance requirements for each of the upcoming releases. This is explained in more detail later in this chapter.

Proactive Planning for SOA

Conducting a capacity and performance assessment for each SOA initiative is necessary, but it is more important to adopt a proactive approach to capacity and performance planning to support SOA. The proactive approach is a process that monitors the platforms and pipes and takes proactive action to ensure that defined thresholds are not exceeded. Working with the SOA application management and monitoring governance body, the enterprise SOA infrastructure and capacity architect establishes baseline capacity and performance levels for all the platforms in each layer of the architecture and baseline bandwidth utilization levels for the network connections across the platforms. These baselines will be different, depending on the type of components running on the platforms and the size and volume of the network traffic generated between the components. Components that have a relatively low volume of small data packets moving in and out of them but require a significant amount of processing power for the business logic will require platforms that have high CPU compute speed and lots of memory, but not necessarily high I/O bus speed and network bandwidth. Database servers, however, need to move large volumes of data over multiple connections; therefore, I/O capacity and network bandwidth are most important. A message ESB is moving relatively small packets of data but may be performing a significant amount of translation, aggregation, and mapping logic that requires a lot of memory and CPU speed.

Step 1: Understanding and Defining the Environment

The key is that each layer of the architecture should utilize the technologies and platform architectures that are most efficient for the type of work performed at that layer. Back-end legacy applications and databases may utilize massively parallel versus symmetrical platforms and have multiple high-speed network connections. Service and composite application layer platforms may use clusters of multithreaded servers to optimize performance. Channel layer platforms are often front-ended by load balances and appliance servers (e.g., encryption/description appliances) to improve performance.

Understanding the platform architecture is the first step in the capacity and performance assessment process. Understanding how those platforms scale is the next step. Platforms such as massively parallel processor (MPP) scale vertically (i.e., adding more CPU and memory to the existing frame). Other platforms, such as clusters and those front-ended by load balances, can scale vertically by adding CPUs or memory to each server or horizontally by adding another server.

It is also important to know if the servers have local disks or are on a storage area network (SAN). If both are utilized, do you have a policy to ensure that local disks are dedicated to system services (operating system, application platform code, network monitoring agents, etc.) and SAN disks dedicated to business application data? If the programs of the deployed components resides on local disks, this capacity has to be understood as new components are added.

Finally, it is important to know all the high-availability and fail-over configurations that exist in the environment as well. If warm or hot servers exist in a second data center, whether they are active-active or active-passive for the platform where SOA components are deployed, capacity assessments have to include these platforms as well.

Step 2: Understanding the SOA Application Components

The second step in the process is to understand the components deployed on the platforms and how those components (and the technologies that support them) utilize and consume resources. Are the SOA components CPU intensive? Memory intensive? I/O intensive? Are there large or small volumes of data moving in and out of the component? What is the frequency of data moving in and out? Where is the data coming from and where is it going? Does the technology running the component (e.g., an ESB product or an application server platform) provide caching? Multithreading?

Step 3: Monitoring the Environment for Baseline Metrics

The next step is to monitor and compile statistics associated with the various platforms and the bandwidth utilization of the pipes between them. Samples should be compiled long and often enough to provide a reasonable and acceptable representation of the average and peak utilization. These initial samplings will become the basis for establishing the baseline capacity and performance measures for the capacity and performance planning process. The utilization table in Exhibit 10.1 is used to summarize these statistics.

Each server or cluster of servers will be defined and maintained by operations. This information includes:

- The name of the server and the cluster it resides in if applicable.
- The number and speed of the CPUs.
- The amount of memory and how that memory is allocated (i.e., pooled or allocated to individual CPUs).
- The number of I/O connections and the I/O bus architecture and speed.
- The number of network connections on the server, the speed of those connections and their configuration (duplexed? Pooled? Allocated?).

EXHIBIT 10.1   Server Utilization Table

Item	Average Utilization	Utilization Window	Peak Utilization	No. of Peaks in Utilization Window	Average Length of Peak Utilization	Longest Peak Utilization
CPU(s)						
Memory						
I/O						
Network						

Average Utilization: The average usage as measured within each sample for all the samples taken.

Utilization Window: The SLA-defined supported uptime for the item (e.g., M–F 8 AM–8 PM, or 24/7).

Peak Utilization: The highest utilization captured in the samples.

No. of Peaks in Utilization Window: The number of times the peak utilization was captured and the time stamps of those peak periods.

Average Length of Peak Utilization: The average length of time sustained by the peak utilization.

Longest Peak Utilization: The longest peak utilization encountered and the start and stop time stamps of that duration.

Utilization tables should exist for every server or cluster configuration defined by operations. The inclusion of time stamps on the peak utilization provides the ability to look at all four items being monitored to see if these peaks align. In other words, are CPU and memory spiking at the same time? Are I/O and the network spiking at the same time? Are all four spiking at the same time? This information is also valuable to identify the peak periods of usage by the business. The detail logs used to compile the summary table should also contain the list of processes that were running during the samplings. Looking at these logs and the processes running during the peak utilization periods will help identify what components or class of components are being used by the business during these periods.

Several samplings should be done for different time cycles: for example, at the beginning, middle, and end of the month. Several samples should be taken during those periods: for example, at the start of business, midday, and close of business on Monday, Wednesday, and Friday.

Two other areas need to be monitored and incorporated into the capacity planning process. The first is direct access storage device (disk) utilization and capacity. The second is the data center footprint and capacity analysis.

DISK CAPACITY AND PERFORMANCE ANALYSIS   Disk monitoring includes monitoring each server or cluster's use of local disk and any shared area network disk space. In most cases, the operating system files and the compiled code for all the application-level components will be stored on the server's local disks with the business data used by the applications stored on the SAN or NAS. Any temporary files created by the applications while they are running, as well as temporary files created by the operating system, would use the local disk as well. Many of these files are swapped in and out of memory during the process. Even though these files are deleted when the process is completed, the storage capacity needs to be there when the process needs it. Therefore, analysis of how much temporary storage each process requires and how many of those processes could potentially run simultaneously needs to be conducted to accurately size the local disk requirements. This is especially important to understand on multithreaded platforms that can spawn additional processes to handle load. Each spawned process will also spawn its own set of temporary files.

Analysis of the growth rate of disk utilization should be conducted for local and networked disk. Knowing how much and how fast the disk capacity is being consumed is necessary to determine future capacity requirements. The final piece of information needed for disk analysis is the archive and purge specifications for the applications using the disks.

The server utilization table (Exhibit 10.1) should be the *local* disk utilization table. This table contains:

- Server name
- Current disk capacity
- Available disk capacity without swap-out
- Available disk capacity with swap-out
- Current disk consumption:
  - Permanent
  - Temporary
  - Total
- Amount and percentage of current capacity available
- Historical monthly disk capacity consumption percentage and volume
- Projected monthly disk capacity consumption percentage and volume

This information will be used as the baseline to establish the local disk threshold levels defined later in this chapter.

For disk analysis of SANs or NAS frames, the process involves analyzing both the disk capacity and the access speed. The IT operations department should have a current definition of the SAN or NAS platforms and the configuration of those platforms. This includes the number of frames, the current utilized capacity within those frames, the current available disk space, and the available expansion disk space. These definitions should also include the total number of connection ports on the frame, the speed of those connections, and the available ports and their speeds. Some NAS technologies can be front-ended by other technologies that allow single high-speed ports to be multiplexed into multiple slower ports. The advantage of these technologies is that they allow more servers to attach to the network storage, especially when the normal high-speed port capacity would be overkill for those servers.

Policies for using and paying for network storage and a procedure for requesting increases in allocations should also exist. Use policies may include primary versus secondary (backup) storage requirements. They may include requirements to have archiving, retention, and purging specifications clearly defined and documented.

Payment policies might include organization charge-backs and billing rates. Charge-backs at a department level worked well when stovepipe applications were "owned" by departments. This model no longer applies under SOA. Since SOA is a service-based approach, charge-back mechanisms ultimately need to be service based as well. SOA charge-back mechanisms will be very similar to the billing models used for cell phones. You will have options for base fees, for ranges of usage up to unlimited use. Alternatively, you can opt for pay-as-you-go models for consumers of lower volumes. Service *consumers* will pay for use, as opposed to the older model where Service *providers* paid for the use. The service rate will include the fixed cost allocation as well as the variable rate allocation. On cell phones, the fee paid includes the variable costs associated with the number of air minutes used or text messages sent as well as fees to cover the cell phone network and infrastructure. From an SOA perspective, the billing of services may include monies to:

- Recover the initial cost of building and deploying the service components.
- Cover the cost of the resources used while the service is being consumed.
- Share in the cost of all the fixed infrastructure costs in the service environment.

Note

If you are in an organization that requires charge-backs for IT assets and services, you need to address this issue strategically in your SOA business strategy and roadmap document. This document is defined in Chapter 14. From a strategic perspective, you need to define the new charge-back model that will be employed for SOA applications and obtain executive approval for this model along with the rest of the SOA business strategy and roadmap document.

You also need to incorporate these requirements into the development frameworks and design patterns developed and published by the enterprise SOA Technology Governance Committee. Just as SOA transactions must be logged and audited at an enterprise level, using a shared logging service requires a development framework and component design patterns to ensure that charge-back requirements are addressed in the design of every SOA transactional component. A similar development framework needs to be defined to describe how charge-backs are captured and processed. The component design patterns have to incorporate the specifications for capturing and calculating the charge-backs and processing them through the shared framework components.

DATA CENTER ANALYSIS   Data center footprint analysis involves understanding of the server rack space; rack expansion space; available ports on the network distribution frame; power (including backup); and heating, ventilation, and air-conditioning (HVAC) capacities. Again, the SOA paradigm changes the way we need to approach managing these capacities. At the SOA initiative level, there is no accurate way of knowing that a new server or increased memory will be needed when the components of this initiative are deployed, even though we went through the exercise to determine what these needs would be. The reason is that the initiative has no way of knowing how much of the existing shared capacity in each layer of the SOA enterprise architecture stack will be absorbed by SOA components being deployed in other initiatives before the SOA components of this initiative are deployed. Thus, putting the responsibility of acquiring new capacity and ensuring that the data center has the capacity to support it on the initiatives is not only unrealistic but also extremely risky. For this reason, each SOA initiative estimates the capacity and performance requirements of each new or reused component in its initiative; the release manager uses this information to determine when the capacity needs to be available. The release manager capacity assessment process is defined later in this chapter.

The enterprise SOA infrastructure and capacity architect monitors the data center footprint and capacities on an ongoing basis. Any plus or minus changes to the available footprint or capacity should be reviewed and approved by this architect. He or she uses this information when working with solutions architects to help them scope and estimate SOA initiatives. The enterprise SOA infrastructure and capacity architect also uses this information when working with the release management team in IT operations so its members plan and procure capacity for the scheduled future releases.

IMPACTS OF VIRTUAL MACHINE TECHNOLOGIES AND GRID COMPUTING ON SOA I want to comment briefly on two specific technology concepts and how they impact SOA. The first technology is virtual machine technology. This technology allows for the creation of multiple servers within a single server. While each of these virtual servers logically represents the equivalent of a fully self-contained physical server, not all the resources may be 100 percent dedicated to each virtual server. They may share a common I/O bus or common network connections, and/or have partitions on common local disks. Therefore, all the applications on these virtual platforms need to be monitored and managed as one. The process is similar to the approach needed for server cluster technologies.

Grid computing presents a different set of issues and opportunities. A grid approach for SOA has not been perfected as of the writing of this book. Grid computing requires the ability to tightly manage the resources, data, and application code distributed to the available platforms in the grid. The distributed functions are typically fully self-contained and do not rely on multiple interactions with other distributed functions on the grid. The whole SOA philosophy is based on distributed functions that are loosely managed and require extensive interaction with other distributed SOA components while they run. Grid computing is a lower-level technology that focuses on managing and leveraging physical computing assets. SOA is an architecture that focuses on managing and leveraging logical business service assets. Grid computing implements capabilities to leverage *physical computing resources* at the *operational* level. SOA implements capabilities to leverage *logical business services* at the *design* level. Therefore, distributing SOA components through grid technology is at a minimum risky and in many instances not technically feasible.

This does not mean that grid computing cannot be used in an SOA environment. Many lower-level foundational capabilities that are self-contained can leverage grid computing. In the earlier billing and charge-back example, the process that compiles all the accumulated charges for the month and generates the charge-back amounts and the entries against the budgets could easily take advantage of grid computing.

PERFORMANCE AND CAPACITY BASELINE ASSESSMENT SUMMARY The IT operations associates supporting the SOA application management and monitoring governance body are responsible for conducting all monitoring samples and maintaining the infrastructure configuration sheets for all the data center assets. Network services is responsible for maintaining the network topology diagrams and current capacity and utilization levels. Network services also works with the SOA application management and monitoring team to coordinate monitoring and sampling activities. The enterprise SOA infrastructure and capacity architect uses the information provided by these two groups to establish ongoing baseline performance and capacity statistics for the entire computing infrastructure. These baselines become the basis for setting the capacity and performance thresholds described later in this chapter. These baselines are reviewed and updated on an ongoing basis. Any changes to the baselines will require revalidation of the associated thresholds.

Step 4: Analyzing the Data and Establishing Capacity Thresholds

The enterprise SOA infrastructure and capacity architect working with the SOA application management and monitoring team analyzes the data to establish performance and capacity thresholds for each platform. These thresholds are incorporated into the monitoring and alerting tools used to monitor the production environment. The thresholds are used to trigger alerts so action can be taken. Thresholds should be set to trigger alerts at a level that allows enough time to correct the issue before it reaches an unacceptable severity level. In the case of shared network disk utilization by a database, it may take only minutes to allocate more space to the database. In the case of alarming increases in the sustained utilization of CPUs, memory, or network connections, the resolution will take longer. Examples of threshold triggered alerts include:

- Notifications if average CPU, memory, local disk, or I/O utilization goes above a specified percentage beyond the established baselines.
- Notifications of increases in the number and duration of peak utilization.
- Notification of network utilization above defined thresholds.

Multiple threshold alert levels with increasing levels of escalation can be established in the monitoring tools.

Step 5: Formalizing the Monitoring and Alerting Process

A formal capacity and performance monitoring and alert manual describing the policies and procedures just defined should be compiled and published. This manual should include the policies and process for:

- Documenting the assets in the IT infrastructure.
- Establishing baseline and threshold levels.
- Frequency of sampling and revalidating the baselines and thresholds.
- Alert escalation and notification lists.

The currency and publication of this manual is the responsibility of the SOA application management and monitoring team. The SOA application management and monitoring governance body is responsible for compliance enforcement.

Step 6: Funding, Acquiring, and Implementing the Capacity Improvements

The enterprise SOA infrastructure and capacity architect facilitates the approval of capacity acquisitions with the enterprise SOA Technology Governance Committee and incorporates these acquisitions into the enterprise SOA technology plan. The enterprise SOA Technology Governance Committee funds these acquisitions through its annual enterprise SOA technology plan budget and, if necessary, seeks additional funding from the enterprise SOA Portfolio Plan Governance Committee if it is unable to fund acquisitions from its own budget.

HANDLING ISSUES AND EMERGENCIES The enterprise SOA infrastructure and capacity architect will work with the other enterprise architects, the operations service-level agreement (SLA) governance teams, and the release managers to resolve issues and assess alternatives when necessary. Examples of these interactions include working with:

- The enterprise data architect to relocate or redistribute databases to improve processing or I/O efficiency.
- The enterprise integration architect to set up additional schemas or integration service instances to support the increased volume and spread the volume across more servers or schema instances.
- The enterprise channel architect to increase cluster and load-balancing capacities of the channel.
- Network services to increase the main distribution frame, intermediary distribution fames, local, metropolitan, and wide area network capacities as needed.
- Configuration management to redeploy code to redistribute SOA components to less utilized platforms or adjust service contract quality-of-service levels to allocate more resources to critical services and reduce resources for less critical resources.

These are just a few examples of the interactions and assessments that are required to support the capacity and performance dynamics of an SOA environment. While the processes just described seem like a lot of work, the investment pales in comparison to the risk and financial exposure of a major outage of production business capabilities. One negative I have come across many times is a fear or lack of comfort with the ability to monitor the SOA environment and maintain uptime SLAs. In most cases, these problems arise because companies have not really done anything to monitor and manage the environment. Or, if they have, they have tried to do so through the traditional approach using the old techniques. I hope the information provided in this chapter presents you with a comprehensive approach for achieving an effective capacity management process under the new SOA paradigm.

Capacity and Performance Planning for Releases

As mentioned earlier in this chapter, the responsibility for managing the production capacities needed for each SOA initiative resides with the release managers. They are the ones who know exactly what is being deployed and when it is being deployed; therefore, they are the most qualified to manage these activities.

In the SOA system development life cycle discussion in Chapter 9, we defined a release process where:

- SOA initiatives can be delivered into production in one or more than one release.
- Each release may contain production deployment of capabilities from one or more that one SOA initiative.

In addition, each release will contain newly developed or acquired SOA components that have never been deployed into production. Some, if not all, of these new SOA components will increase capacity and performance demands on the existing production SOA components they interact with through reuse or leveraged sharing. Thus, the release manager working with the solutions architects responsible for the initiatives extracts the capacity and performance estimates for the new and shared SOA components in those initiatives and compiles them by the release that delivers them. Working with the enterprise SOA infrastructure and capacity architect, the release manager determines the total capacity and performance requirements for the release and identifies the capacity and performance improvements needed in production to support the requirements of the new release.

These capacity enhancements are reviewed and approved by the enterprise SOA Technology Governance Committee and added to the enterprise SOA technology plan. As the SOA initiatives move from original approval estimations into design, then development and certification, these estimates are fine-tuned and revised if necessary. If any changes are made to the release schedule or if there is a change to the initiative SOA components delivered in a release, these estimates, acquisitions, and schedules need to be revised.

The release manager manages the enterprise SOA technology plan capacity project associated with the release. Doing this includes adding all the capacity enhancement activities to the release project plan and ensuring their completion by the end dates on the project plan. The SOA infrastructure and capacity architect oversees these activities and reports their status and progress to the enterprise SOA Technology Governance Committee.

Not all technology acquisitions related to SOA initiatives and their associated releases will be managed by the release manager. For example, say the initiative is the first one to use a portal technology at the Web channel adapter layer of the SOA enterprise architecture and requires that the portal technology be acquired installed and certified. This project would be on the enterprise SOA technology plan but would be managed by the enterprise SOA channel architect, utilizing the center of excellence resources and team. The portal platform technology needs to be certified and available well before the release date for the channel developers to begin coding. Training and certification of the design and development resources that will design and code the portal will have to occur before the design phase begins. The release manager will not be involved in the setup and certification of the production portal environment. He or she will get involved only when the first application using the portal platform gets released into production.

Application-Level Monitoring in Production

Monitoring the availability and wellness of SOA components in production is not the same as monitoring the infrastructure for capacity and performance. Infrastructure monitoring is more a physical resource monitoring mechanism (i.e., enough physical disk storage and enough physical memory or network bandwidth). Application monitoring in a distributed environment like SOA is more of a logical resource monitoring mechanism. For example, are all the SOA components needed to support a specific business interaction operating and available? Are these SOA components able to find each other and interoperate properly?

In a distributed environment like SOA, there are many moving parts, which increases the possibility of one of the parts having a problem. Many things can go wrong. Some may be caused by human error. Coding errors may cause others. Vendor bugs in the operating environment can cause some. Namespaces (containers that hold defined values used by an operating system or application) can be changed or overlaid. Processes can be inadvertently terminated and not restarted. Ports or memory heaps may not get closed or flushed properly.

Mechanisms to monitor the SOA components at the application level need to be implemented to ensure the wellness of the SOA application environment. Monitoring the SOA environment involves more than monitoring Web services. Monitoring Web services is important. In many cases, Web services are the most fragile link in the SOA application chain. However, they are only one piece of the environment.

Mechanisms to monitor the application components at the channel level need to be developed. For Web applications, this may simply involve mechanisms to periodically invoke the application's URL and alert if any "404 - Page not found" errors are encountered. On an EDI channel, it may involve pinging an FTP server and notifications if no new files are found in the FTP directories.

At the Business Process layer, mechanisms to monitor process execution and orchestration can be embedded within those processes (in band) or created as separate processes to monitor the process (out of band). A word of caution is needed. Embedded activity monitoring code adds overhead to the process. The more monitoring that is performed, the greater the impact on resources used and performance of the process. Therefore, a careful balance and pragmatic trade-offs are needed when developing in-band monitoring components. Out-of-band monitoring techniques can shift this resource and performance consumption off the process application platform. The drawback to this approach is that out-of-band monitoring does not have the capability to correct the problem or restart the process automatically. Out of band will simply alert that the problem has occurred. Out of band may not be completely out of band. In some cases, it will be. In other cases, you may need to add a small amount of code to the business process to generate status messages to the out-of-band monitoring process.

The next example highlights the distinction between in-band and out-of-band monitoring. In an in-band monitoring process, failure of the invocation of a process step, such as invoking a Web service, can include decision logic to attempt to discover alternative service locations and reinitiate the invocation process. Alternatively, the process could generate an error message to the enterprise exception-handling module and either continue or terminate the process, depending on the exception-handling response returned. Under this second alternative, a separate out-of-band process provides a central mechanism to handle process exceptions using data provided through a centralized logging system. In cases where the exception is less severe (e.g., warning messages), these can be logged for handling by the enterprise process, allowing the business process to focus on completing business tasks.

At the Business Service and Integration layers, standalone or platform-supplied tools to monitor Web services, the ESB, and messaging systems should be utilized. For example, messaging technologies like Java Message Service (JMS) and IBM Websphere MQ provide monitoring and management capabilities that handle asynchronous as well as synchronous message persistence, queuing, and recovery. Events from these processes can be captured and handled through almost all the industry-standard monitoring platforms.

Many application servers provide monitoring capabilities as well.

Summary

This chapter described some of the unique characteristics and complexities of SOA that make capacity planning and performance monitoring distinctly different. Unlike traditional capacity planning, SOA capacities need to be managed layer by layer, but with an enterprise utilization perspective rather than an application-by-application localized utilization perspective.

Under the old approach, many legacy applications had their own dedicated platforms; therefore, planning for their capacity was much simpler. Under the new model, capacity is absorbed on a daily basis by a host of independent activities whose actions are tightly woven and dependent. Under SOA, capacity planning and management must be proactive and enterprise driven. Under SOA, SLAs that specify business utilization criteria, especially where the utilization is "seasonal" or not linear, are critical to the capacity and performance management processes.

Acquisition of new management and monitoring tools designed to support SOA components should be seriously considered to support this process. The investment in these tools will be well worth it. Think about it this way. Most of us have spent hundreds of thousands of dollars over the years on HVAC in our data centers to keep the equipment at the right temperature to avoid a hardware failure, yet, when it comes to spending money on technology to make sure our software is kept at the right operational level to avoid a failure, we resist. The reality is that *any* failure is a failure. Do you think the business feels better if it was a software failure rather than a hardware failure?

Finally, architecture development frameworks and design patterns should be established to build SOA components with capacity and performance monitoring capabilities embedded within them. This investment will not be required for every SOA component developed. Mission-critical SOA components requiring 24/7 availability must be constructed with these capabilities.

CHAPTER 11

People Involved in the SOA Process

So far, I have defined the SOA~EAF™ and its relationship to other architecture frameworks. I have defined the SOA development approach as well as the governance model and processes for managing it. In this chapter, I focus on defining the roles, responsibilities, and capabilities of all the human resources that have been identified as participants in these processes. While many of these responsibilities have been identified elsewhere in this book, this chapter provides a mechanism to review and understand those roles holistically and identify their distinguishing characteristics. I am sure that I have missed some of the things that these people do in their unique environments. You may decide to split some of the identified roles and responsibilities differently across your resource pool. That is okay. What is important is that all the roles, responsibilities, and capabilities are represented by resources in your environment and they can be clearly distinguished and identified, so that no confusion exists as to who is responsible for what.

Architecture Resource Requirements for SOA

This section defines the various types of architects who should exist in the architecture practice and their organizational structure, roles, and responsibilities.

Enterprise SOA Architects

Enterprise SOA architects are either horizontal or vertical architects. Horizontal enterprise SOA architects are responsible for the horizontal domains of the SOA enterprise architecture framework. They are enterprise SOA:

- Channel architects
- Business services architects
- Integration architects

  Vertical enterprise SOA architects are:

- Security architects
- Data architects
- Infrastructure and capacity architects

Responsibilities of the vertical enterprise SOA architects transcend vertically across all the horizontal domains and share the security, data, and infrastructure responsibilities with enterprise SOA architects at each layer. Their role is to ensure consistency and accuracy of these assets across all the domain layers.

Enterprise SOA architects provide guidance and direction to solutions architects and project architects throughout the design and development phases of the SOA system development life cycle. They also assist these other architects in assessing and estimating initiatives submitted to the enterprise SOA Portfolio Plan Governance Committee for review and approval. Finally, they help these architects in identifying and resolving noncompliant architecture issues and obtaining variances from the enterprise SOA Technology Governance Committee when appropriate.

Enterprise SOA architects support the chief architect in the development of the enterprise SOA business strategy and roadmap. This document is, in fact, the IT business plan for implementing and supporting the SOA enterprise architecture transformation defined in this book. This document is defined and explained at the end of Chapter 14. It is there for a reason. You need to read every part of this book before you begin building this document. It will, however, be the first deliverable you produce and the first document that gets approved by the company executives. Enterprise architects are responsible for establishing and maintaining the SOA reference architecture. This includes all the development frameworks, design patterns, and standards defined within the reference architecture. Therefore, the policies and procedures that govern and define every aspect of the contents of the Reference Architecture column of the SOA~EAF are the direct responsibility of the enterprise SOA architects.

All enterprise SOA architects are members of the enterprise SOA Technology Governance Committee. See the "Enterprise SOA Technology Governance Committee" section in Chapter 8 for an explanation of the roles and responsibilities they play in that committee.

ENTERPRISE SOA CHANNEL ARCHITECTS Enterprise SOA channel architects are responsible for setting and maintaining all the policies, standards, and technologies used at the Channel Domain layer. They specify the specific products and technologies used at the Channel layer. This includes Web server platforms, portal platforms, intelligent voice recognition (IVR) platforms, electronic data interchange (EDI) platforms, and so on. They also define the architectural frameworks for using these technologies, including the frameworks for the adapter and interface sublayers. They define the design patterns and design standards to be applied when coding at this layer. Enterprise SOA channel architects are responsible for maintaining all the reference architecture artifacts and metadata compiled at the Channel Domain layers of the SOA~EAF. They work with business architects and solutions architects to help them understand the capabilities of the channels and the requirements for their usage. They also work with:

- Security architects to define all the policies, procedures, and standards for user authentication for each channel.
- Data architects to define data standards and semantic data formats for the channel presentation layer.
- Infrastructure and capacity architects to establish channel capacity monitoring standards, performance monitoring, as well as the other channel policies and standards for defining and supporting business SLAs.

Enterprise SOA channel architects should be technically competent in all the channel technologies and the applications of those technologies. They should also be knowledgeable about the heuristics and human ergonomics associated with presentation layer design, including the choreography of presentation layer interaction and work flow.

ENTERPRISE SOA BUSINESS SERVICES ARCHITECTS   Enterprise SOA business services architects are responsible for setting and maintaining all the policies, standards, and technologies used at the Business Process and Business Service Domain layers. Technologies they manage include business process management systems (BPMS) and ESB technologies. They define the architectural frameworks for using these technologies, including the framework used by the Channel Interface sublayer to invoke business process and business service contracts. They define the design patterns and design standards to be applied when coding at these layers. Enterprise SOA business services architects are responsible for maintaining all the reference architecture artifacts and metadata compiled at the Business Process and Business Service Domain layers. Enterprise SOA business services architects work with the business architects and solutions architects to help them translate business requirements into appropriate technical solutions. They also work with:

- Security architects to define all the policies, procedures, and standards for user authorization detection and enforcement for each exposed business process and business service.
- Data architects to define data standards and semantic data formats for the Process and Service layer business logic as well as the interoperability data standards for invocation service contracts with the layers above and below.
- Infrastructure and capacity architects to establish business process and business service capacity monitoring standards, performance monitoring, as well as the other policies and standards for defining and supporting Business Logic layer SLAs.

Enterprise SOA business services architects should be technically competent in service design, service orchestration, and business process design technologies and approaches. These approaches include:

- Understanding of service contracting and service contract stubbing methods to support multiple channel invocation mechanisms.
- Business process and business service modeling techniques.
- Process and service persistence and interoperability with channel layer session recovery mechanisms.
- Transaction persistence including distributed application architecture commit and rollback techniques.
- Service and process performance tuning techniques.
- Process and service activity monitoring techniques.
- Logging, auditing, and exception-handling techniques.

ENTERPRISE SOA INTEGRATION ARCHITECTS   Enterprise SOA integration architects are responsible for setting and maintaining all the policies, standards, and technologies used at the Integration Domain layer. Technologies they manage include integration transport technologies such as MQ Series; legacy application programming interfaces (APIs); access points, such as remote procedure calls and data integration; and transformation tools, such as extract-translate-load (ETL) technologies. They define the architectural frameworks for using these technologies, including the frameworks for the Integration Adapter and Legacy Adapter sublayers. They define the design patterns and design standards to be applied when coding at this layer. They also work with the vendors of the underlying legacy application technologies and legacy application maintenance teams to establish and maintain integration interoperability. Enterprise SOA integration architects are responsible for maintaining all the reference architecture artifacts and metadata compiled at the Integration Domain layers. They work with the business architects and solutions architects to help them identify and leverage the legacy system integration assets. They also work with:

- Security architects to define all the policies, procedures, and standards for user authorization pass-through to the underlying legacy security Systems.
- Data architects to incorporate the defined semantic models and legacy data translations and mappings into the Integration layer services.
- Infrastructure and capacity architects to establish Integration layer capacity monitoring standards, performance monitoring, as well as the other policies and standards for defining and supporting Integration layer and Legacy Application layer SLAs.

Enterprise SOA integration architects should be technically competent in middleware, messaging, and ESB technologies. They should also be competent in data extraction and data manipulation technologies, such as ETL tools. Finally, they should be knowledgeable about all the technology and techniques used with the legacy applications to facilitate integration. This includes:

- All the application's APIs.
- Transaction mapping and transformation modeling techniques.
- Remote procedure calls and exit routines.
- Stored procedures and triggers.
- Web services.
- Embedded messaging services (JMS, MQ).
- Embedded data services (ODBC, JDBC, SQL, Hibernate, etc.).

ENTERPRISE SOA DATA ARCHITECTS   Enterprise SOA data architects are responsible for setting and maintaining all the policies, standards, and technologies used for all the business data used at each domain layer. They define the architectural frameworks for constructing and representing data at each domain layers. This includes semantic data standards and formats, data mapping and translation standards, and logical data models. They define the design patterns and design standards to be applied when structuring and using data including formatting like XML. They identify and specify regulatory or industry-standard formats to be used, such as X-12 EDI data standards, ACORD standards, electronic funds transfer (EFT) standards, and so forth. They specify and enforce data naming conventions and maintain all corporate Metadata for all the data stores and data structures in the portfolio. Technologies they manage include data modeling tools, ETL tools, and metadata repository tools.

Enterprise SOA data architects work with all the horizontal enterprise SOA architects to define the data policies, procedures, and standards for each layer. They are responsible for the integrity of the corporate business data as it moves up and down the components in each layer. This includes naming conventions, validation and edit rules, and referential integrity of the data. It also includes semantic data structures and their compliance to internal or external standards as well as their mapping relationships to the proprietary formats of the application data stores. Enterprise SOA data architects are responsible for creating and maintaining the enterprise data model and the common information model that relates all physical data to the enterprise data model.

The common information model also identifies the system(s) of record for each data element and the data flow mapping of those elements into other data stores. This mapping includes the resolution of the physical naming structures and formats of the elements to the enterprise data model definitions. For example, the element name in the enterprise data model is "Customer_Number" and is defined as a 12-digit alphanumeric field. The element name in the order application database is "Cust_No" and is defined as an 8-digit numeric field. The field in the data warehouse is "Customer_Number" and is defined as a 12-digit alphanumeric field. The field in the semantic data model used in the "Enter Order" service is "Customer_Number" and is defined as a 12-digit alphanumeric field, but with an associated validation rule that restricts entry to 8 digits with no alpha characters with "zero fills" in the first four spaces.

This example reflects an enterprise need to expand the capacity of the customer number field and to support the industry's move to support alphanumeric customer numbers. Hence the enterprise model has been defined to support these requirements. All new data structures, such as the data warehouse and semantic model of the "Enter Order" service, are implemented using this standard. In order to accommodate the restrictions on this element imposed by the older legacy data stores, all new components that create or update this element are restricted to the validation rules of the old systems by the validation rule associated with the semantic model. When these old legacy systems are replaced or enhanced, the rule in the semantic model can be removed.

Enterprise SOA data architects work with the solutions and project architects to ensure that data standards, relationships, and rules like those in the preceding example are understood and applied. Enterprise SOA data architects work with other enterprise SOA architects to ensure that these data policies, procedures, and standards are incorporated into the design patterns and development frameworks they produce.

Enterprise SOA data and integration architects also work together to standardize and modernize the legacy system-to-system or application-to-application integration mechanisms. These activities are necessary to:

- Extend the logical isolation of the physical legacy applications.
- Streamline the back-end processes and make the integration of the applications into the higher layers more standardized and efficient.
- Facilitate the migration and ultimate replacement/modernization of these applications.
- Support the elimination of duplicate data stores.

Refer to Chapter 12 for more information on this process.

ENTERPRISE SOA SECURITY ARCHITECTS   Enterprise SOA security architects are responsible for setting and maintaining all the policies, standards, and technologies used for all the security components used at each domain layer, including the Legacy Application layer. Technologies they manage include directory servers, such as lightweight directory access protocol (LDAP) and active directory (AD); and access authentication and authorization policy systems, such as Computer Associates' Netegrity Siteminder or Sun Microsystems' SunOne Access Manager. They define the architectural frameworks for using these technologies, including the frameworks for integrating and synchronizing legacy security systems and technologies for provisioning. They define the design patterns and design standards to be applied when coding at this layer, including security assertion markup language (SAML) standards; other token standards; and authentication standards, such as digital certificates, user IDs, and passwords; as well as change and reset policies. Enterprise SOA security architects are responsible for maintaining all the reference architecture artifacts and metadata related to the core security components at all the domain layers.

Enterprise SOA security architects work with:

- Enterprise SOA data architects to define and manage any encryption, masking and de-identification policies, procedures, and standards applied to the corporate data.
- Enterprise SOA channel and business service architects to define the authentication and authorization privileges policies, procedures, and standards applied in the channel domain.
- External channel intermediaries to define and standardize the security standards and framework to provide security interoperability between the entities.
- Business application vendors to standardize the security interoperability with their system.
- Enterprise SOA business services architect to define the policies, procedures, and standards for authorization detection, challenge, and enforcement at the Process and Service layer levels.
- Business and solutions architects to help them understand and define the roles within each constituency and the rules for authentication and authorization applied to those roles. They also help these architects understand the relationships of these consumer-centric roles to the underlying legacy security systems and the requirements for authentication and authorization interaction between them.

ENTERPRISE SOA INFRASTRUCTURE AND CAPACITY ARCHITECTS   Enterprise SOA infrastructure and capacity architects are responsible for setting and maintaining all the policies, standards, and technologies representing the physical hardware and operating systems in the IT portfolio. This includes all network components and appliances. Their responsibilities include understanding all the capacity and performance requirements of all the SOA components in the releases scheduled on the enterprise SOA portfolio plan and making sure that the required capacity is there when needed. This includes servers, CPUs, primary memory, and local and shared disk storage. It includes data center rack space, network hub ports, and monitoring agents. It also includes any license requirements associated with those components (database licenses, server and CPU-based licenses, etc.). Chapter 10 addressed the capacity issues associated with a shared distributed environment like SOA and how to analyze and manage these types of environments.

Enterprise SOA infrastructure and capacity architects assist the solutions architects in assessing the capacity requirement estimates for the SOA initiatives. They also assist production support and IT operations in managing the ongoing capacity. Enterprise SOA infrastructure and capacity architects should have strong expertise in the server hardware and operating systems used in the corporation. They should understand the entire network topology and the components within the network. They should be knowledgeable about all the network, system platform, and application monitoring and management tools. They should be experts in server (CPU, memory, I/O), network storage (SAN/NAS), and network bandwidth utilization analytical and management tools and techniques. These architects also need to be well versed in the interplatform and internetwork relationships of the multiplatform, distributed SOA application architecture. They need to utilize tools and develop mechanisms that let them not only assess the capacity and utilization of the servers in each layer of the framework but also trace that utilization to SOA components running on the servers in the layers above and below.

Enterprise SOA infrastructure and capacity architects work with the other enterprise SOA architects to define and implement:

- Load balancing and clustering standards.
- Procedures and standards for activity monitoring and spawning and decommissioning of additional instances of services.
- Policies, procedures, and standards for high availability, redundancy, and disaster recovery.

Enterprise SOA infrastructure and capacity architects work with IT operations and production support to:

- Plan and manage capacity enhancements and changes.
- Establish policies, procedures, and standards for maintenance outages, operating system upgrades, and patches.
- Define the service levels to be supported and the mechanisms for monitoring and meeting those service levels.
- Define and administer any charge-back mechanisms, if so decreed, by the corporation.

SOA Business Architects

SOA business architects work with business unit(s) to define the business architecture and business requirements for their initiatives. The business architect helps the business conceptually define:

- Which constituents will use the capabilities being delivered.
- Which channel(s) they will use.
- What specific capabilities (services) they will use.

After the business architecture is drafted, these architects work with the solutions architects to define the proposed architecture for the solution and assist the solutions architects in calculating the time and cost estimates for the initiative. Business architects should be embedded in the business units they support. They are required to have a comprehensive understanding of the business functions performed by those units and the system capabilities that already exist to support those functions (enterprise, departmental, or personal systems). They also should have an understanding of the business unit's strategic business plans and how those plans relate to the corporate strategy. They represent the face of IT in the business community.

On the flip side, they must also have a strong understanding of the SOA enterprise architecture and the business value propositions it promotes. They must have a strong understanding of:

- The components that exist in the channel, business process, and Business Service Domain layers.
- Whether those components are already used by their business unit.
- If they are not in use, assessing whether they have potential value to their business unit.

They also have to have a strong understanding of the existing legacy applications, how the capabilities within these applications support and relate to the business unit, and whether that functionality has been adapted and exposed to the SOA Integration layer. They need to understand what capabilities of these systems are leveraged within the SOA framework and which capabilities are consciously being isolated and eliminated.

Along with strong business acumen, they need to possess great communication and presentation skills. They need to have strong persuasive and mentoring skills to help the business analysts and business subject matter experts transform their thought processes and analytical approaches from a bottom-up, stovepipe system mentality to a top-down, shared, consumer-driven mentality. They must have strong relationship-building skills, not only to forge new relationships between service consumers and service providers, but also to build consumer-to-consumer and provider-to-provider relationships. Business architects must be the drivers who transform the relationship between the business and IT from a bottom-up, service provider ownership approach to a top-down, enterprise-owned, and consumer-driven model.

Business architects work with the business to identify and document initiative opportunities and requirements on an ongoing basis. This is not an end-of-the-year scramble to get ready for next year's budget. It is part of the normal day-to-day management of their unit. Most initiatives compiled by the business unit will be submitted for approval and funding during the annual budget process. Under this new relationship with the business architects, these have already been compiled, estimated, and documented. The business unit leader can determine which of the initiatives are most important to his or her unit and in what order to push for them. Some of these initiatives may have been structured by the business architects with several business unit sponsors. These unit leader sponsors will or have already negotiated their commitment and support to these initiatives. These will be valuable initiatives, since those with multiple business unit sponsorship will have greater chances of approval; it is the unit leaders and their leaders who will make the approval decision. Hence, business architects work with other business architects and other solutions architects when documenting initiatives that have multiple sponsors and span multiple business units.

Once an approved initiative begins its initiation phase, the business architects work with the business analyst and solutions architects to define the detailed business requirements.

Business architects work with the other business architects and the business leaders within the Horizontal Consumer Governance Subcommittee, within the enterprise SOA Portfolio Plan Governance Committee. This is to validate that the proposed business architectures are consistent with each other and comply with the horizontal strategy for servicing and supporting the various constituents. This is especially important when the proposed initiative impacts multiple constituencies.

Business architects are responsible for compiling all the information in the SOA initiative proposal as specified in the template in Appendix A. They are responsible for reviewing the completed document with the initiative's business sponsor(s) and obtaining sign-off. In addition, they are responsible for scheduling the review and approval of the initiative with the enterprise SOA Technology Governance Committee. After this is done, they are responsible for submitting the proposal to the enterprise SOA Portfolio Plan Governance Committee for review and approval and for coordinating the presentation of the proposal to the committee with the business sponsors.

It is the responsibility of the business sponsors to present the proposal to the enterprise SOA Portfolio Plan Governance Committee. Both the business architects and solutions architects attend the presentation to support the business sponsors and answer any architectural or technical questions committee members may have about the proposal. Business architects are responsible for documenting any takeaways from the presentation, facilitating their resolution with the appropriate parties and reporting the results back to the committee. If there are multiple issues, the committee may request a second presentation after they are resolved. Business architects coordinate this meeting as well.

You may decide to structure your SOA portfolio plan review presentation to be delivered independently to the horizontal consumer-centric subcommittee and the vertical provider-centric subcommittee to isolate and address the issues of these groups separately. It will depend on how sophisticated these subcommittees are and how detailed their evaluations are. The final review would then be conducted by the whole committee, without the business sponsors or the architects present, since the sponsors themselves or their leaders as well as the chief architect are members of this committee.

It is the responsibility of the enterprise SOA Portfolio Plan Governance Committee to present the proposed initiatives to the Business Domain Governance Committee if appropriate. Conditions where this may occur include:

- The amount needed to fund the initiative exceeds the funds available in the enterprise SOA portfolio plan budget and a budget override for additional funds is needed.
- The initiative proposes a change in strategic direction not previously approved by the Business Domain Governance Committee, such as the acquisition of a new channel technology or a contracted partner relationship with a new intermediary channel provider.
- The initiative will impact the delivery date of another initiative, and this issue cannot be resolved at the enterprise SOA Portfolio Plan Governance Committee level.

If none of these issues exists and the enterprise SOA Portfolio Plan Governance Committee can make agreed-on adjustments to the budget and schedules to accommodate the initiative, then approval will occur at this level.

Another critical role performed by business architects is the education of the business regarding all aspects of the SOA model. This includes educating people on how initiatives and requirements are documented and why they are documented that way. The architects also must educate company members on how the progress and status of their initiatives will be reported and how to interpret those reports. They need to educate people about constituent and channel differences and why the distinction is important. Most important, they steer plan users' entrenched beliefs around the monolithic grouping of functionality, stovepipe solutions, and physical application ownership toward the new paradigm of discrete, self-contained and self-sufficient services; shared capabilities; and shared (enterprise) ownership.

Business architects need to have excellent communication and presentation skills and be able to talk to businesspeople at every level, from the actual individual who consumes the service up to the unit vice president level.

SOA Solutions Architects

Solutions architects use the business architecture diagram developed by the business architect, along with the preliminary data in the SOA initiative template provided by the business, to develop the high-level technical implementation proposal for the initiative. They refine and add the technical aspects to the initiative, including the nonfunctional requirements not specified by the business but required by architecture. They identify all the components needed to complete the solution at a high level and categorize those components into one of these groups:

- The component exists in production and can be used by the initiative with no additional coding (although configuration changes will most likely be needed),
- The component exists but will require some enhancement coding (e.g., a new service invocation stub for the service) to support the initiative.
- The component is a new component (i.e., a new channel, a new business process or business service, a new integration service to a new or existing legacy system).
- The component is a purchased or leased application service provider's business application with a set of business capabilities that needs to be integrated at one or more levels of the architecture (i.e., at the integration level for integration at the data or API level, at the service level if the application supports Web services, or at the business process level if the product is a BPMS-based solution).

Note

Integration should never occur at the Channel layer unless the application supports the processing of functions through an existing and supported channel adapter (e.g., the ability to send and receive EDI transactions through an FTP channel).

- Enhancements required to an existing legacy application to support the initiative.
- The porting or replacement of a legacy system to a more modern technology platform (e.g., the replacement of a legacy COBOL insurance rating application with rules engine–based solution).
- The acquisition or building of a new major back-office system to be added in at the legacy domain layers.

This last condition (major new legacy application) should be very rare. If it does occur, serious consideration should be given to complete this implementation as a separate project first and then address the rest of the initiative after this legacy application is completed.

These categorizations help facilitate the time and cost assessment needed to compile the initiative estimations. The solutions architect will have to involve different resources to assist in the assessment of the effort for each component, depending on the category. Different assessment criteria will be applied to each category. For example, assessing the cost and time to build a new business service may be based on the cost and time frame it took to build similar services in past projects. Cost and time to enhance a legacy application or install and integrate a new business application may be a unique set of assessment criteria.

The resulting cost estimates can be added to the other nondevelopment costs to come up with the total estimate for the project. These other costs include:

- Project management, project architecture, business analyst, and testing resources.
- Infrastructure costs, including technology acquisitions and capacity expansions.
- Support and operation cost allocations for operation in production for N periods, if required.

Arriving at the delivery time frame is a bit more complex. All the identified components need to be laid out on a prerequisite and dependency matrix similar to a project Gantt chart. The estimated time efforts for each component need to be mapped out on a single timeline based on their dependencies and prerequisites to arrive at the total estimated timeline for the initiative. Variations or alternatives of this timeline can be developed if a phased release of the initiative is desirable or feasible. This will be useful for large initiatives with many components. Examples of a phased release approach include:

- Developing all the business services and business processes, but deploying them to one channel and/or one constituent at a time.
- Delivering a subset of services to a subset of constituents or a subset of channels in each release.
- Merging some of the capabilities into the release schedule for other initiatives impacting the same constituents or channels.
- Any other combination that makes sense to the business and the architects.

Solutions architects are experts in SOA application architecture and design. They have a full and comprehensive understanding of the enterprise SOA reference architecture and all its layers. They also have a full understanding of all the existing components that have been developed within those layers. Solutions architects have access to all the metadata and artifacts in all the layers in all the columns of the SOA~EAF and are the largest users of these artifacts and metadata. They need to understand the conceptual, logical, and physical attributes of the architecture and the explicit and direct relationships among them. They must be able to understand and communicate the logical and physical implementation of existing components back to the conceptual business requirement.

Within each layer of the logical and physical architecture, they need to understand the components from their lowest level of granularity to their highest level of aggregation. In other words, they need to know that at the lowest granular level, a service exists to "Get Customer Credit Limit" and how this service is (logically) consumed and (physically) deployed. They need to know that this service is encapsulated in a higher aggregated service to "Increase Customer Credit Limit." This service is consumed within several business processes, one of which is the "Manage Customer Account" process. This process is a composite application that has been deployed as a data link layer (DLL) within the Windows-based "Customer Support" application. Only employee constituents with the role "customer account administrator" are authorized to use this composite service.

With this understanding, the solutions architect can evaluate the conceptual business requirement to allow customers to request and obtain higher credit through the customer self-service application. If the requirement was just to let customers check their credit limit, the solution would be easy to support. A new service stub based on a new service contract would be created to allow the "Get Customer Credit Limit" service to be consumed by the customer constituency through the Web-based customer portal. Configuration changes to the security policies would be made to add authorization to this service to the contract administrator role within the customer constituency. Unlike the service stub used by internal customer account administrator, which allows the "Account Number" field data to be entered, the new service stub restricts data entry of the account number and populates the field from the authenticated users' security profile records.

Note

This account number profile attribute can be stored in a directory service data store like LDAP or AD. Alternatively, it can be stored in a user profile database. For efficiency and performance purposes, this data should be cached by the security framework service that provides this data so subsequent calls by the business service can be supported efficiently. Refer to Appendix C for more information on this process.

For this particular business requirement, however, solutions architects recognize that a new business process that will contain business logic to potentially allow automatic increases in credit limits is needed. They also recognize that this process may involve the participation and interaction of both the external customer contract administrator and the internal customer account administrator employee when the credit increase cannot be approved automatically. They know the solution will require the development of a new business process that will interact with customers through the Web-based customer portal channel and with customer account administrator through the Windows DLL-based customer support application. They also know that this interaction needs to be real-time and iterative.

This analysis is being conducted by solutions architects during the initiation assessment phase. The detailed business requirements have not been documented yet. While the specific details of this interaction have not been defined, the conceptual representation on the initiative's business architecture, conversations with the business architects who created the conceptual architecture, along with the solutions architects' knowledge of the logical and physical assets should provide sufficient enough information for the solutions architects to get to this level of detail and come up with a high-level cost and time estimate.

Solutions architects also include the assessment of any nonfunctional requirements in their estimates. These can include things like logging credit increase approval transactions and storing them in an audit database.

Finally, solutions architects working with business architects will conduct the enterprise SOA portfolio *impact and opportunity assessment process*. This includes looking at other scheduled releases within the enterprise SOA portfolio plan and seeing if there are any opportunities to merge or combine pieces of this initiative into those releases. See Chapter 8 for more information on this process.

SOA Project Architects

SOA project architects oversee the work and deliverables of the developers. They participate in every development project under the SOA initiative and:

- Provide the development framework, design patterns, and design standards documentation needed to create the design specification of the required components.
- Oversee the code development activities and conduct the code review process.
- Interact and communicate with the other project architects within the same initiative and project architects on other initiatives with commonalties, dependencies, or prerequisites.
- Oversee the delivery of the components into the preproduction certification environment.
- Manage the component interoperability and certification process.
- Support the release management team in aggregating, integrating, and preparing the release components.
- Manage and coordinate the change control activities to move the components from environment to environment.
- Assist production support, IT operations, and the release manager in the deployment of the release into production and, if necessary, the rollback of the release if a problem or failure is encountered.

Project architects are to the technical management of the projects as project managers are to the administrative management of the projects.

Project architects are different from solutions architects in that their focus and domain of expertise is concentrated on a particular layer of the architecture. Remember that we split our initiatives into multiple projects to address the development/enhancement of legacy enhancements, integration components, service and process components, and channel components. Project architects supporting projects developing integration components are intimately knowledgeable about all metadata and assets across all the architecture columns at the Integration layer. They are experts in the design patterns and design standards that are applied at the Integration layer. They are experts in the development tools and deployment platforms for components at this layer. They also understand all the requirements and specifications for all the horizontal and vertical development frameworks that interact with the Integration layer. Project architects ensure that integration assets are reused when possible and that existing assets are aggregated when possible. They ensure that no duplication occurs when new components are built. They address and manage any versioning requirements that arise and present these requirements to the enterprise SOA Technology Governance Committee for review and approval. They also interact with business and solutions architects on an ongoing basis to validate what is being developed against the business requirements and the original conceptual and logical definitions of the initiative.

If project architects encounter an issue that requires a variance to the logical or physical architecture, they work with the solutions architect to resolve the issue with the enterprise SOA architects. If necessary, they obtain one or more governance committee approvals (i.e., SOA Technology Governance for technical exposures, the PMO for business or project plan schedule exposures, or, if necessary, the enterprise SOA Portfolio Plan Governance Committee for financial or delivery time frame exposure). If the issue is with the ability to technically support a business requirement, project architects work with business architects to resolve these issues. Business architects work with the business representatives on the project, the initiative sponsors, and, if necessary, the enterprise SOA Portfolio Plan Governance Committee to resolve the issue.

Ultimately, project architects are responsible for ensuring that the code developed meets all the functional and nonfunctional requirements of the business. Therefore, they should be involved with the solutions architects in the iterative development of the business requirements right from the start. Working with solutions architects, project architects review business requirements as they are documented and begin to frame up the approach (the specific design patterns, development frameworks, and standards) they will use for coding the components that support the requirement. This process also offers the opportunity for clarification and validation of the requirements by the technical teams while the business requirements-gathering process is still open (before sponsor sign-off). This is much more desirable than to have a business requirement technical compliance issue identified and resolved during the design phase (after requirements have been signed off) or, worse, during user acceptance testing, especially if scope or financial changes are involved.

Project architects also identify instances where specific design patterns, design standards, or development frameworks are missing. This will occur more often in the early stages of SOA adoption. Project architects work with the appropriate enterprise SOA architects to establish and document missing material as the need arises. They meet with their peers, as well as with enterprise SOA architects and the solutions architects, to discuss issues, practices, and lessons learned. Their feedback is addressed by the enterprise SOA architects and incorporated back into the architecture policies, procedures, and standards as part of the ongoing process improvements of the SOA quality program.

Project architects need to have extensive knowledge of and experience with the tools, platforms, and development models for the layer(s) of architecture they support. They need to have extensive experience with the coding languages and standards deployed at their domain layers. Project architects must be familiar with all the data standards and models established by enterprise data architects for their domain layer. This includes any industry-standard semantic models. They also need to have a strong understanding of the interoperability requirements with the domain layers above and below their own.

Development Resources

Under the old stovepipe model of application development, the entire application was self-contained, as were the development resources. Exceptions to this model began to exist when integration development started to be supported by separate developers. Under the new SOA model, none of the application is self-contained. It is spread out all over multiple platforms and multiple technologies. The value of structuring dedicated pools or teams of resources to address development at each layer of the architecture has been well documented in earlier chapters. This section describes these different resources and their development capabilities.

Not surprisingly, we can classify our development resources into one of these categories:

- Channel development resources
- Process and service development resources
- Integration development resources
- Legacy application development resources
- Enterprise framework development resources

Channel Development Resources

Channel developers write all the code needed to set up and run the channel and the channel adapters. For the Web channel, this includes the portal server code for portals, MVC or Spring code for nonportal Web applications, and the code to support static and dynamic content (dynamic content being distinctly different from business processes and transactions). On the IVR channel side, it includes the voice recognition and keypad scripting code. On an EDI channel, it includes the FTP and file scripting code.

Channel developers also write the service invocation code in the channel and code or configure the presentation layer services needed to handle those services as the channel consumes them. Channel developers also write the code for integrating with the enterprise SOA security framework for authenticating the user. They are responsible for coding all session and state management needed by the channel *and* the underlying service frameworks. They are also required to code the mechanisms to pass session and state data to the lower layers and the enterprise SOA security framework. Finally, they are responsible for the code needed to close the session when the user logs out, reestablish a connection if the user times out, and, if required, reinitiate the session in the event of a channel or network failure. Enterprise SOA channel and security architects define all the design patterns, development frameworks, and standards used by these developers as well as the programming tools they use.

Process and Service Development Resources

Process and service developers write all the code for all the business process and business service SOA components. They are responsible for coding all the service contracts and invocation stubs associated with the process or service. They are also responsible for writing the invocation code to consume services from the lower layers. They are responsible for coding all the hooks to the development frameworks used by services. For security, this includes the code to invoke the policy detection and challenges for authorization and use. For foundational services, such as exception handling, it involves the code to invoke the enterprise logging and monitoring services to deal with the exceptions.

Even though business processes and business services are referenced as distinct separate layers in the architecture, they are purposely merged and managed together for development purposes. This is done because:

- There is a fundamental relationship between a business process and a business service. For example, a business process has no purpose if it does not contain business services.
- The tools used to develop processes and services overlap and may, in fact, be the same.
- The platforms they are deployed on are often the same.
- Tight versioning control is required between services and processes.
- Not all services will be embedded in and deployed through business processes. In the earlier customer credit limit example, the "Get Customer Credit Limit" service is consumed by a "Manage Customer Account" process, but can also be deployed at the more granular Service layer out to the customer channel to allow customers to check their limits themselves.

Thus, there is significant commonality and overlap associated with the design of components at both of these layers. The separation of the Process and Service layers on the framework is critical when communicating with and educating the business. There are distinctions, but developing these two layers separately diminishes efficiency and value. It is, however, important that the business understands the distinction between these layers from a conceptual perspective and that the artifacts and metadata within the framework are structured to support these distinctions. If you refer back to the description of enterprise SOA business service architects, you see that their responsibilities govern these two layers.

Integration Development Resources

Integration developers write all the integration code. They write the encapsulation code on top of the legacy systems. They develop all the message and data transport mechanisms. They write the code to incorporate integration framework services, such as legacy data code translations and message persistence and queuing. They build and maintain the legacy data to semantic data model mappings and any translation or validation rules between the two. They write all the code to ensure that updates to the legacy systems are processed correctly and committed correctly. They write the code to the exception handler framework and the notification alerts needed by the Business Service layer to handle them.

They may also write the code to aggregate data whose system of record population is spread across more than one legacy system and manages all the CRUD (create, read, update, delete) activity across those multiple stores.[1] The most important aspect is that they develop integration code that isolates the physical characteristics of the underlying legacy systems. This allows for these legacy systems to be enhanced or replaced with no or minimal impact to the higher layer business services.

Legacy Application Development Resources

Legacy application development resources represent the remaining pool of enhancement and maintenance resources in the old legacy environment. They continue to make the required changes to the legacy systems to support non-SOA initiatives. These resources, however, must be very much aware of the SOA integration components that have been built on top of the application and which of those integration components integrate at the database (or data store) level versus the Business Logic level. They must also be aware of any business logic that may have been coded at the Presentation layer of those legacy applications, such as field validations and table look-ups in JavaScript or client DLLs. They must be aware of all the functionality performed by security embedded in these applications and how that security is supported at the Integration layer.

These resources must now be provided with an additional set of design patterns, design standards, and development frameworks for development consideration. They cannot add new roles or other security profile information within these systems without addressing and resolving them with the enterprise SOA security framework. They cannot create new stored procedures to replace business logic within the application without identifying that the use of that business logic is provided in a message API. They cannot modify and replace APIs or remote procedure calls without approval from enterprise SOA integration architects to ensure the changes will not impact existing integration services.

Note

While legacy developers would not intentionally make changes to legacy applications that impact integration layer services, it does happen, especially when installing new releases of purchased or leased legacy business applications.

Enterprise Framework Development Resources

While SOA components are built for each layer of the architecture, the enterprise frameworks supporting those components, either within a layer or across layers, have

SOA components as well. Each channel will have its own unique SOA components, but the service those channels invoke for logon or to maintain the user profile are common shared services used by all the channels. These services were coded leveraging the capabilities within the security products implemented and deployed as components within those platforms. Similarly, the SOA component that logs all the exceptions thrown by a service is a shared service that exists independent of any services that use it.

These SOA components should be developed and maintained by dedicated resources as well. The ability to understand how current security provisioning services work, along with what it takes to add additional provisioning capabilities to those services, is not necessarily knowledge and experience that a channel or Integration layer developer would have. There is intellectual capital associated with enterprise frameworks as well. This intellectual capital is even more critical than that at the individual layers, since these components represent highly leveraged and shared capabilities that can impact many services in and across layers. Also, many of these components have prerequisites and dependencies across multiple projects and multiple initiatives in various states of development. Attempting to coordinate these efforts through different development teams is risky.

For these reasons, these components should be designed, built, and enhanced by a dedicated team.

Risks of an Outsource Development Model under SOA

As more development is completed within each layer, developers in those layers will become more knowledgeable about the design patterns, design standards, and development frameworks they use. In addition, their reliance on and involvement with project architects will diminish. If you are using outsourced development resources, you need to incorporate into those relationships the necessary management and oversight processes to ensure that the development process they use is the same as the process used by internal development resources. Ideally, having the same outsourced resources dedicated to your account minimizes this impact. Building the requirement for the outsourced vendor to supply dedicated architecture resources to the account and embedding those resources into the architecture practice also help to minimize and mitigate risk.

Outsourcing development can have a perceived savings in full-time equivalent costs, but if architecture compliance is not enforced, these savings can rapidly disappear. Once again, you have to think about the new model you are operating under. Architectural risks from stovepipe applications built by an outsourced developer are much less than the risks to SOA components built by an outsourced developer. The use of outsourced developers will increase the amount of involvement and oversight required by project architects.

Test and Quality Assurance Resources

Most test approaches used for traditional application development do not work for SOA developments. Under the SOA model, technical tests are conducted at the individual component level (similar to unit testing), at the component integration level (interoperability testing), and at the release level (performance and regression testing). User acceptance testing occurs at the business service and business process levels (business functional testing) and at the channel level (business presentation heuristics and ergonomic testing).

Under SOA, there is no big-bang user acceptance testing. As each service or business process is placed in a prerelease environment, the validation of the business logic within that service or process can be performed by the business through a stubbed-out test version of it. The stubbed-out version can access test regions or test environments of the underlying legacy applications, sample representative data in a test data store, or a combination of the two.

Many business processes or aggregated services may be using other services that have already been deployed to production and are being used by the business already. There is no need to retest the business functionality of these services. This functionality has already been tested and approved by the business. What needs to be tested is how these existing services interact with the new higher-layer services that are consuming them. This is done by IT when interoperability testing is performed and by the business when it performs its acceptance testing on the higher-level service. The next example highlights these characteristics.

In the customer credit example mentioned earlier in this chapter, we talked about how an Integration-layer service called "Get Customer Credit Limit" was consumed and encapsulated into a higher-layer business service called "Increase Customer Credit Limit" which, in turn, was consumed and encapsulated in a higher-level business process service called "Manage Customer Account."

Depending on the type of customer, the current credit limit amount is stored in one of three contract systems (national account contracts, government account contracts, or local account contracts). The Integration-layer service uses a shared index table to determine the customer type based on a customer number or a contract number and retrieves the credit limit amount from the appropriate contract system. This logic is hidden from the higher layer consuming the service. All the higher layer needs to supply is either an account or a contract number. If the customer or contract number is invalid, this service also throws an exception response to the integration exception handling services which returns the exception message to be passed back to the consuming service and logs the exception in the integration service exception log file.

This service was deployed several years ago and is being used in production by many higher-level SOA components and several other legacy applications. The business validated the business functionality of this service when it was initially deployed, and it has been vetted through operational use over many months.

When the "Increase Customer Credit Limit" business service was developed months later, it consumed and used this existing "Get Customer Credit limit" service. There was no need to retest the business functionality of this "Get Customer Credit limit" service by validating all the permutations of customer and contract types that exist. This had already been validated. What was tested is how the "Increase Customer Credit Limit" business service invokes this service and how it processes the responses (a valid response of an amount or an exception message).

Months later, when the new composite application to "Manage Customer Account" was developed, this composite application consumed and integrated the "Increase Customer Credit Limit" business service. Once again, there is no need to retest this business service or the underlying integration service. In this case, the only thing tested is the validation the composite application successfully launched the "Increase Customer Credit Limit" business service and returned the user to the expected location when the "Increase Customer Credit Limit" business service was completed.

If the composite application to "Manage Customer Account" is initially deployed to the internal customer support associates on one channel and later deployed directly to the customer through a different channel, all that needs to be tested is the security and role modifications that were implemented to restrict access to the specific account (assuming no other modifications were made to the business logic).

If this had been a new monolithic application where the functionality within the "Manage Customer Account" and "Increase Customer Credit Limit" business service was duplicated in new code within the new application, the entire service would have to be revalidated by both IT and the business.

This example is one of the cost-saving advantages that SOA provides. It is not just the cost savings of development resources to develop the duplicate code but the savings on testing, deploying, maintaining, and supporting the duplicate code.

It is critical that the business be educated in this new testing approach and is comfortable with it. The business resources involved in traditional application testing will want, by their nature, to retest and revalidate all this reused functionality. If this is allowed to happen, both the cost and delivery timeline for the initiative will increase.

As the example implies, testing resources have to have knowledge of the SOA component approach to application design and of the different phases in the development process where testing occurs. They will have to be trained on understanding what needs to be validated during a test and what does not need revalidation. They will need to provide and work with standard test data sets to be used over and over again in reused components when testing higher-level functionality. They will be responsible for maintaining these data sets and must readily understand how they support their testing processes.

The test scenarios and resources should be aligned with the SOA model; for example, testers and test cases should be focused on service provider validations and on service consumer validations. Service provider tests focus on validating components from the Business Service layer down. Service consumer tests focus from the Business Process layer up. Under this approach, most or all of the service provider testing will be performed before the components reach the prerelease state. And most or all of the service consumer testing will be performed after the release is aggregated and staged.

Project Management Resources

The SOA model defined in this book adopts a totally new and different approach to development projects, requiring a totally different set of requirements and responsibilities for project managers. To revisit our house builder example, on-site builders usually have a project manager who manages all the activities for a single house. This manager manages the process from the initial clearing of the lot to the final inspection by the homeowner. Each house has its own self-contained project plan.

The modular home builder may have a (project manager) supervisor for each of the crews (framing, plumbing, etc.) and a (initiative manager) floor manager who is overseeing the completion of all the houses in various states of completion on the line. This supervisor's job is to make sure that crews are working on the right components in the right order so that each house module flows off the assembly line in the right order. A third (release manager) supervisor may be taking the completed components as they roll off the line and aggregating all the pieces that need to be shipped together. A fourth (production support) team is sent out to the site to assemble the components there and to answer any questions the homeowner may have on how to "use" the house.

Under SOA, a project manager may, for example, be managing one or more projects to build Business Service layer components to be used by one or more initiatives deployed through one or more releases. This project manager is accountable to each of the initiative managers to ensure that the components needed for their initiative will be delivered. This project manager is also accountable to the release manager to ensure that information about the components and the components themselves will be delivered when needed and be available in the environments they are needed in when they are needed.

Under this model, project managers need to have extensive experience working in a distributed, matrix-managed environment. They need to be exceptional at managing their own project plan as well as managing deliverables they need from other project managers. They need strong influencing and motivational skills. They need to be adaptable and accommodating and to be very strong team players.

As a side note, PMO business leaders who manage the administration of project managers need to understand the new process and model as well. Under the new model, the critical success factor is getting releases out on time. Getting an individual project completed on time or having the initiative come in under budget has to take a backseat to getting the releases out on time. Therefore, all project managers should be evaluated and compensated on their contribution to meeting release schedules. Having one piece of one initiative delayed hurts the business, but having multiple pieces of multiple initiatives delayed *really* impacts the business and the bottom line.

Initiative Business Resources

Business resources that participate in SOA initiatives and their underlying SOA projects represent another area where a significant paradigm shift needs to occur. In reality, the individuals who perform these roles today will probably be the most difficult to reeducate and to gain acceptance and commitment from. They will be asked to come way out of their comfort zone. They will be asked to contribute in areas where they have not contributed before and to refrain from contributing in areas where they have done so in the past. These resources need to understand, at least at the conceptual level, the distinctions among the layers of the architecture and the different responsibilities they have when dealing in those layers. Perhaps the most difficult thing they need to do is to retrain their thought process from a system functionality perspective to a consumer-driven service mentality. Businesspeople have evolved and become accustomed to defining their requirements in the context of the systems they already use. Their reference point is in terms of implemented functionality rather than conceptual views of their business practices. IT has been one of the biggest culprits in helping them evolve to this point. IT must now transform them away from this comfort zone.

You will need to establish new groups of business resources that have responsibilities that transcend their traditional business unit lines of authority. New groups of subject matter experts who focus on consumer-centric requirements need to be established. Business representatives will need to develop new enterprise delivery relationships with all the other business units to negotiate and build consensus around shared delivery of capabilities.

Remember that we are transforming the power model from a provider power base, where the owner of the applications had the power over what was delivered, to a consumer power base, where the consumers are now deriving what is being delivered. Doing this will not be easy.

The first step that needs to be taken is to develop a comprehensive education and selling plan to communicate the new process and the associated roles and responsibilities. This should be augmented by evaluating all the existing business resources to identify the best candidates for adopting and championing the process. These will be individuals who think strategically rather than tactically. They will be individuals who think at an enterprise corporate level rather than at a department or functional level.

Another approach would be to bring in outside expertise with a top-down commitment from the business unit leaders to drive the transformation process. Experts in organization development with business practice and business modeling expertise should be tapped for this role. Experts in IT application development should not be used to fill this role. Even if they understand the role from an account executive level, there is a high probability the resources they deploy to perform the task will be as rooted in the old approach as the businesspeople themselves. Unless they can provide you with documented customer references of similar implementations, they should be avoided. OD experts will approach the engagement with an open mind. They will deploy resources skilled in organization process engineering and organization design. IT application vendors will deploy resources skilled in application engineering and system process design.

Business analysts and subject matter experts will be most affected by the transformation. They both need to move from a functional system-oriented approach to a conceptual model approach. Subject matter experts will need to describe what they know, without including any system or technical implementation descriptions. Business analysts also need to document the business requirements without including the same system or technical implementation descriptions. They need to transform the way they describe and document requirements from a monolithic front-to-back (Presentation layer–to–Data layer) holistic description, to a very segmented, loosely coupled set of capabilities that can be mapped to the layers of the business architecture. They need to be very conscious of delineating discrete subsets of capability that not only have value to the current requirement being defined but have or may have value to other requirements as well. The business architect needs to play a critical role in helping these individuals transform to the new model.

Release Management Resources

Release managers must have experience in the production support and IT operations areas. They must have experience with the process of moving large-scale distributed applications into production and maintaining those applications once they are placed into production. They must have a strong understanding of physical IT infrastructures and the change control practices and processes used to manage those environments.

These are not the same types of individuals who have managed software releases for a software vendor. While some of their skills (especially around aggregating and packaging up the release) are valuable, they may be missing other critical skills, such as understanding how to deploy to an environment where some of the components being used already exist.

A resource that has experience deploying multitier, distributed applications with new and existing components would be preferred.

Production Readiness Resources

Production readiness resources are those that make up the SLA governance bodies. They make sure that everything is in place to deploy the SOA components into production and support those components in production. The leaders of the production support teams participate in each release production readiness meeting. The release deliverables should have a status of "complete" before the meeting is held. Uncompleted deliverables will almost always result in failure to attain production readiness approval.

The team is comprised of business representatives who represent the sponsors of the business capabilities as well. They provide the final affirmation that the capabilities being deployed were fully tested and accepted by the business. If necessary, this includes validation that all training is completed and that notification of change communications have been made to all the affected constituencies. This notification and training may be a business written statement that appears on the landing page of the channel adapter component informing users of the changes and provides a link, tab or button that takes them to content that provides more information and instructions about the changes.

Note

An SOA service change notification framework can be defined by the enterprise SOA channel architect who handles these notifications using a set of enterprise notification services. The framework can be designed to continue to show the notification to all users when they log on until they use the service or invoke the "Do Not Show Me Again" option.

Production Support Resources

Production support resources should be aligned with the technology platforms where the SOA components reside. Intellectual capital needs to be fostered with these resources as well. Resources that install and maintain the technology platforms should be the same team resources that deploy and configure the application code deployed to those environments. For example, the resources that install, update, and maintain the ESB platform should be the same resources that deploy the SOA components to the ESB.

Teams with expertise in the platforms at each layer of the architecture should be established as well as any enterprise framework platforms, such as the Security Access Management, Directory Services, and Provisioning platforms.

One specialized resource group that should be established is the change control group and a configuration manager. Deploying multiple components on multiple platforms that need to interoperate with each other is a very complex process. As mentioned earlier in this book, having a dedicated team that manages the change control process across all the platforms reduces the risk of errors or out-of-sync situations occurring. The configuration manager works with the release manager to help the latter document all the configuration changes that need to be made as the release moves from the prerelease environment through the other environments and, ultimately, into production. The configuration manager also manages the change control process to ensure that the changes are made at the proper time, in the proper sequence.

Another set of specialty resources is the SOA application monitoring group. This team is responsible for ensuring that all the production SOA components are running and meeting the established SLA levels. It is also responsible for taking the appropriate action when a fault condition occurs. This team should have a set of standard and specialized monitoring tools at its disposal to accomplish these activities. Several SOA monitoring tools are on the market, but as of the writing of this book, none of them has a comprehensive and mature solution for handling the monitoring requirements for all the layers of the architecture defined in this book.

What is more likely is that monitoring capabilities coded within the components using the development environment platform that generated the component will be integrated with other monitoring and notification tools (like IBM Tivoli or HP Operations Manager) to provide these capabilities.

Similar to the SOA change notification service, an enterprise service framework for providing this integration can be defined by the SOA enterprise architects, so all SOA components can use these monitoring and alerting integration capabilities. The design patterns used to develop the SOA components would contain the component specification requirements to use these services. Just as every business service component design pattern specifies how to insert an authorization challenge upon invocation and how to call the security SOA service to validate the challenge, the design pattern can specify the specification for periodically publishing a monitoring status to a publish/subscribe message bus. The enterprise monitoring and alerting service that subscribes to this message can begin the alert process if an expected publication does not occur.

> ## Note
>
> The enterprise framework scenarios mentioned in this section are two more examples of why an architectural approach to SOA is important. These capabilities do not automatically happen out of the box when using a technology to develop SOA components. They need to be designed and implemented by following an architectural methodology. Knowing that you need these capabilities and incorporating them into the development frameworks and design patterns before you develop your first components saves money and time that would be needed if you had to go back and incorporate these capabilities in production components at a later date.

Governance Business Resources

Business resources are involved in all the governance committees. The percentage of the business resources to the total number of participants and the level of their authority will depend on which committee they belong to. As stated in Chapter 8, as you go from the SOA Business Domain Governance down to the SOA SLA Governance bodies, the focus moves from strategic to tactical. Therefore, business participation is higher at the strategic level and lower at the tactical level. There is executive-level involvement at the strategic levels and entry-level management and supervision at the tactical levels. IT resources participate at all the levels as well. Their involvement goes from executive-level participation on strategic committees to operational management–level participation on tactical committees. Business participation is greatest on the two highest committees (Business Domain Governance and Portfolio Plan Governance). The remaining lower-level committees have a larger IT resource participation.

SOA Business Domain Resources

Business executives from all the business units are the representatives on the SOA Business Domain Committee. The president or chief executive officer chairs the committee. As stated in Chapter 8, their responsibilities while participating in this committee are to:

- Set the strategic direction and objectives for the enterprise SOA Portfolio Plan Governance Committee.
- Approve the IT budget for the enterprise SOA Portfolio Plan Governance Committee.
- Resolve any issues that cannot be resolved at the enterprise SOA Portfolio Plan Governance Committee level.

Enterprise SOA Portfolio Plan Governance Committee Resources

The enterprise SOA Portfolio Plan Governance Committee needs to decide which initiatives to approve based on the strategic plans and objectives of the corporation.

It needs to determine the priority of these initiatives using those same strategic plans and objectives. The SOA Business Domain Committee provides these plans and objectives. The enterprise SOA Portfolio Plan Governance Committee also needs funding to accomplish the initiatives in the enterprise SOA portfolio plan. Finally, it needs the authority to make final and absolute decisions when they cannot be reached in lower-level committees.

Thus, the people on this committee need to be the company's top-level management. They need to be the same people who set the corporate strategy and vision. They also need to be those managers with approval ownership of the corporate budget. The members of this committee should be identified as the executive business sponsors of the SOA initiatives. Realistically, business unit leaders may not be able to support the full-time commitment needed to participate in all the activities of the enterprise SOA Portfolio Plan Governance Committee. In these cases, they should have *one* senior-level designee to participate in their absence. This representative must have the full decision-making authority of the business unit leaders when representing them in this committee.

One recommended strategy for these leaders is to plan on participating in the governance meetings during the annual portfolio reset process and whenever new initiatives are being presented. Their delegated representative would attend all other meetings where the conversation, in general, is around the status of the initiatives and releases and the resolution of any yellow or red flags within those activities. If the committee generally meets twice a month, one of those monthly meetings can be limited to status reviews with the other allowing presentations of new initiatives. If an emergency meeting needs to be called for budget or business strategy issues, business unit leaders should attend. The designee can be in attendance for all other issues.

SOA Technology Governance Committee Business Resources

As stated in Chapter 8, the business should have representation on the enterprise SOA Technology Governance Committee with a limited number of business participants rolled over on a quarterly basis. I recommend that businesspeople targeted to participate in this process are:

- Business analysts who document the business requirements of SOA initiatives.
- Subject matter experts who provide the requirement details documented by the business analysts.
- Leaders who function as the sponsor's management representative on SOA initiatives.
- Corporate (not business unit) liaisons with external constituents.

If you decide to have, say, four business representatives, you should try to have one from each of the listed categories in each rotation. You should also try to avoid having representatives of the first three categories from the same business unit. This will help to ensure that questions and opinions will be garnered from all the different business resource perspectives and that a single business unit will not intentionally or unintentionally overly influence the process.

SOA Project Governance Business Resources

The business sponsor's leaders assigned to the initiative may be asked to attend the project governance meetings when issues relating to projects supporting the SOA initiative are discussed. These leaders should have the full authority to make project-level business decisions. This includes decisions to reduce documented scope, deny expansions caused by undocumented scope changes, or pursue approval for additional scope. They also need the authority to approve deferring the delivery of capabilities to later releases in the event that unrecoverable slippages occur in the initiative's projects or in projects in other initiatives that the initiative depends on.

This resource should be a senior-level manager or director with the authority approval of the initiative's executive-level sponsor(s) to make these decisions.

Summary

This chapter identified all the key people involved in the SOA architecture practice and the processes defined by the practice. It defined the roles and responsibilities for these individuals as well as the qualities, skills, and experience characteristics they should possess. The success you have implementing this SOA enterprise architecture model and methodology will be directly attributable to the quality and capabilities of the resources defined in this chapter. When acquiring new personnel, you need to hire the highest-quality, most experienced resources available. When reallocating, realigning, and retraining existing resources to fill these new or different roles, you need to commit everything needed and necessary to ensure their success. Nothing will be more devastating to the success of implementing this SOA strategy if resources who agree to come out of their comfort zone and learn a whole new approach do not get the full support of their leaders and the education and training to help them achieve this objective.

Something that I have found helpful, especially in the early adoption stages of the model, is the creation of an SOA FAQ section on the corporate employee intranet. Every employee can go here to see the types of questions being asked about SOA and the responses to those questions. The source of the questions should be anonymous. I recommend organizing the questions by resource type (what they are, what they do, and how they do it) and the different SOA processes (governance, SDLC, the release process, etc.). In addition, a general SOA FAQ section providing information about the SOA strategy, why it was adopted, and the benefits and values it is expected to return should be developed.

Finally, a process to develop, deliver, and improve all the communication and training materials used to transform the company and run the new practice should be fully integrated with and supported by the company's training organization.

Note

1. An insurance company may have multiple claims systems or a bank may have multiple checking account systems. Each record in each system is unique, but the total population of claim records or checking account records is distributed over these systems.

CHAPTER 12

Leveraging SOA to Decommission, Replace, or Modernize Legacy Business Applications

M ost companies, especially those that have been around for many years, have significant investments in their legacy business applications. Many of these applications took years to implement. Many have been in production for 10 years or more. While many "experts" predicted the end of the mainframe over 20 years ago, the mainframes and the business applications that run on them are still alive and well.

SOA architects recognize that these legacy investments have to be treated as an asset as much, if not more, than any other business application asset in the environment. Devising an architecturally driven process that focuses on replacing and decommissioning or modernizing these legacy systems is as critical to achieving all SOA can deliver as the multichannel service distribution model defined in Chapter 4.

There is a reason the framework and methodology defined in this book are called the SOA~EAF™ with the *EA* standing for *enterprise architecture*. One of the biggest failures encountered in SOA implementations done without an enterprise architecture approach is bad legacy application integration approaches that have no strategic assessment of the best approach for legacy systems integration and migration going forward.

Remember, most SOA technology vendors and SOA development consultants want you to get SOA up and running as soon as possible. Therefore, they will try to convince you to use the easiest integration approach and whatever is available to get the proof of technology or pilot application up and running as soon as possible.

The problem with this approach is that it sets several very bad precedents. All of these bad precedents set the false business expectation that you do not need an enterprise architectural perspective to do SOA. These precedents impact the higher layers of the SOA~EAF but also the legacy layer as well.

We have already explained the value of an architectural SOA approach to the layers of the architecture, in terms of reuse and leveragability, and the advantages this approach has over a vendor-driven technology approach. What do you think the chances are that the proof of technology or pilot application just mentioned showed how to build a shared enterprise security framework for all SOA channels and services? How many of these pilots included a shared infrastructure framework for logging transactions and handling exceptions? How many captured usage statistics and used a common enterprise framework for managing billable information and charge-backs? In other words, how many of these vendors asked you to identify what you wanted to achieve from SOA from business strategy and IT architecture perspective?

SOA Architectural Approach to Legacy Applications

An architectural perspective needs to be applied to the Legacy Application layer of the architecture as well. The architectural approach does not ask, "What is the easiest and fastest way to integrate the legacy application?" Rather, an architectural approach considers:

- To what degree the legacy application needs to integrate with the SOA enterprise architecture at an enterprise level.
- How effectively these legacy applications integrate with and support the defined SOA architecture.
- What integration methods and standards are to be used for integrating the application.
- Whether it allows us to expose and integrate the underlying business logic and data at a discrete and granular enough level, enabling us to build the right services at the right functional level to support higher-layer services and processes.
- Whether the application can be modernized to be more SOA compatible or compliant.
- What the strategy will be to decommission the application and replace it, if it cannot be modernized.

Thus, there are three specific areas of architecture focus for managing the legacy application integration and migration:

1. The isolation and abstraction of the physical legacy connection through the Integration Service layer of the architecture
2. Move as much processing logic into the Business Services and Business Process layers of the SOA enterprise architecture as possible
3. Modernize or replace the core functional capabilities within the legacy application with new flexible and configurable modules with technologies that can deploy these modules as loosely coupled, service-enabled components.

Isolation and Abstraction of the Physical Legacy Connection through the Integration Service Layer

The Integration Service layer translates the proprietary and sometimes cryptic data and business logic of the legacy application into a set of standardized data and business rules. It presents this standard data structure and standard business rules as a logical representation, not a physical representation.

> ## Note
>
> An Integration layer service may be accessing the underlying application's data store directly or calling a subroutine or API that provides both Data and Business Logic layer processing of the data. Regardless of the approach, however, the integration service should be presenting the result using a standard, semantic data model and a standard set of access and usage rules. The Integration layer service needs to be designed so it can handle the processing of the rules associated with the semantic model as well as the rules associated with the legacy system nonsemantic model.

The Business Service layer component consuming the integration service has no knowledge of the physical application behind that service. Therefore, if the source of the information in the integration service is changed, this will be completely undetectable by the component at the Business Service layer. Having this logical abstraction from the physical legacy implementation allows the legacy system to be replaced by a new application and shut down in the future. Alternatively, it allows modernization enhancements (e.g., replacing the applications old nonrelational data store with a relational database technology) to be made without impacting all the Business Service layer components consuming the Integration layer service. Only the code and semantic data model mapping between the integration service and the legacy application needs to be changed.

Moving Processing Logic into the Business Services and Business Process Layers

The biggest problem with old legacy applications is that they require extensive analysis and significant coding to change them, which usually takes a lot of money and time. Most of the changes required in these systems do not relate to the data and the rules around controlling the data. Most changes relate to the process flow of a transaction or an interaction within the system. It is rare, for example, to have a requirement to add new data to an order or an invoice record. Adding new data to an order or invoice record can have significant impact to the processing logic that uses that record. It is not rare, however, to add a new step or conditional paths to the "Place an Order" or "Pay an Invoice" processes. Orders exceeding a certain dollar amount may require different levels of approval, depending on the amount. The "Pay Invoices" process may incorporate a process to handle disputed line items on the invoice. The problem is that coding these changes in the legacy application is costly and time consuming because the changes need to be embedded in one or more large, monolithic programs that were not designed as isolated and discrete business functions. This monolithic, programmatic approach used to build applications make them very inflexible. If we want to tweak or change the dispute line item process, once again we have to enlist coding resources and wait too long for the change to be completed.

The goal of an SOA enterprise architecture is to have the entire process orchestration capabilities in the SOA layers above the legacy application. It is also the goal of an SOA enterprise architecture to have the ability to "code" business rules in several layers of the architecture, not just in the legacy systems layer. The technologies used at the higher layers are designed to support flexibility and adaptability by, in many cases, providing configuration-based business rules rather than code-based business rules. They are designed to provide the capability to maintain business rules using configuration modules, not just coding.

Hence, the architectural model to adopt is one where the legacy applications are leveraged for their ability to perform low-level business functions and to maintain and control the data from a system-of-record perspective. We want the legacy system to manage the process of creating, reading, updating, and deleting a record (CRUD responsibility). We want the rules that orchestrate the process to move from one record to another, from records in one system to records in another system, and from processing business rules in one component to another component to be developed in the SOA layers above the legacy application.

Referring back to Exhibit 3.1 and the black hole example in Exhibit 3.2, our business processes are complex and often supported by many legacy systems. Each legacy system provides a subset of functionality or a piece of the information needed to complete the process. Finally, the "code" that manages the navigation of these systems from the beginning of the process to the end is the "human computer" in the middle of all the applications. The SOA application architecture allows us to automate these human process management capabilities in the Business Service and/or Business Process layers of the architecture. Once we have the process automated in the higher SOA layers, we can enhance and change the process flow rapidly. We can pull in additional business services and integration services from other legacy applications to support those enhancements and changes. Finally, we have the option to write new business rules outside the legacy application when needed and when it makes sense to do so.

An example in my past was a situation where the legacy application enhancement team was asked to estimate the effort to restrict the ability to deliver a specific health service to a single physician practice group unless the service was delivered in an emergency room situation. This required two enhancements:

1. An enhancement to the referral/authorization system to deny authorization of this service outside the specified practice group.
2. An enhancement to the legacy claims adjudication system to reject claims for this service not submitted by this group except for claims identified as emergency room claims.

The estimate returned by the legacy enhancement team was 20 development month equivalents and over $1 million. The problem here is two relatively simple requirements (from the business's perspective) are being resolved using modifications to massive amounts of complex COBOL and assembler legacy program code. Of the 20 person-months, 11 of the quoted months were devoted to figuring out how to make the changes to the legacy programs; 9 person-months were required to actually make the changes, test them, and put them into production.

The business, which initially thought this would be a minor request, had gone directly to the legacy enhancement team with the request. After receiving the estimate, it was forced to submit it as a major IT project through the traditional funding process, which triggered a review by the enterprise SOA Technology Governance Committee.

The SOA architects recognized that, as a result of HIPAA compliance, all referral/authorizations were now being processed through a new SOA service component to support the electronic data interchange (EDI) X12 278 transactions for referrals and authorizations and a new SOA component to support all claims through EDI X12 837 (claims) transactions. These transactions were all being processed through business services implemented at the Business Service layer and a HIPAA translation service implemented at the Integration Service layer of the architecture. This service translated the formats of the referral/authorization and claims transaction coming in and out of the system to and from the proprietary and standard formats. It also provided business logic rules used to translate and cross-reference the semantic data element values to the proprietary data element values used in the legacy system as well as rules to validate the format and structure of the data.

The architects quickly recognized that new rules could be added at the Business Service layer to solve the business need described at significantly less cost. One rule would be added to the 278 transaction service to look up each health service in a cached "Restricted Service" table. If the health service was found, the requesting provider number on the 278 transaction was compared to the authorized provider list for the service in the table. If a match was not found, the Integration layer would generate the 278 denial response without invoking any of the legacy system logic in the Legacy Application layer below.

The 837 claims transaction used this same table to compare all the health services on non–emergency room claims and insert a "claim line item Rejection Code" on the claim record line item if the rule was violated so the claim would be processed as a rejection by the legacy claims adjudication system. The legacy claim system would simply see the claim line as in a reject status and process it accordingly by using the rejection reason description entered into its code table when the new code was created.

The total cost of these changes was $80,000, and they were completed in less than two weeks. The solution was accomplished by implementing configuration tables that could be maintained by the business instead of being hard-coded in the back-end legacy applications. This allowed the business to:

- Add or remove services in the "Restricted Service" table.
- Add or remove authorized providers from the services in the table.
- Add or remove claim types from the "Restricted Service Exempt Claims Type" table.

This example highlights one of the key advantages of the SOA architectural approach and a key governance tenet to remember. The key advantage is that the SOA enterprise architecture provides alternatives and opportunities to build business logic at different layers of the architecture, often providing more flexibility and adaptability for less money and in less time. The key governance tenet is that the SOA architects and the enterprise SOA Technology Governance Committee should be involved with and review all IT initiatives, even if they are perceived by the business or the other IT departments as non-SOA projects. If not for a gatekeeper funding restriction that raised this project to higher visibility, a significant amount of money would have been spent needlessly.

The other advantage of the solution implemented besides the money and time savings was that this process and the logic to perform it would not have to be recoded when the old legacy systems were replaced or modernized. This approach also allowed the new rule to be applied against national account claims that were adjudicated in a different claims adjudication system.

Value of Legacy Isolation and Logic Shifts to Higher Layers of the Architecture

The legacy isolation and logic shift approaches just described play a critical role in the ability to migrate legacy applications to new, more modern platforms and to decommission the old systems. The isolation provided by the Integration layer allows new systems to be installed in the legacy layer by mapping their interfaces to the logical, semantic interface within the Integration layer service. In fact, the new and old systems can be mapped to the interface concurrently, allowing an evolutionary migration from the old platform to the new instead of requiring a big-bang replacement. Logic would be added to the Integration layer code to provide the data access rules to determine which legacy application will source the request. This data access logic should itself be a separate enterprise service in the Integration layer in order to allow all the integration services supporting the two systems to leverage this multiapplication access logic.

Adding or building new business logic in the layers above the legacy application is in fact the start of the migration of those legacy applications. The more new code built or old code migrated to the higher layers means less code to replace when the legacy application is replaced or modernized. In the "Restricted Service" process described, the expensive, inflexible, and nonadaptable aspects of the legacy application were avoided and the new business capability was delivered using a modern, flexible, and adaptable solution on a modern technology platform.

Modernizing and Replacing the Core Functional Capabilities within the Legacy Applications

Employing these legacy isolation and business logic shift concepts is a key strategy to achieving SOA. Being able to modernize or replace the all core functional capabilities within the legacy application with new flexible and configurable modules as loosely coupled, service-enabled components will remove the last obstacle to achieving a completely flexible and dynamic SOA application environment.

WHEN TO START THE LEGACY MODERNIZATION AND REPLACEMENT PLAN   While integration isolation and code shifting practices should begin immediately after starting the SOA enterprise architecture practice, developing and managing a legacy modernization and migration plan does not start at that time. This plan should be initiated after the SOA processes and practices are well established and the breadth and depth of the SOA platforms and business components are fairly substantial.

This is important for two reasons:

1. Most, if not all, of the platforms and SOA components needed to support the modernization will already be in place and mature.
2. Experience with the platforms and the comfort level with their reliability and performance will reduce the risk to the business and alleviate any concerns it may have about replacing mission-critical core processing systems.

One caveat to this recommendation: If there is an immediate, pressing need to replace a core legacy system, the possibility of building or acquiring a modern SOA-compatible solution should be studied and, if feasible, implemented. Recognize, however, that this initiative will be significantly larger than if it were initiated later in a more mature SOA environment. This is because many of the higher-level components, such as channels, may not exist yet and must be funded and implemented to support the new replacement solution.

APPROACH FOR EVALUATING AND PRIORITIZING THE MODERNIZATION AND REPLACEMENT OF LEGACY APPLICATIONS   Evaluating the legacy application and prioritizing its modernization and replacement is assessed from two perspectives:

1. Business value perspective
2. SOA enterprise architecture perspective

The business value perspective evaluates the importance and value of the application to the business, the business's perception of how effective or ineffective the application is to adapt to business changes, and the completeness or incompleteness of the business functionality automated by the application.

The enterprise SOA architectural perspective evaluates the ability of the legacy application code, the technologies used by the application, and the platforms they run on to interoperate with the SOA enterprise architecture. It also evaluates the ability of the legacy application to support the design standards and development frameworks defined by the SOA enterprise architects. The enterprise SOA architectural perspective also evaluates the life cycle of the legacy application technologies and platforms that may be reaching or past an unsupported or obsolete status.

Business Value Assessment   The business value assessment focuses on gathering metrics around:

- How effectively the application supports the business; what it does well and what it does poorly.
- How flexible and adaptable the application is to changing business needs.
- How many people use and rely on the application. Does this include external users, or are they restricted due to shortcomings of the system?
- How many additional people could use the application if a more flexible and controlled access existed.
- How it could be improved to meet the business need.

Gathering this information can be accomplished through a questionnaire completed by the business architects and subject matter experts (SMEs) supporting the business unit that maintains the legacy application and those who support system users outside the business unit that maintains the application. The responses from the business architects and SMEs should be reviewed and validated by the business leaders before they are used to evaluate and prioritize the applications.

Business Assessment Questionnaire   An example of a business assessment questionnaire is provided in Appendix A. The questionnaire provides the information to answer these questions:

- What business functions does the application support?
  - Which of these functions does it do well?
  - Which functions does it do but does them poorly?
  - How critical are the functions from a corporate enterprise perspective?
- What functionality, if any, is it missing?
  - Is another, different system used to provide this functionality? If yes, which systems and what functions?
- How many people use the system?
  - Are they all internal users?
  - If yes, is there a business desire to provide some or all of the functionality to external constituents, but restricted for technical reasons?
  - If no, is the external access flexible and effective?

In addition, general statements from the business on how the application could be changed or improved to support its needs and its (subjective) overall rating of the application's ability to support its business needs should be solicited and recorded.

The questionnaire is completed for each legacy application starting with the applications that the business perceives as mission-critical core processing systems. These are the systems that have the highest value to the SOA enterprise architecture adoption and, more than likely, have the most integration with the SOA environment.

A scoring scale and ranking matrix should be used to rank and prioritize the results of the questionnaires. The structure and criteria used for ranking and prioritizing the applications from a business perspective will vary from company to company. These variations will be based on:

- The number of legacy systems and the complexity of those systems.
- The business and IT organization model. (See Chapter 13 for more information on business and IT organization models.)
- The diversity of legacy system ownership in the company.

At a minimum, however, higher ranking (priority for modernization) should be given to applications that:

- Have a higher number of functions performed by the application.
- Provide a high level of core or mission-critical functionality.
- Have a strong business requirement to extend application functionality to more internal or external users.

- Impact the business's ability to adapt and support changing business conditions.
- Are very costly to operate and maintain.

SOA Enterprise Architecture Assessment   The SOA enterprise architecture assessment focuses on gathering metrics around:

- The ability to adapt the application to the SOA framework.
- The integration openness of the application.
- The granularity of the integration points.
- The age and versions of the platform and technologies used by the application and the vendor support life cycle of those platforms and technologies.
- The age and version of the application itself.
- The ability to adapt the platform to the SOA framework.

The presence of SOA capabilities in a legacy application or the underlying technologies those applications run on often depends on the age of the application and the platforms it is built on. The expectation should be that newer business applications, whether they are custom built or purchased packages, will contain some SOA-enabling capabilities, such as integration services built as Web services, loosely coupled business processes built using business process management technologies, and business logic coded using rules engines and, most important, platform agnostic presentation services. In other words, all newer built or purchased business applications should be created using the same standards and open platforms compliant or consistent with our SOA Reference Architecture. Business applications that do not offer these capabilities and design features should be targeted for migration.

Integration Openness of the Application   The integration openness of the application assesses the integration capabilities at each layer of the application (Data Logic, Business Logic, and Presentation Logic layers) and the standards used in those layers. The openness of the security capabilities of the application in terms of standards-based integration and interoperability is also assessed. This assessment looks for the application's use of open standards, such as XML, SOAP, BPEL, WSDL, SAML, and WS-Security. It also looks for use of de facto standard technologies, such as IBM WebSphere MQ and ActiveX, as well as underlying platform standards, such as JMS, ODBC/JDBC, LDAP, and Hibernate. The use of these standards by the application or their presence in technologies used by the application increases the interoperability with the SOA architecture. Applications that do not use these standards or run on platforms that do not support them should be targeted for migration.

Granularity of the Integration Points   Being able to integrate the business application is important, but being able to integrate it at the level of granularity that provides the highest level of adaptability and flexibility to the higher SOA layers is even more important. In other words, an application that exposes a very complex business process is valuable, but an application that also allows smaller functional pieces to be exposed is even more valuable. On the other side of the coin, applications that let you integrate at the lowest granular level (the data level) but then require all or most of the data access logic and a significant amount of business logic to be duplicated outside the application have very little value to the higher levels.

For example, some old legacy applications stored data in their data stores in an "unreadable" format because of the high cost of storage space when they were first built. Some are even still based on 80-character punch card formats and utilize multiple record types within the same record layout. The translation of the bytes into intelligent data is buried inside the programs that use it. Attempting to read and parse these old multiple record format flat file structures and translate the contents into data poses a significant risk and a large sunk cost investment. The risk is that changes to the legacy access programs are not duplicated in the integration code or are implemented inaccurately. Structured procedural code on one platform may act very differently from object-oriented code on another platform.

The sunk costs lie in the fact that the replicated data access logic is physically tied to the legacy system. This data interpretation logic has no value if the legacy application is replaced. For these reasons, writing remote procedure calls that create data access routines leveraging the existing data access logic in the legacy programs is the better alternative if the investment needs to be made. This approach will eliminate dual maintenance of the data access logic and the requirement to shut down all the duplicate Integration layer data access logic when the application is replaced.

Vendor Support Life Cycle for Mature Platforms and Technologies   Companies have legacy applications that have been around for a long time. The platforms these applications were deployed on and the technologies used to build or operate the applications will be old as well. While porting these applications to newer platforms appears reasonable, especially if the platforms and tools used to support and develop the application were based on open standards, experience and reality have shown many of us that Company H's UNIX is not necessarily identical to Company I's UNIX. We have learned that Company S's relational database technology is not exactly the same as Company O's relational database technology. In some cases, the tool used to build the application does not exist anymore. You may still have the original tool in-house, but its capabilities have not been modernized. This has forced you to abandon the tool and maintain the application at the source code level using other integrated development environments.

For these reasons, many of these applications have been left alone out of fear that porting them to newer platforms using newer technologies may cause them to break, resulting in an outage in the business continuity. While this may be perceived as the safe route, it is actually just the opposite. Many of these platforms will have reached or be close to reaching obsolescence or unsupported status.

For hardware, being unsupported means that replacement parts may no longer be available and hardware interoperability with peripheral components may not be supported on newer peripherals. Anyone remember SCSI?

From a software perspective, obsolescence or unsupported status means lack of support of new standards or new versions of standards in the operating system. It may impact the availability and support of other software components, such as monitoring agents or device drivers.

Prior to adopting an SOA enterprise architecture strategy, the only alternative to porting these applications to new platforms was to write new applications to replace them. While the tools used to write the new applications and the platforms those applications were deployed on were modern solutions, the replacement application was still a stovepipe solution. Because of this approach, the replacement applications were almost always big-bang replacements, requiring all the functionality of the old system to exist in the new system before it is deployed. The deployment of the new system coincides with the shutdown of the old system. Unfortunately, this is the most complex and risky approach you can take.

Under an SOA enterprise architecture, we have options and capabilities to move these applications off older platforms and technologies incrementally through a pragmatic and manageable migration plan. An example of this incremental approach to migration is provided at the end of this chapter.

Applications supported by platforms and technologies that are obsolete should begin their SOA migration process immediately. Applications whose platforms or technologies are targeted for obsolescence by the vendor (i.e., no newer version or upgrade path is being offered) should be added to the migration plan so their migration can be completed before the vendor's obsolescence date passes. Any applications on older versions of platforms or technologies where these older versions are approaching an unsupported status date should go through a cost and impact assessment to determine whether upgrading to the newer versions is a more cost-effective or a less risky alternative than migrating the application.

Age and Version of the Application Itself Even if the platforms and technologies supporting the application have been modernized and have version currency, the business application code itself may pose significant risks to the business. This is true for both purchased and built business applications, although the risks of the two are different.

For purchased business applications, not keeping current with the new product releases may put the application itself in an unsupported status. From a business perspective, critical business capabilities in newer versions may impact the business if the upgrades are not performed. More important, from an architectural perspective, improvements in the application to support more integration and interoperability with the SOA enterprise architecture will not be available unless the upgrades are implemented.

From an SOA strategy perspective, purchased applications that are moving toward a more open, loosely coupled approach and incorporating SOA standards and principles should continue to be upgraded and supported. Purchased applications that are not moving in these directions should be targeted for replacement by purchased solutions that are moving in these directions or by internally built solutions.

For built applications, the readability of the code and the accuracy and currency of its documentation and operational manuals may be at risk. Certainly, as mentioned throughout this book, the adaptability and flexibility of the application is most likely impacted by the programming language used and coding techniques employed when the application was initially designed and built. The older the application, the more restrictive it is likely to be. Therefore, applications that are written using older programming languages and older design principles should also be targeted for SOA migration. These applications, as currently designed, will not be able to support the adaptability and flexibility that SOA can offer.

Legacy Migration Assessment and Approach Summary The SOA enterprise architecture practice should make sure that several policies have been documented and are in force to support the technical justifications for migration. These include policies that require:

- All unsupported and obsolete technologies are removed from the environment.
- All applications on unsupported or obsolete technologies are migrated.
- Applications with limited or no access to the application's core functionality and are not modular and open, allowing all or part of the application to be exposed, are migrated.
- Applications that do not allow their embedded security mechanisms to be accessed and managed by a separate enterprise security and authorization framework and a centralized provisioning mechanism are enhanced to do so or replaced if they cannot.
- All purchased business applications are upgraded so that they are never more than one version behind the current general availability version.
- Business applications from vendors that are not adopting a loosely coupled modular approach with embedded SOA capabilities in their future releases are replaced with solutions from vendors that are adopting these strategies. If no such vendor solution exists, in-house solutions are built on the SOA platforms.

These policies should be accepted and backed by the top executives of the company. The benefits for adopting and supporting these policies should be clear after reading this book. Commitment to these policies will have the largest positive impact on the adaptability, flexibility, and total cost of ownership achieved by the company.

Pragmatism must be practiced as well. It took many years and, in most cases, millions of dollars to implement these applications. They will not be replaced overnight. However, taking the steps outlined in this chapter to isolate the application and develop new subsets of business functionality in higher layers will reduce the impact of the migrations and replacements. The trade-off will be how much of this can be done without impacting the business. The architects need to know when it will make sense to code enhancements in the legacy platform to avoid impacting the business.

Making Legacy Application Recommendations Based on the Business and Technical Assessments

The results of the business and technical assessments are compiled and evaluated. Exhibit 12.1 provides a decision flow for evaluating the results for each application.

Applications that fall into the "Replace" decision box should be addressed as soon as possible. Applications in this category should be evaluated against all the SOA initiatives in the enterprise SOA portfolio plan. If any of these legacy systems are required to support SOA initiatives on the enterprise SOA portfolio plan, an assessment of the migration or replacement of these legacy applications should be conducted and incorporated into the SOA portfolio plan impact and opportunity assessment that was conducted when the initiative was originally proposed. The migration or replacement of these applications should be approved if they can be

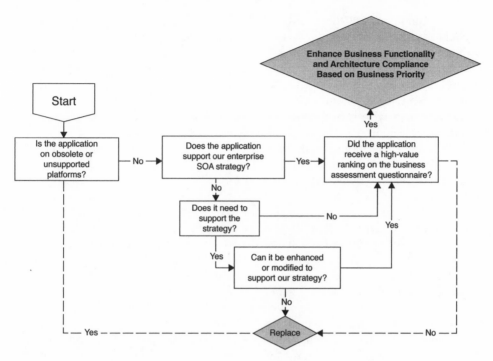

EXHIBIT 12.1 Legacy Application Modernize versus Replace Decision Tree

accomplished without impacting the business operations or the committed delivery dates of the SOA initiative.

Applications that fall into the "Enhance Business Functionality and Architecture Compliance Based on Business Priority" decision box should also be evaluated against all the SOA initiatives in the enterprise SOA portfolio plan. If any of these legacy systems are required to support SOA initiatives on the enterprise SOA portfolio plan, the business functionality enhancements and architecture compliance improvements to these applications should be documented on the SOA portfolio plan impact and opportunity assessment that was conducted when the initiative was originally proposed and approved as part of the initiative.

Legacy Application SOA Modernization and Replacement Solution Example

An example of how the strategy and approach defined in this chapter was used to develop a modernization and migration plan for three legacy insurance rating applications is presented next.

Background

Over several years, Insurance Company ABC had developed three separate stovepipe rating applications. Although the three applications were developed to meet different business conditions, all three had over 80 percent commonality in their business logic and data. Due to this fact, any changes to the rating data or business logic had to be coded in all three systems. This was done by a central group of resources that would make the changes to all three applications simultaneously and manually control the accuracy. Some of these changes were done by the business using the maintenance screens within each of the applications. Other changes were done by IT programmers who would code, test, and deploy the enhancements through the standard application maintenance and enhancement process.

All three applications would generate the rates based on inputted data. The first application (R1) provided the functionality to generate formal quotes in PDF format that could be delivered in printed form or viewed online. The second application (R2) created informal and relatively simple quotes on one of the application's screens. Since the actual customer did not have access to this application, the data on the quote screen would be cut and pasted into one of several quote template documents created with Microsoft Word and stored on a common directory. The third application (R3) had no quote functions. The rates from this application were manually entered into one of the quote template documents just mentioned. Application R1 stored all the quotes it generated in its local database and provided some basic statistics on when it was created, who created it, and when it was "closed." However, it had no mechanism to track the status of the quote in terms of its location in the acceptance and approval process. For the other two systems, storing and tracking manual quotes was a manual process and 100 percent reliant on the person who created them.

Application R1 had a Visual Basic application developed by a programmer hired by the business who used macros within the emulation software used to connect to the legacy policy system's CICS screens. This screen scrapping application provided a presentation layer integration for automating the setup of the new accounts and rates in the back-office policy system for new business. This Visual Basic program used data stored in the quote table of application R1 to process the legacy system updates. These updates were done manually for business sold through the other two systems using the CICS screens of the legacy policy system.

The R1 and R2 applications are used by both internal sales associates and external brokers. The external brokers access these Web applications through the Internet. Security profiles within each of these applications control the functionality available to these two constituents. For example, in application R1, only internal sales administrators can change the status of a quote to "booked" or "closed."

Isolation Activities

The first step taken to architecturally modernize these applications was to create a new rating service at the Business Service layer of the SOA enterprise architecture that provided the capability to return rates for all the different rating scenarios and product lines. This service utilized newly built integration services to each of the three rating systems to process rate requests and return rate replies and data access logic that determined which of the three systems to get the rates from. This logic established application R1 as the preferred source of the rates that existed in the other systems as well. On the consuming side, the new rating service used an industry-standard semantic model for insurance rating that included the standard data formats and the standard rating request and reply message formats. Adopting these standards provided the capability and option to expose the rating service directly to external constituents in the future as well as the option to leverage this service to process any EDI transactions that are also based on these standards.

Users of applications R1 and R2 continued to use the proprietary user interfaces of those applications to generate rates. Users of R3, however, were given access to a new Web application that provided access to a composite application built at the Business Process layer of the architecture that consumed the new rating service. This new interface gave the R3 users everything they needed to replace the capabilities of the old R3 system. The Presentation layer component of this new composite application leveraged the existing SOA authentication and authorization services already deployed through the Web Channel layer to the employee constituency in an earlier SOA initiative.

The second integration step taken was to replace the Visual Basic screen-scrapping application used by the R1 rating application with a new "Create/Maintain Account" service. This service used a newly created API in the legacy policy application that allowed the creation or update of account records and policies without using the CICS 3270 screens. A new screen and JAVA program was added to application R1 that allowed the user to "Create or Update Policy Application Account and Group Information" for quotes that were flagged as "booked." This new JAVA program consumed the new "Create/Maintain Account" service to perform this task. Since application R1 was also a Web application that had its URL realms authenticated through the enterprise security access management tool, the user security information stored in the Security Token was sufficient and used to authorize the users consumption of the "Create/Maintain Account" service.

Activities to Move Process Logic to Higher SOA Layers

The next step in the modernization process was the development of a new "Quoting" service at the Business Process layer. The composite application built previously at this layer to allow the R3 application users to get rates was enhanced and expanded to include a quote generation process and a quote tracking process.

The quote generation process allowed the user to select one or more of the rates returned by the rating service and incorporate it and customer information into a selected quote template. The text for the quote in the selected quote template was extracted from a content management system that used a work flow and business rules to extract the appropriate paragraphs that make up the template. The multiple Word template documents previously used to manually create quotes were decomposed and stored at the paragraph and section level in the content management system. Since 70 to 80 percent of the content across all these templates was the same, the new streamlined content management solution simplified the quote template maintenance overhead that occurred in the past and automated the dynamic construction of the quotes. The content stored in the document management system was in HTML format with embedded XML to support the incorporation of the variable customer and rate information.

All compiled and generated quotes were stored in a new quote database. The composite application was also enhanced to track the status of all the quotes in the database from initial generation to final booking or closure. All authorizations for getting rates, generating quotes, and managing the quote status are based on roles provided by the enterprise SOA security framework module.

The final step added in the composite business process was the consumption of the "Create/Maintain Account" service that was created during the integration activities just mentioned. This service would now provide automatic updates to the legacy policy system for all booked quotes. The process also provided a real-time work flow mechanism to handle any errors or problems encountered with the policy system updates.

The composite application was configured to operate differently and provide different capabilities based on the role of the authenticated user. The three internal roles driving the three internal configurations were internal sales representative, sales manager, and sales administrator. Two external roles (broker and broker administrator) defined two external configurations of the composite application.

After these changes were made, the application was redeployed in a release that also deployed a new broker registration and logon application in the enterprise SOA security framework module. With this deployment, the proprietary user interfaces of the R1 and R2 applications were decommissioned by shutting down the presentation layer logon screens in them. The user roles still needed to be maintained in these systems to allow the credentials passed through the rating service token to be validated in the systems' security modules.

With this release, all internal and external users of the three rating applications were now using the new rating and quoting composite application. All rate requests were being processed by a shared service. All quotes were being automatically generated and stored in a single quote database. All quotes were now being tracked and managed through a single tracking work flow, and the setup of the accounts and groups were being automatically processed for all booked quotes. The three rating applications were now providing just one function through a single rating service. The only direct user interaction with these applications was the application administrators who maintained the rate tables.

Activities to Modernize and Replace the Core Functional Capabilities within the Legacy Applications

The final step in the evolutionary SOA migration of the rating applications was to replace the three hard-coded rating applications with a single, user-configurable solution. A rules engine technology was acquired to provide this capability. Although the initial use of the rules engine platform was to provide ratings, the platform was evaluated and purchased from an enterprise perspective. This platform was expected to provide rule capabilities to many more initiatives and legacy modernization initiatives down the road.

A new SOA rating application was developed using the rules engine platform. This application provided a single system of record and single source of rating data and rating business logic. The new rules-based rating application allowed business users to maintain not only the rating data but also all the business rule changes through a configuration module, eliminating the need for IT developers to perform these changes. This configuration module allowed the business to add new data and new business rules as needed. Empowering the business to make the changes themselves not only significantly reduced the cost of maintaining the data and making the code changes but also rapidly accelerated the ability to deliver rate changes, which were often under tight regulatory or business delivery time schedules.

The existing Integration layer components of the rating service that managed the connections and data access logic to the three legacy rating applications were enhanced to replace these connections with a single connection to the new rating rules engine application. Since this rating application was new and built with knowledge of the insurance industry's data standards for requesting and returning rates, the mapping and translation complexity between the internal data structures and the semantic industry standard format exposed by the previous version of the rating service was eliminated. The semantic document received by the integration service was passed directly to the back-end rating engine, which used the same semantic document.

After the new rating application was released into production, the three legacy rating applications were decommissioned and removed from production. Most of the infrastructure resources that supported these three applications were reutilized to support additional capacity for other applications.

Legacy Application Modernization Example Summary

It is hoped that the example just presented shows the value of adopting an SOA enterprise architecture and applying architectural principles to migrate these legacy applications. The example shows how the first two architectural principles of isolation through integration and business logic shifting help to make the third principle (core functionality modernization) easier to achieve.

It is also hoped that this example clearly shows that investing in the migration of legacy applications has tremendous value to the business agility and a significant return on investment. The rating migration example has delivered these benefits:

- A significant reduction in business and IT maintenance costs
- Rapid, low-cost delivery of changes to rating data and rating business rules as regulatory or business changes arise
- Improved accuracy by eliminating redundantly maintained rating data and rating rules
- The replacement of three proprietary user interfaces and security systems with a single composite interface module controlled by the enterprise SOA security framework module
- The replacement of dedicated infrastructure resources for three stovepipe applications with SOA components distributed across a shared multilayer environment
- The ability to create additional channel stubs to the composite interface module and deploy the application through other channels
- The ability to configure new roles and business process flows based on those roles to support use of the application by new constituents (e.g., accounts) or new roles within the existing constituents (e.g., internal sales support agents)
- The ability to leverage the SOA assets not only at the composite Business Process layer but at the Business Service layer as well (i.e., reusing the rating service to process EDI rate requests)

Finally, this example shows that the SOA approach provides an alternative to the big-bang replacement approach traditionally needed when replacing legacy stovepipe applications with new stovepipe applications. The migration in the example was accomplished over two years through four releases.

Summary

This chapter explained how non-SOA legacy applications, which still make up a significant percentage of companies' application portfolios, need to play a key role in delivering SOA-enabled capabilities. How to evaluate and prioritize the modernization or replacement these legacy applications from both a business and a technical perspective was presented. Finally, an SOA enterprise architecture framework approach to accomplishing the modernization and replacement of these legacy applications through a phased, pragmatic approach was provided. The big-bang approach of replacing one stovepipe solution with another is no longer necessary or required. We can modernize and replace these systems gradually, over time, in a way that does not impact the business but in fact improves system capabilities and efficiencies with each step taken.

PART IV

Developing Your Plan for Achieving Service-Oriented Architecture

Implementing an Effective SOA Strategy under a Decentralized Business or IT Model

D ifferent companies have different organizational models for how they organize and manage their business. They also can have different organizational models on how IT is organized and managed to support the business. These organizational structures have a direct impact on the ability of the enterprise architecture team to implement a SOA enterprise architecture strategy and to maximize the benefits achievable by the strategy. This chapter describes the four variations of these organizational structures and their impact on an SOA strategy. It also identifies the conditions and situations to look for under each model and recommends appropriate actions based on those conditions and situations.

Business and IT Organization Variations

There are four variations of how the business and IT can be organized, as depicted in Exhibit 13.1. The four variations are:

1. A centralized business model and centralized IT model
2. A centralized business model and decentralized IT model
3. A decentralized business model and centralized IT model
4. A decentralized business model and decentralized IT model

A centralized business model is one in which all the business units roll up to a single management team. The budgets for each business unit are part of an overall corporate budget and can be adjusted or reallocated among the business units at any time at the discretion of the executives. The company has a single common mission and strategy, and every business unit has business plans in support of this common mission and strategy. There is a significant amount of interaction and cross-functional activities between the business units. The customer, partner, and vendor relationships are at the corporate level (i.e., the relationships and contractual obligations are managed by corporate-level resources).

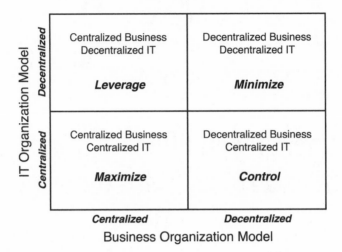

EXHIBIT 13.1   Business and IT Organization Models

A decentralized business model is one where the business units and, in many cases, separate business entities exist as completely autonomous entities. These entities can have their own business missions and strategies as well as their own profit and loss statements and budgets. There may be very little interaction and cross-functional activities between the business entities, with the exception of some common corporate services (human resources, general ledger, or payroll). The customers, partners, and vendors may be completely different in each business entity with their relationships and contracts managed within each of the different entities. This is the model usually associated with large conglomerates that are holding companies for multiple businesses. Many times these business entities are acquired through mergers or acquisitions of companies that already have established business models and practices. Companies that have entities that participate in different markets or industries will often have different customers, partners, and vendors.

A centralized IT model is one where all the IT resources are controlled and managed by a single, central management team. The IT budget and the allocation of the budget spending are governed by a single governance process with representation from all the business units. All business application development or acquisition initiatives are managed with and implemented by shared corporate resources that can support any initiative from any business unit. The vendors and partners used by IT to supply infrastructure platforms and development tools, provide consulting or development resources, and provide operations and production support are governed and managed by the central IT organization.

A decentralized IT model is one where the IT resources are disbursed into the business units and dedicated to those business units. Each business unit has its own IT budget and can spend that budget autonomously. The business units may have their own IT infrastructures, share a common infrastructure, or a combination of the two. Even in a decentralized IT model, some, if not all, of the IT policies, procedures, and standards are established at a corporate IT level and consistently applied and enforced within the decentralized IT organizations.

Centralized Business Model and Centralized IT Model

If your company currently has a centralized business model and centralized IT model, you have the best situation for implementing and maximizing an SOA enterprise architecture and strategy. This type of business structure is already accustomed to doing things at a corporate level. It is accustomed to sharing resources and participating in cross-functional and multi–business unit activities. The IT organization is accustomed to functioning at an enterprise level and has the structure and business support mechanisms in place to address and implement systems at a global enterprise level. The ability to retool and realign the IT resources to the layered architectural development approach, as well as the ability to transform to a release approach to business application delivery, is much better facilitated when IT and the business are centrally organized. From an SOA business strategy and roadmap perspective, a centralized business and IT organization model should be seen as a positive asset and leveraged to accelerate the transformation to the SOA architectural model.

Decentralized Business Model Considerations

When a decentralized business model exists, attaining all the benefits that a highly leveraged and shared SOA enterprise architecture has to offer may not be possible. Clearly, the objective should be to maximize the benefits to the extent possible within each of the decentralized business entities. Some key strategic assessments, however, need to be made at the corporate level to determine if any business organizational alignments should be established at the corporate level or if any IT budgets and assets should be pulled under a centrally controlled umbrella. The most critical strategic assessments that need to be made revolve around the commonalties and similarities between the different business entities. These questions need to be asked:

- Are the business entities in the same industry or different industries?
- Do they share the same customers or have different customers?
- Do they share a high number of support resources or use completely different support resources?
- Are they sharing any IT resources?
- Are they in regulated or unregulated industries that restrict or control their organizational and corporate relationships?
- Are they a mix of for-profit, not-for-profit, or nonprofit businesses that have financial or incorporation restrictions on how they operate?
- Were cultural or country differences a major factor and driver in establishing the decentralized entity approach?

Other questions that need to be addressed include:

- Do any of the entities sell complementary products or services? Competing products and services? If yes, are they selling to the same customers? Is there a strategic desire to cross-sell or up-sell to these shared customers? Do these customers see these different business entities as "one company" and get confused or frustrated when they are unable to address needs or issues that cross or transcend these businesses? Have customers provided feedback that reflects these concerns?

- Do any of the business entities use the same suppliers, partners, or vendors? Are these relationships contracted at the corporate level or within each business entity? Are their financial benefits relating to contract management and volume economies of scale that can be achieved by moving these relationships to the corporate level? Do these suppliers, partners, and vendors have the same confusion and frustration that customers have when dealing with separate entities within the same company? Do supplies and resources provided by these suppliers, partners, and vendors ever get transferred between business entities? Do these transfers cause tracking and billing problems?

From a strategic SOA perspective, if any customers, suppliers, partners, or vendors are common across business entities, the SOA application components related to the Service Consumer layers of the architecture and the management of those layers and components should be realigned to a centralized management model. This means that the services consumed by these constituents and the channels they use to consume them should be developed and managed as corporate enterprise services.

For customers, this is important if the strategic direction is to have the ability to up-sell or cross-sell products or services to them or if the direction is to have the ability to provide holistic support to those customers, whether through internal resources or self-service capabilities directly accessible by them. At a minimum, this holistic approach would facilitate the ability to support and reflect the position and status of customer relationships with all the different business entities.

For suppliers, partners, and vendors, the holistic view provides your company with the ability to manage and monitor relationships with these constituents at an enterprise level. It allows these constituents to use a common and consistent mechanism to interact with all the business units and the ability to process and manage cross-business unit services, such as volume discounts and corporate-level invoicing through a common set of services. The company benefits by being able to monitor and validate purchases. Discounts can be moved from a back-end postinvoicing audit function to an up-front proactive validation when purchase orders are placed. It also provides a common enterprise framework for all suppliers, partners, and vendors to use, eliminating the need for each business entity to develop and maintain its own mechanisms.

The easiest way to facilitate this transformation on the business side is to establish constituent representatives in each business entity for each consuming constituent those entities interact with. These representatives will make up the horizontal consumer strategy subcommittee within the corporate SOA Portfolio Plan Governance Committee. This is the exact same approach in the centralized model where constituent representatives are established to represent the needs of consumers. The distinction here is that not every business unit in the centralized model will have a representative for each constituent, whereas each business entity will if it has a relationship with those constituents. The second distinction is that the money, and perhaps the development resources to build or acquire the enterprise services and channels, needs to be allocated from the individual business unit's profits and losses to the corporate level to support these services.

This transformation also requires that the platforms for the shared services and channels, as well as the management of the release into production of SOA application components on these platforms, be at the corporate enterprise level.

Under this approach, all the service provider activities related to the back-end legacy systems in each business unit continue to be funded and administered autonomously by each of the business entities. The development of Integration layer components and Service layer components can also continue to be developed and funded within each business entity. These developments, however, need to be governed by a corporate-level enterprise SOA Technology Governance Committee and overseen by solutions and project architects within the enterprise SOA practice. All activities related to the SOA migration (isolation, code shift, and technology modernization) of the legacy applications in each business entity should be governed and overseen by these enterprise resources as well.

At the lower Legacy Application layer of the architecture, business entities that have systems that perform the same basic functions (either within their business entity or in other business entities on similar systems) should be required to incorporate these applications into a corporate-level SOA legacy migration plan. While it may not be feasible or legal to incorporate the modernization and replacement of these systems with an enterprise shared SOA solution, the assessment and evaluation of this approach should be conducted and implemented if possible.

A Word about Multinational Corporations

Many companies operate globally today. Both centralized and decentralized corporations operate at a global level. As a result, there are many differences in how a company operates in different countries. The business applications they use need to operate differently as well. One major common factor is language. Applications used by people who speak only French need to provide everything displayed in French. Another factor is different government and regulatory requirements. The laws for selling insurance in Germany need to be enforced in the systems used in Germany to book and administer the insurance. A third variable is currency. Countries that use the euro need systems that store currency as euros.

A properly defined SOA enterprise architecture with the appropriate development frameworks, design patterns, and design standards can accommodate all these variables across all the shared and leveraged components. This does not happen by chance, however. The way these variables are handled needs to be evaluated by the enterprise SOA architects *before* any of the SOA application components are built and must be documented in the development frameworks, design patterns, and design standards they publish. See Appendix B for more information on this subject.

Decentralized IT Model Considerations

If your company has a decentralized IT model, you will need to push hard to change it to a centralized model. A decentralized IT model works well when the architectural approach is for fully self-contained stovepipe applications in a stand-alone environment. About the only cross-functional or enterprise focus applied under this approach is data management and, to a lesser degree, integration management. This model does not work for building enterprise SOA applications utilizing a multitude of shared and leveraged components across multiple layers of a distributed architecture. It just will not work. Managing three separate project teams making coding or configuration changes to existing service components to be deployed by three isolated and uncoordinated deployments is almost impossible. The risk that changes made by one team to a component will impact the changes made by another team to that same component is high. The ability of all these teams to understand what components already exist in every layer and how to properly use them or, worse, avoid duplicating them is a massive responsibility. Web service definition languages (WSDL) help developers understand what a Web service provides and how to consume that capability, but not every interface in every component in every layer will have a WSDL. While the documentation needed for them to use an existing component will exist in the artifacts and metadata stored in the SOA~EAF™, the task of understanding how to use the information in the framework when it is maintained in multiple separate frameworks will be difficult to accomplish.

Another issue is how shared components get developed and deployed effectively under this model. Will two separate project teams attempt to build and deploy their own customer portal to support their applications? How can this be avoided? Setting up a process to identify these situations within all the distributed projects being developed by the distributed resources and managing the projects so these situations do not occur is, in fact, a step toward a centralized model. If you think about it, the best way to handle this issue is to merge the two projects into one and allocate resources from both the projects to design and develop the portal component of the applications based on a merged set of business requirements. The reality, as shown by this example, is that adopting the SOA architectural approach will either eventually end up with a centralized IT model or you will have a very complex, convoluted, and conflicting portfolio of SOA applications with very little reuse or leveragability. If you look at the next list of decentralized IT characteristics, you will see that none supports the SOA architectural paradigm, with the possible exception of a decentralized budget if enterprise developments can be charged back to those decentralized budgets.

The undesirable characteristics of a decentralized IT model are decentralized:

- Development teams
- Infrastructures
- Architecture practice
- Project management
- Budget
- Project approval

Summary of the Four Variation Quadrants of the Business and IT Models

As stated, if you have a centralized business model and centralized IT model, you have the most effective models for implementing and maximizing your SOA enterprise architecture strategy. Gaining support and approval of your SOA business strategy and roadmap will be easier since you will not have to politic and sell the strategy to multiple, highly autonomous business entities and IT organizations. Implementation will be quicker because the business and IT are already used to working at a cross-functional enterprise level. Therefore, the strategy is to *maximize* these benefits to achieve the strategy.

If you have a centralized business model and decentralized IT model, you need to transform the IT model to a centralized model. This will cause contention within the business, as people are used to controlling their IT assets and spend. Business leaders need to be convinced that the agility and flexibility they will gain along with the ever-increasing amount of capabilities being delivered faster, for less money, significantly outweighs the value of the control they are relinquishing. Business leaders also have to understand that the corporate objective is to offer the most compelling and competitive experience to the consuming constituents and customers. Continuing to operate under an inward-looking-out mentality will lose that competitive advantage. The perceived goal can no longer be what is best for a particular business unit or what that business unit wants. It must be what is best for the customer and what the customer wants. Since all business units share the same customer, they should share responsibility for providing the best possible service to those customers. Therefore, the strategy here is to *leverage* this shared responsibility to the customer to reorganize IT and move toward a shared resource model.

For companies that have a decentralized business model and centralized IT model, the strategic assessment defined above in the section labeled "Decentralized Business Model Considerations" needs to be conducted. If there are commonalties among the customers, suppliers, partners, or vendors that exist in these decentralized businesses, there is strategic value to managing these relationships holistically. This is accomplished by establishing the enterprise SOA Portfolio Plan Governance Committee at the corporate (enterprise) level. The constituent-driven horizontal consumer strategy subcommittee within this enterprise-level committee will be used to facilitate the transition to an enterprise-level, consumer-centric SOA approach. The centralized IT resources can then be rapidly reorganized to support this model. If there is no strategic value to creating a corporate-level horizontal consumer strategy (i.e., no shared customers, suppliers, partners or vendors and no strategic need to build shared relationships with them), then the model should be applied separately in each of the business entities. The centralized IT organization will be an asset to help implement these models across each business unit and to ensure they are consistently applied and governed. Therefore, the strategy for this model is to gain corporate enterprise-level *control* of the horizontal consumer strategy and the delivery management of the initiatives that impact the consumers. If there is no value to this approach, the strategy is to use the centralized IT organization to *control* the independent SOA implementations in each of the autonomous business entities to ensure consistency of SOA policies, procedures, standards, and practices.

If you have a decentralized business model and decentralized IT model, the same decentralized business model assessment described earlier should be conducted with the same actions taken for the outcomes explained in the previous paragraph. The IT model changes described there should be adopted for the business model as well. If the result is that both the business and IT models remain decentralized, the strategy should be to *minimize* the impacts and risks of these models. These impacts and risks include:

- Wasted money on duplicate or competitive technologies when the same technology could be used and at a lower cost if enterprise licensing contracts were negotiated.

- Duplicate time and money spent on designing and building duplicate capabilities. A security framework and the technologies used to build the modules within that framework should be able to be designed once on a standard platform and implemented separately in each business entity.
- Inconsistent and conflicting use of technologies (e.g., two entities settling on different messaging technologies and, subsequently, unable to support a corporate requirement to send corporate information using a third messaging technology).

These are a few of the impacts and risks that this model presents. These impacts and risk are best minimized through the use of standardized IT policies, procedures, standards, and practices implemented and enforced in each of the business entities.

Summary

The way a business and its supporting IT resources are organized impacts our ability to implement an SOA enterprise architecture strategy and may limit the value returned from that strategy. The four variations presented in the chapter will help you identify the models deployed in your company and determine what changes you should attempt to make to improve your SOA enterprise architecture implementation and success. These four examples represent the four extremes of the models that can be deployed. In many cases, shades of gray may exist in the business or IT, where some things appear to be centralized and others appear to be decentralized. In these cases, you should apply the analysis described in this chapter at a more granular level using the criteria that most aligns with the characteristics of the item being evaluated (e.g., decentralized IT model criteria for granular IT functions or services that are decentralized).

CHAPTER 14

Assessing the Organization's SOA Maturity and Developing Your Company's SOA Business Strategy and Roadmap

Congratulations! Now that you have completed the first 13 chapters of this book, you can use this information to create your business model of what your transformed SOA-focused company will look like. You have now seen all the pieces of the SOA enterprise architecture model and how they all fit together. You have seen how the SOA~EAF™ and methodology work together to facilitate the operation of an SOA-driven architecture practice. This book has provided you with everything you need to successfully implement an enterprise architectural approach to SOA. This chapter describes what you need to do to make it happen.

The final step in the process, before you embark on this SOA journey, is to understand where your company is today in terms of the capabilities defined in the previous chapters and what is necessary to close the gaps to achieve these capabilities. This final step is to evaluate your current people, process, platform, and practice capabilities against the ones described in this book, identify the differences, and develop a plan to close those differences. I refer to these capabilities as the 4Ps (people, process, platforms, and practices) throughout the remainder of this chapter.

Each of the 4Ps is evaluated in terms of the current capabilities and how they map to the 4Ps of the SOA model in this book. For each of these Ps, the results identify people, process, platforms, or practices that:

- Do not exist in the current environment and need to be acquired or created.
- Exist but have to be modified or "transformed" to the new model.
- Exist but do not fit into the new model and need to be "disengaged."

Each of these assessment results is be the basis for creating an action plan containing the specific activities to create, transform, or disengage these 4Ps. This action plan represents the SOA practice implementation strategy within the SOA business strategy and roadmap document. The number of activities within the action plan that are concurrently initiated and the timing for starting those activities are the basis of the roadmap portion of the SOA business strategy and roadmap document.

What Is the SOA Business Strategy and Roadmap?

As stated earlier in this book, the SOA business strategy and roadmap is a business document, not a technical one. It is not just about acquiring the technologies needed to build SOA applications. These are important but represent only one of the 4Ps that needs to be transformed. The SOA business strategy and roadmap document includes:

- How business and IT organizations may have to change.
- How the practices and responsibilities within both the business and IT have to change.
- The new policies, procedures, and standards that need to be developed and institutionalized.
- The transformation of all the governance bodies to the models defined in this book.
- The documentation of all the templates (forms, project plans, reports, and communication vehicles) used by the new SOA systems development life cycle (SDLC).
- The environmental and capacity management and monitoring capabilities required for the new environment.
- The acquisition or reallocation of human resources to perform the supportive roles defined in Chapter 11.
- The education and training programs needed to educate business, IT, and any other external vendors and partners involved in the processes regarding the new models, policies, standards, and processes implemented under this roadmap and strategy.

This document does not represent the plan for implementing the business applications specified by the business initiatives in the portfolio. It is the plan describing exactly what IT is going to change and when it is going to make those changes to transform IT and the company to the new SOA paradigm.

This is what is sometimes called the plan behind the plan. Like all other business units, IT needs to present and sell its plan to the company's executive leadership. As with plans for all other business units, this plan is incorporated into, and part of, the corporate strategic plan. What better way to support the new business-IT relationship proposed in this book than to elevate the IT organization as an equal business partner in the corporate strategic plan! The other value of this process is that it makes achieving the plan a corporate mission, as all the other business unit plans are. The executive leadership commitment to the IT plan is recognized throughout the company and has their (implicit) full support.

The SOA business strategy and roadmap is the business plan for transforming the company to the SOA enterprise architecture practice model. Exhibit 14.1 summarizes this process.

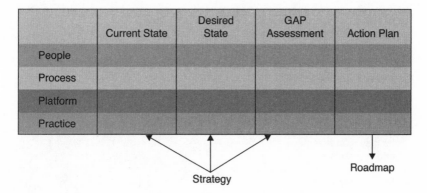

EXHIBIT 14.1   SOA Gap Analysis Matrix

Framework for Assessing Maturity

A maturity model is a guide for process improvement. It is also a guide for planning and managing change. It provides a standard framework for measuring capabilities in a systematic manner so that all the activities conducted to move the organization forward are at the appropriate level at a given point in time. It identifies what the capabilities are at various levels of relative maturity. Where an organization falls on the maturity model determines *what* activities should be conducted to advance the organization up the chain. Attempting to address activities that are more appropriately addressed at a higher layer has a high probability of being less successful. This is because the foundational capabilities of the lower levels will not be mature enough to support the higher-layer initiatives. Building a solid foundation at each layer helps to accelerate the organization up the layers.

A common model used for assessing an organization's maturity is the Capability Maturity Model Integration (CMMI) developed by Carnegie Mellon University. (See Exhibit 14.2.)

Level 1 reflects an environment totally reactive, unpredictable, and uncontrolled. Awareness of SOA is limited and, where it exists, highly misunderstood. Few, if any, activities are centered on SOA. No formal SOA enterprise architecture development frameworks, design patterns, or design standards exist. Most of the policies, procedures, and practices are designed to support the traditional bottom-up systems approach to business applications. No SOA architectural considerations are made when purchased or leased business applications are being evaluated. No one in the business, from the leaders to the individual users of applications, feels he or she has any accountability or responsibility for systems architecture. They all perceive conversations around architecture as barriers or obstacles to their business objectives instead of benefits to their business strategy.

Level 2 reflects an environment that is still heavily reactionary, but pockets of managed focus on architecture and SOA exist on a project-by-project basis. Unfortunately, an SOA enterprise architecture practice and the supporting policies, procedures, and standards to support that practice are still nonexistent or informal. Therefore, the infusion of technical SOA characteristics in these projects has very little architectural or strategic value to the company. Since most of these capabilities

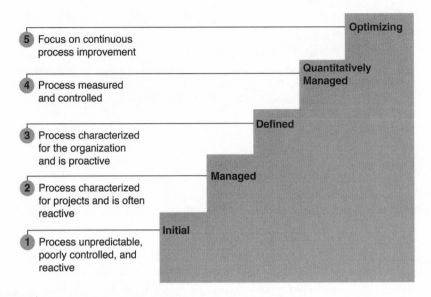

EXHIBIT 14.2　CMMI Maturity Model

Source: © 2005 by Carnegie Mellon University.

were built at a project level, bounded by project-level business requirements and project-level budgets, few, if any, of these SOA components can be leveraged within the enterprise SOA architectural framework defined in this book.

Level 3 reflects an environment where the focus has moved beyond the project level, and proactive activities are occurring at the enterprise level. At this level, the SOA enterprise architecture practice is established and operational. The policies, procedures, and standards to support the practice have been documented and communicated. The human resources, defined in Chapter 11, are on board, and the roles these people perform are under way. The SOA SDLC process and the governance bodies overseeing it have been implemented, and the first SOA initiatives are being cycled through the process.

At Level 4, the process has moved beyond the effective tactical implementation of SOA initiatives and is heavily focused on maximizing reuse and the strategic values of SOA. A tipping point has occurred where existing SOA assets are influencing and, in some cases, driving the business strategy instead of the other way around. The business is recognizing, at an enterprise level, the increased competitive advantages that can be gained by leveraging the SOA assets and is driving the company in that direction. The architecture is "owned" by the business, and everyone supports 100 percent compliance to it.

When you reach Level 5, the focus of both the business and IT leadership is on continuously improving the SOA~EAF and methodology. At this level, almost every IT Initiative will be an SOA initiative. Heavy focus will be placed on the modernization and replacement of the remaining non-SOA business applications with solutions that take advantage of all the benefits of the SOA environment.

The critical point to remember is not to attempt to accomplish activities at Level 5 when the impacted organizations and resources are at a Level 1 or 2. Attempting to roll out an SOA quality improvement program in the early stages of your SOA business strategy and roadmap is doomed to fail.

This does not mean that all of the 4Ps or different capabilities within the 4Ps will be at the same maturity level. They will not. Some of your IT assets across these 4Ps will be, and should be, at a higher maturity level than the business. You should strive so that IT and, if possible, the vendors supporting IT are always at a higher maturity level than the business until Level 5 is reached. This will pre-position them to focus on bringing the business to the next level rather than both attempting it together.

At Level 1, communications and training focus on understanding SOA and learning about the processes and people roles being established. At Level 1, the objective is to begin awareness of a formal set of processes and practices.

For Level 2, the focus shifts to communicating early successes of the process and programs to create and promote more instances of the processes in a repeatable fashion.

To move to Level 3, the education and training focus is on ensuring that every business unit is participating in the process and that enterprise-wide SOA initiatives are occurring.

At Level 4, communication and education is all strategic. The process is well established and running smoothly. The business is developing corporate strategies and business plans that are designed to maximize the value of the SOA assets in the portfolio. It has taken complete control of the process and is driving communication and education around maximizing the business value of SOA.

At Level 5, every part of the process is constantly being evaluated for improvements. The programs being developed are quality improvement programs, and communications are focused on reminding and enforcing the tenets and values of SOA.

As stated earlier in this book, the first action that needs to be taken is to get the architecture resources established and aligned to the SOA enterprise architecture roles defined in Chapter 11, at least for the chief architect and enterprise architecture roles. These resources need to be established before the SOA business strategy and roadmap is developed, since they are the resources that need to develop it. It will also be beneficial to utilize organization development consulting services that are skilled in the application of the CMMI to assist in developing the SOA business strategy and roadmap.

People Assessment

The *people* assessment involves comparing the roles, responsibilities, and capabilities of all the people resources defined in Chapter 11 to the current associates in the company. The goal is to identify all associates who have the capability, or potential capability, to perform the desired roles. For these individuals, the objective is to get them to accept these new roles and help them acquire any new skills and capabilities to perform in those roles. Examples would include taking seasoned application architects and placing them in a solutions architect position, or taking seasoned project managers and placing them into SOA initiative management roles. For roles where no internal associates meet the criteria, the action plan identifies requirements to hire resources to fill those roles. This may include a need to fill the enterprise infrastructure and capacity architect position with an external resource with extensive knowledge of highly distributed, multiplatform environments.

The people assessment will also include the redistribution of responsibilities within existing associate roles. This action plan will require activities to communicate these changes to these associates and their leaders and get their buy-in and commitment. Next, it will require an education program to help the associates understand and perform these new responsibilities. This education includes explaining the new processes where these responsibilities will be applied and the associates' participation in those processes. It will include redefining business associate roles around *consumer* and *provider* responsibilities.

The first step in the people education process is to change the way the business thinks about systems. Traditional thinking of a business application that encapsulates multiple business processes into a monolithic deliverable needs to change. The service model approaches system design from the perspective of consumers and the business processes (or services) that support those consumers. Each of these processes is viewed from cradle to grave without restrictions imposed by organizational or even corporate boundaries. Each process is further decomposed into the activities within it. Those activities are evaluated and classified as to whether they are unique to the specific business process or represent activities performed in other processes as well. This evaluation is not limited to the processes within the current consumer domain. All consumer domains are evaluated. Evaluating if a process or service has value to other constituents or other interactions with the same constituent allows the enterprise assessment to maximize the value of the investment. Educating business members so they understand these concepts is critical to moving forward with the SOA transformation. Some of this education (especially at the executive level) will be in the form of communications and presentations. At lower levels of the organization, these tools, as well as formal training sessions, will be involved. Examples based on the SOA Business Architecture framework should be used to facilitate the training process. To be most effective, these examples should be based on actual business conditions within your company.

Examples of communication and education programs that need to be developed and disseminated are presented next. The comprehensiveness of this list and the programs themselves will be based on your current maturity level assessment of the individuals participating in the programs. These programs will change as you move up the maturity level model. Additional programs may be identified as you advance through the process.

Executive-Level Communications
- What is SOA, and what is its value to the business?
- How to perform strategic business planning from a consumer-centric Service Domain perspective
- Defining the roles of service consumers and service providers
- The SOA governance process and its importance to the success of SOA

Initiative and Project Manager Programs
- Explaining the SOA SDLC development and management model
- Constructing SOA initiatives and developing SOA project plans to support those initiatives

- Initiative and project governance processes under SOA
- Matrix project management requirements and skills
- Understanding the release approach to business application delivery
- Setting the scope of SOA initiatives and projects
- Resource planning for SOA projects
- Establishing the funding and expenditure model for SOA
- How to manage an SOA business requirements–gathering process
- How to manage the SOA design, development, test and release processes

Business Analyst and Subject Matter Expert Programs
- Understanding the SOA governance process
- Using the SOA SDLC development and management model
- Understanding the Business Architecture framework
- Understanding the release approach to business application delivery
- How to develop business requirements using a top-down, multichannel, consumer-centric approach
- Understanding the distinction between local and enterprise business capabilities
- How to identify and leverage shared business capabilities

IT Operations and Support
- Developing monitoring, performance, and capacity utilization service-level agreements (SLAs) for SOA applications
- Understanding the release approach to business application delivery

Application Development Resources and Vendors
- Understanding the SOA~EAF.
- Using the SOA application development and integration guide
- Understanding the development frameworks, design patterns, and design standards within the SOA~EAF

These are a few examples of the communications and programs that will be needed in the early rollout stages of the SOA strategy. Similar rollout programs need to be developed for other business entities, such as procurement (or the entity that handles business software procurement through requests for information and requests for proposals) and finance (which manages and maintains the IT budgets).

Process Assessment

The *process* assessment analyzes current processes and how they differ from the desired end-state processes defined in this book. These processes include:

- Comparing the current development life cycle to the SOA development life cycle.
- Comparing the current program and project management processes to the SOA program and project processes.
- Comparing the current governance processes to the SOA governance model.
- Assessing the vendor contracting and business software procurement process.

Other comparisons include the strategic planning, business planning, and budgeting processes.

The action plan produced by this analysis will define the activities to reengineer current processes to new processes. This will include the modification of existing policies or the creation of new policies to govern and support the new processes. Finally, it will identify steps to define and implement the new metrics, measures, and management controls within those processes. Examples of some of the defined activities out of this assessment include:

Governance
- The creation of the five governance processes defined in Chapter 8 (or transition of existing governance processes)
- The enrollment of the participants in the governance processes and the formal definition and acceptance of their roles and responsibilities
- The establishment of the governance evaluation criteria and metrics used to make governance decisions
- The definition of the input and output documents of the governance processes and the reporting mechanisms for status and resolution

SOA System Development Life Cycle
- The rollout of the SOA SDLC process
- The creation of the formal process for documenting and submitting SOA initiatives
- The official implementation of the:
  - Initiative scope process
  - Resource planning process
  - Business requirements–gathering process
  - Project scope process
  - Configuration management and change control process
  - Release process
  - Testing processes
- The development of the SOA initiative and SOA project plan templates

Delivery Assurance
- The implementation of the SOA release certification and deployment process (production readiness process)
- The creation of the SLA monitoring and management process
- The incorporation of the business application vendor architectural compliance process into the existing vendor solicitation and contracting processes

Platform Assessment

The platform assessment assesses current versus desired capabilities from four perspectives:

1. The platforms (as specified by the chief architect, chief technology officer [CTO], and enterprise architects) that are needed to design, develop, deploy, and operate SOA components at each layer of the architecture

2. The hardware and operating system platforms that those deployed SOA components run on
3. The resources needed by operations to monitor, manage, and support the SOA components in production
4. The tools needed to manage, maintain, and leverage the enterprise SOA artifacts and assets

Specific platform recommendations may include the acquisition of:

- New channel or channel adapter technologies to support the Strategy.
- Middleware and enterprise service bus (ESB) platforms.
- Extract, transformation, and load platforms.
- Security and provisioning platforms.
- Service repository and service discovery platforms.
- Business process modeling (BPM) and business activity monitoring platforms.
- Business intelligence platforms.
- SOA management and monitoring platforms.

The acquisition of some of these platforms will be identified as foundational and will be required before the SOA development approach is started. Others can be deferred until business initiatives requiring them are identified.

The platform assessment also includes the evaluation of the legacy application integration capabilities. What integration capabilities exist? Are any integration tools or technologies in use? Are these capabilities, technologies, and tools supportive of the SOA Enterprise Architecture Integration layer design standards and development frameworks? If not, what tools or capabilities are needed to support or improve legacy integration?

The action plan developed from this assessment defines the activities to acquire and implement the identified platforms and tools. This action plan is slightly different from plans in that the timing and priority of these activities can be tied to the projected SOA initiatives. Not all platforms and tools will be needed at the same time. Depending on the initiatives, certain platforms may or may not be required. For example, if the first SOA initiative is deploying simple services and does not require a business process or work flow capability, the acquisition of a BPMS platform would not be necessary at that time. If none of the early SOA initiatives requires a Web portal platform, that purchase can be deferred as well.

While the acquisition of these technologies can be deferred, the decision on which platforms will be acquired should not be deferred. These decisions should be made as soon as possible for two major reasons.

1. To ensure that the selected platforms comply with all the standards and interoperability requirements established by the enterprise SOA architects.
2. To avoid a rush decision or the holdup of an SOA initiative if a business driver changes the priority of an SOA initiative that does require them.

These decisions should be revisited annually by the enterprise architects if they still have not been acquired to validate that the product is still the best available solution.

The platform action plan is also different from the other action plans in that this plan becomes the basis for creating the first version of the enterprise SOA technology plan. The SOA technology plan is the technical document that supports the business-driven enterprise SOA portfolio plan. Once the new process is up and running, all the entries on the enterprise SOA technology plan map directly to initiatives on the enterprise SOA portfolio plan as technical prerequisites or dependencies. During start-up, however, the enterprise SOA technology plan may contain technology acquisitions that are not directly linked to a specific business SOA initiative. Examples of these acquisitions include:

- New SOA design, development, deployment, and code management tools.
- New SOA capacity and performance monitoring tools.
- New framework platforms, such as security or layer platforms (such as an ESB).
- An architecture metadata repository to electronically manage the documents and artifacts contained within the SOA~EAF.

These tools and the capabilities they provide are critical to implementing and maintaining a service-oriented architecture. They need to be explicitly identified as prerequisite requirements to implementing SOA in the SOA business strategy and roadmap. As a business strategy, the SOA business strategy and roadmap defines these as foundational capabilities required to achieve the strategy. Attempts to achieve the strategy without them will in all probability fail. Engineers of an auto manufacturer would not recommend going forward with building a completely different type of automobile they designed if they knew that the new technologies and manufacturing processes needed to build it would not be funded. Business executives need to understand that asking architecture and IT to implement SOA based on the value propositions they have put forth without funding the technology infrastructure needed to achieve it will set them up for failure.

When establishing your people resource plan, do not forget that all tool and technology acquisitions also require resources to support and maintain them. The acquisition of a new tool or technology may require a skill or training not found in current operations. The acquisition of these resources, the cost of education and training programs and of vendor-supplied support contracts should all be included in the action plan.

Practice Assessment

The *practice* assessment evaluates how the business operates and how those practices can positively or negatively impact your ability to achieve SOA success. These practices include how:

- IT relates to, interacts with, and influences vendors.
- The business and IT evaluate and build partner relationships.
- Technology and application vendors interact with your business and who owns those relationships.
- The business and IT are organized, as explained in Chapter 13.
- The customer relationship is managed in the company.

These are a few of the common practice areas that impact IT abilities. The practice assessment is really an evaluation of the culture and politics of the organization and how they can impact your ability to succeed. The practice action plan is focused on the modification and creation of corporate business policies that drive different business practices. It is also focused on activities to build executive commitment and enforcement of those policies and practices.

The practice assessment also includes assessing IT's current capabilities. Do current IT practices support the SOA model? Are there IT functional areas that are missing or not scaled properly to support the practices necessary to support SOA?

Practice action plans include:

- Development and institutionalization of the SOA~EAF methodology.
- Enterprise architecture SOA practice.
- Creation of the software release and quality assurance practices.
- Development of the legacy SOA modernization practice.

The practice needs to incorporate the resources to develop, communicate, and maintain the key SOA documentation for supporting the model. The architects need to make sure that these documents are approved by all the executives and institutionalized so everyone participating in the process is on the same page.

These documents include:

- SOA~EAF model—how its content is populated and used.
- Development of your company's unique reference and platform architectures.
- Documentation of the SOA development frameworks, design patterns, and standards.
- Publication of the SOA application developers' reference guide.
- SOA testing model and approach.

In addition, formal adoption of the new IT practices by the other support organizations, such as finance and procurement, need to be established.

Determining the Current Maturity Level of the 4Ps

In terms of an architectural approach to SOA, especially one that adopts the framework and practices defined in this book, it is highly unlikely that your organization's people, processes, or SOA enterprise architecture practice are above a Level 2 maturity. The only exception may be platforms that already provide all the capabilities to achieve the SOA architecture defined in this book. Whether that capability is being maximized from an architecture perspective is a different story.

If the people, process, platform, or practice do not exist (maturity Level 1), the focus of your efforts will be on communication, education, and training. At this maturity level, you are creating awareness for the need and building support and commitment at all levels to move forward.

If some of the 4Ps address SOA at an informal or tactical level (maturity Level 2), these activities need to be expanded and formalized. The resources involved in these informal activities can be leveraged to expand awareness to other resources that are less mature and to help the architects document and prove out formal policies and procedures. The goal at Level 2 is to:

- Define and establish all the people roles.
- Define and vet all the processes.
- Establish and formally recognize the SOA architecture practice team.
- Have in place or funded the platforms, tools, and technologies needed to support the defined SOA initiatives.
- Have formally documented and approved all the policies required to support, govern, and enforce SOA.

When conducting your gap analysis, you need to separate *what* is being done from *how* it is being done. If a formal process or activity is not established, you need to establish one. If a formal process or activity does exist, you need to determine how similar or different that process is from the one you need to implement. In the first case, the action plan is for a new process development. In the latter case, the action plan is for a process improvement. If you already follow a formal SDLC process, you will assess how that SDLC process maps to the one defined in this book. Activities to enhance the existing process to adopt the SOA model would be documented in your SDLC enhancement plan. If no formal process for gathering business requirements exists, one needs to be developed. A formal requirements-gathering process is one where all requirements are gathered using the same structure and format and following a defined, repeatable process. Simply requiring that business requirements be documented is not a formal process.

Some governance activities may be formally established. Some of these bodies may align fairly closely to the governance committees defined in this book. An existing executive governance body should map fairly well to the SOA Domain Governance Committee. There may be a body that performs governance roles similar to those defined by the enterprise SOA Portfolio Plan Governance Committee defined in this book. How they are governing, however, will need to change dramatically. They need to transform from a bottom-up, system delivery model to a top-down, service delivery model. They need to shift the governance focus from a vertical stovepipe delivery of functionality to a horizontal consumer-centric focus.

Throughout this gap assessment process, you need to evaluate the existing policies that are the basis for these activities. You need to determine how these policies must change to support the new processes. Every process, especially governance ones, should be based on policies that direct the actions and decisions that are made. If a policy stating that all new business capabilities delivered to internal and external constituents will use an enterprise authentication and authorization security system does not exist, the enterprise SOA Portfolio Plan Governance Committee will have no basis for requiring that submitted initiatives comply.

Regardless of the maturity level, the initial focus of your efforts will be on:

- Education and communication programs for your associates, leaders, and vendors.

- Process development or enhancement programs to transform SDLC and governance activities.
- Implementation of an SOA center of excellence to support the proof of technology and proof of concept (POC) activities that need to be conducted before the model is officially adopted.

Therefore, the gap analysis grid depicted in Exhibit 14.1 will have action items that address these areas:

For People
- Hiring people with new skill sets
- Transitioning existing resources into new roles
- Restructuring responsibilities within existing roles
- Formally implementing multiple training and education programs for understanding and adopting the new model

For Process Development of New Formal Processes and Activities Not Currently Performed in a Formal Manner
- Enhancing existing formal processes to transform them to the new processes
- Developing new policies or modifying existing policies to support the new processes
- Developing or adaptating all the documentation and artifacts required by the new processes

For Platforms
- Acquiring any platforms required to design, build, test, deploy, and maintain the SOA applications
- Retooling or enhancing existing documentation, monitoring, and management platforms to support the new platforms

For Practice
- Establishing the enterprise architecture SOA practice
- Establishing the SOA center of excellence
- Formalizing the vendor and partner SOA relationship practices
- Creating of the horizontal consumer and vertical provider practices

Starting New or Changing What Exists

As stated earlier in this book, one approach is to leave all the existing practices and processes in place and build the new SOA practices and processes in parallel to run separately from the traditional approach. This approach is recommended if the gap analysis is wide and the maturity levels are low. Under these conditions, the majority of the IT initiatives will continue to follow the old approach because a significant amount of effort will be required to get the company to the point where it can support processing the initiatives through the new approach. If the gap analysis is narrower and the company's maturity level appears very responsive and adaptable to the changes, merging the new processes and practices into existing management practices and processes will certainly help accelerate the transformation. Obviously, some processes, such as portfolio governance, can merge relatively easily, but others, such as the SDLC, cannot.

If this second approach is adopted, you need to make absolutely sure that the differences between the two approaches are clearly defined and followed. As stated earlier, attempting to apply the metrics and rationale of traditional IT projects to SOA initiatives will be unfavorable to the SOA initiatives every time. The reality is there will continue to be a mixture of traditional IT projects and SOA initiatives for some period of time. Even if the same bodies are used, the activities should be separated and the separate inputs, processes, and outputs clearly identifiable.

As a rule of thumb, strategic activities should be merged and transformed faster than tactical or operational ones, since Strategic Activities have a more global and enterprise impact.

Also, the IT organizations should be positioned to support the transformation as fast as the business can absorb the changes. The business adoption will be the slowest and will control how fast the transformation occurs. IT should not wait for the business to evolve to the next level before developing everything required to support it at that level. IT needs to be ready and waiting to help them move forward.

Piloting an SOA Initiative to Shake Out and Evaluate the Model

Most, if not all, of the initial gap analysis around the maturity level of the people and processes in terms of how effective new processes and development approaches will be accepted and adopted will occur behind the scenes, i.e., through an informal observation of existing activities. This should be done prior to the rollout of the formal SOA process. That is not to say that you need to have every aspect of every change defined and documented before you start. It does mean that the architect team must assess what you will need and when you will need it at a fairly detailed level so the initial implementation will be as smooth as possible. The approach I recommend is for the architects to look into the IT development pipeline of projects that have not been submitted or approved for a potential candidate for an SOA initiative simulation pilot. When you do this analysis, make sure to pick a project that has these four characteristics:

1. It has a high business value and a high probability of being approved in the next annual approval process.
2. Its sponsors have a good relationship with IT and have shown openness to IT's input in the past.
3. It involves at least one strategic partner or vendor if those relationships already exist.
4. Its complexity is (relatively) simple in the sense that:
   - At least some foundational capabilities already exist in the environment that can be leveraged.
   - The new technology investment needed is relatively low.

- Its scope is relatively small (one or two constituents using one channel for a small number of services).

After this is done, the business architects should build a sample SOA business architecture to reflect the SOA initiative.

Next, the solutions architects would develop the high-level solution for the SOA initiative, including cost estimates and timelines.

This process should also include the extraction of the corporate strategies and business unit plans that relate to the pilot SOA initiative and populating this information into the Corporate Strategy and Business Unit Plans columns of the SOA~EAF. These straw entries should be validated with the business leader sponsoring the initiative.

Throughout all these steps, the architect team should identify and document:

- The processes used, the people involved, and what that involvement was.
- The changes needed to be made to those processes to get the task accomplished.
- All the architectural and design considerations that were discussed and how they were converted into development frameworks, design patterns, design standards, and so forth.
- The communication and management tools used and what changes were made to those tools (e.g., What did a matrix SOA initiative project plan look like?).
- Changes made to the format, content, or audience of all deliverables.

At the completion of these activities, the architects should conduct a "lessons learned" or postoperative assessment. They must evaluate what went well and what did not and identify if there are any holes in the process or documentation that need to be shored up. The major objective of this step is to assess the SOA maturity of the IT organization. Did you have the right people? Was the communication of what you were doing and how to do it concise and clearly understood? Did you have to bring in outside expertise? Did you accomplish the tasks quickly and efficiently, or was it painful and slow? Was there excitement and enthusiasm, or was there fear and lack of comfort?

The answer to these questions will help to identify strengths and weaknesses of the current resources and environment. This will help the architects determine where they can move ahead at a faster pace (strengths) and where they need to spend more time building their comfort level with the process.

When completed, you should feel comfortable that if the initiative was presented and approved, you would be able to deliver it within the estimated time frame and cost. You need to feel comfortable that if this test run were real, the same outcomes would have been reached. If you are not comfortable, go back through the process until you are.

After all this is done, the IT executives can meet with the rest of the business members. The purpose is not to discuss this specific initiative but to present the new IT business plan for maximizing IT's support of the business. At this point, the business education and "sell" process begins. A successful meeting will be an agreement by the business leaders to go to the next step, which would be to conduct an analysis and come up with a proposal for a pilot SOA initiative.

> **Note**
>
> If a particular executive suggests that you simulate one of his initiatives, agree to assess it. If it seems too large, will take too long to assess, or appears not to be a project that can be addressed through SOA, work off-line with the executive to get him to agree to use another project. If it is a candidate for SOA and can be assessed in the allotted time, take the opportunity to do so and have two alternative pilots to present. This second assessment should be much quicker because you can leverage all the procedural and analytical documentation produced during the first simulated assessment.

The pilot should be sold as a POC. The proof, however, is not just the proof that SOA as a technology can deliver what the business needs. It should be a proof of the architectural approach to SOA. The pilot is proof that the new processes and practices have high value to the business and IT. It is proof that the new approach helps the business achieve better alignment with what IT is delivering and a clearer understanding of the alignment of those deliverables with the corporate strategy. The business should be able to understand not only the capabilities delivered by the pilot SOA implementation in terms of the business value, but also why it was designed the way it was and the strategic value of that design to future initiatives.

Throughout the delivery of the POC, discussions with the business about how the channel implementation can be leveraged to deliver additional services or be deployed to other constituents in the future should be held and documented. How the development frameworks, such as security, will be a foundation for expediting the delivery of new capabilities in the future should be understood by the business leaders, who should fully embrace the value of these development frameworks.

The business participants in the POC should include strategic thinking leaders as well as subject matter experts. The best outcome of the POC would be having these business leaders carry the results of the POC to the executive leaders of the company and expound on the virtues and values of the approach. The architects need to play a key role in making this happen. They need to do everything possible to position these leaders to see the value and take ownership for carrying those values forward.

The information gathered from this process will help you assess how capable the organization is and how easy or difficult it is going to be to make the significant cultural and organizational changes that need to be made. If things go well, it may be possible to accelerate the number of SOA initiatives addressed in the next wave. If things go poorly, you will need to focus on identifying what the barriers and issues were and getting them completely resolved before the next SOA initiative is proposed.

You need to constantly reinforce that the commitment to the SOA approach and the whole rationale for undertaking such a major transformation should not change because of the cultural and organizational difficulties encountered. Nobody said transformation is easy. Sometimes things that return tremendous value take a lot of effort to achieve that value. If it was easy, it would have already been done.

This gets back to the whole premise of this book. Implementing a technology is relatively easy. Implementing an entirely new business model where the business and IT create new synergies, efficiencies, and competitive advantages takes a little more effort.

Structure of the SOA Business Strategy and Roadmap

The enterprise architects support the chief architect and the CIO in the development of the SOA business strategy and roadmap. This document is, in fact, the IT business plan for implementing and supporting the SOA enterprise architecture transformation defined in this book. This document is defined in this last chapter for a reason. You need to read every part of this book before you begin building this document. It will, however, be the first deliverable you produce and the first document that gets approved by the company executives.

It is important that this entire document be reviewed within IT as well as with all the other business unit leaders before being proposed at the executive level. The vetting process with the non-IT leaders is to make them aware of the new model and get their buy-in and commitment to the entire process. The CIO, CTO, and chief architect need to expend a significant amount of time and effort with all the company leaders to help them to understand at a high level what IT is attempting to accomplish, what they will be asked to commit to, and why it is important for them to buy into it. No corporate executive or business unit leader should be surprised when IT presents its formal business plan.

If your company has a formal format for documenting and submitting business plans, you should use that format for the SOA business strategy and roadmap. The roadmap represents IT's business plan submitted to the formal corporate strategy group with all the other business unit plans. It should start with an executive overview, explaining why IT is undertaking this radical transformation and how that transformation will help the company achieve its strategy. It should provide a high-level overview of what is going to change (the 4Ps) and how long it is going to take to make those changes. It should identify which changes are going to occur first and why those were chosen as the first priority for change. Finally, it should identify:

- Which of these changes will be made over the next year (or *N* years if defined as such by the business strategy unit) and the resource and funding commitment needed.
- The measures and metrics that will be used to evaluate the success of those changes.
- How the executives will be informed as to the progress of those changes.

The next section of the document should be a business justification section. This is IT's business justification. It should explain how business and technology have evolved and how the corporate business applications are no longer bounded by corporate walls. It needs to explain how the external entities that the company interacts with are now heavily involved in the use of those business applications as well. The greater their involvement becomes, the more influence they feel they have the right to exert on how those business applications work. Draw on the information in the first four chapters of this book to make this justification. This section has to make a compelling argument that staying with the old status quo approach will drain the company's resources, continue to make the environment more complex and rigid, and ultimately become a competitive disadvantage to the corporation.

The next section should be the current environment assessment, which defines the way the company currently operates as it relates to the acquisition and/or development of business applications. It should identify what is good as well as what is bad. This section should document examples of existing formal processes and practices that are solid foundations for building on going forward as well as examples of waste, duplication, and rigidity caused by complexity created by the old approach.

The next section should define the new desired end state and introduce the new business model. The focus should be a business focus, not a technical one. It should introduce the concept of the business architecture and how it is driven from a top-down, consumer-centric perspective. It should show how the corporate strategy and business unit plans can be structured in a similar fashion to drive the evaluation and priority of initiatives reflected through a business architecture and how those conceptual views expand and evolve as more capabilities are delivered. It should describe the higher-layer governance activities and how the new SOA model helps the business better understand their capabilities and make better business decisions when it comes to business applications.

The next section should be the results of the gap analysis and the action plans defined as a result of that analysis. Each section of the action plan should have defined deliverables and a brief description of the effort and resources involved. The approach I recommend is to use the framework depicted in Exhibit 14.1, but create separate ones for the processes and practices defined in this book. Under this approach, a people, process, platform, and practice gap analysis will be developed for the:

- SOA SDLC process.
- SOA governance process.
- Business application acquisition or lease process.
- SOA capacity planning and infrastructure monitoring process.
- Business and IT organization model.
- Legacy application assessment and modernization process.

Some of these categories may be broken down to a more granular level. In the SDLC process, for example, each phase, from initiation to deployment, may have its own gap analysis framework with action items specific to the gaps in those phases.

The final section of the business plan lists the action plans that will be addressed first and the priority for addressing them. Once again, these plans would have been vetted with all the leaders and their agreement to the activities and the priorities already established. The list should cite the activities that will be undertaken first, once the SOA business strategy and roadmap is approved and through the period of years specified by the corporate strategic plan. These action items are defined in detail, including the IT and business resources needed as well as any funding and acquisition of resources required. Following the recommended approach in this chapter, the initial activities will focus around setting up a center of excellence, acquiring foundational SOA technologies and platforms, and identifying a pilot SOA initiative for a proof of concept. In parallel, the roadmap may include resources to develop and deliver educational and training capabilities to be rolled out across the enterprise after the pilot is completed.

Summary

This chapter defined how to assess the current people, processes, platforms, and practices in your company compared to the ones outlined in this book and developing a SOA transformation action plan. Examples of the types of communications and training programs needed at the different maturity levels were provided. Also provided was a model you can use to assess your company's maturity level to gauge how fast you can move the transformation along and what critical activities to focus on, based on how mature the organization is.

The gap analysis tells you how far you are from where you need to be and the actions needed to get you there. The maturity level assessment helps you determine if those gaps are at the lower level of the maturity spectrum, the higher level, or somewhere in between. At the lower layers, the activities focus on setting up formal processes and practices that do not exist. The focus is heavily on education and training. At the higher layers, the focus is on process enhancement and improvement of exiting formal processes and more on communication than training.

You may think the SOA transformation I am recommending is overwhelming. Others may think this book is Nirvana and not achievable. To be truthful, it is overwhelming and, to some degree, it is Nirvana. The reality is it will take years to effect all the changes presented in this book. The most important thing you can do is to forget how daunting the tasks in front of you are and just begin! Pick areas where you feel you have the best chance of being successful and start there. Start slowly and expand as rapidly as knowledge, skills, and understanding grow through the corporation. Look for allies and partners who show an interest in the SOA concepts, can see the value it offers, and are open to change.

You are trying to effect an SOA transformation that will affect almost everything your company does. Transformations are not easy. Transformations are risky. Transformations are scary to those who do not understand their rationale or those who are comfortable with the status quo. As with most transformations, however, the end result is often enlightening and extremely valuable. I can only tell you that the farther you advance, the more visible the value becomes, and less frustration and resistance will exist. If you persist, you will reach a tipping point where you will transition from trying to drag the business along to where you are struggling to keep up with them. This will be a good thing!

Obviously, the stronger the executive commitment and buy-in, the better your chances of success. If the CIO of your company is driving the changes within the IT organization, they will be the easier to achieve, since the CIO has a position of influence and power over the organization. Even with this, however, it will not be easy. It may require letting go good committed people who do not have the right skills and are not interested in acquiring those skills. It may require that some resources lose responsibilities and power while others gain them.

Assessing the SOA maturity of the IT organization will not be the most difficult evaluation you make, but it will be the most critical in terms of establishing a foundation to build on. The last thing you want to have happen is for the business to buy into the SOA transformation and not have your IT organization ready to support it. The IT organization has to be well ahead of the business in terms of SOA knowledge and capabilities. Holding up an initiative while IT figures out how to do it will mean certain death for the SOA transformation effort. SOA preparedness includes not only the skills and capabilities of the IT personnel, but also the technologies, development frameworks, design standards, and design patterns needed to implement the SOA initiative successfully.

If you are unsuccessful in getting your company to commit to such a major transformation, I hope you can use the concepts and ideas described in this book to improve your SOA capabilities at a micro level through grassroots efforts. Adoption and use of the SOA~EAF by your architects will help them infuse some of the architectural principles for SOA design into individual projects. Leveraging the concepts in this book to get traditional business applications to use common framework capabilities will have measurable benefits that can push commitment to the higher levels of the company. Getting some key business leaders comfortable with looking at their business applications from a conceptual business architecture perspective will provide a way to carry their business application requirements to the next level. If you can build alliances with your key constituents, vendors, and partners who also see the value of the approach, you can build influence outside of the internal IT organization to push and promote the values of adopting the SOA model.

Finally, it is hoped that once this book is published, more companies will begin the adoption of the model. I hope that, through my blog (www.soaistheway .wordpress.com), the experiences of these companies and the lessons that they provide will help all of us get better and succeed. I welcome all of you to use this site and learn from each other as you embark on this scary but wondrous journey!

SOA~EAF Documentation Templates

This appendix contains blank templates of the documents described in this book that are used to capture, compile, and communicate information used in the service-oriented architecture (SOA) practices and processes. These documents are provided to assist you in setting up your own documents for your own practice. Feel free to use them within your company as is or modify them to suit your own business needs. If you are using the templates or variations based on them for commercial reasons or include them in documents distributed to entities outside your company, I ask that you honor the copyright laws and include the following copyright disclosure at the bottom of each template page.

Electronic versions of these templates for you to use can be downloaded from my blog (www.soaistheway.wordpress.com).

The templates provided in this appendix are:

- SOA Initiative Template
- Legacy System Business Assessment Questionnaire
- SOA Business Architecture Diagram Template

SOA Initiative Template

This appendix contains a template that can be used to structure SOA initiatives and facilitate their submission through the governance review and approval processes. You can use this template as is or as a guide to help you build your own template. I encourage you to incorporate any key criteria that your company uses in its existing IT assessment and approval processes if it is not within this template or to eliminate information that is perceived as of lower value or not important by your corporate culture.

Sections III through VI and Section VIII, however, should not be eliminated and should be completed to the best level of detail possible within the time frame allotted for compiling and submitting the initiative. That said, the entire document should not exceed 10 pages and the executive summary should be no longer than 2 pages.

Remember that the intent of this document is not to provide the full set of requirements or the full detailed specification of the initiative. Its intent is to "sell" the initiative as a valuable proposal that should be approved when compared to all the other proposals being submitted. Adopting and enforcing a template for the initiatives ensures that proposals are evaluated using an apples-to-apples comparison so that the members of the enterprise SOA Portfolio Plan Governance Committee and the SOA Business Domain Governance Committee have a consistent and fair way of conducting their evaluations.

I. Initiative Description

Initiative Name: _____

Tracking ID: _____ **Version Number:** _____

Sponsors:

Name	Organization	Review Status

Review Status = Under Review, Approved, Rejected

Initial creation date: _____/_____/_____   **Last modified date:** _____/_____/_____

Requested production implementation date: _____/_____/_____

Requested implementation date justification:

Regulatory/Legal requirement _____ Market/Customer commitment _____

Competitive exposure _____ Audit/Security exposure _____

Other (Explain): _____

_____

_____

Status: _____ Incomplete _____ Sponsor review _____ Sponsor approval

_____ Technology Governance review _____ Technology Governance approval

_____ Portfolio Governance review _____ Portfolio Governance approval

_____ Domain Governance review _____ Domain Governance approval

_____ Portfolio Governance rejection _____ Domain Governance rejection

Solutions architect:
Name _____   **Phone** _____   **E-mail** _____

Business architect:
Name _____   **Phone** _____   **E-mail** _____

II. Executive Overview

Initiative Overview

This overview contains a brief explanation of what the initiative is, the business processes and services it provides, and the expected business value of these processes and services.

Strategic Alignment

This section contains specific summary statements as to which strategic objectives of the corporation and business plan objectives are addressed by the proposed initiative. The detailed explanation of these strategic statements is contained in Section VII of this template, "Detailed Business Justification and Return on Investment."

Critical Success Factors

The specific metrics and measures that will be used to evaluate the success of the initiative are defined in this section.

ROI Summary

This section contains a brief summary of the detailed information in the ROI portion of Section VII of this template.

Alternatives

This section summarizes alternatives considered and the benefits and drawbacks of each one.

III. Business Architecture

Initiative-Specific Business Architecture

This section contains a business architecture diagram depicting only the components developed or used by the proposed initiative.

Portfolio Plan Impact Assessment and Alignment

This section overlays the components within the initiative onto the current approved portfolio plan, including the slotting of the deliverables of the initiative into one or more releases on the portfolio plan.

IV. Technology Components

New Technology Acquisitions

This section identifies requirements for any *new* technologies not currently used by the company to support the initiative and when they will be needed. It includes:

- New application development tools (JAS, Eclipse, Maven, .Net).
- New operating platforms (portal servers, application servers, Web servers, business process management systems [BPMS], enterprise service bus [ESB], etc.).
- New monitoring or management tools.

Capacity Enhancements

This section identifies requirements for any incremental purchases of *existing* technologies to support the capacity requirements of the initiative and when they will be needed. It includes:

- Storage area network (SAN) or network attached storage (NAS) disk space.
- Server CPU and memory upgrades.
- New cluster or stand-alone servers.
- Additional network components (racks, hubs, network interface cards, etc.).
- Additional licenses for non–enterprise licensed software (operating systems, database management systems, web application servers, etc.) deployed on additional servers or CPUs.
- Additional human resources to run expanded data center activities.

Note

These requirements should be incorporated into the annual capacity planning analysis for initiatives approved during the annual process. For out-of-cycle submissions of initiatives (new ones that arise during the year and are submitted for approval outside the annual process), these requirements should be validated against the established capacity plan. See Chapter 10 for a description of the capacity plan and the capacity planning process.

Training and Operational Support Requirements

This section identifies needs for training on new applications or new technologies, increased support staff to run and operate the data center, and so on. It includes:

- User application training on the new business processes or business services deployed.
- New certifications of employees.

- Technology-specific training (e.g., portal development training).
- Training of data center employees on the installation, operation, and support of new technologies.

V. Component Summary

This section gives a brief description of all the components that need to be built or enhanced at each layer of the architecture. It also identifies the existing components that will be used by the initiative without coding modification.

VI. Cost Breakdown and Delivery Time Frames

This section summarizes the estimated costs for developing or enhancing the components described in Section V and the estimated full-time equivalents needed to complete the development/enhancements. It also identifies the estimated cost savings that are realized through the reuse of existing components and the leveraging of enhancements to existing components.

The section also defines the projected future releases that will deploy the components of the initiative and which components will be in each of those releases.

VII. Detailed Business Justification and Return on Investment

This section documents the detailed business justification of the initiative, including how the initiative helps to achieve the strategic plan of the corporation and the supporting business plans of the sponsor organization(s).

It also includes a formal return on investment (ROI) analysis of the initiative. This is often developed by the finance department or a financial arm of that organization within the IT or sponsor organizations. This ROI also includes qualitative measures expressed in the business justification. It includes such things as competitive advantage, customer satisfaction, and quality improvements.

VIII. Architecture Value Proposition and Justification

This section documents the architecture practices rationale for recommending the proposed approach and design. It should include references to architectural benefits to other approved initiatives or other initiatives not yet approved. It should point out any efficiencies or savings opportunities that could be realized in the future.

Most important it should highlight how the approach and solution increases flexibility and business agility going forward. It should identify how it expands the options and alternatives the business will have at its disposal to address new and future needs.

Legacy System Business Assessment Questionnaire

This section provides a legacy system business assessment questionnaire that can be used to obtain the business's view of the functionality and capability of legacy systems. This information is critical when assessing the business value of the legacy applications and determining if they should be modernized or replaced and in what priority. The information gathered from these questionnaires along with the results of the technical assessment drive the decision process using the decision tree depicted in Exhibit 12.1.

The questionnaire should be completed by the business architects during interviews with the business. The interviews should be conducted with both the people who own the system and people in other business units or external entities that use the system. Input from this second group (users) is the most critical to the assessment of the application as they represent the service consumer view. It should not be completed by the business directly, especially without business architect assistance. This is a business assessment questionnaire. Information about the specific platforms and programming technologies underlying the applications should be compiled separately when conducting the technical assessment of the application.

The information gathered from the questionnaires should be compiled in a database or spreadsheet where questionnaires on the same application can be aggregated and compared to aggregated results on other applications.

SOA Modernization: Legacy System Business Assessment Questionnaire

Name of application being evaluated:
Version being evaluated:
Date evaluated:
Name of person completing the questionnaire:

☐ Owner　　　☐ User　　　☐ Administrator

Involvement with application:
If other, specify:

Specific Business Process and Business Function Assessment

List the business processes and business functions the application supports.

For each business process or function, please rate how well or poorly the application supports the process or function. Use a rating from 1 to 5 where:

    1 = Minimal or ineffective support

    2 = Less than acceptable support

    3 = Acceptable level of support

4 = Supports the process or function well

5 = Exceptional support for the process or function

Using the same 1-to-5 rating scale, please rate how critical each process or function is from a corporate enterprise perspective where:

1 = Minimal criticality

2 = Below-average criticality

3 = Average criticality

4 = Above-average criticality

5 = Highest level of mission criticality

General Application Assessment

What functionality, if any, is it missing?

Is another, different application used to provide this functionality? If yes, which applications and what functions?

How often do you use the system?

Do any external constituents you support have direct access to the application? How is this provided? Is the external access flexible and effective?

Are you aware of any external constituents who would benefit by having direct access to the processes or functions performed by the application?

If yes, is there a business desire to provide some or all of the functionality to external constituents but restricted for technical reasons?

General Statements from the Business on How the Application Could Be Changed or Improved to Support Its Needs

Complete the following statements:

The thing I like most about the application is . . .

The thing I like the least about the application is . . .

If I could change the application I would change it to . . .

Overall Rating of the Application's Overall Ability to Support Its Business Need

Overall, I am (check one):

___Very satisfied

___Satisfied

___Somewhat satisfied

___Somewhat dissatisfied

___Dissatisfied

___Very dissatisfied

with the application.

Service-Oriented Architecture: Business Architecture Template

This template provides a framework for documenting the conceptual business architecture diagrams for SOA initiatives. I recommend creating a default page layout of this template in a drawing tool like Microsoft Visio and building custom Visio drawing objects for each layer. For example, if you create stick-figure objects for constituents, you can drag them onto the page and place them at the constituent layer. These objects can then be connected to channel objects you have created. Besides creating a constituent and channel object for each constituent and channel that exists, you should create an object in each category labeled "New." This will allow the business architect to draw diagrams representing new business relationships or requiring new channels but, more important, highlight a potential disconnect between a business unit and the corporate strategy. All constituents and channels should exist in the corporate strategy column of the SOA~EAF™; therefore, the need to document a new constituent or channel should never arise at the business architecture level.

Constituent	Consumer Domain Provider Domain
Channel	
Business Process	
Business Service	
Integration Service	
Legacy Application	

Service Categories and Types

No book on service-oriented architecture (SOA) would be complete without a discussion of services. Services have been defined in many different ways by different individuals writing about SOA. Despite all the variations, the definitions all cover the same basic points.

The service definitions I use and the way I slice and dice those definitions into categories and types are provided here. It is not coincidental that the way I classify services is consistent with the architecture layers and frameworks that have been described throughout this book.

I included these definitions as an appendix so you could find and reference them easily. Business analysts and business architects should use the definitions to help them understand and explain why requirements are gathered and structured in a certain way based on the type of service being defined. Solutions architects should refer to them to help them in defining and estimating project costs and scope and to produce the high-level design architecture on SOA initiatives. Project architects will use them when describing the detail design and development characteristics with the systems analyst and programmers. Finally, all the design patterns and design standards that the enterprise architects develop will have characteristics that align with the different service categories and types.

Service Categories

The major service categories are:

- Business Domain services
- Enterprise framework services
- System or utility services

The Business Domain services include:

- Channel services
- Business process services
- Business services
- Integration services

Enterprise framework services are comprised of consumer and provider services. Consumer enterprise framework services include:

- Security services
- Identity provisioning services
- Personalization services
- Profiling services

Provider enterprise framework services include:

- Logging services
- Audit services
- Billing services
- Exception processing services

System or utility services include:

- File transfer services
- Encryption/decryption services
- Data format transformation services
- Monitoring services

Business Domain Services

Business Domain services are those that exist within a specific horizontal layer of the service-oriented architecture (SOA) enterprise architecture framework (SOA~EAF). Their purpose is to provide business capabilities. Business Domain services handle all the presentation logic, business logic, and data logic defined by the business.

Channel services manage:

- The access and use of a channel.
- The invocation of policy enforcement points for processing authentication services provided by the enterprise SOA security framework.
- The session and state (if supported by the channel) of the user while using the channel.
- Any presentation layer characteristics defined by any personalization or profiling attributes provided by those frameworks.
- The presentation and invocation of the lower-layer services the user is allowed to invoke based on its authenticated user's profile.

Business process services are the most comprehensive and complex services. They are multistep, multibranching process flows that manage a defined business process from start to completion. They consume and orchestrate multiple lower-level business services that are required to complete the defined business task at hand. While many business process services will be consumed directly by a user through a channel, they do not have to be. Business process services can be designed to perform complex background processes with no human intervention. A business process that gathers and compiles all of a user's utilization statistics over a defined period of time and generates a bill for that utilization is an example of a background business process service.

Business services are more granular than business process services. They provide discrete, bounded units of work more in line with a business function than a business process. Business services represent the lowest level of granularity exposed to a consuming constituent. Everything that happens below this layer ultimately should be completely invisible to the consuming constituent.

Integration services:

- Manage the physical characteristics and restrictions of the non-SOA legacy application environment and isolate the higher-layer services from them.
- Provide isolation and abstraction from the physical legacy systems.
- Handle semantic data model mapping and translation to the proprietary formats of the underlying legacy systems.
- Handle the routing of requests to multiple systems and if necessary multiple systems of record, when they exist, and handle all CRUD (Create, Read, Update, and Delete) activities associated with those systems.
- Integrate with the enterprise SOA security framework services to acquire and provide the appropriate profile attributes for authentication and authorization by the proprietary security systems within the legacy application environment.

Enterprise Framework Services

Enterprise framework services are vertical services. They transcend the horizontal layers of the SOA~EAF and provide supporting interaction capabilities needed between the services at each layer. They represent shared capabilities that need to be managed and monitored holistically. They eliminate the requirement for coding the integration of these vertical capabilities within every service at every layer and the creation of thousands of point-to-point integration and interoperability code sets.

Consumer Enterprise Framework Services

Security services manage the security policy enforcement specified and required at each layer of the architecture. At the Channel layer, the enterprise SOA security framework provides services to authenticate the user and establish authorized service privileges. At the Business Process and Business Service layers, it provides services to validate credentials and authorize the use of the process or service invoked. At the Integration Service layer, the enterprise SOA security framework provides the appropriate individual or group security profile attributes required for access to the underlying legacy system's embedded and/or proprietary security system.

As you can see from this description, the design pattern and design standards used to invoke the security services by services at each horizontal layer are different. The enterprise SOA security framework also has distinct design patterns. It has to manage what credentials and attributes are established at each layer and if and how those credentials and attributes are needed by services in other layers. Each service has a design pattern that ensures that every service in the same layer invokes the enterprise SOA security framework services the same way and uses the same consistent set of credentials and attributes.

Identity provisioning services are enterprise services that maintain all the credentials and profile information of the enterprise SOA security framework as well as any remaining stovepipe security systems in the legacy environment. These services are used to create the security profile for a new user in the enterprise SOA security framework as well as in any underlying legacy systems that require user authentication and authorization from integration services accessing the legacy application's application program interfaces or data stores. Provisioning services are used to synchronize security data across these security systems to support events like password changes and resets. Provisioning services are also used to disable the user's security in all the systems if the relationship with the user is terminated.

The security and provisioning services just described are not a single-sign-on (SSO) solution. SSO is a user presentation layer login and logout synchronization technology. It facilitates user access to multiple applications with multiple authentication logon mechanisms. SSO's value proposition is predicated on the basis that multiple embedded stovepipe security systems will continue to exist and grow. The security and provisioning components of an SOA framework provide support of and migration to a single enterprise SOA security system designed to control access to all services through all channels by all constituents. The enterprise SOA security and provisioning frameworks provide a mechanism to handle the support of the security requirements of the underlying legacy applications for as long as they exist. The SOA's goal is for all these stovepipe security systems to go away as legacy applications are modernized or replaced. The expectation is that ultimately all the core business applications—regardless of if they are custom-built in-house, purchased, or leased—will expose services through the enterprise SOA security framework utilizing a federated security model.

The security and provisioning frameworks discussed here and throughout the book are architectural design approaches that are critical to achieving the SOA strategy and realizing its benefits. The success of your SOA strategy will be based on your ability to facilitate the delivery of any service through any channel to any constituent as efficiently as possible with no or minimal additional coding investment. Having an enterprise SOA security framework that every user authenticates through and every service authorizes against is the only way to achieve this objective. Since you are adopting an architectural approach to SOA, you understand this requirement and apply these frameworks to all SOA developments from the beginning.

Personalization services manage the attributes associated with user-configurable customized offerings within your applications and provide this information to all SOA components that use it. An example of a personalization capability is language preference. When a language preference is specified, all services use this attribute supplied by the personalization service to display all fixed data in the language specified. An architecture framework designed to support this capability is defined by the enterprise architects. The design patterns for all services with exposed presentation services specify how to interpret the personalized attribute and display the correct language. Under this approach, each service would construct XML templates for the fixed-format presentation layer data in each of the supported languages. When the service is invoked, the fixed data template for the specified language would be used by the presentation layer logic.

An alternative approach would be to have all the fixed text stored in English and have each service use a translation service to translate the text to the appropriate language. There is a performance trade-off with this second approach. The architects may determine that both approaches are allowed with performance considerations determining the appropriate one to use.

Regardless of which approach you use, if you want to support multilingual capabilities in your SOA applications, the architects should design and implement language management and maintenance services within a personalization management framework. This framework would allow for adding new language templates to existing services and new language translation rules to a language translation service. It would also allow for word replacement or substitutions in existing templates and rules when necessary.

The personalization management framework is to the personalization framework as the provisioning framework is to the security framework. The security framework assumes the security profile has been provisioned in the legacy system so the credentials it provides to the integration service will work. They work because the provisioning services have created the profile and synchronized the data within the profiles. The personalization framework assumes the language template or translation rules the service needs to support the specified language are in place. This framework created them, so they will be in place.

Building SOA applications from an architecture perspective takes the consideration of requirements like personalization from a tactical point solution or afterthought to a strategic level where they can be designed and embedded into an architecturally driven development approach. If you want to build SOA applications to support global or multilingual usage, you need to architect how to do this up front. If you do not, you will be forced to create new versions of all the services to accommodate these needs in the future. The implication of a tactical approach will become evident if you need to consider additional personalization capabilities and profiling capabilities in the future. The impact of these changes will be significant as each service would have its own framework for handling personalization and profiling. If you do not architect these frameworks up front as part of your enterprise SOA strategy, you will be forced to follow the same duplication and redundancy model that you are trying to eliminate through your SOA approach.

Profiling services are different from personalization services in that they are not determined and set by individual users. Profile services manage attributes that apply to a group or set of users based on conditions unique to that group. Examples of profile attributes are "customer status" and "monetary currency."

You may decide to have platinum, gold, and silver customer levels and provide different services or levels of service to these customers. An order business process may automatically give free priority shipping to a platinum customer whereas gold and silver would have to select and pay for it. Using this profile attribute, the order business process will completely bypass the "select shipping method" activities with the work flow when a platinum customer is using it.

A currency profile service would determine that any currency fields embedded in the service need to be displayed, captured, and processed as euros rather than dollars, for example. The integration services would use this profile information to understand that in one case the legacy system of record stores currency in euros, and in another case, dollars. Alternatively, the integration service would need to know that the legacy system stores currency in multiple formats and needs to be told which one to return or update.

Other profiling attributes can change the business rules used within the business process or business service. Orders placed by overseas constituents may have restrictions on which products can be sold or shipped to that country. Some states or countries may require that a disclaimer or disclosure statement be read and accepted by the consumer before the order is accepted.

Following the logic of all the services just described, you can see that the design of architectural SOA frameworks allows you to:

- Authenticate users and authorize services through a shared, common enterprise SOA security framework.
- Deliver those services customized to the personal preferences of consumers and to support the unique conditions based on their profiles.

I can guarantee you that none of this would be possible at a strategic enterprise level if you did not take an enterprise architecture approach to SOA.

Provider Enterprise Framework Services

Logging services provide the capability for business domain services to log a usage event. This framework is designed to allow service logging for domain services at any layer. Entries created through logging services can be accessed by other services in the same or different layers that are interacting with the service that created the log entry. A logging service framework can be designed to support logging of traditional flat-file records or logging events within a publish/subscribe framework.

An example of a traditional logging service is the Channel layer logging a record for each user who logged on through the channel specifying who the user was, when he or she logged on, how long the user was logged on, and potentially all the services the user invoked during that session. This type of log record could be used by an audit service or a billing service at a later time.

An example of a publish/subscribe service is one where a shipping service publishes a record of each order shipment. The customer notification service would subscribe to this publication and generate a shipping notification e-mail to the customer.

Having logging services through a common shared framework provides the capability for any new service in the future to log transactions through these services and use any existing logged records or publications to support its processing needs.

Audit services provide capabilities to monitor and manage information about the entire SOA application environment. Audit services can be designed as ad hoc, scheduled, or dynamic. They can be utilized by other business services, other framework services, and other stand-alone tools and platforms used to monitor and manage the application, platform, and network infrastructure. For example, a channel adapter may create an audit record periodically to notify a socket "listener" of its availability. Alternatively, an out-of-band service may interact with the channel and create the audit record on its behalf. In the case of an FTP server supporting an EDI channel, this could be as simple as a response to a ping or a file lookup in one of the FTP directories.

A billing services framework provides enterprise capabilities to capture and maintain utilization data necessary for billing external constituents for utilization or generating charge-backs to internal business unit budgets for internal utilization. A billing services framework should leverage logging and audit services to capture and compile the utilization data needed to calculate the utilization charges. This framework may also include fixed overhead costs and standard rates for charge-back of that overhead.

A billing services framework is essential for companies that need to charge individual departments or business units for the cost of the information technology infrastructure and support resources. The stovepipe application model with dedicated servers and bounded user populations no longer exists. The cost of a shared portal server or enterprise service bus (ESB) platform will need to be allocated back to the business units that use the portal channel adapter and consume ESB services.

Exception processing services are another critical framework within the SOA enterprise architecture framework. In an SOA application, the exception may be thrown by a service in one layer but handled by a service in the same or different layer. Under SOA, exceptions that are common and occur in multiple services may be handled through an additional common service that handles the exception for all the services. Having an exception processing framework prevents every service from having to redundantly code exception handlers and potentially prevents consumers of the service from having to understand and handle the service. This is not to say that consumers will never need to handle exceptions, but the framework provides the capability to handle the exception outside the consumer's realm if possible.

Examples of exception processing services that could be provided by the exception processing framework are presented next. Assume that an order business process submits an order to be created on the legacy order system that will return a confirmation number upon successful creation. The "CreateAnOrder" business service invoked by the order business process in turn invokes an integration service to create the order. If there is a network or application failure and the legacy order system is not responding to the integration service request, the timeout failure could be reported back to the "CreateAnOrder" business service, which could apply a rule to attempt to resubmit the order two more times and if unresolved inform the order business process, which may apply rules to hold the order at the Process layer level until it can be successfully submitted and generate a follow-up confirmation e-mail to the customer.

The problem with this approach is that a complex and resource-intensive business process initiated through a user login session now has to maintain its state after the user exits the process and more than likely after the user close the session by logging out. Because it is being managed at the Business Process layer, it must reinvoke the Business and Integration layer services over and over again until a successful commit is received.

If, alternatively, the integration service consumed a service from the exception handling framework that (1) queued the request for resubmission and commit by the legacy application and (2) published a notification containing the commit results and confirmation number using the logging framework services, the integration service could notify the business service of this exception. The "CreateAnOrder" business service can now invoke the exception handling service that will maintain its state until the commit from the exception service is published. Once the commit is published, the "CustomerOrderNotification" service can generate the customer notification e-mail. The "CreateAnOrder" business service notifies the order business process of this event, which in turn triggers the process to tell the customer about the e-mail that will be received. When the user exits the order process, the business process and the "CreateAnOrder" business service can be closed and shut down.

System or Utility Services

System or utility services are services that perform discrete, low-level processes. Many SOA documents classify some of the provider framework services listed earlier as utility services. If described in the context of designing and implementing a service, they are utility services. If described in the context of an enterprise architecture approach, however, they are much more than a utility. As described earlier, they not only provide the shared capabilities that utility services provide but also play an intricate role in the interoperability of services. Utility services are not designed to provide interaction mechanisms with other services beyond the service that invoked them. Utility services have little or no routing or decision logic embedded in them. They do not apply any business rules and perform a task one way with no variations.

File transfer services move files from one location to another. Many traditional applications use scripting languages or other tools outside the applications realm to handle file transfers. Under SOA, we need a service mechanism to provide these capabilities. Some ESB technologies provide these capabilities, as do some ETL tools. An ESB or ETL platform that can wrap FTP/SFTP activities in Web services would be the best solution.

Encryption/decryption services can be used to process lower-level encrypted data. In the health industry, the Health Insurance Portability and Accountability Act is requiring "personal health information" (PHI) to be encrypted when it is stored or transported. This means that integration services accessing data stores containing PHI directly need a mechanism to decrypt the data being delivered. Encryption/decryption services at the system data level can be developed to support this requirement.

Data format transformation services are those that transform data from one format to another (e.g., flat file to XML and vice versa). For transaction and low-volume data, this can be provided by an ESB. For higher volumes of data and large file transformations, this is better handled by the use of an ETL tool.

Monitoring services are low-level system services that provide useful information to higher-level SOA services. A monitoring service to "check available disk space" may be used by a logging service to validate space availability for log entries. Building these as services isolates the service consuming them from any physical changes that may occur later on.

Service Types

Service types apply to the Business Process, Business Service, and Integration Service layers. Since services in these three layers fall within the Business Domain category of services, they reflect the different variations of business activities. Services of the same type have common characteristics that are reflected in the design patterns developed by the enterprise architects. Services constructed in each of these three layers should have a design pattern developed for each of the service types defined below. When a developer is developing a service that is one of type *transactional* in the Business Service layer, the design pattern for transaction services at the Business Service layer defines all the core capabilities required for those transaction services.

The service type definitions are also helpful to solutions architects when estimating the scope and cost of initiatives. More complex service types take longer and cost more to develop; therefore, the cost estimates and delivery timelines for these services will be higher and longer. Over time, experience gained from developing the different types of services and the postinitiative "lessons learned" analysis will help you to fine-tune the data used for estimating services, resulting in more accurate estimates.

The service types are:

- Transaction services
- Inquiry services
- Data services
- Reporting services
- Image services
- Content and document services

Transaction Services

Transaction services are those that result in the creation, update, or deletion of business records in the core transaction systems of the company. They involve changes to the official systems of record within the company. In an SOA environment transaction services need to ensure that all of the system of record changes are completed and in the proper order. Transaction services need to understand what actions need to be taken in the event that a failure in a commitment occurs, including the capability to roll back previously successful commitments in other systems. SOA applications may also have to accommodate the fact that the SOA transaction service may be available even when the underlying system of record is not available.

Since three Business Service Domain layers (Business Process, Business Service, and Integration Service) may be involved in processing a business transaction, all three layers will be involved in handling exceptions encountered when processing the transaction. As the example provided in the "Provider Enterprise Framework Services" section suggests, there are multiple ways transaction exceptions can be handled. There may be significant performance hits if not done properly. If you do not have a defined exception handling framework and defined transaction service design pattern at these three Business Domain layers, every transaction process developed may handle exceptions differently.

Transaction services design patterns at each domain layer will ensure that transaction processing activities, including exception handling, will occur at the right level and be consistently applied at those levels.

The Integration layer design pattern for transactions should specify that updates or commits to individual systems or databases are controlled by Integration layer logic. Resolutions to exceptions to those individual system commits should be handled at this layer as well through the use of Integration-layer exception handling framework services. Specifications for the number of retries when individual system connections cannot be established, metadata about system of record availability windows, transaction queuing mechanisms for persisting updates during outage windows, and submitting them once the system is back on line should all be specified in the Integration layer transaction service design pattern.

The Business Service layer design pattern for transactions defines how to handle transaction processing and exception handling activities that occur above the Integration layer and below the Process layer. If a Transaction business service invokes more than one transaction integration service or other transaction business services, it must manage the commit and exception handling process defined for all those services as a group. For example, assume that a specific transaction business service calls an integration service to update one system of record and another transaction business service (which in turn calls another integration service) to update a second system of record. The two integration services will handle any exceptions at the individual system commit level. The second business service invoked may provide specific actions that were undertaken to provide an alternate resolution to the exception. If the business rule specifies that both of these systems of record updates need to be committed, and if one fails, the other needs to be rolled back, this exception process needs to occur at the Business Service layer.

> **Note**
>
> An Integration layer service should never be consumed directly by a Business Process Service layer. It should always be consumed through a business service.

The design pattern at the Business Process Service layer defines how business transactions are choreographed from start to finish. Any exception handling or rollbacks occurring at this level are at a coarse business process level.

In the Business Process Service layer example, assume the two updates were to:

- Create an account record in the account master file for a new customer.
- Set up a credit limit for the customer.

The customer had been recently acquired but decided to create a new account for its subsidiary, even though the subsidiary was planning to order under the parent's volume discount contract.

This business service was consumed in the first step of the business process.

After this step is completed, the user can invoke the process step that invokes the "PlaceAnOrder" business service. A rule in the "PlaceAnOrder" service threw an error exception after determining that a different customer account from the one entered on the order was associated with the volume discount contract number entered. The user entered the parent's account number, and the order was validated and placed. The business process should take the user back to the "Create/Maintain Account" business service used previously to set up the subsidiary account invoking the revalidate account option within the service. The revalidate account rules in the service determine that the reason it was invoked was to resolve a duplicate account number. The exception record in the exception handler log file provides the subsidiary, parent account, and contract number keys as well as the order exception reason. The business service will ask the user if the user wants to keep the new subsidiary account or delete it. It will inform the user that no volume contract exists for this account. If the user elects to delete the subsidiary account, the account number record previously created needs to be deleted. The "Create/Maintain Account" business service will accomplish this by calling the integration service for deleting account master file records.

Inquiry Services

Inquiry services simply provide read access to the data in the legacy systems of record. There are no create, update, or delete actions involved. Inquiry services do not have to be persisted or committed. Inquiry service design patterns seldom queue inquiry requests that fail due to system availability windows. They can, however, invoke other actions to accommodate for these outages. They can be designed to provide data from a near-time data store when the primary system is unavailable. For example, an order operational data store (ODS) can provide an order status that is up to four hours old during the four-hour batch processing window of the order system.

Therefore, the Integration Service layer design pattern for inquiry services that need or will need higher availability than the primary source system should specify a second source to provide the data during the outage period. This design pattern should also specify that the higher-layer service consuming the Integration layer inquiry service is informed that the data was retrieved from the secondary source and why the secondary source was used (batch window, scheduled maintenance window, or unavailability reason unknown).

The design pattern at the Business Service layer defines the rules to accept the secondary source or issue a new request if the reason was not a batch or maintenance outage. The design pattern may also specify a lookup in the exception log for an entry generated by the inquiry integration service and use this information to help make the decision.

The design pattern at the Business Process layer will support a combination of a system- and user-driven decision process. If the cause is a batch or maintenance window, the user will be given the near-time value and will be informed to try again at a later specified time if more accurate status is wanted. If the reason was due to a system outage, the user can accept the status that is up to four hours old or initiate a new request.

The design patterns for Integration and Business Service layer inquiry services should specify a framework for caching data where appropriate. For example, a business service that could potentially involve multiple product description and pricing lookups should be designed to cache the product price file (or a subset of the file) to improve the performance of the service.

If an inquiry integration service uses translation tables to convert cryptic code values stored in the system of record to intelligent values in the semantic data model, these code tables should be cached as well.

The design pattern for inquiry services should specify integration with the enterprise SOA security framework to provide role-based policy challenges when the inquiry service is invoked at the Business Service layer.

Data Services

Data services are either data distribution or data acquisition services. Data distribution services place bulk data produced from an SOA component to a specified location or locations. Data acquisition services provide bulk data to SOA components for further processing or to support the processing of other transactions.

Data acquisition services are different from inquiry services in that data acquired through an inquiry service is designed to support one transaction or event whereas data acquired by a data acquisition service is designed to support multiple events. For example, a customer's order history inquiry could return a substantial number of order records, but the records would be only for that customer and only as a reply to that single inquiry request. A data acquisition service initiated by a district office associate that extracts and downloads all the orders processed by that district office during a specified time period to a local reporting server would be a data acquisition service. This data will be used multiple times for analytical and reporting purposes.

Design patterns for data acquisition services include specifications for:

- Full refresh or incremental acquisition.
- Encryption/decryption services for transport of the data.
- De-identification of data.

Design patterns for data acquisition services specify integration with the enterprise SOA security framework for controlling authorization to the service and to restrict the destination of the data being acquired (i.e., places the data in a secured directory or database where user access is restricted to authorized employees). Data acquisition services may reside on top of underlying data manipulation tools, such as ETL tools that can aggregate data from multiple sources, provide transformations of the structure and format of the data, and manage the full commit to the target location.

An architecture framework for data services should be based on a Common Information Model (CIM) that delivers standard canonical definitions utilizing standard semantic models wherever possible. This framework would also include standard rules for calculating and producing derived data that is commonly used by the business.

The architecture framework should specify that data services utilize, whenever possible, ODS, data warehouse (DW), or DW marts to source the data provided rather than the core transaction system of record for the data to minimize the performance impact on these systems. These secondary stores also help to isolate the proprietary data structures and nonsemantic formats that exist in the legacy transaction systems.

Ultimately, SOA Data services provide a standard mechanism for all data distributed throughout the corporation. All data is defined through a CIM and delivered in standard formats based on the enterprise data model defined by the CIM. The

CIM should be based on industry-standard terminology and definitions if they exist. The high-level entities defined in the CIM will represent the enterprise data model of the corporation.

Reporting Services

Reporting services are services that deliver defined sets of data through a presentation layer delivery mechanism. Reporting services are different from data services in that they are directly usable by the consuming constituent without additional manipulation or formatting. Data services require additional processing capabilities to convert the data to viewable information. Reporting services provide the logic for presenting the data as information to the constituent. Data services deliver data that is intended for further processing by the business service or business process consuming it. The data delivered by a data service may never be seen by the person using the service, even if it was delivered to support a business process.

Reporting services can be scheduled or ad hoc. They may also provide options for sorting, limiting, or restructuring the formats the service provides. Reporting services can also be designed to provide extracts of the report data into formats like Excel or delimited files for further processing by the user or into formats like PDF that cannot be processed further.

The design pattern for reporting services should specify integration with the enterprise SOA security framework to provide role-based authentication of the consumer. Depending on the underlying reporting tool used to generate the report and the security granularity it supports, the authorization can occur at the report level, at a defined sublevel of the report, or at the report line level.

You should think of a reporting service as a "container" that:

- Encapsulates the formatted report data generated by the reporting tool.
- Manages the integration of the enterprise SOA security framework with the security platform within the reporting tool platform.
- Provides the service invocation stub and its associated service contract used by a business service or a business process to invoke the reporting service.

The value of this approach is to provide a loosely coupled abstraction from the underlying reporting tool platform. If the reporting tool is replaced or the report is generated from some other tool in the future, the only changes necessary will be at the service provider side with no impact to the service contract exposed to the service consumer.

Image Services

Image services provide an SOA framework for capturing, storing, and delivering images to SOA applications. If your company processes a lot of scanned or faxed documents and multiple business units or multiple business processes use those documents, you should develop an architecture framework to support image services.

Image services are similar to reporting services in that they:

- Encapsulate the image display retrieved from the image storage location.
- Manage the integration of the enterprise SOA security framework with the security implementation within the imaging tool platform.
- Provide the service invocation stub and its associated service contract used by a business service or a business process to invoke the image service.

Image services are different from reporting services in that they provide the capability to capture new images to be stored as well as services to retrieve the images.

How you set up your image services will depend on whether you are using an image management or a document management platform underneath the services. If you are using one of these underlying technologies, you should follow the encapsulation approach described in the previous section. If you do not have an underlying platform for imaging, you can build generic services to provide image processing capabilities to your SOA applications. This generic framework should provide a set of services for business users to:

- Define a new image document type to be acquired, including defining the search and retrieval keys as well as user access role policies.
- Allow an image to be acquired and stored.
- Allow a stored image or groups of images to be retrieved and viewed by a business service or business process.

This generic framework would be designed to support path- or URL-based indexing for images stored as files, primary key indexes for images stored in a database system, or both solutions if necessary. The primary index and alternate key values should be represented through XML structures that allow:

- The image acquisition services to automatically generate the primary key and accept user-entered search keys.
- The image retrieval services to retrieve the image or images using the primary or secondary keys.

Generic enterprise SOA image retrieval services would provide access to stored images based on the image document type defined by the administrator who configured the initial setup for the image. The service would utilize the enterprise SOA security framework to authorize access to the images based on the role(s) set up by the administrator in the configuration file for the specified document image type and the role(s) in the security profile of the authenticated user invoking the image retrieval service.

The generic enterprise SOA image retrieval services should be designed to support:

- The retrieval of a single image based on a provided primary key.
- The caching of multiple images when alternate keys are used for retrieving images with next and previous display capabilities.

- The presentation of a summary table of images retrieved using an alternate key with the ability to drill down to the individual image represented by each summary line. The summary table should include the primary key value, the specific alternate key used to select the retrieved images as the primary sort of the table, and the other alternate key values defined for the image.

The service should also allow the consumer to re-sort or subsort the table list based on any of the other key values.

Content and Document Services

I am specifically distinguishing content services from document services from an SOA service type perspective even though from a technology platform perspective these terms are heavily overlapped.

Content services deliver readily viewable text, usually in HTML, ASCII, or RTF format, that is readily usable by the consuming service or process. HTML content can be augmented with scripting capabilities and XML to provide dynamic data embedded with the content. Content services can be structured with different service stubs to support the delivery of the content through JSP, ASP, XML, and so forth.

Content stored on and supported by an underlying content management system can be dynamically constructed and delivered. In the health insurer quote generation example used in Chapter 12, hundreds of highly duplicative quote documents stored in word processing format were replaced with individual quote paragraphs dynamically assembled by the content management system's work flow engine and merged with data within the application to produce a customer quote.

Another example of content services would be the storage and retrieval of user support information like frequently asked questions and how-to guides.

Document services deliver content that is not readily usable by the consuming service or process. COTS (commercial off-the-shelf) applications or a COTS plug-in viewer must be invoked to open and view the documents, including word processing, spreadsheet, and presentation documents and PDFs.

Creating SOA content or document services provides these benefits:

- A layer of isolation and abstraction from the underlying platforms.
- A mechanism for integration with an enterprise SOA security framework.
- Session layer management to maintain state throughout higher-level processes.

How this is accomplished depends on many factors including the capabilities of the underlying content or document management technology. Older technologies have the same characteristics and shortcomings as described earlier when discussing older image technologies. Platforms with these characteristics are treated the same way: as non-SOA-compliant legacy systems with their proprietary APIs wrapped in integration services.

Like newer image technologies, newer content and document management technologies provide integration capabilities at higher layers of architecture through support of Web services and BPEL-compliant process engines.

Enterprise SOA Perspective of Imaging and Content/Document Management Systems

Throughout this book we described the core corporate portfolio of business applications as legacy applications. We defined them as such because they were not SOA enabled. They had to be wrapped in higher-layer integration and business service components to be SOA enabled.

We talked about how purchased and leased business software can fall anywhere from the bottom legacy application layer of the architecture for non-SOA-enabled purchased or leased applications to fully integrated software-as-a-service (SaaS) solutions that integrate at the business service, business process, or even channel layer of the architecture.

We need to conduct the same architectural assessment of our imaging and content/document management platforms as well. The enterprise SOA framework defined in this book is predicated on the belief that any business data or any business function has the potential to be leveraged in any business service or business process and also that any data or function may have value to multiple constituents. We need to recognize, however, that it is not just electronically processed data that has these values but any stored business information, including images and documents.

We presented the value of the SOA approach for a health insurance company that provides a claim status service that can be consumed by:

- A provider service representative answering a provider's request over the phone.
- The provider directly over the Web.
- A member service representative answering a member's request over the phone.
- The member directly over the Web.

If the claim status was "Pending Medical Policy Review," would the letter from the provider providing its justification for the medical policy override not be just as important to the members, providers, and service representatives?

The letter may have been sent by mail and scanned into an image file. It could have been faxed and stored as a fax image file. It could have been an attachment in an e-mail in any one of several different formats (word processing, text, PDF, etc.) The claim status service may have an option to invoke a "Find Attachments" service, which would invoke imaging services to search provider correspondence and member correspondence image and document management systems for records with the claim number of the pending claim.

The higher-level business process may also invoke a service to get a status from the medical policy system or medical policy tracking system to further qualify the status of the claim. The status may be "Correspondence Received; Under Medical Director Review."

Just as our framework for data services supports data stored on different platforms and different formats, our image, content, and document services need to support different platforms and formats. Supported platforms need to include file management structures, database management systems, and hierarchical storage management systems. Supported formats need to include, for example:

- JPEG and TIFF for images.
- XML, HTML, ASCII Text, and RTF for content.
- Office document formats and PDF for documents.

Under our enterprise architecture approach to SOA, any information needed to support a business service or business process, regardless of how it is stored, should be made available. No developer, system analyst, or technology vendor is going to even think about this type of architectural approach to image and content management integration. The enterprise SOA architects are the only ones capable of establishing these types of frameworks for the SOA environment. Once again, an enterprise architecture approach to SOA that defines these frameworks up front and incorporates them into the SOA developments from the beginning results in significantly more valuable solutions for the business and eliminates any throwaway of SOA components designed without the frameworks.

Older technologies in this space tend to be similar to the prevalent architecture design principles of the time (i.e., they tend to be deployed as self-contained stovepipe solutions). We need to treat technologies in this space in the same way we treat our other non-SOA-enabled business applications. We need to treat them as legacy platforms and legacy layer solutions. I will use an imaging technology solution as an example.

Traditional imaging platforms were comprised of these components:

- The integration with an image acquisition platform, such as a scanner to capture the images. This often included software to index the image and create alternate keys for access to the document. Today bitmapped images are transformed into machine-readable data through OCR/ICR software, direct integration with other technology platforms such as fax to acquire images, and support for expanded image formats beyond TIFF.
- An underlying data repository for storing the images, indexes, and access keys.
- A work flow engine for building image process applications. This work flow engine was also embedded in the administration capabilities within the platform for setting up the security and access privileges associated with the images and the work flow applications.
- The resulting applications were stovepipe solutions providing a self-contained solution, including the presentation layer. These solutions provided capabilities to incorporate data from other sources, such as core legacy systems, to provide more robust solutions. Unfortunately, they were designed just like all the other legacy applications. They forced the application's designer to replicate and duplicate data and business logic in the work flow to provide the capability needed. Content and document management technologies used this same approach.

These technologies produced applications just like the other legacy applications with their own Security and presentation layer delivery mechanisms.

Under SOA, we need to treat these technologies the same way we treat our non-SOA-compliant legacy applications. We need to decouple the acquisition components of the platform from the distribution and use capabilities. We want to be able to use any captured image or document in any SOA business service or SOA business process we develop. We want to eliminate the use of the platform-specific presentation layer capabilities and incorporate the image or document into the presentation layer services produced at the higher layers of the architecture. We want to control the access privileges to secured images or content through our enterprise SOA security framework.

To do this, we need to stop building applications for the delivery and use of the images or content utilizing the embedded work flow engine in the imaging technology and build the work flow capabilities with the orchestration and business process capabilities in the higher layers of the architecture. We need to leverage the application programming interface (API) capabilities of the platforms to build integration services to access the underlying images or content at a much lower granular level.

This results in the creation of a portfolio of integration services that provide a layer of isolation and abstraction on top of the image and content/document management platforms and make the image or content available to any higher-layer service. It also allows for retrieval from multiple back-end platforms or from new replacement platforms without impacting the higher-layer services.

Newer image and content/document management platforms are more SOA en-abled and provide the capability to integrate at higher layers. Some platforms provide the APIs as Web services that can be deployed at the Business Service layer of the architecture. Others provide BPEL-compliant process engines that allow the built-in subprocesses to be integrated with BPEL-compliant business processes built at the Business Process layer of the architecture.

Newer technologies with these capabilities can also be leveraged to provide SOA-enhanced acquisition capabilities. The business process within the image or content/document management platform for acquiring a defined image or document can be designed to accept new images or content from a scanner, fax, FTP server, or Web service.

The Web service could be one deployed at the Business Service layer of the architecture that can be used by a higher-layer business process service or deployed directly out to one or more channels to one or more constituents. Under this ap-proach, correspondence from a customer received through the mail is processed through the scanner channel. Correspondence faxed is processed by the same busi-ness process through the fax channel. Correspondence in JPEG, PDF, or any other accepted format uploaded from the customer self-service application would be pro-cessed through the Web channel.

External Services

Many SOA publications define external services as a distinct type of service. External services provide access to systems and applications of external partners and vendors (e.g., credit card authorization, shipment tracking, or stock quoting service). While external services have unique characteristics that need to be dealt with, the services themselves should fall into one of the defined service types discussed earlier. For example, shipment tracking and stock quoting are inquiry service types; credit card authorization is a transaction service type. A credit card authorization requires the approval of the transaction based on an available credit level and generates a trans-action confirmation ID to confirm the commitment and provide an audit trail key for the transaction.

When dealing with consuming an external service, the first step is to determine which of the defined service types it falls into. Once this is determined, the next step is to learn how the vendor's or partner's implementation of the service complies with your internally defined development frameworks and design patterns for those service types. Does the service support a federated authentication and authorization framework? Are multiple service invocation stubs supported to provide access through different protocols and formats?

In all but rare instances, the best enterprise architecture approach to external services is to encapsulate them in internally developed services that can augment their functionality with additional capabilities defined by your SOA framework. For example, the service consumed from the vendor or partner may be available only in English. The service wrapper built internally to consume the external service can incorporate language translation services to support the multilingual capabilities of the SOA profiling framework.

As more vendors move toward delivering SaaS, the integration with customers will occur through open standards–based interoperability at the architectural level rather than the service level. This means that vendors will provide options to integrate and interoperate at the ESB and business process platform level instead of at the service invocation level. This means that your ESB or BPMS platform can call orchestrated services and business processes defined and operating on the ESB and BPMS platforms of the vendor's customers. It will allow those customers to control and define how those services and processes operate by exposing configuration modules to (technical) administrators at each client.

What this is all heading toward is vendors and partners providing SaaS capabilities that will augment their current service consumer–centric delivery model with a service provider–centric delivery model. SaaS vendors provide directly consumable services because most customers do not have the SOA infrastructure or SOA enterprise architecture framework to support integrating these services at the service provider level. As more customers develop these capabilities and become more mature from an SOA perspective, the demand will shift to SaaS interoperability at the service provider level rather than the service consumer level.

This evolution is not unlike other technology evolutions of the past. Many companies bought fully self-contained Web applications because they did not have the Web capabilities and a defined Web architecture and strategy. Today many of these companies have developed Web strategies based on portal technologies to provide a single entry point to the Web and a single view of all Web capabilities. These companies now demand that vendors provide alternative access mechanisms to their functionality besides their proprietary Web client. This was in fact one of the major drivers for the Web service and SaaS approaches. Eventually customers will have the infrastructure and capabilities to support multiple service invocation stubs for the delivery of services through multiple channels using multiple formats. They will want this same capability for external services as well. They will also develop the capabilities to integrate below the Web service invocation level utilizing BPMS and ESB interoperability standards.

As enterprise SOA architects, you should be actively discussing these concepts with your SaaS partners and with your BPMS and ESB vendors.

APPENDIX **C**

SOA Security Development Framework

D evelopment frameworks are a key component of an SOA. Developing SOA applications from an enterprise architecture perspective requires that all these development frameworks be documented and embedded in the reference guides provided to every developer. This appendix describes the architectural characteristics that are needed in an enterprise SOA security framework to support the enterprise delivery of SOA applications. While this example is specific to security, the same architectural concepts and principles can be applied to the other development frameworks you define. The information provided in this appendix is representative of the security framework documentation that would be included in an SOA architectural design and development guide provided by the SOA enterprise architecture team to every SOA developer.

Traditional versus SOA Approach to Security

In the traditional stovepipe application approach, each application was built with its own embedded security. These applications required the user to sign in to gain access (authentication). These applications also controlled what the authenticated user could do within the application by limiting the functionality exposed to that user through various mechanisms, including screen masks, database record locks, and defined roles.

Under an enterprise SOA application development model, security needs to be designed so that it can provide authentication services and authorization services to *any* SOA component in the SOA enterprise requiring them. Note that the SOA enterprise includes internal SOA components built in compliance with the defined SOA reference architecture and purchased, leased, or SaaS SOA components integrated to the SOA enterprise architecture through a federated security model. Once these credentials have been validated, they need to be available throughout the session so other services can validate against these credentials without invoking duplicate user interaction. Caching these credentials in the enterprise SOA security framework application improves performance by reducing subsequent calls to the security profile data store.

As we architect our SOA application approach, we need to understand and resolve the implications just expressed. We need to understand and document how security is going to be performed going forward. We need to understand and document how we are going to handle the issues of our many and multiple legacy security systems while they still exist in our portfolio. Finally, for each channel in our SOA environment, we need to define and document from a security perspective what that security is and what it needs to capture to integrate with the SOA layers below it. This applies not only to our internal channels but to our external intermediary channels as well. In some cases you will be able to dictate these conditions to the intermediary. In other cases you will not be able to do so. For those that you cannot dictate, you need to understand how you will handle their approaches.

SOA Security Framework Requirements

The enterprise SOA security framework needs to provide these capabilities:

- Constituent authentication services
- Constituent role and service privileges identification services
- Service authorization services
- Service validation services
- Security pass-through services
- Security detection and enforcement policy configuration services

In addition, the enterprise SOA security framework needs to be supported by an Identity Management and Provisioning Framework that provides these capabilities:

- Constituency setup and configuration services
- Role creation and configuration services
- Constituent SOA user profile setup and configuration services
- Legacy application security provisioning services
- Legacy application security synchronization services
- User provisioning services
- SOA user profile management services

Finally, the enterprise SOA security framework needs to integrate with other enterprise SOA provider development frameworks like "logging" and "exception handling" and enterprise SOA consumer development frameworks like "personalization" and "profiling" for support of these capabilities.

Enterprise SOA Security Framework Is an Application

Each of the capability statements just listed ends with the word *services*. That is because all of these capabilities are SOA services that you need to design and implement. These implemented services in total make up the enterprise SOA security framework application. The logical SOA Security Development Framework defined in the Enterprise SOA Reference Architecture column of your SOA~EAF™ is directly mapped to the physical service components, technologies, and platforms in the Enterprise SOA Physical Architecture column of your SOA~EAF that were implemented based on the reference architecture specification. These capabilities are based on and leverage the capabilities of underlying security and provisioning technologies but are constructed as custom-built SOA services to:

- Create a layer of abstraction from the physical underlying technologies providing the capability to support multiple technologies or replacement technologies if necessary.
- Allow for multiple custom service invocation stubs to support multiple protocols and standards used by service consumers.
- Provide the capability to integrate with other enterprise SOA development frameworks.

In fact, we treat security technologies no differently from any other technology in the SOA environment. Using the application programming interfaces (APIs) of the security technology directly is no different from using the APIs of a legacy business application directly. Just as we wrapped the legacy APIs in integration services so we could add value-added capabilities to them and deliver them in multiple formats through multiple protocols, we need to wrap security technology applications for the same reasons.

The same approach should be used for integrating provisioning technologies or any other technology underlying any SOA component. Failure to do so will ultimately result in inflexibility and nonadaptability caused by technology platform lock-in of the SOA components.

Enterprise SOA Security Framework Architecture

The enterprise SOA security framework will have service components that operate at each layer of the Enterprise SOA Framework. The service components at each layer are described in the next subsections. The enterprise SOA security framework is the mechanism for managing the interaction persistence among the components invoked in each layer.

Channel Layer Security Services

The Channel layer is where user authentication and role identification occurs. The enterprise SOA security framework defines all user authentication mechanisms and specifications needed to support authentication of all constituents through all channels. It also specifies the authentication standards and mechanisms for providing services through channel intermediaries and for consuming secured services from external partner entities.

The authentication mechanism specified for a constituent in one channel may be different from the authentication mechanism for that same constituent entering through a different channel. For example, a doctor submitting claims through an electronic data interchange (EDI) file transfer from his practice management system may authenticate to the FTP server using a user ID and password. The same doctor submitting a claim through an insurer's Web portal may authenticate using a digital certificate.

Even though authentication happens primarily at the Channel layer, lower-layer business processes and business services can reinvoke authentication challenges to provide a further layer of security protection. For example, even though a doctor has been authenticated to the insurer's provider portal application, the doctor may be challenged to answer a security question if the URL for the "Provider Payment Information" service is invoked.

Five general categories of authentication scenarios that occur in a typical company. From an SOA perspective, these can be described as:

1. A user authenticates to an internal channel.
2. A user authenticates to an external intermediary channel.
3. An internal application (component) authenticates to another internal application (component) to consume a service.
4. An external application (component) authenticates to an internal application (component) to consume a service.
5. An internal application (component) authenticates to an external application (component) to consume a service.

Therefore, at a minimum, you should have at least five Authentication Frameworks defined:

1. Authentication of an individual constituent to an *internal* channel.
2. Federated authentication of an individual constituent through an *external* intermediary channel.
3. Authentication of one internal application system to another internal application system (A2A) for service invocations.
4. Authentication of external application systems to internal application systems (B2B) for service invocations.
5. Authentication of internal application systems to external application systems (B2B) for service invocations.

The key to the enterprise SOA security framework is that regardless of which channel invokes the authentication or which Authentication Framework is used, once authentication has been established, the roles associated with that authenticated user stored in the enterprise SOA security profile system are now available for processing by any of the SOA components invoked through that channel while the security framework session is still active.

The services within the enterprise SOA security framework application can provide to any SOA service at any layer:

- The roles defined for the authenticated user.
- The services authorized for each of those roles.
- Additional security profile data that are needed to consume individual services within each role.

> **Note**
>
> In many instances, invoking services to obtain data from other frameworks (personalization, profiling, etc.) will be performed at this same point. For this reason, all the SOA user profile data (security, personalization, profile) should be stored in a common enterprise SOA user profile data store and placed in a common cache that can be shared by all these framework services.

This process requires that the channel invoking the authentication service is responsible for shutting down the security session when the user logs out of the channel or the channel session times out. This is accomplished by invoking the "Close User Security Session" service during the logout or time-out process. This service terminates the authenticated user's security token and flushes the cached user security profile record. A new user security profile record will be cached if the authentication is reinstated.

Some channels may hard-code the service invocation mechanisms for every authorized service into the Channel layer presentation logic. Other channels may dynamically build the list of authorized services based on the service privileges defined under the roles in the user's security profile. Some channels may use a combination of the two. For example, an IVR application providing access to services for health insurance members may have all the service offerings hard-coded into the IVR's scripting logic soliciting members to "Press 1 for Claim Status," "Press 2 for Address Changes," "Press 3 for New ID Card Request," and so on. The member self-service portal however, may not expose the "Add a Dependent" service invocation link on the landing page if the authenticated user has the role "Dependent," since only the member with the role "Subscriber" can add a dependent.

Hard-coded invocations at the Channel layer improve the performance of generation of the landing page but require enhancements to the Channel layer presentation logic when new services are added or existing services are removed. These changes need to be made on all the channels where the service is offered.

Dynamic generation of the service invocation links slows the presentation layer processing but automatically accommodates displaying or removing services when they are added or removed to the roles in the enterprise SOA security framework through configuration. Even new roles can be dynamically consumed and processed by the channel if this capability was specified in the design patterns published for the channel components.

The next desktop operating system analogy will help you better understand hard-coded versus dynamic service configurations. Some of the "services," such as access to the local hard drive on the desktop computer and a locally connected printer, are hard-coded at the operating system level (i.e., they are physically connected to the local computer) and appear every time the computer is turned on. Other services, such as access to a remote high-speed printer or a home drive of a file server, are dynamically made available based on the authentication credentials and privileges of the person logging onto the desktop computer. If different people logged onto the same desktop computer, they would have access to the same local drive but will have a different home drive and perhaps a different remote printer.

Applying this same principle to a health member self-service portal, some services, such as "Claim Status," may be available to all members, and the links to invoke them could be coded within the portal server to place them on the member portal landing page that appears after successful authentication of the member. Other services, such as "Add a Dependent," are authorized only for members who are the policy holders (subscribers). The link to invoke this service would be dynamically generated and displayed on the member portal landing page only if the authenticated user had the role "Subscriber." The enterprise SOA security framework not only returns the role value of "Subscriber" but also the invocation URLs for the authorized subscriber services, one of which is the "Add a Dependent" service. This is the same as the desktop computer acquiring the network path to the remote home drive or remote printer.

There are many ways to set up and maintain the integrity of the invocation links to the SOA services associated with constituent roles. These solutions may include directory servers, access management platforms, identity management platforms, and perhaps even domain name system (DNS) and Universal Description, Discovery, and Integration (UDDI) platforms. These details are too complex to attempt to address them here. What is important is that the enterprise architects, leveraging the capabilities of the center of excellence, evaluate these options and alternatives and develop the best solution for your unique environment.

Business Process and Business Service Authorization Services

User authentication and service privilege identification are components and standards that are specified in terms of their design and utilization in the *Channel* layer of the SOA enterprise architecture framework. *Service authorizations* are components and standards that are specified in terms of their design and utilization in the Business Process and Business Service layers of the SOA enterprise architecture framework.

The previous example of the "Address Change" service is a Business *Service* layer SOA component with its invocation mechanism exposed directly to the Channel layer portal application. The "Add a Dependent" service is a Business *Process* layer service with its invocation mechanism exposed to the Channel layer portal application. When either service is invoked by the authenticated user logged into the portal application, the first step performed by the "Address Change" service or "Add a Dependent" process is to call the "Service Authorization" service of the enterprise SOA security framework application. This is a policy enforcement point that validates that the authenticated user role is authorized to use the service.

Under this approach, each individual Business Process or Business Service manages the authorization of the service it performs, not the channel. The channel simply exposes the service invocation mechanism but does not authorize its use. You may wonder why this is necessary and whether the channel can authorize access to the service. There are three reasons why this approach is necessary.

1. If the service invocations are hard-coded into the Channel layer, there is no way to validate that the services are still authorized for the role.

2. There may be additional qualification data that restricts use of the service. For example, while members with the role "subscriber" are authorized to add a dependent, some accounts may want to restrict their employees to adding their dependents through the account's human resources system, which sends the updated information to the health insurer through one of the insurer's account constituent channels. Incorporating this logic at the Presentation layer of the channel could have significant performance implications.

3. Performing this authorization process at the Service or Process layer means that it is invoked only when and if the service is used; if performed at the Channel layer (so that the service invocation mechanism can be eliminated from the displayed list of available services), it would be invoked every time the user authenticates.

The design patterns for enterprise SOA security framework services invoked at the Business Process and Business Service layers specify that the service use a cached SOA user profile record containing the SOA user profile information and an authenticated user's security token generated by the underlying security technology. If the authenticated user's security token does not exist, one of two conditions has occurred. Either the service is being invoked from an unauthorized, unauthenticated source or the "Close User Security Session" service was initiated by a logout or time-out process. Regardless of the cause, the service authorization should be denied by the enterprise SOA security framework application's authorization service if this condition occurs.

Integration Layer Security Services

The Integration layer provides a layer of abstraction on top of the back-end legacy business applications. In many cases, the Integration layer may have to authenticate to the back-end legacy system's security module before any Integration layer requests or replies are processed. Many of these systems will have their own proprietary format and structure for authenticating Users. In some cases, a "SuperUser" or group-level authentication mechanism can be used, allowing access to most if not all of the functionality of the system. In other cases, the specific authentication credentials of the individual user logged in at the Channel layer need to be provided. In most if not all cases, the authentication credentials used at the Channel layer will be different from those needed by the legacy application.

The enterprise SOA security framework provides centralized services for authentication within the back-end legacy applications. How this is accomplished depends on the legacy application's security mechanism and process. Examples of some of these options include:

- A service to log the user into the legacy application security system and pass the generated security token to the Integration layer service for incorporation into the integration service request.
- Establishing a federated trusted relationship with the legacy application for the integration services to use.
- Providing the encrypted authentication security credentials used by the legacy application security system to be passed within the integration service request.

When integration is through APIs exposed by a purchased or leased legacy application, the specific security mechanism used will be specified by vendor in the API documentation. Integration at the database level may specify the security mechanism as implemented by the database developer leveraging the database platform's security capabilities (e.g., record locks, field locks, secured views, etc.).

The enterprise SOA security framework provides these capabilities by integrating with the Enterprise SOA Provisioning Framework and leveraging services from that framework to obtain the necessary credential data and processes. For example, the provisioning technology is used to:

- Set up the user credentials for new users in all the legacy applications they are authorized to use.
- Process password resets and password synchronization across those systems.
- Inactivate or remove the security in each system for users no longer authorized.

These technologies provide these capabilities by providing adapters to commonly used legacy security systems such as IBM's Resource Access Control Facility (RACF), integration with directory server platforms such as Microsoft's Active Directory and the lightweight directory access protocol, or by emulating the security administration consoles of proprietary security platforms. Therefore, the provisioning system knows the user credentials for all these systems and knows how to access their security functions.

The enterprise SOA security framework leverages these provisioning capabilities to obtain user authentication and authorization data for each legacy application and to obtain security session tokens used by the protocols supporting those legacy applications.

The Integration layer services can also leverage the user security profile record to increase the security of the integration service. This is accomplished by using data stored in the authenticated user's security profile record rather than soliciting the information from the user through data entry. For example, when a health member registered online for self-service, a security profile record was created. In addition to storing the member's user ID, password, and secret questions and answers, the registration program also added the member's account's policy number and member ID number to his or her security profile record. This information was extracted from the legacy policy and membership system. When this member logs into the member self-service portal and invokes one of the self-service transactions requiring either the user's member ID or account's policy number, the service will extract these data elements from the security data that was returned with the authentication or authorization service reply message. There is no mechanism for the logged-in user to enter this information. This process not only eliminates the need for validation edits on these fields but also minimizes the amount of data entered by the user.

If the legacy claim system is keyed off the subscriber ID, which is the same first 9 digits of the 11-digit member ID, the claims returned in the integration service reply would be for all the members under the subscriber. The Integration layer service would apply a data filtering rule to reply only with the claims belonging to the authenticated member. This would be accomplished by using data in the authenticated user's profile to determine which of the returned claims belong to him or her. This data could include elements like first, middle, and last name; date of birth; gender; and so forth. This is an example of a transaction validation service. The legacy claims system does not recognize a member ID and keys all records using the subscriber ID. This was not a problem when the person viewing the claims was an employee of the insurer. The employee applied the filtering rule and communicated the claim information only for that particular member. This is another example of a business rule black hole, as depicted in Exhibit 3.2, when this service is exposed directly to the member. The SOA integration service for claims was able to leverage the enterprise SOA security framework to close this hole by writing a simple "Transaction Record Filtering" business rule at the integration layer rather than embarking on a seven-figure enhancement of the legacy claims system to index claims at a member ID level.

Long-Term Legacy Security Approach

Ultimately, all the legacy applications are replaced with applications that either (1) use the enterprise SOA security framework application and no longer have their own embedded security systems or (2) modernize their security systems to support standards-based federated security services.

As legacy applications migrate toward the first approach, the integration services will no longer need to provide the security pass-through services as the new or enhanced legacy application will acquire these directly from the enterprise SOA security framework.

For applications adopting the second approach, which in most cases will be purchased, leased, or external SaaS applications, the security will be federated at the layer where the interoperability occurs (i.e., Business Process layer, Business Service layer, or Integration Service layer).

Value-Added Extensions to an Enterprise Security Framework

When an enterprise SOA security framework is applied to SOA, additional value-added capabilities can be incorporated into or facilitated by that framework. Examples of these value-added capabilities are profiling and personalization.

Profiling involves the identification of specific characteristics associated to a group for which the authenticated user participates in or has been categorized into. Profiling may be the identification of the authenticated user as a preferred or platinum customer to whom special services are offered. These profile attributes may be passed from the framework to lower layers of the architecture in order to be interpreted by lower-layer business processes or business services and customize the way they operate.

Personalization involves the identification of specific characteristics uniquely associated to the authenticated individual. Personalized characteristics may include specifying a language preference, the automatic invocation of specific services that the user has subscribed to, or preferred mechanisms for delivering notifications and other communications.

The enterprise SOA security framework authenticates the logon to the channel through a logon service provided by the framework itself, not the channel. The initial user registration process and SOA user profile maintenance of their security profile are also services of the enterprise SOA security framework. The security profile records for each registered user are managed and maintained by the enterprise SOA security framework. This profile database can be extended to contain profiling and personalization attributes as well. These attributes can be maintained by the user through the user registration and SOA user profile maintenance services, by provisioning administrators within the company, or provisioned automatically by the Enterprise Provisioning Framework using triggers from other systems, such as the customer contract application (which stores the customer status classification).

The advantage of incorporating these into an enterprise SOA framework is they can be made available to and used by any service delivered through any channel. When the amount of profiling and personalization is minimal, incorporating these into an enterprise SOA security framework eliminates the need to define and set up separate comprehensive frameworks to support one or two services. Under the traditional stovepipe approach, the logic to maintain and use these characteristics, and in many cases the data itself, had to be duplicated in every application that wanted to use them. Under SOA, profiling and personalization are just another set of loosely coupled services available to every business service and every channel.

Thus, your architecture framework for SOA defines an enterprise SOA user profile record stored in an enterprise SOA user profile database that contains all the SOA user profile data needed by the SOA security, personalization, and profiling services. Any constituent using any service through any channel would have an enterprise SOA user profile record.

The enterprise SOA user profile database may not be one database. For added security, you may have a database for each constituency or one for the employee constituency and a second for all other constituencies. It all depends on your security requirements and risk tolerance level.

SOA user profile records for external constituents, such as customers or accounts, may be created and maintained by the individual user through the user registration and SOA user profile maintenance services provided by the Enterprise SOA Provisioning Framework. Internal employee constituents may be restricted from any access to their SOA user profile record. These records would be created and maintained by employees with security administrator roles in the enterprise SOA provisioning system using services within the enterprise SOA Provisioning Framework.

Thus, the SOA user profile record stores all the data needed by the SOA security, personalization, and profiling services. If your company allows a significant amount of personalization and performs a significant amount of profiling that requires a fairly significant amount of data to be stored, you may wish to construct separate services for these capabilities. If there is a minimal amount of personalization and profiling data to be stored, you may decide to simply add these services to the services within the enterprise SOA security framework application. This could be accomplished by passing the personalization and profiling data within security replies, providing two additional services within the framework ("Get User Personalization Attributes" and "Get User Profiling Attributes"), or a combination of the two. The separate service alternative should be employed to provide personalization and profiling data to unsecured services. For example, a campaign management application may use the "Get User Personalization Attributes" service to determine which language should be used on a mass mailing of a notification to all customers. This application has no authority to see the security attributes of the customers but does need their language preference from their SOA user profile record.

Summary

This appendix described the enterprise architecture development and design principles that need to be considered so that effective development frameworks are in place to develop enterprise SOA applications successfully. It discussed these principles using the enterprise SOA security framework as an example. It also discussed how a single framework or a common SOA user profile repository can be developed to support different framework services—in this case, merged Security, Personalization, and Profiling frameworks.

The purpose of this appendix is to show how important development frameworks are to SOA and why they need to be defined at an enterprise level and published before any SOA initiatives are started. Nothing in an SOA vendor's documentation or technical SOA documents will describe or discuss these requirements. These frameworks are the benefits of an architect-then-build enterprise approach to SOA versus an architect-while-building approach or, worse, a build-then-architect approach. Neither of the last two approaches will achieve anywhere near the long-term success of the first one.

Glossary

Accredited Standards Committee (ASC X12) Also known as ANSI X12. The official U.S. standards body responsible for developing and maintaining Electronic Data Interchange (EDI) standards.

American Standard Code for Information Interchange (ASCII) Standard character encoding scheme for representing text in a machine-readable language.

Application Service Provider (ASP) A business that provides computer-based services on systems it hosts to customers over a network.

Application to Application (A2A) A term to describe the interoperability of one application with another application.

Association for Cooperative Operations Research and Development (ACORD) A global, nonprofit standards development organization serving the insurance industry and related financial services industries.

Bulletin Board System (BBS) A computer application that allowed users to log in through a terminal service to access application functionality.

Business Process Execution Language (BPEL) A open-standards language for the formal specification of business processes and business interaction protocols.

Business Process Management System (BPMS) A platform for developing and implementing applications based on the business process management philosophy of leveraging and reusing assets through higher level process orchestration.

Business Service Provider (BSP) An application service provider company that offers state-of-the-art business applications over the Web using Web services designed with modern security, management, and identity standards to facilitate plug-and-play integration.

Business to Business (B2B) A term to describe the interoperability of one business's application with another business's application.

Center of Excellence (COE) From an SOA perspective, a COE is a fully functional technology lab staffed with technology experts who evaluate and certify the capabilities, efficiencies, and interoperability of the technologies used to design, build, deploy, and manage SOA components.

Commercial Off the Shelf (COTS) Software or computer products that are ready made and available to the general public. "Shrink-wrapped" software is a COTS product.

Common Information Model (CIM) An open standard for defining data and metadata about data that allows internal and external applications to understand and use the data without previous knowledge of it. A CIM uses industry-defined and standards-based common data definitions, if they exist. The CIM metadata provides knowledge of the defined common data and hides the proprietary format and structure of the physical implementations of the data.

Computer Telephony Integration (CTI) A technology platform that allows interactions between a telephone and a computer application to be synchronized and interactive. CTI provides for routing an inbound call and an associated application screen pop to a specified telephone extension and desktop computer, respectively.

Create, Read, Update, Delete (CRUD) A term that reflects the four basic functions of data management.

Domain Name System (DNS) A hierarchical naming system for computers, services, or any resource connected to the Internet or a private network. It associates various information with domain names (e.g., us.gov) assigned to each of the participants. Most importantly, it translates domain names meaningful to humans into the numerical (binary) identifiers associated with networking equipment for the purpose of locating and connecting to these devices worldwide.

Electronic Data Interchange (EDI) Standards-based structured transmission of data between organizations by electronic means.

Enterprise Service Bus (ESB) An architectural concept where all services are delivered through a common enterprise delivery mechanism. Technology vendors have adopted the term to refer to their products that provide message processing, including transporting, transformation, and orchestration of message formats and protocols.

Extensible Markup Language (XML) A World Wide Web Consortium (W3C) Standard that defines a set of rules for encoding documents electronically.

File Transfer Protocol (FTP) Standards-based protocol for transferring files on top of the Internet protocol.

Full-Time Equivalent (FTE) A standard way to represent the level of participation of a resource. An FTE of 1.0 means the resource is full-time committed (100 percent). An FTE of 0.5 means the resource is half-time committed (50 percent).

Health Insurance Portability and Accountability Act (HIPAA) U.S. government law passed in 1996 setting standards for the exchange of health information for all health entities that interact with government health agencies. It also set standards for defining "personal health information" and the security policies for protecting that information.

Integrated Development Environment (IDE) A tool providing a single, comprehensive mechanism for developers to build applications.

Intelligent Character Recognition (ICR) A more advanced form of optical character recognition that can interpret different bitmapped font and handwriting styles and translate them into machine-readable format.

Intelligent Voice Recognition (IVR) Interactive telecommunications technology that allows a computer to detect voice and keypad inputs.

Java Database Connectivity (JDBC) A Java API that enables Java programs to execute SQL statements.

Java Message Service (JMS) A Java API for sending messages between two or more clients.

Lightweight Directory Access Protocol (LDAP) An Internet protocol for accessing distributed directory services that act in accordance with X.500 data and service models.

Model-View-Controller (MVC) An architectural approach for building applications where the data and logic (model) is isolated from the presentation logic (view) and managed by a common central control mechanism.

Network Access Storage (NAS) An architecture that uses file-based protocols, such as Network File System (NFS) or Server Message Blocks, where it is clear that the storage is remote, and computers request a portion of an abstract file rather than a disk block.

Open Database Connectivity (ODBC) Microsoft's strategic interface for accessing data in a heterogeneous environment of relational and nonrelational database management systems. Based on the Call Level Interface specification of the SQL Access Group, ODBC provides an open, vendor-neutral way of accessing data stored in a variety of proprietary personal computer, minicomputer, and mainframe databases.

Operational Data Store (ODS) A database designed to integrate data from one or more operational transaction systems to improve reporting and analysis without straining the performance of the online transaction processing systems.

Optical Character Recognition (OCR) Software used to scan and interpret bitmapped images and translate them into machine-readable text.

Portable Document Format (PDF) A file format created by Adobe Systems providing a standard document interchange format.

Program Management Office (PMO) The corporate organization that defines and maintains the policies, procedures, and standards related to project management, quality management, and delivery assurance.

Proof of Concept (POC) A limited-scope, not necessarily fully functioning, application of concepts, ideas, or processes to test their viability and accuracy. From the SOA perspective defined in this book, a POC is a test SOA application development exercise to ensure that the defined SOA policies, procedures, and practices will produce the expected results.

Proof of Technology (POT) A limited scope, not necessarily fully functioning, application of technologies, standards, and architectural design principles to validate they operate as expected and produce the expected results.

Quality of Service (QoS) The ability to provide different priority to different applications, users, or data flow, or to guarantee a certain level of performance to a data flow.

Relational Database Management System (RDBMS) A database that maintains a set of separate, related files (tables), but combines data elements from the files for queries and reports when required. The concept was developed in 1970 by Edgar Codd, whose objective was to accommodate a user's ad hoc request for selected data.

Request for Information (RFI) A process less formal than a Request for Proposal where vendors or suppliers are not asked to bid but to provide specific information about their products or services.

Request for Proposal (RFP) A formal invitation for suppliers or vendors to submit proposals bidding for the delivery of specific products or services. The process provides a mechanism to evaluate competing offerings using a standard set of questions and qualifications.

Rich Text Format (RTF) A document format developed by Microsoft for cross-platform document interchange.

Secured File Transfer Protocol (SFTP)   Protocol for transferring files over a secured shell connection.

Security Assertion Markup Language (SAML)   An XML-based standard for exchanging authentication and authorization data between security domains, that is, between an identity provider (a producer of assertions) and a service provider (a consumer of assertions). SAML is a product of the OASIS Security Services Technical Committee.

Service-Level Agreement (SLA)   A negotiated agreement between two parties where one is the customer and the other is the service provider. The SLA defines a common understanding about services, priorities, responsibilities, guarantees, and warranties. Each area of scope should have the level of service defined. The SLA may specify the levels of availability, serviceability, performance, operation, or other attributes of the service, such as billing. The level of service can also be specified as target and minimum, which allows customers to informed what to expect (the minimum) while providing a measurable (average) target value that shows the level of organization performance. In some contracts, penalties may be agreed in the case of noncompliance of the SLA.

Simple Object Access Protocol (SOAP)   A protocol specification for exchanging structured information in the implementation of Web services in computer networks. It relies on XML as its message format, and usually relies on other Application layer protocols (most notably Remote Procedure Call [RPC] and HTTP) for message negotiation and transmission. SOAP can form the foundation layer of a Web services protocol stack, providing a basic messaging framework upon which Web services can be built.

Single Sign-on (SSO)   A technology platform that sits on top of multiple application security implementations and synchronizes the logon to and logoff from those applications through a single user entry mechanism.

Small Computer System Interface (SCSI)   Set of standards for physically connecting and transferring data between computers and peripheral devices.

Software as a Service (SaaS)   Software licensed by a vendor for use on demand.

Storage Area Network (SAN)   An architecture to attach remote computer storage devices (e.g., disk arrays, tape libraries, and optical jukeboxes) to servers in such a way that the devices appear as locally attached to the operating system.

Universal Description, Discovery, and Integration (UDDI)   A platform-independent, XML-based registry for businesses worldwide to list themselves on the Internet. UDDI is an open industry initiative, sponsored by the Organization for the Advancement of Structured Information Standards (OASIS), enabling businesses to publish service listings and discover each other and define how the services or software applications interact over the Internet.

Web Application Server (WAS)   A server platform that hosts business logic and business processes. The most common application server platforms are those based on the Java 2 Platform, Enterprise Edition (J2EE) Standard and Microsoft's .Net framework

Web Service Descriptive Language (WSDL)   An XML format for describing network services as a set of endpoints operating on messages containing either document-oriented or procedure-oriented information. The operations and messages are described abstractly and then bound to a concrete network protocol and message format to define an endpoint. Related concrete endpoints are combined into abstract endpoints (services). WSDL is extensible to allow description of endpoints and their messages regardless of what message formats or network protocols are used to communicate.

Web Services Security (WS-Security) A communications protocol providing a means for applying security to Web services.

About the Author

Rick Sweeney was the chief architect for Blue Cross Blue Shield of Massachusetts, where he was instrumental in the design and use of a service-based architecture and philosophy across all major internal and external systems. Through his architectural framework he laid the foundation for a true service-oriented architecture to support the multitude of health industry partnerships and information-sharing initiatives that were on the immediate horizon as well as the flexibility and nimbleness to support the parallel migration of its core claims and memberships systems to a new platform. He has established an architecture vision and practice that has returned significant year-over-year cost savings to Blue Cross.

Prior to joining Blue Cross, Mr. Sweeney was an independent consultant providing technical and business application consulting services to customers in the banking, government, and high-tech industries.

Mr. Sweeney was also employed at Wang Laboratories Inc., where he implemented 15 major systems in 9 months to support the sales, accounting, and operations of Wang's wholly owned captive finance subsidiary, Wang Credit Corp.

Mr. Sweeney has also been an adjunct professor at UMass Lowell where he has taught several technology courses for the Continuing Education Program.

Index

A

Application interoperability, advances in, 13

Application Service Provider (ASP), 107

Architecture practice, justification for, 7–8

Author's blog, xvi, xvii, 302, 303

B

"Black hole," in communication, 25, 106, 258, 339

BPMS. *See* Business process management systems (BPMS)

Business and IT organization model assessment:

  centralized business model, 275

  centralized IT model, 276

  decentralized business model, 276, 277–279

  decentralized IT model, 276, 279–280

  multinational business considerations, 279

  overview of variations, 275–276

  undesirable characteristics, 280

Business application:

  definition of, 24

  inherent flaw of design, 24–27

Business application vendors:

  architecture commitment example, 111

  architecture compliance criteria, 110

  evaluation criteria, 108–110

  SOA advantage, 107

Business architects, 233–236

  technology governance role, 154–155

Business architecture:

  definition, 27

  as a driver for application design and planning, 27–31

  template, 310

  value of, 29

Business domain governance. *See* Enterprise SOA business domain governance

Business domain services, 312–313

Business process management systems (BPMS), 99, 291, 306, 329

Business requirements. *See also* SOA SDLC Phase IV

  bad examples of, 16

  business analyst control of, 248

  capturing strategic requirements, 53–57

  deliverables, 204

  framework for capturing, 202

  roles and responsibilities, 202–203

  strategic assessment of, 294

  use case approach, 19

  value of an SOA approach, 20

  vetting requirements, 16

Business service provider (BSP), 107

C

Capacity planning for SOA:

  application capacity monitoring, 225–226

  approach, 213–215

  assessment process, 215–216

  baseline metrics, 217–221

  data center capacity, 220–221